AF633024

SYNTHETIC RESINS TECHNOLOGY WITH FORMULATIONS

With Directories of Present Manufacturers/Dealers/Suppliers of Synthetic Resins, Raw Material Suppliers and Suppliers of Plant & Machineries

Books on Paints, Plastic, Adhesive, Paints & Inks

HAND BOOK OF ADHESIVES WITH THEIR FORMULAES

The book covers almost all the basic and advanced details to setup own unit of Adhesives & Gums etc., Manufacturers & suppliers of machinery & equipments and suppliers of raw materials & chemicals used in adhesive, glues & sealants industries. Apart from these, present manufacturers, dealers & suppliers of glue & adhesives have also been provided.

PAINT PIGMENT VARNISH & LACQUER MANUFACTURING

The book covers Paint & Enamels, Solvent & Plasticisers, More Other Important Details on Solvent and Plasticisers, Thinners, Powder Coating, Bituminous Paint, Synthetic Enamel Paints, Emulsion Paints, Distempers, N.C. Lacquers, Pigments & Extenders, Varnishes, Paints Formulaes, Varnish Formulaes, Important Formulations of Ready Mixed and Stiff Paints, Insulating Varnishes and Wire Enamels, Testing & Evaluation of Paints, Project Profiles, Suppliers of Plant, Equipments and Machineries, Suppliers of Raw Materials, Details of Plant Equipments and Machineries etc.

RUBBER CHEMICALS & PROCESSING INDUSTRIES

The Book covers Natural & Synthetic Rubber, Acrylic Rubber, ABR, Butyl Rubber, Nitrile Rubber, Silicone Rubber, Urethane Rubber, Rubber Powder, Rubber Reclamation, Pigments and Colours, Rubber Blowing Agents, Latex Dipped Goods, Latex Foam Products, Latex Based Adhesive and Rubber Solution, Rubber Moulded Articles, Rubber Beltings, Rubber Rollers, Rubber Footwears, Tyres & Tubes, Rubber Gaskets, Seals and Washers, Rubber Auto Parts, Various Other Important Formulaes, Polymers Related to Rubber, Compounding, Processing Methods, Testing, Trade Names & Chemical Compositions, Suppliers of Plant & Machinery, Suppliers of Raw Materials, Project Profiles, Details of Rubber Process Equipments & Machineries etc.

MODERN INKS FORMULAES & MANUFACTURING INDUSTRIES

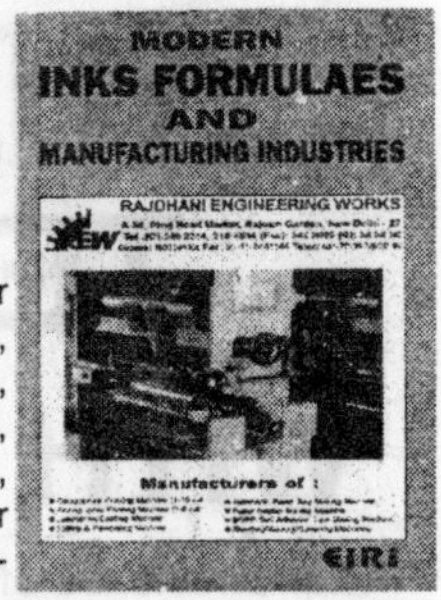

The book contains Colour Matching, Raw Materials, Waxes & Additives, Typographic Inks, Formuations, Photogravure Inks for Three & Four Colour Reproduction, Screen Process Inks, Ball Point Pen Inks, Testing of Finished Inks, Formulae, Toner Inks for Automatic Machine, Printing Inks, Screen Printing Inks, Offset Printing Inks, Stamp Pad Inks, Flexographic and Rotogravure Ink, Printing Inks (Flexographic Inks), Duplicating Ink, Ball Pen Refill Ink, Plastic Ink (Flexographic & Rotogravure Ink) and Golden Silver Paste, Suppliers of Plant & Machinery, Suppliers of Raw Materials etc.

PLASTIC PROCESSING & PACKAGING INDUSTRIES

The book Introduction, Technical Specifications, Plastic Processing, Injection Moulding, Extrusion, Blow Moulding, Other Processes, Compounding of PVC, Processing of PVC, Applications of PVC, Improving Moulding Through Melt-Flow Oscillation, Polymides to Extend High Wear, Applications to Replace Metal, Polyurethanes, Project profiles and directory section. The book is covering with the 54 fully detailed and exhaustive chapters excluding a directory section which covers various addresses of Plant and Machineries suppliers and manufacturers of Plastics Processing and Packaging Industries.

Books Available at :

ENGINEERS INDIA RESEARCH INSTITUTE
4449, Nai Sarak, Main Road, Delhi-6
Ph:. 3918117, 3916431, 3920361, 3960797 * Fax: 91-11-3916431
*E-Mail : eirisidi@bol.net.in

SYNTHETIC RESINS TECHNOLOGY WITH FORMULATIONS

With Directories of Present Manufacturers/Dealers/Suppliers of Synthetic Resins, Raw Material Suppliers and Suppliers of Plant & Machineries

Written By

EIRI Board of Consultants & Engineers

ENGINEERS INDIA RESEARCH INSTITUTE

4449, Nai Sarak, Main Road, Delhi - 110 006 (India)

Ph:. 91-11-3918117, 3916431, 3920361, 3960797

Fax: 91-11-391 6431

*** E-Mail : eirisidi@bol.net.in**

*** Website: www.startindustry.com**

Sole Distributor :

Indian Institute of Consultants, 4/27, Roop Nagar, Delhi - 110 007

PRINTED & PUBLISHED BY

ENGINEERS INDIA RESEARCH INSTITUTE

4449, Nai Sarak, Main Road, Delhi - 110 006 (India)
Ph:. 91-11- 3918117, 3916431, 3920361, 3960797
Fax: 91-11- 3916431
E-Mail : eirisidi@bol.net.in
*** Website: www.startindustry.com**

DISTRIBUTED BY

SMALL INDUSTRY RESEARCH INSTITUTE
INDIAN INSTITUTE OF CONSULTANTS

© Copy Reserved by Sudhir Gupta, Delhi.

ISBN : 81- 86732-40-3
Printed in New Delhi (INDIA)

The book is sold subject to the condition thac it shall not, by way or trade or otherwise, be lent, resold, hired out, or otherwise circulated without the publisher`s prior written cinsent, in any form of binding or cover other than in which it is published/compiled and without a similar consent including this condition being imposed on the subsequent purchaser and without limiting the rights under copy rights reserved above, no part of this publication may be reproduced, stored in or introduced into a retrieval system, of transmitted in any form or by any means (electronic, mechanical, photocopying or otherwise), without the written prior permission of both the copyright owner and above mentioned publisher of this book. While the book has been prepared carefully, yet the publisher`s, printer and compiler do not hold any responsibility on the subject of the book. All disputes regarding this book are Subject to Delhi Jurisdiction only

Rs. 800.00 in India or US $ 150.00 in Overseas Countries

Printed & Published by Sudhir Gupta for **"Engineers India Research Institute"** 4449 Nai Sarak, Main Road, New Delhi - 110 006 and Printed at Swastik Offset, Shahadra, Delhi - 32

SHANKAR DYES & CHEMICALS

SDC

HEAD OFFICE :
1209, Shankar Buliding, Gali No. 11,
Sadar Bazar, DELHI - 110006
Ph. 3673462, 3558239, 3616830
Fax : 3558239, Mob: 9810355592

BRANCH OFFICE :
119, Tilak Bazar, DELHI-110006
Ph. 3970589,3959574,3912061
Resi. 7492678, 7495359, 7490135
Mobile : 9811014659

E-mail: djeswani@sattiya.net.in
Website : http:./ www.shankardyesandchemicals.com

Wholesale Dealers : Printing Auxillaries as Binders, Fixer, D.A.P. : Emulsifiers; Full Range of Ranipal, Golden Powder (All Grades)

Mfg. : Pigment Paste Emulsion also I.D.I.S.C.I. Colourchem & P.D.I.

Deals in : All Kinds of Colours Chemicals Pigments & Dyes

Specialists in : Plastic Colours, Plastic Brightening Agents, D.O.P., D.B.P., D.M.P., C.P.W. Waxes, Resins, Titanium, (All Grades) Calcium, P.V.C. Medium, Epoxy Resins, Hardeners, All Stabilizers Fluorescent & Pigment Colours Pearl Powder & Paste, Foaming & Defoaming Agents, D.J. Fog Fuel Chemicals for musical parties.

All Over Delhi Distributors:
"Orien Metal Powder Company PVT. LTD.
Always use Luxmi Brand Colours Intermediate.
Top Quality Luxmi Gold Bronze Powder®
Top Quality Luxmi Pigments Emulsion®

*** Specialist in :** ALL TYPE OF CHEMICALS & DYES PRODUCTS
ALL KINDS OF CHEMICALS & DYES PIGMENTS..........

*** NEW RESEARCH CENTRE**
WE SOLVE ALL CRITICAL PROBLEMS IN DYES & CHEMICALS

Contact :
Dr. Nirmal Kumar (M.Sc.Chemistry)
Master Mind of High Tech Chemicals & Dyes
Dilip Kumar (B.Sc. Chemistry)
Master Mind in Chmeicals & Dyes

Preface

*The book '**Synthetic Resins Technology with Formulations**' covers almost all the basic and advanced details to setup own resin unit including Alkyd Resins, Acrylics, Epoxy Resins, Ion Exchange Resins, Melamine Formaldehyde Resin, Phenol Formaldehyde Resins, Polyesters, Polyvinyl Acetate, Polyvinyl Alcohol, PVC Resins & Plastisols, Silicons, Urea Formaldehyde Resins, Project Profiles on various allied resins, Present Manufacturers/ Dealers/ Suppliers of Synthetic Resins, Raw material Suppliers and Suppliers of Plant and Machineries.*

The book has been written for the benefit and to prove an asset and a handy reference guide in the hands of new entrepreneurs & well established industrialists.

Director

ENGINEERS INDIA RESEARCH INSTITUTE

Nai Sarak, New Delhi (INDIA)

E-Mail : eirisidi@bol.net.in

दीपक

Chowdhry Rubber & Chemical Co.

STOCKISTS • EXPORTERS • IMPORTERS

1403, Pan Mandi, Sadar Bazar, DELHI- 110 006
Phone : 3634153, 3634380, 3673373, 3616098
Resi : 5105883, 5936016 Fax : 91-11-3634153

Corporate Office :
19/310, Shehzada Bagh, Old Rohtak Road, Near Daya Basti Rly. Stn., DELHI - 110 035.
Tele-Fax : 3658709, 3659055, 3656680, 3646014, 3646374, 3645081 **Resi:** 5105883, 5936016
Gram : RUB CHEM * **E-Mail** : anshdeep@del3.vsnl.net.in

Bahadurgarh Branch
30.8 KM Stone, MIE, Delhi-Rohtak Road,
Bahadurgarh (HR)
Ph. # 367560, 367505

Ghaziabad Branch
Delhi-Meerut Road, Old Chungi in
Ranjeet Singh Compound,
Ghaziabad (U.P) Ph. # 4735978

Distributors / Authorised Stockist / Agents for :

Ethyl Vinyl Acetate (EVA) Polymer 2825/1802/1202	National Organic Chemical Ind. Ltd., Mumbai
Industrial Chemicals	National Organic Chemical Ind. Ltd., Mumbai
Rubber Chemicals	National Organic Chemical Ind. Ltd., Mumbai
Pigment Powder/Fine Paste	Clarient Colour Chem Ltd., Mumbai
Carbon Black	Hi-Tech Carbon (A divn. of Indian Rayon & Inds. Ltd., Mumbai)
Silicone Rubber/Emulsion/Oil	Reliance Silicones India Ltd., Mumbai
Precipated Silica	Insilco Ltd. (Degussa India Pvt. Ltd. Group)
Calcium Carbonate - All Grades	Lime Chemicals Pvt. Ltd.
Calcium Carbonate - Precipated	Indo Chemicals Pvt. Ltd.
Blowing Agents - All Grades	High Polymer Labs Ltd., Ballabhgarh
Ultramarine Blue	Ultramarine & Pigments Ltd., Chennai
Dispersing Agents	Auchtel Products Ltd.
Foam Stabilizers	Organo Vinyl Pvt. Ltd.
Strearic Acid & Glycerine	Nahar Industrial Enterprises Ltd.
Stearic Acid (Wonder Brand)	Ritesh International Ltd.
Alumina Hydrate	Marathwada Chemical Inds. Pvt. Ltd.
Stearates/Zinc Oxide Dolphin	Anshdeep International
Silicone Products (Update Brand)	Chowdhry Industries
Zinc Oxide (Swagat Brand)	Chowdhry Industries

Titanium Dioxide, Dicumyl Peraoxide, Magnesium Oxide, Magnesium Carbonate, Poly Butadine/Neoprene/EPDM/Viton/Nitrile/Oil & Resins.

Our Associate Concern:

DEEPAK INTERNATIONAL (INDIA)

19/310, Shehzada Bagh, Oil Rohtak Road, Near Daya Basti Rly. Stn., DELHI- 110 035
Tele-Fax # : 3658709, 3659055, Resi : 5936016, E-Mail : anshdeep@del3.vsnl.net.in

DEEPAK-ANSHDEEP GROUP

HAND BOOK OF DAIRY FORMULATIONS PROCESSES & MILK PROCESSING INDUSTRIES

The book is covering Introduction, Manufacturing, Technologies, Packaging, Statistical, Figures & Formulations of various Milk & Milk Based Products, Project Profiles on Dairy & Milk Products, Directory Section.

FOOD PROCESSING & AGRO BASED INDUSTRIES

The book is covering 31 detailed and exchaustive chapters including dairy, confectionery, fruit juice, chocolate, frozen desserts, honey, chewing gum, tomato products, jams and jellies, chutney, dehydration of fruit and vegetables, packing of food & alllied products, new development in technologies for food processing, aseptic packaging of food and beverages, packaging of dairy & milk products, breads, buns, pies, pasta products, cakes, biscuits and other allied bakery products. Among all the project profiles on different

AGRO BASED INDUSTRIES HANDBOOK (PLANTATION & FARMING)

The Book Covers almost all the lucrative Plantation Cultivation & Farming methods related with Piggery Farm, Aquaculture Shrimp Farming, Poultry & Broiler Farming, Dairy Farm & Dairy (Milk) Products (Pasteurised Milk, Butter Ghee & Paneer), Teak Tree Plantation, Suger Cane Plantation, Floriculture (Cut Flower-Rose) with Green House Technology, Silk Cocoon Cultivation (Growing of Silk Cocoon From Silk Worm), Mushroom Growing & Processing by Deep Freezing Method (Export Oriented), Papaya Cultivation and Papain Manufacture.

World Importers Directory of Agro Based & Food Processing Industries

The Directory provides Importers addresses of food & Agro Based industries with their Phone and Fax number alongwith complete addresses. This will help to find global overseas customers to the traders/exporters/ manufacturers.

START YOUR OWN COLD STORAGE UNIT

The major chapters in the book are Special features of Cold Storage Project, Selection of the location for the Cold Storage production details and process of manufacture, Operating Conditions, Selection of the Refrigeration Plant Capacity & Machinery, Main Features of Ammonia Compressors

HAND BOOK OF HERBS, MEDICINAL & AROMATIC PLANTS CULTIVATION

The book is covering allmost all the Herbs, Medicinal & Aromatic Plants cultivation details.

Manufacture of Snacks Food, Namkeen, Pappad & Potato Products

The book covers Manufacturing of Potato Chips, Pappad, Snacks Food, Namkeen, Ready to Eat Food Products, Project Profiles, Manufacturers of Machinery & Raw Materials.

Hand Book of Essential Oils Manufacturing & Aromatic Plants

The book covers trade of essential oils, rose oil distillation method, cultivation of matricaria chamomilla, extraction of essential oils, essential chemical constituents profile in tree spice, folk medicinal, essential oil bearing plants status, promising aromatic plants of industrial value, essential oil industry waste utilization, fractionation of essential oil in perfumery & turpentine industry, citronella oil, ginger oil, jasmine rose & lily oil, jasmine flower oil etc.

Books Available at :

ENGINEERS INDIA RESEARCH INSTITUTE

4449, Nai Sarak, Main Road, Delhi-6

Ph:. 3918117, 3916431, 3920361, 3960797 * Fax: 91-11- 3916431

***E-Mail : eirisidi@bol.net.in**

Contents and Subject Index

Chapter 11

Chapter 12

New Detailed Project Reports available on SPICES, FOOD ETC. INDUSTRIES @ Rs. 3675/- each

LIST OF READILY AVAILABLE DETAILED PROJECT REPORTS

- ASAFOETIDA (HING)
- ASAFOETIDA (SYNTHETIC)
- AJOWAN EXTRACTION FROM AJOWAN
- AMLA PLANTATION & PROCESSING (E.O.U)
- AMCHUR
- BLACK PEPPER
- BEE KEEPING
- BIO-FERTILIZER
- BREWERY & DISTILLERY
- CASHEW NUT SHELL LIQUID & KERNEL
- CHILLI OIL
- CORE OIL FROM CASHEW NUT OIL
- COCONUT PRODUCT & BY PRODUCTS
- CHILLI POWDER
- CARDANEL FROM CNSL
- CLOVE OIL
- COLD STORAGE & ICE
- DRYING OF RED CHILLI, HALDI, DHANIIA, PEAS ETC.
- DAIRY FARM & PRODUCTS
- DRY GINGER POWDER & OLEORESIN
- DRY GIBGER FROM GREEN GINGER
- EXTRACTION OF LARGE CARDAMOM
- FISH FARMING
- FLORICULTURE (CUT FLOWER)
- HERBS CULTIVATION
- HERBS DRYING
- GINGER PROCESSING
- GOAT & SHEEP FARMING
- GOAT FARMING
- GUAR GUM
- GARLIC OIL
- GARLIC POWDER
- GARLIC ACID
- GARLIC FLAKE & POWDER DEHYDRATION
- GINGER OIL
- GINGER OIL & GINGER DUST
- GINGER STORAGE
- MAIZE & ITS BY PRODUCTS
- MUSHROOM
- MINERAL WATER
- MUSTARD POWDE
- PAPAYA
- OLEORESIN FROM CHILLI & GINGER
- OLEORESIN FROM CHILLI
- ONION FLAKES
- SPICES WITH PACKAGING & FORMULAES
- STARCH
- STRAWBERRY CULTIVATION
- THYMOL FROM AJOWAN OIL
- TOMATO CHILLI & SOYABEAN SAUCE
- TARMARIND JUICE CONCENTRATE
- TARMARIND SEED
- TURMERIC POWDER
- TURMERIC PLANTATION
- TURMERIC OIL OLEORESIN
- WATER COCONUT SWEET

*Each 'EIRI' ***Market Survey Cum Detailed Techno Economic Feasibility Report (Detailed Project Report)*** covers Introduction, Properties, Market Survey, Process of Manufacture, Cost Economics with Profitability Analysis, Suppliers of Plant & Machineries and Raw Materials, Cash Flow Statement, Repayment Schedule, Depreciation Chart, Projected Balance Sheet etc.

*Price **Rs. 3675/-** (Rs. Three Thousand Six Hundred Seventy Five Only) for Each Report. Send Draft/M.O./Cash in favour of **"ENGINEERS INDIA RESEARCH INSTITUTE", DELHI. (Payable In India) (Delivery within Two Days)**

ENGINEERS INDIA RESEARCH INSTITUTE

4449, Nai Sarak (D), Main Road, Delhi - 110 006 (India)

Ph:. 3918117, 3916431, 3920361, 3960797 Fax: 91-11-3916431

E-Mail : eirisidi@bol.net.in * Website:www.startindustry.com

• Chapter 1 •

ALKYD RESINS

INTRODUCTION

The term "alkyd" was originally used by Kienle in 1927 to describe the reaction products of polyhydric alcohols and polybasic acids. Extensive commercialization of special classes of polymeric esters which are not recognised as alkyds has forced a more limited definition. For example, among the polymeric esters which are alkyds by Kienle's definition are the unsaturated polyesters reacted with isocyanate, and the so-called "Super" linear polyesters of terephthalic acid. The term "alkyd" now tends to specify polyester products composed of polyhydric alcohols, polybasic acids, and monobasic fatty acids. These materials are used chiefly in the coatings industry. In this industry the terms alkyd, alkyd resin, and alkyd solution are used interchangeably, even though most alkyds are handled as solutions in hydrocarbon solvents (30 to 70% by weight of alkyd resin).

The term "modified alkyd", which formerly was used to describe these products, now is associated with chemical modifications which are carried out during alkyd preparation, and which incorporate chemical agents of types other than those included in the definition. For example, if resin (a mixture of diterpene resin acids and non-acidic components; is added as part of the monobasic acid in an alkyd preparation, the alkyd is considered a rosin-modified alkyd. When no fatty acids used, or whn they are completely replaced by other typres of acid, the products can be considered as "Oil-free" alkyds. Resin is used to replace the fatty acids in a wide variety of commercial products. Other commercial "oil-free" alkyds include glyceral terephthalates and water-soluble resins such as the glycol esters of1,3,5- benzene tricarboxylic acid or the glycol maleate ester of pentarythritol.

The term "alkyd blend" is used for the physical mixture formed by "cold cutting" an alkyd solution (mixing with it another resin or polymer solution at moderate temperatures). For example, an alkyd solution cold cut with nitrocellulose will be considered an alkyd-nitrocellulose blend.

In fact and practice, even in the coatings industry, these definitions are by no means precise and often are interchanged.

CLASSIFICATION OF ALKYD RESINS

The alkyds, as finished solutions, are ready for cold blending with other resins or polymer solutions for use clear finishes, or for use as vehicles in which to grind pigments prior to blending with other resin or polymer solutions for use in clear finishes; or for grinding with pigments to form finished alkyd paints. More than 90% of the alkyds produced are handled in one these ways to produce some type of paint, varnish, or lacquer for industrial or home consumption. About half of the alkyds made are sold by their producers to others who carry out the final operations of manufacture of a paint or other coating material. The remainder of the alkyds are converted direstly by their manufacturers to finished coating products. The bulk of these finished coatings are sold as pigmented products.

Because of the wide variety of commercial alkyds, they are further classified by the coatings industry. The following widely used classification is related chiefly to the kind of monobasic fatty acid in the alkyd.

1. DRYING

The monobasic fatty acid has an unsaturated structure present in sufficient quantity to cause a thin film (1-3 mils) of the alkyd to polymerize in the presence of oxygen at room temperature to give coherent, solid film.

2. NON-DRYING

The amount of unsaturated structure in the monobasic fatty acid is so low that little or no polymerization occurs with oxygen.

The drying alkyds are often used alone in coating vehicles, non-drying alkyds are blended with other polymeric materials to give finished products, obviously these classifications are somewhat arbitrary and various degrees of drying can exist. As a matter of nomenclature, alkyds which are intermediate in behaviour are sometimes considered semi-drying.

The monobasic fatty and content of and alkyds may be added,

as such, or it may be added in the form of a glyceride, which is commonly referred to as an oil. Vegetable oils such as soyabean or soya oil are currently the predominant oils used in alkyds.

Alkyds are also classified according to the amount of oil and phthalic anhydride present in the alkyd. The generally recognized compositions are as follows.

Type of oil	Oil content, %	Phthalic anhydride,%
Short	35-45	735
Medium	46-55	30-35
Long	56-70	20-30
Very long	71 up	L 20

The content of any ingredient in an alkyd may be defined and determined by the following expression.

Content as wt. % of

$$X = \frac{\text{weight of recharged to alkyd}}{\text{Theoretical weight of finished alkyd}} \times 100$$

Where x may be phthalic anhydride, oil, monobasic fatty acid, polyhydric alcohol (also called polyol), or other reagent. Since water is lost in the esterification, it is possible for the percentages of the ingredients to add up to more than 100. Use of the oil content classification and the drying or non-drying concept leads to alkyd descriptions such as a 60% oil-drying alkyd, or with less precision, a long drying alkyd.

When monobasic fatty acid is used instead of an oil, yet another type of nomenclature is required. For example, an alkyd prepared from tall oil acid, pentaerythritol, and isophthalic acid might better be described by per cent fatty acid content. This classification is enjoying a greater degree of popularity, especially as inexpensive tall oil fatty acids have been used in alkyds in increasing amounts in recent years. However, the alkyd contains 60% fatty acid pentaerythritol isophthalate alkyds.

CHEMICAL REACTION

The basic reaction involved in the preparation of all alkyd resins is esterification, one of the most familiar of organic chemical reactions. As an equilibrium system the reaction is reversible as shown below.

$$R'COOH + ROH \rightleftharpoons R'COOR + H_2O$$

Linear polymer result if both the acid and alcohol have only two reactive (functional) groups each. However, as any one ingredient with more than two reactive groups is introduced, so is the possibility of introducing of chain-branching in molecules and cross-linking among various molecules.

Many of the ultimate coating applications of alkyds have the implicit requirement that the alkyd be capable of gelation. However, such a gelation is desired only after the paint or other coating vehicle has been applied to the substrate. Cross-linking to the point of gelation before application is undesirable because such insoluble, infusible resins are intractable. Some possibilities for branching and crosslinking when the functionally of one of the reagents is greater than two.

Etherification is another reaction by which the alkyd resins can be made. It has been in fact found that at the temperatures alkyd processing (typically 210-250 C), reactions other than esterification can occur with relative ease. Etherification of the polyols may occur.

$$2\,ROH \rightarrow ROR + H_2O$$

At 280° C Brett found as much as 27 per cent etherification with glycerol as the polyol but he found this amount only during alcoholysis when an excess of glycerol and an alkaline catalyst were present. At a more conventional temperature, 240° C, he found less etherification-8 per cent with glycerol. He reported little etherification with pentaerythritol at 240° C. Sorbitol is more prone to etherification than glycerol because it is capable of internal etherification.

MANUFACTURE

As discussed earlier, the preparation of alkyd resins is essentially an esterification process in which the polybasic acids and polyhydric alcohols are reacted with various oils or fatty acids and modifying agents in a reaction kettle. When a fatty acid is used, the process chiefly involves direct esterification. When an oil is the fatty acid source, an alcoholysis or ester-exhchange reaction between the oil and the polyhydric alcohol is usually carried out before the esterification step.

Four basic methods for manufacturing alkyd resins are recognized; the fatty acid method, the fatty acid oil method, the oil dilution method, and the alcoholysis method.

FATTY ACID METHOD

The entire charge of fatty acids, polyhydric alcohols, and dibasic acids is heated to reaction temperature (usually 210-250°C but as high as 280° C may be used) and maintained until alkyd specifications are achieved. A variation in which the polyol is reacted with the dibasic acid before addition of the fatty acids gives rapid viscosity rise, wide alkyd molecular-weight distribution, poor stability with driers, a tendency towards surface drying, and often gel formation in films.

FATTY ACID-OIL METHOD

The entire charge of fatty acid-oil-polyhydric alcohol and dibasic acid is added to the reaction kettle, and the temperature is raised to 210-280°C and maintained in this range until specifications are reached. Alkyds made by this method give coatings with more rapid top-drying and slower through drying than those from the alcoholysis method. It is important to have the correct ratio of fatty to oil; otherwise partial gelation can occur.

OIL-DILUTION METHOD

The base alkydis prepared by either the fatty acid, fatty acid-oil, or alcoholysis method. This alkyds is diluted with oil at elevated temperatures to the desired oil concentration. Alkyds prepared by this method usually exhibit better brushing characteristics but produce somewhat softer coatings with poorer colour retention and durability than do alkyds made by the fatty acid or alcoholysis method.

ALCOHOLOYSIS METHOD

A large proportion of alkyds are made by alcoholizing triglyceride oils, such as soyabean and linseed, with pentaery-thritol or glycerol as the additional polyol. After redistribution of the fatty acid groups, the partial esters, which now have free hydroxyl groups, are esterified with dibasic acids such as phthalic anhydride. In comparison with the fatty acids method, the alcoholysis method gives the following differences in alkyds; higher and more rapidly attained viscosity and gelation at low degrees of esterification; and softer and slower drying coating films.

The general alcoholysis method proceeds as follows: the oil is heated to 230-250° C, the sublimed litharge and then the polyol added, and the mixture is reheated to 230-250° C. One way to follow the course of the alcoholysis reaction in anhydrous methyl alcohol, whereas the monoesters are soluble. When at least two volumes of methanol per volume of alcoholysis mixture give a clear solution, the phthalic anhydride is added and the alkyd is completed at a reaction temperature of 210-250° C to the desired specifications.

FUSION VERSUS SOLVENT PROCESSING

Any of the four methods described above, which vary only in order of addition or source of ingredients, can be further modified in point of technique during the esterification cycle. If any of the four is carried out as described, the process is called a fusion process, a term which presumably signifies that the fluidity of the mass is developed by heat. The technique of adding an azetropic liquid as an aid to removing water during simple esterification reactions can also be used in alkyd processing. When this is done, the process is referred to as a solvent or azeotropic process.

In the fusion process, the evolved water of esterification is vented to the atmosphere or is collected in a fume scrubber system. In the solvent process the amount and king of solvent present (aromatic types are preferred), usually 3-10 per cent of the batch charge, is adjusted so that a vigorous refluxing occurs at the desired esterification temperature. The vapours are condensed and collected in an automatic decanter which removes the water and returns the solvent to the reaction kettle. Aliphatic solvents are generally not used in the solvent processing of alkyds because they are poor solvents for phthalic anhydride, which can sublime and plug the reflux condenser tubes.

In solvent processing of alkyds made by the fatty acid method, the usual procedure is to charge all the ingredients and the solvent. In alcoholysis, the solvent is withheld until after the alcoholysis is completed. The solvent is then added after the dibasic acid.

GENERAL PROCESSING AND DESIGN CONSIDERATIONS

In designing a plant for the manufacture of alkyds, the following properties of the finished product must be considered.

(1) The resin must be homogeneously polymerized. Unpolymeried or overpolymerised portions and surface skins must be eliminated.

(2) Colour should be as pale as possible.

(3) Free acidity should be minimum.

From an economical point of view the design should be such that every type of alkyd resin can be made in the installation, and these vary considerably in their constituents and characteristics. Moderately polymerised resins of medium and long types which are quite liquid when hot, do not present any special difficulty in removal from the reaction vessel but highly polymerised or hard resin-modified types require modifications in design. Resins which are taken to a high state of polymerisation, often near gelation point, necessitate rapid cooling to prevent further polymerisation, and rapid removal from the reaction vessel. The introduction of hard resins, like rosin, rosin ester, copaleaster or phenol formaldehyde resins, in large quantities, may mean modification of stirring equipment, and probably also the method of heating.

The cover of the reaction vessel must be such that it possesses both flanged connections for addition of liquid raw materials, and a large aperature manhole for the solid ingredients. Preferably two flanged connections should be included in the cover, to allow the simultaneous addition of two liquid ingredients if desired. This will reduce the charging time considerably. The manhole can be fitted with a temporary, loose fitting deflector, which is inserted during filling. With this, lumps of solid raw materials can be gently projected against the side of the vessel, and not allowed to crash on to the bottom. If internal electrical heating elements or heating coils are used, the lumps of raw material can be directed to avoid them. If the manhole deflector is adjusted, the lumps can be sent against different parts of the inside of the vessel to avoid wear or mechanical damage at one stop.

Some of the raw materials are volatile at the reaction temperature, and condense on the cooler parts of the reaction vessel and on the underside of the lid. Phthalic anhydride and maleic anhydride condense to form solid or crystalline incrustations. These cakes absorb oily vapours and in process of time darken, and sometimes fall back into the bulk of the molten reactants below. This causes unnecessary darkening of the resin, and, moreover increases the time required for cleaning. This accumulation of solid condensate can be avoided or considerably minimised by lagging that part of the vessel above the jacket if such be used, or above the jacket liquid. The outer surface of the cover should also be lagged. This simple expendient of lagging these exposed areas to maintain their temperature above the melting point of the solid condensates cited, but conserves heat put into the reaction vessel. It is obvious that a jecket which extends the full height of the vessel is a

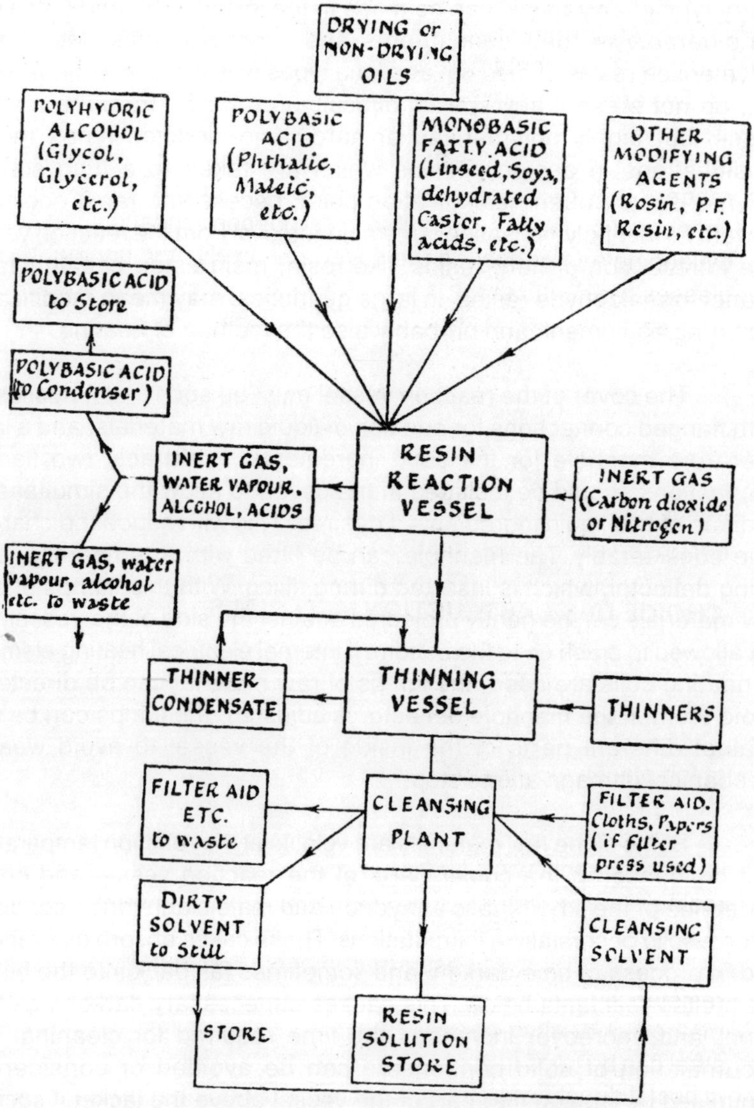

Fig. 6.0 : Materials Flowsheet for Alkyd Manufacture

distinct advantage. It may also be considered good practice to attack electric strip heaters to the outside of the vessel cover, instead of or in addition to lagging.

At certain stages in the reaction, appreciable frothing occurs, and it is convenient to observe this through sight glasses fitted into the lid. Two are necessary-the one to provide a source of light for the interior illumination of the vessel, and the other for visual observation. Often these sight glasses, which can be valuable aids to reaction control, are rendered useless because they are almost constantly obscured by condensation inside. Much of this interior condensation can be removed by lagging and/or heating the cover effectively, and by heating the sight glasses by electrical means.

This characteristic property of these two anhydride constituents, of condensing in solid form also indicates that the vapour removal duct must be kept hot, if choking is to be prevented. This is usually achieved by supplying the duct with electric strip heaters on the outside, or by fitting a jacket for pressure steam or hot liquid circulation. Any values in the vapour removal circuit should be jacketted also. If this precaution is not observed it will be impossible for them to function properly.

CHOICE OF CONSTRUCTION MATERIALS

It is acidic constituents which have the greatest tendency to attack the metals of the plant, and metals such as copper and steel, which yield coloured salts, should be avoided. This is true of every part of the plant which is contacted either by liquid reactants or hot vapours-stirring shaft and arms, valves, bolts, rivets etc.

The following metals or alloys have given good service in alkyd resin reaction vessels: stainless steel, monel, nickel inconel, aluminium.

Of these,stainless steel, monel, and aluminium show the best resistance to attack, with monel next and nickel somewhat inferior. If the method of heating permits, stainless steel, clad steel, or inconel clad steel can be used in place of the solid metals, with an important reduction in cost if direct firing is employed solid stainless steel or inconel will give vessels with excellent resistance to scaling at high temperatures.

AGITATION

An efficient stirrer is a vital accessory for alkyd manufacture.

Apart from the fact that efficient stirring leads to an increase in the rate in reaction, the individual components of an alkyd resin vary widely in specific gravity.

Natural connection from application of heat is not violent enough to cause adequate mixing. With direct heating in absence of mechanical stirring, it is usual for the lower layer of liquid to become heated above its boiling point. Equilibrium may then occur suddenly with great evolution of energy on occasions with glycerol as the lower layer.

The stirrer should be designed, therefore,to force the heavy lower layers of liquid upwards and in constant and intimate circulation with supernatent layers.

REMOVAL OF UNREACTED RESIN CONSTITUENTS

As with most organic chemical reactions, that of alkyd formation does not proceed to completion. The process of resin formation is followed and controlled by withdrawing samples at known intervals and examining them for viscosity and acidity. Whilst in the earlier stages of the reaction, determinationsof the free acidity fulfil the purpose of a safe guide to the progress of the reaction, it is the viscosity of the product which usually determines the end point. The viscosity of the resin in the suitable solvent is accepted as a good criterion of the degree of polymerisation. Thus it follows that when a resin has been satisfactorily polymerized, it is hazardous to continue the heat treatment in the hope that this will reduce the free acidity to the specified limits. With a sluggish resin, many hours of further heating are required to reduce the acidity.

Alkyds are mainly made at temperatures above 220° C, and if a moderate, vacuum, represented by a pressure of 10 mm. only is applied at these temperatures, it is sufficient to remove, to a substantial degree free fatty acids, polyhydric alcohols and phthalic and maleic anhydrides.

ADMINISTRATION OF INERT GAS

Although inert gases obviously do not enter into combinations with other reactants to form the resins, they are, nevertheless, consumed in appreciable amounts. Either carbon dioxide or nitrogen is employed as the inert gas, the former being the more popular. Most of the inert gas involved in the manufacture of alkyds or, for that matter, in the manufacture of most other resins and varnishes, is used without due regard for its effectiveness.

it is a very common practice to deliver inert gas to the bottom of the reaction vessels. Satisfactory agitation of 1-ton batches or alkyd resin, by means of gas bubbles would require a great flow of gas, and this would have to be continued for the many hours required by the reaction. Low level administration of inert gas does not assist water vapour removal to an appreciable extent. Unless large volumes of gas are removed, the scrubbing effect will be of small magnitude, and in any case gas bubbles will assist the removal of volatile reactants, which even under volatile conditions are lost to substantial degree.

Inert gas is injected below the surface of the resin reactants by inserting one or more vertical delivery tubes through the cover of the vessel. Other modifications are similar tubes containing a large number of small perforations for a foot or so at the bottom, or a vertical tube terminating in a flat perforated coil. A better arrangement is rotating sprayer, and this gives better gas distribution. It consists essentially of a perforated tube, fixed horizontally at the end of the agitator shaft, so that it rotates with this, distributing the gas as it revolves.

If is recalled that the reaction temperatures are of the order of 220° C, it will be realised at once that any formed as a result of reaction will be in vapour form. Because of the prevailing temperature, the water vapour bubbles will be in an expanded, rarefied condition, and will naturally and rapidly find their way to the surface of the liquid.

A conglomeration of extra pipes or coils in a reaction is always a disadvantage, although a sprayer fitted to the end of an agitator shaft is not affected by this.

The most satisfactory way of introducing inert gas is by one or two small tubes, located at the top of reaction vessel above the maximum operating level of the reactants. They are arranged so that they project downwards a few inches on to the surface of the liquid and towards the outlet for the vapours on the other side. In this way a stream of inert gas hits the surface of the liquid on one side of the vessel and travels as a protective blanket to the other, sweeping air and water vapour above it.

Carbon dioxide should be introduced as soon as the process of resinification is started, to expel all the air from the vessel and, its flow should be increased during the initial stages when most of the water is liberated. When bubbling of the reactants ceases, supply of carbon dioxide can be reduced.

The carbon dioxide injector tubes should be fitted so that they can be easily removed by cleaning and, if several are installed, one can be removed for cleaning if required, without interrupting the flow of gas during a particular process.

FURTHER FACTORS INFLUENCING PLANT DESIGN

Most of the foregoing of plant design arise from a consideration of the raw materials utilised and their properties. The following factors relate to the individual processes, and in a similar way they have a very important bearing on the design.

REACTOR

The usual shape of the vessel is cylindrical with a dished bottom and fitted with a domed cover. Direct fired pots are used but the better types of plant include indirect heating.

If indirect heating is used electrical immersion heaters, or a jacketed vessel for fluid heating a draw off pipe can be weided on to the bottom of the inner vessel, and can pass through the outer jacket.

With direct heated pots the resin can be cooled quickly by passing water through a coil immersed therein, or by moving the vessel and its contents by overhead tackle from the furnace setting and placing it into a large water bath or in a position where it can be sprayed on the outside with water. The water sprays can be substituted by a storng blast of cold air, made to travel round the vessel, and contained by an outer jacket entering near the base and leaving at the top. One ton resin can be cooled from 270° C to 195° C in about one hour, and from 195° C to 140° C in a similar time. This may be considered sufficiently rapid for most operations without undue risk of gelation. Alternatively if the vessel is heated by a hot liquid circulating in a jacket, the hot liquid can be replaced by cold when cooling is desired.

The time required for discharging the resin mechanically will depend upon the internal diameter of the discharge pipe and the power of the pump, and these should be arranged to effect a discharge within half an hour.

The beat types of alkyed vessels are designed to function under vaccum, and the joint between the flanges of the cover and the shell of the reaction vessel should be a tight one.

It has been stated already that the blades of the stirrer should be so shaped and located that they keep the heavier reactants in constant movement and dispersed in other reactants, but in addition the blades should pass very near the surface of the vessel at the bottom to ensure that solids are kept freely moving.

Temperature measurement and control are of great importance in alkyd manufacture. Thermostatic control is advisable in large installations, and two thermometers at different levels in the liquid are a precaution against failure with a single thermmometer.

TEMPERATURE AND TIME OF REACTION

Most alkyds are made at temperatures at or in excess of 220° C, but in designing a plant the heating arrangement should be such as will attain much higher temperature, if desired, in a reasonable time.

Some modified alkyds, for example, are readly two-stage product. In the first stage the alkyd is prepared as such at the usual temperatures, and in the second stage it is cooked with drying oil at 280° C or slightly higher. If the heating capacity of the plant is fully extended in raising the temperature to 220-230° C for the first stage of the alkyd resin, it will never attain 280° C for the final stage.

It is very convenient to raise the temperature of the reactants to the reaction temperature in 1 to 2 hours, and this is the average time required for this part of the process. The reaction is then conducted at a fixed temperature, or within a small deviation on either side of this, for a period of hours depending on the type of resin. Some reactions, once the reaction temperature is attained, involve 3 to 4 hours treatment only; others include a long cooking occupying 42 hours or more.

REACTION CONTROL

The extent to which the reactions involved in alkyd production have progressed is followed on the work's scale, as mentioned already by the determination of the free acidity and viscosity of the reaction mixture at regular or known intervals of time. Viscosity determination are of little value until the reactants have combined to give a homogeneous mixture, and a clear solution in a suitable solvent. This stage is easily determined when a drop of the hot mix, cooled on a piece of glass, remains clear and transparent when cold. Known weights of resin mix and solvent are then thoroughly blended and checked for viscosity, either alone by any of the usual methods, or by comparison with a bubble-tube containing a solution of finished resin.

When an alkyd resin has been transferred from the plant and several batches have been made on the work's scale, the control by determination of free acidity can be relaxed, and the reaction controlled by viscosity determinations at regular intervals. If desired a final check on acidity can be made just before discharging the finished resin, to check the efficiency of the vacuum treatment for removal of excess acid.

It is evident, therefore, that provision must be made just before discharging the finished resin, to check the efficiency of the vaccum treatment for removal of excess acid. When the plant is not operating under vaccum this is a simple matter if a cock is provided in the side of the reaction vessel below the liquid level. When under vacuum, however, a special arrangement of cocks is necessary.

After the resin has been made it is kept in concentrated form or thinned. For varnish makers who prepare their own resins for use in cold mixes with formaldehyde, melamine fomaldehyde, or other resin solutions it is most economic to thin the alkyd resins to a convenient extent with a suitable tinner. This eliminates the difficulty of removing concentrated resin from kegs and the necessity for reheating. Production of resin solutions is also popular with synthetic resin manufacturers, but for transportation reasons many resins are kept in concentrated form. Alkyds which are to be further processed with oil and other agents, are either sent directly to another vessel for this treatment whilst still hot to avoid waste of heat; or processed in the reaction vessel itself which means a corresponding reduction in the size of the alkyd produced initially; or filled out into kegs. Resin manufacturers have, of course, to adopt this last procedure.

If the final lacquer or varnish composition made from the alkyd has to be filtered or centrifuged in any case, there is no need to cleanse the resin or its solution. On the other hand, the hot concentrated resin can be sent directly to a centrifuge or a jacketed or heated filter press. The same procedure can be adopted for resin solutions except that a jacketed or heated press is unnecessary unless the solutions are very viscous. It is a great advantage to cleanse the resin solutions whilst they are still hot. because the effectiveness of the process is greater and the output is higher.

FORMULATIONS FOR THE PREPARATION OF ALKYD RESIN

As mentioned earlier, the alkyd resins may be considered as the fatty acid modified polyesters obtained essentially from a dibasic acid and a poly functional alcohol. A wide variety of alkyds can be manufactured by varying the amount and type of fatty oils, alcohols, and acids. Out of the various raw materials employed for the manufacture of alkyd resins, the most common ones include phthalic anhydride, maleic anhydride, glycerine, pentaerythritol, propylene glycol, linseed oil, soyabean oil, castor oil, and dehydrated castor oil. Some formulations based on alkyd resins are given here.

1. LINSEED OIL PENTAERYTHRITOL ALKYD RESIN

Ingredients	*Parts by wt.*
Refined linseed oil	850
Pentaerythritol	185
Phthalic anhydride	320
Lime	2
Mineral spirit (thinner)	865

Refined linseed oil, pentaerythritol and lime are heated 450 F and this temperature is maintained until the alcoholysis is complete. A vigorous agitation is essential during this operation in order to keep the pentaerythritol to react than that by glycerine. Phthalic anhydride is then added and the temperature maintained at 450° F until the acid number drops below 10. The reaction is carried out in a reaction kettle. A vapour duct is provided with the kettle to carry the water vapours along with some amount of phthalic anhydride which sublmes at the reaction temperature. The phthalic anhydride going with the vapours is condensed in a specifically designed phthalic anhydride condenser.

The reaction is carried out at atmospheric pressure. Vaccum is applied to the kettle after the reaction is completed.

2. LINSEED OIL GLYCREINE SHORT OIL VARNISH ALKYD

Ingredients	*Parts by wt.*
Phthalic anhydride	200
Glycerine	140
Refined linseed oil	100

Glycerine (secondary)	100
Turpentine oil (thinner)	325

Glycerine and refined linseed oil are poured into reaction kettle and heated. The temperature is raised gradually to 250° C and then up to 280° C. The batch is constantly agitated and inert gas is bubbled through the batch. When monoglycerides are formed the batch is cooled to 180° C and phthalic anhydride added at once. The temperature is again raised to 210° C and maintained at that. Continuous heating and stirring is carried out, till the acid value drops below 20. The batch is then allowed to cool at 150° C and agitation stopped.

Barring the temperatures at different steps, all other operations remain the same as in the last process. The resin is thinned with turpentine and filtered, the quantity of the thinner being about 3/4 of that of the pure resin.

3. SOYABEAN-OIL ALKYD MODIFIED WITH MALEIC ANHYDRIDE

Ingredients	*Parts by wt.*
Refined soyabean oil	850
Glycerine	205
Phthalic anhydride	320
Maleic anhydride	20
Zinc acetate	2
Mineral spirits	880

Heat the soyabean oil, glycerine, and zinc acetate at 450° F until alcoholysis is complete. Add the phthalic anhydride and meleic anhydride and maintain the temperature at 450° F until the desired acid number is obtained. Bubble carbon dioxide through the batch during the reaction and stir constantly. Reduce with the mineral spirits.

4. DEHYDRATED CASTOR OIL-PROPYLENE GLYCOL ALKYD

Ingredients	*Prats by wt.*
Dehydrated castor oil	1100
Propylene glycol	425
Calcium naphthenate	2
Phthalic anhydride	512
Maleic anhydride	100
Mineral spirits	1285

Heat the dehydrated castor oil, propylene glycol, and calcium naphthenate at 350° F for 30 minutes. Add the phthalic anhydride and maleic anhydride, and maintain the temperature at 450° F for 2 hours. Reduce with mineral spirits.

5. SOYABEAN OIL PENTAERYTHITOL ALKYD

Ingredients	*Parts by wt.*
Refined soyabean oil	850
Pentaerythritol	185
Zinc acetate	2
Phthalic anhydride	320
Mineral spirits	865

Heat the soyabean oil, pentaerythritol and zinc acetate to 450° F and hold at this temperature until alcoholysis is complete. Stirring should be quite vigorous during this operation in order to keep the pentaerythriol in motion. More time is generally required for pentaerythritol to react than for glycerine. Add the phthalic anhydride and react at 450° F until the acid number drops below 10. Thin with mineral spirits.

The resulting alkyd resin solution has several improved characteristics over its glycerine equivalent. The viscosity is higher, the drying faster, and the water resistance materially improved.

6. NATURAL-RESIN-MODIFIED ALKYD

Ingredients	*Parts by wt.*
Alkali-refined linseed oil	680
Glycerine	185
Zinc acetate	2
Phthalic anhydride	320
Rum congo resin	500
Mineral spirits	1600

React the linseed oil, glycerine, and zinc acetate at 450° F until the glycerine layer is taken up. Add the phthalic anhydride and heat again to 450° F. Hold the batch at 450° F until a clear batch is obtained on cold tin. Then introduce the run congo and hold the resin at 450° F for 2 hours. Finally add the mineral spirits.

This resin solution dries in about 2 hours with suitable driers to a hard, abrasion-resistant film with excellent water resistance and adequate flexibility. It can be used for floor mattings, traffic paint and,in general, where quick drying and wear resistance are important. The nonvolatile content of the resin is 50 per cent with about 20 per cent phthalic anhydride.

7. NON-DRYING ALKYD

Ingredients	*Parts by wt.*
Castor oil	680
Glycerine	185
Calcium naphthenate	2
Phthalic anhydride	320
Xylol	700

React the castor oil, glycerine, and calcium naphthenate at 450° F until homogeneous. Add the phthalic anhydride and hold the batch at 450° F for 2 hours. Allow the temperature to drop below 350° F and reduce the batch with the xylol.

The presence of castor oil prevents the resin from drying even with the addition of driers. This type of resin is useful as a plasticizer in a lacquer formulation.

The castor oil may be replaced by other non-drying oils such as coconut, cottonseed, or palm oil. Similar plasticizing alkyds may be obtained by using the fatty acids of the non-drying oils of saturated,shorter-chain monobasic acids, such as pelargonic, and by increasing the molar proportion of the esterifying agent to compensate for the increased amount of free acid.

APPLICATIONS OF ALKYD RESINS

Alkyd resins exhibit excellent outdoor durability, quick drying, inherent flexibility and water resistance. This makes them ideally suited for surface coating purposes. These are, therefore, extensively used for protective and decorative coatings for metals, wood and paper. Following are some of the examples of applications of alkyd resins in surface coatings.

1. High grade architectural enamels

2. Primers and undercoaters
3. Interior and exterior enamels
4. Trim and trellis paints
5. Marine paints
6. Industrial finishes
7. Baking enamels
8. Automotive finishes
9. High temperature baking white enamels in combination with urea formaldehye resins
10. Plasticizers for nitrocellulose
11. Emulsion paints

Alkyds, however, cannot be used successfully where resistance to alkali or other strong chemicals is required. Since alkyd resins are essentially esterification products alkalis will cause saponification with resultant disintegration of the film.

In architectural, automotive and industrial finishes alkyds flat vehicles perform the function of a binder for flat paints which can produce uniform finish on all types of surfaces in one coat and are washable. Alkyd resins are also finding wide applications in adhesives, printing inks, rubber compounding, floor covering etc.

1. WHITE ARCHITECTURAL ENAMEL

Ingredients	*Parts by wt.*
Titanium dioxide	500
Calcium carbonate	200
Long-oil-soyabean alkyd (60 per cent nonvolatile)	1000
Dipentene	25
Mineral spirits	125
24 per cent lead naphthenate	10
6 per cent cobalt naphthenate	4

GREEN TRIM AND TRELLIS PLANT

Ingredients	*Parts by wt.*
Chrome green	200
Zinc oxide	100
Maleic modified long-oil soyabean alkyd (60 per cent non volatile)	700
Mineral spirits	100
24 per cent lead naphthenate	10
4 per cent cobalt naphthenate	3

Trim and trellis paints based on alkyd resins dry quickly to a hard, glossy finish which retains its lustre and is very weather resistant.

3. OUTSIDE WHITE HOUSE PLANT

Ingredients	*Parts by wt.*
Anatase titanium dioxide	100
White lead	300
Zinc oxide	300
Magnesium silicate	100
Refined linseed oil	400
Long-oil linseed alkyd (70 per cent nonvolatile)	200
Mineral spirits	30
24 per cent lead naphthenate	8
6 per cent cobalt naphthenate	3
6 per cent manganese naphthenate	3

The alkyd resin shortens the time of drying and imparts gloss and gloss retention to the paint.

4. TRAFFIC PAINT

Ingredients	*Parts by wt.*
Lithopone	200
Titanium dioxide	100
Magnesium silicate	200
Mica	50
Pumice	50
Congo-resin modified	600

Linseed oil alkyd (50 per cent non-volatile)	
Mineral spirits	300
24 per cent lead naphthenate	8
6 per cent cobalt naphthenate	3
6 per cent Manganese naphthenate	3

A very fast drying product can be obtained with no pick up after 1/2 to 1 hours, by using natural-resin-modified alkyds with 15 to 20 per cent phthalic anhydride based on the solid resin.

5. FOUR-HOUR TYPE BLACK INDUSTRIAL ENAMEL

Ingredients	*Parts by wt.*
Carbon black	25
Medium-oil linseed alkyd (50 per cent non-volatile)	350
Mineral spirits	50
24 per cent lead naphthenate	6
6 per cent cobalt naphthenate	3

This is a typical formulation for a quick-drying, general purpose, industrial finish or 4-hour enamel.

6. WHITE BAKING ENAMEL

Ingredients	*Parts of wt.*
Titanium dioxide	285
Zinc oxide	15
Short-oil dehydrated castor oil alkyd (50 per cent non-volatile)	950
Xylol	75
6 per cent cobalt naphthenate	0.8
8 per cent zinc naphthenate	5

Reduce to spraying viscosity with xylol. Bake at 250° F for 30 minutes.

Hard glossy finishes on a short baking schedule are obtainable by using the short oil alkyd. The dehydrated castor oil is effective in retaining colour during the bake.

7. WHITE MARINE PAINT

Ingredient	*Parts by wt.*
Nonchalking titanium dioxide	200
Zinc oxide	80
Magnesium silicate long-oil soyabean pentaerythritol alkyd (60 per cent nonvolatile)	600
Mineral spirits	100
24 per cent lead naphthenate	9
6 per cent cobalt naphthenate	2

The outdoor durability and water resistance of the long-oil pentaery-thritol alkyds make them outstanding for marine application.

8. QUICK-DRYING RED-LEAD PRIMER

Ingredients	*Parts by wt.*
Rutile titanium dioxide	200
Whitener	500
5 per cent aluminium octoategel	20
Alkyd flat vehicle of 40 per cent non-volatile	330
Mineral spirits	160
6 per cent cobalt naphthenate	10
24 per cent lead naphthenate	2

9. (a) EMULSION PAINTS

Ingredients	*Parts by wt.*		
	1	2	3
Type	Short oil	Medium oil	Large oil
Trimethylolethane	843.5	676	-
Ethylene glycol	-	-	186
Pentaertythritol	-	-	435
Phthalic anhydride	1036	867	888
Tail oil fatty acids	1211	-	1386
Soyabean fatty acids	-	778	-
Benzoic acid	-	179	-
Xylene	147	115	136

For 1 to 2 heat at 245° C until acid number is below 10; distil xylene. For 3, heat half of phthalic anhydride and ethylene glycol for 30 minutes, add balance, heat at 190° C for 1 hour, thence 245° C until acid number falls below 10.

The final products are about 50 per cent solids content, of thick creamy consistency, and slight separation can be readity homogenized.

Alkyds 1 and 3 give tough films which dry in about 15 minutes, very slightly longer than a comparable 60 per cent alkyd xylol. Sward hardness, 10, is comparable, but is increased to 18 where the emulsion of alkyd has 1 per cent on alkyd solids of polyammonium acrylate added.

(b) EMULSIFICATION OF ALKYD

Ingredients	*Parts by wt.*
Alkyd resin (any one from 9 a)	400
Nonyl phenoxy polyethoxyethanol, water soluble (Igepol CO-880)	1.33
Nonyl phenoxy polyethoxyethanol, oil soluble (Igepol-430)	2.6 per cent

Add emulsifiers to alkyd, stir at 120° C until dissolved, cool to 90-100° C, ncrease stirring to very high speed, and add water phase at 85-95° C at 3-5 ml per minute until inversion occurs (sudden drop in viscosit), thence increase rate to 10-15 ml per minute.

Water	400
Ammonium hydroxide, 28 per cent	4
Igepol C0-880 (as above)	1.33
Igepol C0-430 (as above)	2.67

The following may be added optionally after first 50 ml of water phase has been added.

Emulsified lead naphthenate	0.5 per cent (Pb on alkyd weight)
Emulsified cobalt naphthenate	0.5 per cent (Co on alkyd weight)
Emulsified manganese naphthenate	0.02 per cent (Mn on alkyd weight)

On baking for 1 hour at 150° C hardness increases to 16 for alkyd 1, and alkyd 2 gives a very good rating of 30. Water resistance tests, and immersion of the stoved films for various times or temperatures shows that there is only slight whitening compared to a solvent based alkyd.

• Chapter 2 •

ACRYLICS

The laboratory history of acrylic monomers began as early as 1843 when acrylic acid was first synthesized.

This was followed in 1865 by the preparation of ethyl methacrylate by Frankland and Duppa, while in 1877 Fitting and Paul noted that it had a tendency to polymerise. By 1900, most of the common acrylates had been prepared in the laboratory and some work had also been done on their polymerisation. In 1901, Dr. Rohm, in Germany, started systematic work in the acrylic field and later took an active part in the industrial development of the acrylic ester polymer in that country. Polymethyl acrylate was the first acrylic polymer to be produced industrially. It was marketed as a solution of the polymer in an organic solvent and was used mainly in lacquers and surface coatings. Later, Roland Hill (of I.C.I) studied methyl methacrylate and its polymerization in detail, while Crowford (also of I.C.I) developed an economic method of manufacturing the monomer.

Acrylics are thermoplastics and are widely used in such diverse industries as building, automotive lighting, sign, appliance and aircraft. The term acrylic not only covers the polymers and resins made from acrylic esters, but also includes polymerizable derivatives of both acrylic and methacrylic acids as well as the acid chlorides nitriles and amides.

Natural gas, compressed air and acetone are the basic raw materials from which monomers for acrylic resins are produced. By combining the carbon, hydrogen, oxygen and nitrogen from the natural gas and air, methanol and ammonia are obtained. These raw materials and intermediates are then converted in several steps to MMA or other members of the broad family of acrylic monomers; polymerization is accompanied by adding organic catalysts and heat to the reactive mixtures through either bulk, suspension or emulsion polymerization.

The major constituent of acrylic plastics is MMA. Acrylic plastics are marketed in the form of moulding powders or cast shapes such as sheet rods tubes and blocks.

CATEGORY OF ACRYLICS

There are generally two categories of acrylics :

(a) Unmodified (b) Modified and acrylic multipolymers.

(a) UNMODIFIED ACRYLICS

These are transparent and extremely stable against discoloration. They have almost unlimited colour possibilities. They exhibit superior dimensional) stability and offer highly desirable structural and thermal properties. They also demonstrate exceptional resistance to weather, breakage and chemicals and are light in weight.

(b) MODIFIED ACRYLICS

Impact modified acrylics are available as sheet and as moulding pellets. Cast sheet retains all the forming and surface quality characteristics of unmodified sheet. The weathering of this material is also good.

Moulding pellets are available both in moderately translucent formulations and in the more recently available transparent formulations. The former provide impact strength up to almost 10 times that of the general purpose acrylics: In addition they have greater elongation at break and more flexible. Moderately translucent acrylics are used primarily in pigment form in piano keys and housings. They have hard surfaces, good resistance to staining and low water absorption.

Acrylic polymers in general have the properties of light transmittance, weather ability, strength, dimensional stability,thermal expansion, heat resistance, chemical resistance, bonding qualities.

RAW MATERIALS

The major raw materials required for acrylic resin manufacture is methyl methacrylate monomer.

METHYL METHACRYLATE MONOMER

It is a colourless volatile liquid; b.p. 101° C; m.p. 48.2° C, sp. gr. (25/25° C) 0.940. It is slightly soluble in water and soluble in most organic solvents. It is readily polymerized by light, heat, ionizing radiation, and catalysts. It can be copolymerized with other methacrylate esters and many other monomers. It is made by the reaction of acetone cyanohydrin, methanol and dilute sulphuric acid. It is marketed as the technical grade.

Methyl methacrylate monomer is not made in India and is imported from other countries.

MANUFACTURE

Methyl methacrylate is readily polymerised by bulk, solution suspension and emulsion polymerisation, Each of these methods is practised commercially with polymerisation being the predominant method. These methods are described below in brief.

BULK POLYMERISATION

Techniques which involve a combination of bulk polymerisation and casting are extensively used in the manufacture of polymethyl methacrylate sheet. In most processes, the first step is the preparation of a partically polymerised material. Typically, the monomer is stirred with benzoyl peroxide (0.5%) at 90° C for about 10 minutes to give a syrup which is then cooled to rear temperature. Colourant. plasticiser and ultraviolet absorber, if required, are added at this point. At this stage, the degree of conversion of monomer to polymer is about 20 g; the use of such a syrup reduces shrinkage in the casting cell and also lessens leakage from the cell. The syrup is then poured into a casting cell, consisting of two plates separated by a rubber gasket. The plates are held together by spring loaded clamps so that the plates continuously move together in response to the shrinkage of approximately 20 percent which occurs on conversion of monomer to polymer. The filled cell is then passed through a heating tunnel wherein the temperature is maintained at 40° C for 15 hours and then 95° C for 1 hour. The sheet is then cooled and removed from the cell. With casting of thicknesses greater than about 2 cm, the exothermic reaction may result in local temperatures above the boiling point of the monomer (100.5+C) and bubbles may form. In such cases, polymerisation may be carried out under pressure so that the boiling point of the monomer is raised.

Rod si also manufactured by casting. In one process, syrup is contained in vertical aluminium tubes which are very slowly lowered into a bath at 40° C. As the lowest portion of the syrup polymerises it contracts and the syrup above moves downward. In this way a homogeneous rod, free from voids, is obtained. Dentures are normally made from a polymer-monomer dough in a plaster mould. Bulk polymerisation carried out in the preparation of sheet, as described above, results in polymer of very high average molecular weight, (10 6).

SOLUTION POLYMERISATION

Solution polymerisation of methyl methacrylate is utilized mainly in the production of surface coatings. Usually polymerisation is conducted in an aromatic hydrocarbon such as benzene or toluene or a ketone such as methyl ethyl ketone. The initiator is generally benzoyl peroxide (0.2-1% weight of the monomer). The reaction is carried out at 90-110° C under slight pressure in a jacketed kettle fitted with a heavy duty stirrer. Since reaction is vigorous, it is common practice to add the monomer gradually to the hot solvent over a period of 1-4 hours. This technique gives polymer with a wide molecular weight distribution; normally conditions are chosen to give an average molecular weight of about 90,000. The final product is a 40-60 per cent solution of polymer in solvent which is used directly in the preparation of surface coatings.

SUSPENSION POLYMERISATION

Suspension polymerisation of methacrylate is used mainly for the production of injecting and extrusion grades of polymer. Suspension polymer is also used in preparation of polymer monomer doughs for dentures. Polymerisation is carried out batchwise in a stirred reactor, jacketed for heating out and cooling; the reaction is capable of withstanding a pressure of 3-4 atmospheres. A typical formulation may be a follows.

FORMULATION

Ingredients	*parts by wt.*
Methyl methacrylate	100
Water	200
Magaesium carbonate (suspending agent)	3
Benzoyl peroxide (initiator)	0.2

Reaction is carried out under nitrogen atmosphere. Typically the mixture is initially heated to about 80° C but the exothermic reaction causes the temperature to rise to about 120° C, with accompanying increase in pressure. Polymerisation is rapid and is complete in about 1 hour. The suspension is cooled and acidified with sulphuric acid to the suspending agent. The beads of polymer are then filtered off, washed and dried in air at about 80° C. The dried beads may be used for moulding without further treatment of they may be compounded with additives (e.g. colourants), exturded and granulated.

Suspension polymerized polymethyl methacrylate normally has an average molecular weight of about 60,000.

EMULSION POLYMERISATION

Conventional emulsion polymerisation of methyl methacrylate is not practised extensively in commercial operations. However, an interesting non-aqueous emulsion technique is used in preparation of surface coatings. A limitation of polymethyl methacrylate solutions is the low solids content (20-30 per cent) which corresponds to an acceptable viscosity for application. Latices, on the other hand, have acceptable viscosities even at solids contents of 50-60 per cent. Aqueous latices, however, give rise to coatings which suffer from such limiations as water sensitivity owing to the high latent heat of vaporisation of water; and lack of control over the evaporation rate of the dilute. Thus aqueous latices are unsuitable for use as automobile lacquers. These difficulaties may be overcome by the use of an organsol in which the polymer is in the form of a stable dispersion in suitable organic liquid. It is not merely sufficient to disperse particular polymethyl methacrylate prepared by conventional emulsion polymerisation in the organic diluent since the resulting coating would still contain hydrophilic surfactants. It is necessary therefore to prepare the organsol by an in situ process involving non-aqueous emulsion polymerisation. This type of reaction system requires the use of a hydrophobic surfactant such as a rubber polymethyl methacrylate.

LABORATORY PROCESS OF EMULSION POLYMERISATION

A typical composition for acrylic emulsion preparation is given below:

Ethylacrylate	30 parts
Water	40 parts
Sodium lauryl sulfate	03 parts
Potassium persulphate	0.3 parts
Sodium metabisulfate	0.3 parts

Monomer emulsion is prepared from 30 parts of ethyl acrylate, 70 parts of water, and 3 parts of sodium lauryl sulphate in a stainless steel kettle equipped with reflux condenser, agitator and thermometer. The emulsion is agitated and the batch temperature is adjusted to 20° C, 0.3 parts of potassium persulphate and 0.3 parts of sodium metabisulfate are then added in quick succession within a period of one and half hour, the batch temperature is achieved in this time. The permissible concentration of the monomer is obviously a function of heat of polymerisation. If enough heat is produced in boiling the water and unreacted monomer, a dangerous situation results. Alternatively, the polymerisation can be affected by adding the monomer to the water and emulsifier at an elevated temperature in the presence of an initiator, for example, ammonium persulphate, with the monomer added at such a rate to prevent a runaway polymerisation.

The following fomulation uses ammonium persulphate as catalyst instead of potassium persulphate as used in the first formulation.

Ingredients	*Parts by wt.*
Water	200
Ethyl acrylate	100
Ammonium persulphate (sufficient to produce polymerisation at reflux temperature)	0.005
Emulsifier	0.5-1
Wetting agent	1-2

Water and water soluble ingredients are charged into a stainless-steel reaction kettle which is equipped with an agitator, reflux condenser and jacket for steam heating. The solution is stirred. The monomer and the remaining ingredients are then added. The contents are heated until refluxing occurs. The kettle is generally filled to 60 per cent of its capacity. Heat is applied intermittently, if needed, to induce polymerisation. If the polymerisation does not start within 10 minutes after refluxing first occurs, additional ammonium persulfate is added. If excessive quantities of catalysts are required, the monomer is not considered to be of the proper purity. The reaction usually proceeds at a rate sufficient to cause refluxing without external heating for 15-30 minutes without flooding the condenser. Heat is then applied, and the refluxing temperature raised to 93-95° C for completion. The emulsion is then steam distilled for 15-30 min.

To detain the polymer, the hot emulsion is run slowly into twice its volume of hot approximately (90° C), rapidly stirred, 3,5 per cent sodium chloride solution. The precipitated polymer in the form of discrete particles is washed with water until free of salt and dried. Polymers prepared in this manner are soluble in organic solvents such as toluene, benzene ethyl acetate, acetone and dioxane, whereas those made with substantially larger amounts of catalyst are not.

If emulsion itself is desired; it is cooled and poured into emulsion paint. A typical stoving schedule will be one hour at 120° C.

APPLICATIONS

The major applications of acrylics are in the field of paints, leather, textile, paper, automobiles, aircraft buildings, sign boards, buildings, automobiles, applianes etc. Historically, markets were opened in major industries in this order : leather, textile, paper, and paint. On a volume basis, however, today's marketing picture inverts this order and puts paints first. Production of new acrylic paints for exterior application on wood is expected to expand this market substantially. The coming years should see a sharp increase in production of paint made with 100 per cent acrylic base (primarily copolymers of methacrylates and acrylates) and of paints based on copolymers of acrylates esters with vinyl acetate or with styrene of special interest is the recent development of thermosetting acrylic emulsions which are certain to find numerous applications in industrial contings.

ACRYLIC EMULSION PAINTS

The properties of polymers and copolymers of acrylic esters render them ideal as media for emulsion paints. They tend to have better resistance to water and to alkaline hydrolysis than polyvinyl acetate and most of its copolymers. Even polymethyl acrylate, the most readily hydrolysed polymer of the series is more resistant to alkali than polyvinyl acetate.

Ethyl acrylate and butyl acrylate are the principal acrylic monomers included in emulsions intended for decorative coatings, and they are normally copolymerised with methyl methacrylate to obtain a film of requisite degree of hardness. Styrene and less frequently acrylonitrile, are used as hardening monomers. Each, however, has some disadvantages. Styrene, unless present in relatively small proportion, gives rise to yellowing on exposure to ultra-violet light. The inclusion of even small quantities of acrylonitrile, which has an efficiency as hardner about double that of styrene, tends to cause complications with the wetting and adhesion of films. Acrylonitrile when present in an acrylic polymer imparts increased solvent resistance.

The odour of the lower acrylic esters is objectionable and there is considerable difficulty in removing the last traces of monomer for the polymerized emulsion. No satisfactory chemical methods have been found to date, and prolonged blowing of air and/or steam through the emulsion is resorted, with sometimes the addition of deodorant.

A polymerisable acid, usually acrylic or methacrylic, is almost invariably included in the polymerisation formulation. The normal quantity is 1-2 per cent which is included in the monomer mix.

Apart from imparting greater stability to the emulsions the acid helps in wetting out the pigments and often assists in increasing the gloss of paint films. An acrylic copolymer including a higher quantity of acid is beneficial when it is desired to prepare paints of high pigment/volume loading.

Whilst polyvinyl acetate type emulsions are usually manufactured with the aid of colliod, acrylics in general have comparatively poor colloid acceptance, other than for certain polyactrolytes. Inclusion of a cellulosic thickner in an acrylic formulation generally produces a product of coarse particle size and impaired stability. Polyacrylates, e.g. sodium polymethacrylate produce, as a rule, more stable products, but their inclusion does not normally enable any marked reduction to be made in the quantity of anionic or cationic surfactants present.

The particle size of acrylic latices is almost invariable much finer than that of vinyl acetate products, and is of the order of 0.1-0.2u. This implies that the individual particles require a much larger quantity of surfactant as 'cover' in order to inpart stability. Thus acrylic emulsion polymers often include a level of surfactant as high as 7-8 per cent.

Correctly formulated acrylic paints are, however, of low viscosity and as a result of the time particle size there is considerable drag on brushing. Careful formulation, both of the emulsions and of the pigmented coatings in necessary in formulating a good acrylie emulsion paint.

Most of the earlier technical emulsions have a composition which is about 62-64 per cent ethyl acrylate, 1-2 per cent acrylic or methacrylic acids, with a balance of methyl methacrylate. Products with solids content of 50 per cent are available commerically, with a pH adjusted with alkali, most frequently ammonia, to about 6-8.5. Various blends of nonionic and anionic emulsifiers are employed, recommended formulations depending on the ultimate application of the final product.

Pigment binding power of acrylic latices tends to be markedly greater than that of vinyls, and thus a high PVC can be employed to give corresponding results, with some redress to the cost of the final paint. A wide variety of pigments can be employed, and equally the paints can be utilised in many different applications, whether exterior or interior, and on a wide variety of substances. They are exceptionally useful as clear sealers for porous surfaces, and as primer sealer, which may be followed by almost any form of top whether a further emulsion coating, or an oil paint, varnish or enamel.

Evidence has been accumulating in recent years that the chalk resistance and tint retention of acrylic emulsion paints can be maintained by using less titanium dioxide than has been customary in the past, a maximum of 2 to 2.5 lb. per gallon being suggested. Above this level, although brightness increases, hiding power does not increase quantities of titanium dioxide, the binder demand of the system is reduced and the pigment volume can be increased. This produces tigbter, stronger, more chalk-resistant paints, with reduced erosion, and improved grain crack resistance.

Acrylic emulsion paints are considered to be outstanding in adhesion to glossy surfaces. They are also excellent with coloured pigments. Conventional additives such as antifoamers and preservatives against mildew, fungus, mould and bacteria may be required, depending on formulation and application conditions.

Coalescing agents (although rather less necessary than with vinyl acetate copolymers) may be included. They are more likely to be desirable in systems with high pigment volume ratios or for application to exceptionally porous surfaces. These coalescing solvents should be first diluted with water before addition to the emulsion system, and since acrylic emulsions normally contain polymerised acid, it is desirable to maintain a constant pH level, which should normally be between 8.5 and 9.5.

Some formulations of acrylic emulsion paints are given below.

1. GROSS EMULSION PAINTS

A. Emulsions	*Stage1*	*Stage2*	*Stage1*	*Stage2*
Ethyl acrylate	59.7	-	-	-
2-ethylhexyl acrylate	-	-	30	-
Styrene	19.9	15.9	20	50
Methacrylic acid	1.5	3.0	1.25	2.5

B. Paint	*Parts by wt.*
Water	100
Daxad 30 (25 per cent aqueous polyacrolyte)	2
Water dispersible lacithin	2
50 per cent aqueous technical defoamer	5
Tributoxyethyl phosphate	14
Phenyl mercuic preservative	0.25
15 per cent solids aqueous casein	65
Rutile titanium dioxide	200

To the above after grinding was added.

Resin emulsion prepared as above and adjusted to pH 9.0 to 9.5 at 50 per cent solids.	200
Water	62
50 per cent aqueous defoamer	5

2. ACRYLIC RESIN EMULSION PAINT

Pigment dispersion	*(1) Gallons*	*(2) Gallons*
Titanium dioxide, rutile	1.82	6.11
Calcium carbonate	8.10	2.08
Borite	8.62	-
Diatomaceous silica	-	4.82
Tamol 731 (10 per cent)	0.92	0.78
Acrylsol A-3 (10 per cent)	0.96	0.78
Ethylene glycol	1.18	-
Diethyleneglycol	-	0.99
Boric acid	0.48	0.53
Acrysol GS (6 per cent)	7.08	-
Triton X-102	-	0.25
Defoamer	0.25	0.25
Water	14.40	14.40

Led-down materials Rhoplex Ac-33

(46 per cent solids)	41.70	46.95
Carboxymethyl celluose (5 per cent)	-	2.02
Water	17.06	15.65
Ammonium hydroxide (28 per cent)	Adjust to pH	9.0
Total solids	53.05%	55.0%
PVC	50.0%	45.0%

3. ACRYLIC EMULSION EXTERIOR PAINTS

Ingredients	*Pounds per gallons*			
	A	B	C	D
Triton CF-10	3.0	2.0	2.0	4.0
Tamol 731 (25 per cent)	15.0	7.8	7.8	8.6
Antifoamer	2.0	2.0	2.0	2.0
Titanium dioxide, rutile	175.0	175.0	175.0	175.0
Titanium dioxide, anatase	75.0	75.0	75.0	-
Calcium carbonate	133.5	185.0	218.9	844.0
Water	-	42.0	42.0	4.3
Methyl cellulose (2% 4000 cps)	41.0	75.0	75.0	98.7
Rhoplex-Ac-33 (46 per cent)	94.0	-	-	-

Add and mix thoroughly:

Put the above through a high speed stone mill and then add:

Rhoplex AC-33(46 per cent)	531.0	569.0	537.4	574.1
Ethylene glycol	30.0	25.0	25.0	25.0
Preservative	9.0	9.0	9.0	9.0
Antifoamer	2.0	2.0	2.0	2.0
Ammonium hydroxide (28%)	1.0	1.5	1.5	2.0
	1146.5	1170.3	1172.6	1149.6
Total solids, % by wt	60%	60%	61%	60%
PVC	30%	35%	40%	35%
pH	9.1	9.1	9.2	9.3

4. EXTERIOR PAINT FORMULATION WITH RHOPLEX AC-34

Ingredients	High TiO_2 Formulation		Lower TiO_2 Formulation	
	White paint	Tint base	White paint	Tint base
Mix in a change can mixer:				
Water	49.0	30.0	73.7	25.6
Triton CF-10	2.0	2.5	2.7	1.8
Tamol 731 (25% aq.)	9.0	8.6	9.8	6.5
Thickener 2% (aq).	100.0	100.0	100.0	100.0
Rutile TiO_2	225.0	171.0	172.0	100.0
Anatase TiO_2	250	-	28.0	-
Tale	-	-	181.5	-
Mica	30.0	30.0	-	30.0
Put above paste through a high-speed stone mill and add:				
Rhoplex AC-34 (46% aq).	547.5	561.6	523.8	576.2
Ethylene glycol	20.0	20.0	20.0	20.0
Preservative	9.0	9.0	9.0	9.0
Antifoamer	4.0	4.0	4.0	4.0
Coalescent	-	-	9.0	-
Water	7.0	8.0	-	-
Ammonium hydroxide	2.0	1.0	-	1.0
Total	1154.5	1132.2	1133.5	1114.1
PVC (%)	35	35	35	35
Solids (%)	57	57	55	57

It is recommended that pigment volume concentrations below 28 per cent should not be used with Rhoplex AC-33 or Rhoplex AC-34 as thickness may result with increased dirt retention. Conventioal thickners of the cellulosic type may be used, but the overall quantity should not be greater than about 0.3% maximum on paint weight.

5. ACRYLIC EMULSION PAINT FORMULATION

Ingredients	High hiding power semi-gloss white	Dripless white
	Pounds weight	
Water	85.8	91.9+21.2
Tamol 731 (25% aq).	9.0	10
Triton CF-10	-	2
Defoamer	3.5	6
Propylene glycol	100	-
Ethylene glycol	40	22
Preservative	0.9	0.5
Pine oil	1.8	-
Polyacrylate thickener	7.5	-
Acrysol G-110 (22% aq)		
Sodium dioctyl sulphosuccinate (60% aq)	2.2	-
Diethylene glycol monoethyl ether	-	10
Rutile titanium dioxide	275	200
Calcium carbonate	16	54
Extenders (mixed clays)	-	157
Hydroxyethyl cellulose high viscosity (2.5% aq)	-	50 (Ist), 197.5 (IInd)
Rhoplex AC-22 (44.5% aq)	550	209
Veegum T (inorganic thixothropic agent) (4% aq).	-	80

The semi-gloss pigment grind can be prepared with pigments, tamol 731, and part of the defoamer with 70 parts of propylene glycol alone. This is followed by all other ingredients, including the emulsion, the thickener being diluted with water.

The dripless grind contains the items up to hydroxy-ethyl cellulose, except where marked (2nd) and about one third of the defoamer, emulsion thickners and the second parts of water and cellulosic solution.

Adjusted pH	-	9.5
Total solids (%)	49.5	54.6
PVC	25.0	61.8
Photovolt gloss (60°)	30.0	-

6. HIGH QUALITY FLAT WALL PAINTS

Ingredients	Pounds weight		
	1	2	3
Water	175	175	175
Hydroxyethyl cellulose (medium low viscosity)	4.2	4.2	4.2
Ethylene glycol	14	14	14
Hexylene glycol	15	15	15
Coalescing solvent	-	12.5	20
Antifoam	35	-	-
Preservative, 10% mercury	2+1	2+1	2+1
	1	1	1
Rutile titanium dioxide	300	300	300
Clay	75	75	75
Silica (Imsil A-25)	50	50	50
Silica (Imsil A-15)	20	20	20
Rhoplex AC-22 (44.5% aq).	470	-	-
Rhoplex AC-388 (50% aq).	-	418.5	-
Rhoplex AC-900 (46.5% aq).	-	-	450
Water	16	37	27
Hydroexyethyl cellulose (medium viscosity 3.5% aq).	48	101	42.9

Hydroxyethyl cellulose is dissolved in water, followed by water solubles, including coalescing solvents and pigments, which are ground together a cowles mixer being advised. This includes the first part of antifoam. Emulsion and thickener are finally mixed. In all cases pH is adjusted to 9.5 with amonium hydroxide.

Total solids	54.2	54.2	54.2
PVC (%)	42.9	41.9	42.9

The Trade Name Rhoplex used in the above formulations stands for acrylic emulsions known in U.S.A. as Primol.

7. PAINT FORMULATION WITH RHOPLEX AC-33 AND RHOPLEX AC-55

Ingredients	*Low cost Semi-gloss*	*Primer* sealer	*White exterior*	*Interior topocast*
Water	15.0	50.0	55.0	60.0
Oratan (Tamol) 731 (25% aq).	8.0	8.0	10.0	15.0
Triton CF-10	2.0	2.0	2.0	2.0
Anti-foaming agent	2.0	2.0	5.0	2.0
Rutile titanium dioxide	175.0	75.0	175.0	200.0
Anatase titanium dioxide	-	-	75.0	-
Amberlac 165 (21% aq)	50.0	-	-	-
Calcium carbonate	-	195.0	165.0	385.0
Barytes	-	-	25.0	-
Methyl cellulose (2% aq).	-	-	50.0	-
Mildewcide, or preservative	0.5	2.0	9.0	1.0
Ethylene glycol -	-	-	20.0	15.0

The above are ground in a roller or ball mill. Thence add:

Water	144.0	315.0	71.0	-
Rhoplex AC-55	301.0	352.0	-	270.0
Rhoplex AC-33	-	-	500.0	-
Rhoplex AC-72	260.0	-	-	-
Diethylene glycol monoethyl ether	50.0	-	-	-
Primal (Acrysol) ASE-60 (28%)	15.0	28.0	-	16.0
Tributyl phosphate	-	-	5.0	-

Some minor modifications may be made, e.g. the anti-foam, preservative or ethylene glycol may be added in the second stage.

Total solids (%)	45.5	46	46.5
Pigment/binder ratio	0.6/1	1.35/1	1.9/1
PVC (%)	13.8	34	

Oration 731 is the trade name for di-isobutylene-maleic anhydride sodium salt; Triton CF-10 is the nonionic wetting agent; Amberlac 165 is the ammonium salt of a water soluble synthetic resin added to give extra hardness; Primal (Acrysol) ASE-60 is an acrylic emulsion thickener, added after pH adjustment to 8.5. Rutile titanium dioxide used in the formulation is a chalk resistant grade containing 97 per cent Tio_2; oil absorption value being 181b/lb pigment.

8. ACRYLIC EMULSION PAINT

Ingredients	*Pounds per gallon*	
Mix in change-can mixer	(a)	(b)
Water	170.68	171.70
Triton CF-10	3.0	3.0
Tamol 731 (25%)	15.0	10.0
Antifoamer	1.0	2.0
Ammonium hydroxide (28%)	4.08	4.61
Talc	90.0	134.50
Tio_2, anatase, free chalking	102.3	75.0
Tio_2, rutile, non chalking	153.5	175.0
Mix thoroughly and grind on high speed stone mill, add:		
Rhoplex AC-33 (46%)	579.0	476.0
Ethylene glycol	20.0	20.0
Preservative	9.20	9.0
Antifoamer	1.0	2.0
Water	8.16	23.50
	1094.12	1106.31
Total solids,% by wt.	55.0	53.5
PVC	28.0	35.0

The preservative must be mixed the ethylene glycol before adding to the paint, and the pH of the final paint should be adjusted to 9.0 with ammonium hydroxide before packaging.

LEATHER

The earliest use for acrylic polymer dispersions was in finishing of leather, as base coats for nitrocellulose finishes, and as components of water finish systems. As base coats for nitrocellulose finishes, acrylic polymers produce permanent flexible and strongly adhering coatings which not only do not require any plasticizer, but are effective in preventing migration into leather of plasticizers present in subsequent lacquer coats. A large proportion of shoe upper, upholstery and garment leather has been finished for many years with arcylic polymer dispersions. There is increasing use of these dispersions as camponents of water based finishes where the acrylic polymer improves washability, adhesion, flexibility, and levelling of the finish.

It is also used as leather paste in animal hides. When such hides are unhaired, tamed, and washed, they are customarily dried by placing them on vertical panels which then move slowly through a drying tunnel. This operation requires several hours. The hides may be tacked periferally to the panels; but drying shrinks the hides, which thus may pull away from the tacks and rip the edges in so doing.

It has become more desirable to paste the hides to the drying panels. This procedure requires a paste possessing good wet adhesion in order to prevent dropoff of oxides in the drying tunnel. The paste must also have relatively poor dry adhesion so that the hides can be readily removed from the dried hide by brushing or by swabbing. Water soluble acrylic polymers have found use in this paste applications, either alone or in conjunction with starch or carbonymethyl cellulose.

In the finishing of leather, base and top coats are applied in order to improve the appearance, feel, durability, and general performance of the leather article. Water-soluble acrylic polymers have been suggested for applications as pigment binders and clear topcoat vehicles in the formulation of finishing systems.

PAPER

In the paper industry acrylic polymer dispersions are used as binders for pigmented coatings as clear grease-resistant coatings as saturants, and as ingredients in heat-sealing adhesives. In pigmented coatings, resins can be manufactured with excellent pick resistance, wet rub resistance, colour, gloss, and printing quality. Principal advantages in clear coatings are resistance to oils and solvents, freedom from colour, and permanent flexibility. These properties also are desirable in many grades of saturated paper. In heatsealing adhesives, acrylic polymers permit considerable freedom in formulating to specific requirements as to flexibility and heat sealing temperatures. The desired properties, once achieved, do not vary with age.

The use of poly (acrylic acid) and some of its derivatives has been suggested for slush stock or beater additive application for the improvement of suspending properties in the stock or performance properties, i.e. dry strength of the formed paper.

Lithographic printing mats have been prepared with the ammonium salt of poly (acrylic acid) applied as a coating on the paper. After suitable treatment, the mat retains a proper combination of ink holdent and rewet properties of function satisfactorily in this applications.

TEXTILES

In the textile field, acrylic emulsion polymers are used in place of rubber latex as binders for the relatively new non-woven fabrics, as backings or automotive and furniture upholstery fabrics, and as bonding agents in pigment dyeing and printing. In these applications excellent binding efficiency, superior stability to light and ageing, and ease of handling give the acrylics advantage over natural and synthetic rubber latices. Many different acrylic emulsion polymers and polymers are used to impart varying degrees of hand and drapability to a wide variety of fabrics from natural and synthetic fibres.

In the textile operations of weaving and knitting, it is often desirable to size the yarn or thread. This is done to reduce machine shutdowns resulting from feuling of the shuttles and other working parts with fuzzballs formed by loose ends and fibrillation of the fibre. Sizing is acomplished by passing the thread through an aqueous bath containing the agent and thus placing a coating on the outside of the fibre.

After drying, the fibre can be woven or knitted, and the size can then be removed by washing, or it may be left on the fabric as a temporary finish or feel-improver. Starch is widely used in the sizing of cotton. Blends of salts of poly (acrylic acid) with starch find application in this and finishing operations by virtue of a plasticizing action imparted to the starch.

With nylon and other synthetic fibres, such as dacron, sizing has been most effectively carried out with poly (acrylic acid) or other suitable water soluble acrylic polymers. Poly (acrylic acid), as suggested earlier, is apparently spor-welded to the nylon and thus serves as an effective sizing agent, which may be readily removed by subsequent washing techniques. Alternatively, a durable finish can be achieved by heat sealing the poly acid, with or without adding glycerine or polyhydroxy compound, before it has been removed.

ADVERTISING SIGNS AND DISPLAYS

Advertising displays constitute the most important use of acrylic sheet in most countries. Whenever display advertising is desired, specially outdoors, acrylic sheet provides a replacing painted metal, wooden and neon signs in many countries. A wide variety of signs displays are fabricated from it. Industrial users in some countries include producrs of oil, beef, salt, drinks, paint, rubber, food, automobiles and chemicals, to name but a few. Many advertisers specify internally lighted outdoor signs made from white translucent acrylic sheet as a background with raised letters in a contrasting colour. Attractive point of purchase displays are also becoming popular in many areas.

In some countries, acrylic sheet is sold to firms that specialise in the production of advertising signs. These firms perform a variety of services that includes painting, installing lighting equipment, and vacuum forming the flat sheets into other shapes.

LIGHTING FIXTURES

Cast and extruded acrylic sheet is used extensively for lighting shields. The light source is given primary direction by the reflection lens or diffuser. The acrylic shields diffuse the light, protect the light source (incandesent, fluorescent or vapour lamp) and minimize direct glare. Both glass and metallic shields have been replaced by acrylic sheet which is lighter and shatter resistant and provides maximum lighting efficiency over a long period. Without discoloration or deterioratino these properties are especially useful for outdoor lighting diffusers.

Acrylic sheet can be formed into various dimensional shapes. Most acrylic plastics tolerate temperatures above 180° F and higher before becoming distorted. It is recommended that the operating temperature be 20° or 25° F below the distortion temperature.

Extruded sheet can be formed and/or embossed to provide refraction light control. A mattle surface can be made that has excellent light-diffusing characteristics. Cast sheet is often specified where optically clear sheet is needed. Injection moulded lighting parts are selected where the desired shape and primatic surface cannot be achieved readily by extrusion or casting.

Most acrylic cast sheet used for lighting is white translucent, although clear and coloured sheets are also used. Matte finishes are gaining in popularity when clear sheets are used, they normally have a patterned surface of matte finish.

ARCHITECTURE AND GLAZING

Acrylic sheet is replacing glass in domes, skylights, swimming pool enclosures, shop fronts, window panes and related applications. Most of the material used is clear sheet, but some is limited to reduce glare. In developing countries, the use of acrylic sheet to replace glass in windows has been tried with success, particularly in industrial sites where breakage is frequent. The specification of acrylic sheet for domed roofs such as those of sporting areas has come to be accepted in many countries. For example, in Houston, Texas, the roof of the Astrodoma stadium was constructed of 9,200 acrylic sheets (about 3,50,000 pounds), each measuring 41x88 inches. The sheets are in two layers, those of the outer layer being 1/8" thick, and those on the inner layer 3/16 inch inch with a light diffusing prismatic inner surface. In England, corrugated acrylic sheet is being used for the entire roofing of some factories and schools.

A more recent development is the use of this material for building facings. Acrylic sheets can be vacuum formed into panels of any configuration and pattern. They are lighter than glass and have better impact resistance, and they weather very well. Acrylic sheet panels can be installed by several methods, including a clip system for formed panels or by curtain wall foaming techniques.

The building code in some countries incorporates strict fire laws which regulate where acrylic sheet can be used. Usually, acrylic sheet is not subject to code regulation when used in exterior structures such as domes or building facings, but interior application such as cellings or lighting fixtures may be regulated.

PLUMBING FIXTURES

Bath tubs produced from vaccum formed acrylic sheet are sold in many parts of the world, including some developing areas. Reinforcing agents such as glass-fibre matting incorporate into their suructure. Significant savings in weight and cost are possible to the heavier traditional materials. This product has become an important export item; for example, one firm in a developing country sells acrylic bath tubs in a variety of colours and shapes for several hundred dollars each. Sales have increased substantially over three years. Countires with favourable wags rates may find this product an attractive possibility. Good contacts with distributors in the importing countries are however, needed.

AIRCRAFT ENCLOSURES

Transparent acrylic sheets enclosures are widely used for commercial and military aircarft, windows, windshields and canopies etc. These enclosures must meet critical optical and strength standards and be resistant to shuttering and crazing. Most of the enclosures are produced from cast sheet that has been stretched. Stretching produce tougher, craze and shatter resistant sheet. Laminated acrylic sheets are also used by the aircraft industry. However, the lack of a local aircraft industry combined with the high level technology required for stretching, all but eliminates this application for developing nations.

LATEX THICKENERS

The thickening of polymer latex systems is required for a variety of applications. Water-soluble acrylic polymers are effective latex thickeners. With any given water soluble polymer, thickening, of the latex is increased with increased molecular weight of the thickener, which indicates some support for the requirement of the thickening the aqueous phase. However, very low molecular weight polymers, which have a relatively small thickening effect in water, may be internally effective in thickening certain latexes.

This variability of thickening action is typical and may be attributed to the various latex compositions, particularly the nature of the emulsifier. The phenomenon is made even more complex with compounded latex formulations in which the thickener may also react with day, pigments, and fillers introduced into the system.

In handling certain rubber latexes, especially natural rubber, a convenient practice is to cream the latex in order to concentrate rubber. The addition of such a creaming agent as a low molecular weight sodium salt of poly (acrylic acid) to a 40 per cent natural rubber latex will result in the separation into a clear serum layer and a more concentrated, approximately 60 per cent latex layer.

In textile applications, the thickening of latexes is required in the backing of rugs for the preparation of resilient, rubberized, nonslip floor coverings. It is also used in upholstery fabric backing. Thickened latexes are also required for dipping operations in which fabric froms may be dipped in thickened rubber latex and the covered form cured to prepare such articles as gloves.

The latex paint field is a rapidly expanding one.The adjustment of such paints to a desired viscosity level is required for brushing and roller and spray application. Viscosity adjustment can be made with water-soluble acrylics. In addition the final formulation must be stable. In both formulation stability and reduction of viscosity drift of the thickened paint are achieved with selected acrylic thickeners. They also serve as grinding media for the preparation of paint pastes.

NONFLAMMABLE HYDRAULIC FLUIDS

There is a real interest in the development of a non-flammable fluid for use in power transmission and actuating devices. Such hydraulic fluids find use in such industrial establishments as foundries. In these cases, since the fluids are under considerable pressure a leak or rupture in the lines results in the formulation of a fine mist of potentially flammable material, if the base for the fluid is a petroleum lubricant or other flammable stock.

One method of reducing the danger of such fibres has been the use of blends of water with ethylene glycol. In order to improve the lubricity of such systems and to adjust their viscosity to the desired level, water-soluble acrylic polymers have been employed. Polymer modification or the addition of antistak agents is required to prevent the formation of hard films at value fittings, such as would be formed by poly (sodium acrylate).

VISCOUS FLOODING

In the secondary recovery of underground petroleum deposits, it is customary to employ flooding techniques. In this operation, an injection well is drilled in a control location in which it is surrounded by producing wells. Water is then injected underground, and this water flood fores the petroleum deposits out toward the producing wells with consequent increase in oil recovery.

Success has been achieved in the addition of surface active agents to such flooding waters. In certain cases, however, where the petroleum crudes are more viscous, the flooding water is incapable of forcing the heavier material ahead of it and the deposit is merely channeled. Some evidence is suggested for the use of water soluble polymers for the thickening of flooding waters to overcome this difficulty. Such viscous flooding studies have included water-soluble acrylic polymers.

The requirements for these polymers are that efficient thickening be achieved at very low polymer concentrations and that this thickening be affected relatively little by dissolved salts and brackish water. Modifications of poly (acrylic acid) are therefore necessary to overcome its known susceptibility to insolubilization with polyvalent metal ions.

The extent of thickening applications may be suggested by the following representative uses. In textile operations thickening of pringing pastes has been carried out with the water-soluble acrylic polymers. Ceramic glazes have been thickened for use as patching compositions, and the thickener subsequently burned. Jelly toothpaste adn shaving cream have been bodied with such polymers. Stabilization of icecream with alkali metal (sodium) salts of poly (acrylic acid) has been claimed.

BUILDINGS

In buildings, acrylics have both functional and decorative uses. These various uses include large area enclsoures for swimming pools, shopping centres, restaurants and botanical gardens. In such applications acrylics offer a combination of transparency, light weight, resistence to breakage, excellent weatherability, ease of maintenance and design flowibility. 2,00,000 sq. ft. of acrylic sheet was used by the united pavillion in Expo 67 in Montreal. The use of textured or formed acrylic sheets as spandrel panels or other facings is also popular. Availability of special colours and patterns has increased utility in this area.

Another applications is for transparent window glazing, particularly in industrial plants and city school buildings where breakage often is a costly problem. Thick acrylic sheets are used for protection of personnel and property in riot areas. In many cities police and fire vehicles are being equipped with such shields as protection against missiles. Bank robberies are being effectively discouraged by enclosing teller booths in heavy gauge sheet that resists penetration by small firearms.

Properly designed tinted sunscreens of acrylic can reduce direct solar heat and air conditioning load by as much as 50%.

Extruded or moulded acrylic light control lenses are light in weight and resist breakage. They provide precise control for effective, comfortable glare free lighting. Special ultraviolet filtering and transmitting formulations are also available. In commercial and residential installations colourful patterned acrlic sheet is used extensively as decorative room dividers. A recent style trend has made acrylics increasingly popular in furniture and lamp applications. A major new use for acrylics in general and impact modified acrylic sheet in particular is in sanitaryware. The acrylics provide a smooth, easily cleaned, stain resistant surface which is reinforced with polyester glass fibre backing for varieties, bathtubs and shower enclosures. In the marine field acrylics are employed widely in boat wind shields and nameplates and instrument components.

SUSPENDING AND DISPERSING AGENTS

PETROLEUM PRODUCTION

One method of drilling for petroleum deposits involves the use of drilling muds. The well is drilled with a bit, the shaft of which is increased in length, as the hole deepens, by adding sections. As each section is added, a section of pipe is also put in place around the shaft so that the drilling mud can be pumped down around the shaft to lubricate and clean the drilling bit. In returning to the surface via the annulus, it also carries cuttings to the surface.

In the preparation of the muds, clays in various formulations are customarily used. The upgrading of such muds can be accomplished by the use of poly (acrylic acid) or its homologs. Such upgrading results in the formation of more barrels of mud from a given quantity of ingredients.

Two other drilling applications will be mentioned here, although the action of such an additive as poly (acrylic acid) or other water-soluble acrylic polymers is more complex than than that of a mere suspending agent. If the drilling mud passes throgh a porous structure in the underground formation as it returns to the surface, appreciable water loss results. This leads to deterioration of the formation and to the loss of raw materials. Fluid-loss additives are employed to seal-up such porous formulations and thus prevent this loss.

Large quantities of starch and carbonymethyl cellulose are used for this operation. As drilling has proceeded to deeper and deeper levels, bacterial and thermal degradation have suggested the use of less susceptible fluid-loss additives. Hydrolysed poly-acrylonitrile has been used and has been able to withstand both bacterial and thermal conditions. However, the susceptibility to insolubilization by polyvalent metal ions has limited its usefulness in this application.

METAL PRODUCTION

In the preparation of copper pellets, poly (acrylic acid) serves as both a dispersant and an activator for the reduction of the copper. In addition, the particle size of the copper pellets is controlled by the same additive.

Poly (acrylic acid) is also used to some extent in nickel-plating processes, presumably by virtue of dispersant activity.

FLOCCULANTS

A great variety of water-soluble polymers function as flocculants for many types of suspended materials. Polymers which have been used in this type of application include cationic, anionic and neutral molecular derived from such monomers as dimethylaminoethyl methacrylate, acrylic acid, and acrylamide, respectively. Because of the divergence of base materials and efficitive polymer types, the action is not explained by a simple mechanism. In has been suggested that best results may come with the use of a fairly long-chain, linear polymer. This functions to encompass a number of the individual fine particles of the dispersed material, attaching itself to the particles at various sites by means of chemical bonds, electrostatic attraction or other attractive force. Relatively stable aggregates are thus produced.

CLARIFICATION

Flocculants have been used to clarify a numer of liquids which have suspended fines contaminating them. Such aggregated materials may be removed by filteration, settling, or other convenient means. Acrylic polymers such as poly (sodium acrylic), have been reported of interest in water clarification and in the treatment of sugar solutions. Fields of application include white water treatment in paper manufacture and sewage disposal problems.

METALLURGY

The water-soluble acrylic polymers have found application in the recovery of ore from suspension in water. In addition to the clarification of the water, a further object in metallurgical processes is to recover the aggregated are fines. The increased speed of settling and the enhanced rate of filteration are responsible for the successful application of these polymers to this type of operations.

This type of aggregation to improve settling and/or filteration rates has been expanded to include other than metallurgical fines. For instance, in the filteration of a precipitate such as calcium sulfate, improved filteration rates are obtained by prior flocculation with such polymers of acrylics.

SOIL CONDITIONING

A few years ago, appreciable publicity was given to the synthetic soil conditioners, materials designed to make stable aggregates in soil to improve the tilth of the soil and plant germination, and to reduce water loss from the soil and runoff of soil in heavy rains. The inability of these polymers to compete economically with other methods of soil treatment does not alter the fact that they do indeed function as very efficient stabilization agents for soil aggregates.

Although many successful field trials were run suggesting that improved soil performance was obtained for certain treated plots as compared with untreated controls, the stabilization effect is readily noted by first forming soil aggregates in the laboratory, treating them with an aqueous solution of the polymer in question and then placing the aggregates on the top screen of a set and then jigging the assembly while it is immersed in water. After a given time, the loss in particle stability is observed by noting the amount of soil retained on each of the sreens in the assembly.

This demonstrated aggregate stabilizing effect has also been suggested for application in erosion control on roadside banks, railrod and temporary construction operations.

In contrast to this type of effect, actual soil stabilization, i.e. the more durable hardening and impermeabilization of soil structures such as walls and dikes, has been achieved by the in situ polymerization of soluble acrylic derivatives, such as blended calcium acrylate and methylene bisacrylamide.

MISCELLANEOUS APPLICATIONS

Acrylics are used in automobiles for tail light and stop-light lenses, medallions, nameplates, dials,instrument panels and signal lights. They are also used as hoods for hair dryers; as knobs in beverage dispensers and in vending machine windows and housings; as display cabinets and transparent demonstration models.

In cosmetics,the water soluble acrylic polymers are of interest in hair-finishing formulations in which they serve to coat the hair and permit setting and styling operations.

The use of poly (acrylic acid) as a film former has been directed toward many applications. Representative of this type is the suggested use of sodium salt of poly (acrylic acid) as the major component of a nonglare coating for headlights.

Another use of acrylic polymer is in binders. In certain applications, it is necessary to impart green strength to moulded articles so that they may retain ressonable dimensional stability after formation in a wet condition until they have been fired or cured to their final form. For convenience, the temporary binder employed for this purpose should be capable of being burned out during the firing operation. Operations requiring such temporary binders include ceramic manufacture, asbestos board preparation, and the formation of vitreous grinding wheels. A specific use is the formation of nickel briquettes in which poly (acrylic acid) is specially effective.

Another application of acrylic polymers is as ion-exhange resins. Water solubility of an acrylic polyacid can be reduced either by reducing the acid content of a copolymer with a hydrophobic comonomer, or by cross-linking the aicd polymer. In the latter case, complete water insolubility can be achieved. Such insoluble polyacids constitute a major group among the ion exchange resins.

Poly (acrylic acid) and certain derivatives have been used as additives for boiler feed water. In this case, they are reported to act as a suspending agent for the developed boiler scale, allowing longer operating time between shutdowns for boiler cleanup and greater efficiency of heat transfer.

In many polymerization processes, a dispersing agent is required to maintain the initial monomer charge and the ultimate polymer particles in relatively stable latex form. For this purpose, such derivatives as the ammonium salt of poly (methacrylic acid) have been reported effective.

• Chapter 3 •

EPOXY RESINS

INTRODUCTION

The word 'epoxy' comes from the greek prefix meaning 'over' or 'between' and the English suffix for oxygen. Thus an epoxy material may be regarded as an 'oxygen between compound'.

Epoxy resins are thermosetting viscous liquids or brittle solids, of which most widely used are those derived from the condensation reaction between epichlorohyrin and bisphenol A. Commercial exploitation was first initiated about the middle of 1930 by I.S. Farben and this work was later followed independently by P. Castan, in Switzerland, and then in U.S.A. around 1938. Development were slowed down by the second world war and relatively high price and scarcity of epichlorohydrin. However, at the end of the war epichlorohydrin, which was then obtained as an intermediate from the production of glycol, became commercially available and led to wider uses for epoxy resins.

The most widely used epoxy resins are made by reacting epichlorohydrin with bisphenol A. However, other polyols, such as aliphatic glycols and novolak resins, can be used in place of the bisphenol.

Epoxy resins are supplied as either liguid or solids, depending on the resin type and end use applications. They are converted to thermoset state by any one of the numerous compounds referred to as curing agents. The conversion is accomplished at room temperature or elevated temperature depending upon optimum condition or desired end properties. A further modification of the properties is possible by the incorporation of reactive diluents, plasticizers, fillers and other additives.

Table 7.0 indicates the approximate molecular weight melting point, epoxy equivalent and average 'n' value fo ECH/B (also called DGEBA-diglycidyl ether of bisphenol A) type of resin.

From the table it is found that as the molecular weight increases a transition from a relatively low viscosity liquid to a high viscosity liquid and finally to a solid material occurs. Together with this increase in molecular weight, the number of hydroxyl groups per molecule and the equivalent weight for the esterification also increases. However, the epoxy value decreases because the distance between terminal epoxy groups becomes greater.

Epoxy resins are soluble in ketone, esters and other alcohols and some chlorinated solvents. The solubility of resins depends on their molecular weight and decreases as the molecular weight increases. The high molecular weight resins are not soluble in alcohol, aliphatic hydrocarbon and aromatic hydrocarbons.

TABLE 7.0

Properties of Epoxy Resins

Approx vol. wt.	*M.P,°C*	*Av. Epoxy value equiv/100 g.*	*Average n value/soluble*
360—380	Liquid	0.54	0.10
370—400	—do—	0.52	0.15
380—420	—do—	0.50	0.21
390—450	—do—	0.47	0.30
460—560	—do—	0.39	0.60
770—1000	60—75	0.23	1.80
850—1100	60—75	0.21	2.20
1750—2050	95—105	0.10	5.50
4000—5000	125—135	0.05	14.40
5000—8000	145—155	0.03	16.00

In general the higher molecular weight resins are not compatible with vegetable oils, alkyd resins, cellulose dērivatives, melmine fomaldehyde resins, silicones or hydrocarbons resins, applied in protective coatings. However, the surface coating types of epoxy resins are compatilble with certain alkyd resins, polyvinyl acetone resins.

The major applications of epoxy resin are in the field of adhesives, surface coatings, lamination and casting.

RAW MATERIALS

The most important commercial epoxy resins are reaction products of epichlorohydrin and bisphenol A. A brief description of these materials is given below.

EPICHLOROHYDRIN

Epichlorohydrin is a colourless liquid with the characteristic odour of many of the chlorinated hydrocarbon solvents such as chloroform. It has the following suructure:

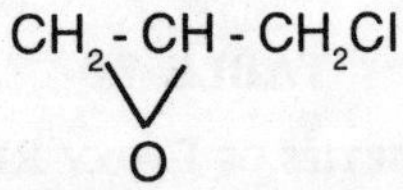

It is made on a chemical scale by the chlorination of propylene.

This material is highly volatile and unstable, miscible with most organic solvents but slightly soluble in water. It is highly toxic by inhalation and ingestion and skin absorption and is a strong irritant. Due precautions should therefore be taken while handling it.

Epichlorohydrin is not produced in India and has to be imported from Japan and other countries.

BISPHENOL A

It is not uncommon to see other terminology used for this material and it is often referred to as diphenylol propane or bis (4-hydroxy-phenol) dimethyl methane.

Bishenol A is normally prepared by combining acetone with phenol. It is the most preferred dihydric phenol because of comparatively low cost. Since in epoxy resins the colour of the resin is of not much importance,bisphenol A need not be of very high puirty. Bisphenol A with 153° C melting point is considereed adequate for most applications.

This material is in the form of white flakes with a mild phenolic odour. It boils at 220° C and has a specific gravity 1.195. It is insoluble in water; soluble in alcohol and dilute alkalies.

Bisphenol A is made in India by a number of units. Some of them are

Arun Rasayan Udyog, Delhi, Cibatui Limited, Atul, Gujarat etc.

CURING AGENTS

The uncured epoxy intermediates are either honey-coloured liquids or brittle amber solids which become liquid when heated. When cured or hardened, the short polymer molecules are jointed to each other to form large crosslinked structures. These final products are thermoset, i.e. insoluble and infusible.

Whether the curing agent is a catalyst or reactive hardener, the cure results in as exotherm or in evolution of heat. In the casting of thick sections, the higher temperatures thus developed result in fäster cures. In adhesive bonding, however,the glue line is ordinarily thin and the heat developed by the curing reaction is largely conducted away into the adherents. Consequently, the fastest hardeners are preferred if no heat is to be supplied to the adhesive joint from outside.

A wide variety of curing agents may be used to cure epoxy resins and there are many ways in which they can be classified. They can be conveniently subdivided at room temperature or high temperature curing agents or by the groups to which chemical curing agent belongs. However,for simplicity it is intended to deal with the subject as follows.

1. Catalytically

(a) Epoxy reaction-The epoxy resins are fairly reactive and because of this the group may be readily opened by tertiary amines. The actual opening is believed to take place as follows.

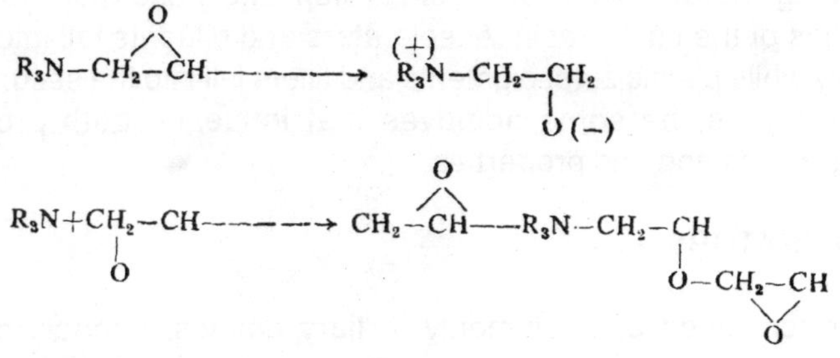

This reaction may continue and result in very long-chain system, although the chain may be terminated by blocking of the final activated epoxy.

(b) Epoxy hydroxyl reaction-Epoxy rings will react with hydroxyl groups that have been introduced into the resin by curing agents or certain modifiers. The reaction takes place as follows.

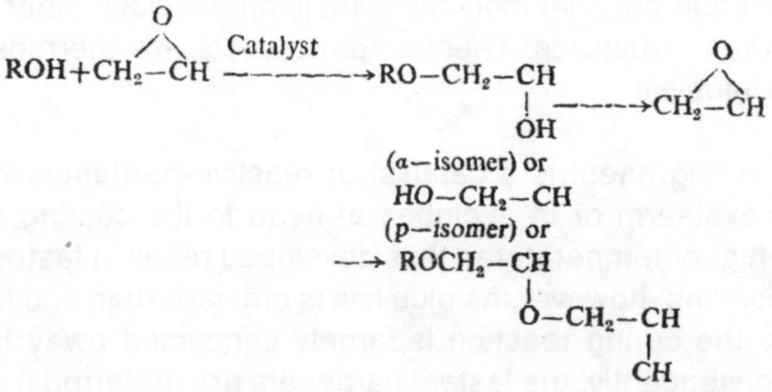

Two isomers are possible and both provide a new hydroxyl group from which further polymerization may take place. A structure very similar to that shown for the epoxy-spray may result and the reaction may continue until a high degree of cross-linking is obtained.

2. Cross Linking Agents

Some commercial curing agents are listed in Table 7.1

ADDITIVES

Two types of additives are used in epoxy resins, those which alter the processing characteristics of a resin system and those which modify the properties of the cured resin. Accelerators and diluents fall into the first category while plasticizers, pigments and fillers fall into the second. There can, of coures, be some additives that influence both processing characteristics and end properties.

ACCELERATORS

Accelerators used are commonly tertiary amines, phenols or amino phenols, the preferred being benzyl dimethyl-amine and tris (dimethylaminomethyl) phenol.

TABLE 7.1

COMMERCIAL CURING AGENTS

Materials	*Amount used in parts per 100 parts of resin*	*Pot life*	*Uses*
Diethylene 5-triamine Triethylene	11 —do—	45 min. at 20°C	General purpose room temp. curing agent
Piperidine	6	90 hr. at 40°C	Castings
Triethylamine	10	7 hr. at 20°C	Adhesives
m-phenylene diamine	14	2.5 hr. at 50°C	Chemical and heat resistant laminates
p, p'–diamino diphenyl sulphone	30	2 hr. at 20°C	—
Phthalic anhydride	30-45	14 hr. at 100°C	Coatings
Hexa hydrophthalic anhydride	80	—do—	Castings

REACTIVE DILUENTS

Reactive diluents are usually mono-epoxy compounds like butyl glycidyl ether, cresyl glycidyl ether or phenyl glycidyl ether,but di-epoxides like 1:4 butane-diol diglycidyl ether and vinyl cyclohexane dioxide are also employed.

PLASTICIZERS

Plasticizers are of two types : external and interanl. Exteranl plasticizers are phthalate and phosphate esters. Internal plasticizers are longchain diols or in some cases the hardener may itself be a long chain di-anhydride or a polymide.

PIGMENTS AND FILLERS

These two types of additives are not very commonly used in composites. Pigments may be used in gel coats or in surface coats to impart colour and fillers like aluminium trihydride sometimes used between layers of glasscloth for self-extinguishing properties.

CHEMISTRY OF RESINIFICATION

Bisphenol and epichlorohydrin first react to form chlorohydrin derivative. This is followed by dehydrochlorinations with a suitable base. The two steps are shown below.

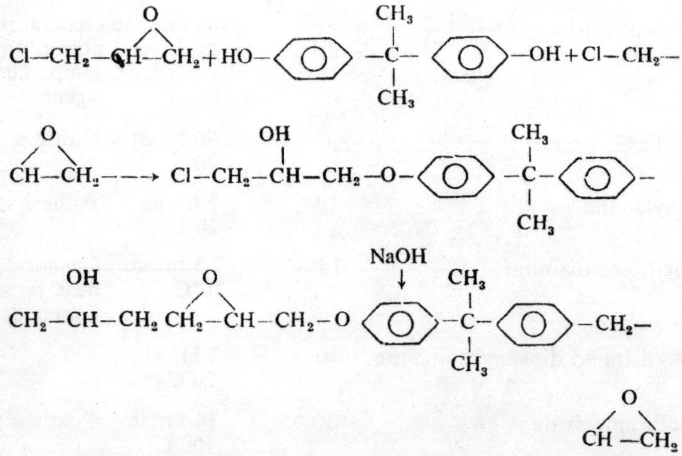

By varying the operating conditions and the ratio of epichlorohydrin and bisphenol A, resins of low, intermediate, or high molecular weight can be prepared. The general structure for an epoxy resin is given below:

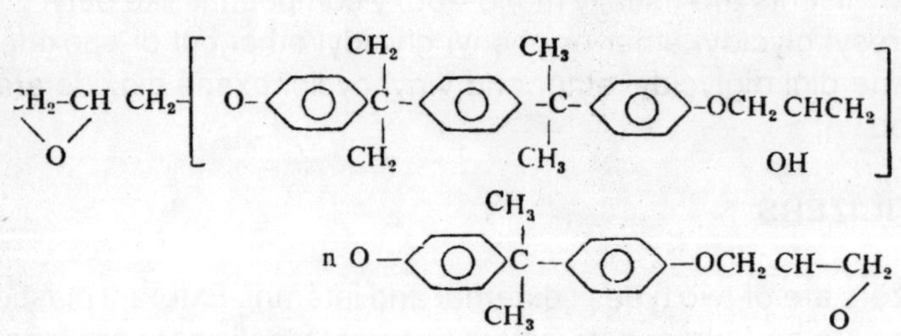

For the liquid epoxy resins, n is generally less than 1, while for the solid types n is generally 2 or greater, although in either case the product is a mixture of various molecular weight resins. An examination of the structure epoxy resin points out the following characteristics:

a. The epoxy and hydroxyl groups are the centres for reaction with curing agents such as amines,acids, anhydrides,aldehyde resins,and other materials.

b. Other than carbon-to-carbon bonds, ether linkages are the only type present.

c. Three types of polar groups are present, epoxy, hydroxyl,and ether. These groups increase the adhesion of the resin.

In manufacture by the non-stage process, epichlorohydrin is reacted with bisphenol A in the presence of sodium or potassium hydroxide. Both of the reactions as described above take place. In the presence of the alkali catalyst, epichlorohydrin will react with the chlorohydrin hydroxyl group to form a product with the following structure.

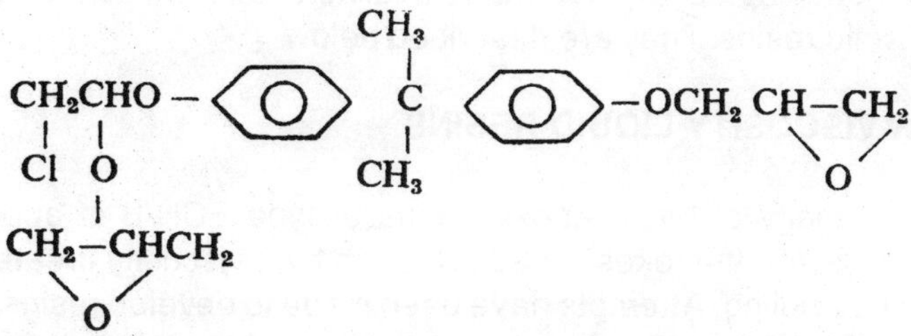

In order to avoid this reaction, temperature are maintained as low as possibl', since elevated temperatures promote the reaction of epichlorohydrin and alcoholic hydroxyl groups.

To produce the lower molecular-weight epoxy resins, large excesses of epichlorohydrin are used, since this will favour the formation of n=0 types of resins. However, this method is not completely effective, and all liquid resins that are not subjected to molecular distillation contain a small percentage of high-molecular-epoxy resins.

The solid or higher molecular weight epoxy resins are prepared in the same general manner, except that less than 2 moles of epichlorohydrin per mole of bishphenol A are used. The product often becomes extremely viscous, and the operation is sometimes referred to as the 'taffy' process.

Two major side reactions take place in this preparation of solid resins, and both contribute to the variable reactivity of conventional epoxies These reactions are branch chain formation and phenol termination.

Branch chain formation results from the reaction of an epoxy group of one molecule and the hydroxyl group of an adjacent molecule. In this reaction epoxy group is eliminated, and the same number of hydroxyl group is maintained. Branch chain formation increases surface tension and melting point, reduces solubility,and contributes to gel formation.

In two stage method for preparing epoxy resins, materials such as stantric chloride, aluminium chloride, and BF_3 complexes have been utilized to effect the condensation of bisphenol A with epichlorohydrin.

TYPES OF EPOXY RESINS

The liquid epoxy resins at ambient temperatures are highly viscous whereas the solid resins when melted at high temperatures also exhibit high viscosity. This problem has resisted their use for many years but recent developments have made available lower viscosity liquid resins and solid resins. They are described below.

LOW VISCOSITY LIQUID RESINS

The viscosity of liquid epoxy resins of type ECH/B is approximately 1000 C.S. (centi-stokes) at 25° C. Such high viscosity creates problem in their handling. Attempts have been made to develop resins with lower viscosities. Two of the better known of these methods have been the addition to the basic resin of either (a) low viscosity plasticizer, such as dibutyl phthalate or (b) a low-viscosity monofunctional dilluent such as butyl glycidyl ether. By these methods, the viscosities are lowered, but the cured resin has inferior properties at high temperatures, as compared with those obtainable from original unmodified resins.

Recently a series totally difunctional low viscosity epoxy resins have developed in which low viscosity is obtained without secrificing the high temperature properties of the cured resin.

LOW-MELT-VISCOSITY SOLID RESINS

Solid epoxy resins are extensively used in the manufacture of cast electric insulation because (a) the shrink of hardening is less than that of liquid resins and (b) the hardened solid resin is tougher than the hardened liquid resins.

These solid resins are used with an anhydride hardener to give a long pot life for the necessary degassing and casting operations. A filler such as silica flour is also normally used, higher filler content gives lower coefficient of thermal expansion.

Recently low-melt-viscosity solid resins have become available having a very closely controlled molecular weight distribution, enabling more filler to be used with these casting mixes. Normally synthetic resins melt slowly over a temperature range of several degrees. The new type of resin melts sharply to give a low viscosity liquid. The result of this is that more filler can be added to these new resins than could be added to their predecessors to produce the same casting viscosity.

The particular point of interest in these results are: (a) the lower viscosity resin has a longer pot life than the standard resin (b) the more highly-filled coatings have lower thermal coefficients of expansion than castings made by using the standard resin (c) a 25 per cent increase in the filler convent can be made to the lower viscosity resin, to obtain the same casting viscosity as the standard resin used with the normal amount of filler.

EPOXY RESINS SYSTEMS FOR OPERATION AT HIGH TEMPERATURES

Epoxy resins which will operate satisfactorily at 200° C, or even 300° C are demanded with increasing frequency nowadays. Normally both a high temperature deflection and a good thermal stability are required. By increasing the number of epoxy groups per molecule the functionality and the density of the cross-linking are incerased and so the cured resin has a higher deflection temperature. Glycidyl ether resins having a functionality higher than 2 and which have been offered commercially are shown in Table 7.2.

Each of the above resins load than does the standard glycidyl ether of bisphenol A, with any given hardener. However these higher functionality, higher molecular weight resins suffer from the general disadvantage of having an even higher viscosity than the standard diglycidyl ether of bisphenol A resin. They are therefore readily used in such technique as hot lay-up laminating and their use has been restricted mainly to applications where they can be used in solution.

Another way of achieving a higher density of cross-linking is to use the standard resin, a hardener of higher functionality like phthalic anhydride, trimellitic anhydride and pyomellitic dianhydride.

However, these higher functionality hardeners are also rather difficult to use, bacuase they are not readily soluble in the epoxy resins. Their use has therefore been restricted. An alternative way to higher deflection

TABLE 7.2

COMPARISON OF PERFORMANCE OF EPOXY RESIN SYSTEMS AT HIGH TEMPERATURES

System Resin Type	Hardener	Tem. of Deflection under Load °C	Wt. Less At 200°C A days	on Ageing for 20 days
1. Liquid glycidyl ether	Phenolic resin	79	2.65	3.18
2. Liquid glycidyl ether	Diamino diphenyl methane	135	2.59	3.60
3. Liquid glycidyl ether	Diamino diphenyl sulphone	168	2.59	3.60
4. Liquid glycidyl ether	Trimellitic anhydride maleic anhydride	176	1.36	2.18
5. Liquid glycidyl ether	Methyl nadic anhydride	202	1.34	1.75
6. Dicyclopentadiene dioxide	Maleic anhydride/ Trimethylol propane	208	1.44	2.79
7. Fpoxidized polyolethin	Maleic anhydride	240	1.80	3.30

temperature is to make a more rigid epoxy resin molecule,this has been done with the cycloaliphatic epoxies e.g. dicylopentadiene dioxide.

Temperature stability is assessed by observing the changes in weight using this as a criteria of heat stability, various epoxy resin systems are compared in table given above, which shows the results obtained both on weight loss determination and on observations on deflection temperatures. It can be seen that a high deflection temperature is not necessarily indicative of great heat stability.

From this table it can seen that the best system is the liquid glycidyl-ether resin hardened with methyl nadic anhydride, for it combines a good deflection temperature with good heat stability. It is therefore currently one of the most useful systems for operations at higher temperatures.

FLAME RETARDENT EPOXY RESINS

In some applications such as to aircraft components or printed circuits in computers, it is particularly important that materials used should not burn at all readily. Consequently a demand arises for flame retardent epoxy resins.

The flame retardance was obtained in earlier systems either by adding a plasticizer which contained halogen or by using a hardner which contained halogen, e.g. chlorendic or HET anhydride. These materials are toxic and if is not readily soluble in normal epoxy resins. On this line, the work has been done to develop epoxy resins which are flame-retardent in their own right i.e. resins which are themselves halogenated. Such resins generally contain chlorine or bromine, and thus they may be based on tetrabromo bisphenol. Such resins are now available commercially.

They have the advantage that being of similar basic structure to normal epoxy resin, they may be hardened with the same hardners as are used with the normal unhalogenated resin. In some cases blends of halogenated and normal resins can be used. Table 7.3 lists a few characteristics of commercially available brominated and chlorinated epoxy resins.

It is noted from the Table that these resins are semi-solids and their main usage to date has therefore been either in solution or in blends with liquid epoxy resins. The halogen content of resin containing bromine is markedly higher than chlorinated resin. This is due to higher molecular weight of bromine and chlorine.

TABLE 7.3

Characteristics of Halogen-containing Epoxy Resins

	Bromine Containing	*Cl_2 containing resin*	*Std. Resin*
Epoxy equivalent	**365**	**260**	**190**
Total halogen content	**% 48**	**28**	**1**
Physical state	**semi-solid**	**semi-solid**	**liquid**
Sp. gr.	**1.49**	**1.38**	**1.16**

NON-GLYCIDYL-ETHER EPOXY RESINS

There are alternative ways of introducing the reative epoxy group into the molecule. One of these is the epoxidation of an unsaturated compounds as show below.

-C = C- $+O_2$ ⟶ -C-C— (with O bridging, \/ O)
(Unsaturated compds.) (usually as H_2O_2 or peracetic acid (Epoxy compoound)

In this case the resulting epoxy compound is not usually a glycidyl-ether, i.e. the epoxy group is not in close proximity to an ether linkage. The epoxy resins made oy the epoxiadation of unsaturated compounds are referred to as nonglycidyl ether resins. These resins may be further divided into two groups: (1) cyclo-aliphatic epoxy resins, i.e. those containing a ring structure and (2) Acylic aliphatic epoxy resins. i.e. those containing no ring structure.

CYCLO-ALIPHATIC EPXOY RESINS

These resins contain both epoxy groups and non-aromatic rings in their structure. A few of these are listed in Table 7.4.

TABLE 7.4

SOME COMMERCIALLY AVAILABLE CYCLO-ALIPHATIC EPOXY RESIN

	Chemical Name	*Physical state*
(1)	3,4-Epoxy-6-methyl cyclohenyl methyl 3,4-epoxy-6-methyl cyclobexane carboxylate	Liquid
(2)	Vinyl cyclohexane dioxide	Liquid
(3)	Dicyclopentadiene dioxide	Solid
(4)	Linonene dioxide	Liquid
(5)	DGEBA	Liquid

The physical properties of these cycloaliphatic epoxy resins differ markedly from those of the standard liquid glycidyl-ether resins. These resins are generally of lower viscosity and of lower epoxy equivalent. The viscosity of some of the cyclo-aliphatic epoxy resins is so low that they may be used as diluents i.e. viscosity reducers for glycidyl-ethers. The improtant difference between the conventional glycidyl ethers and cyloaliphatic epoxy resins is the rate at which they react with different types of hardeners, and this must be appreciated if they are to be used to their fullest advantage. Cycloaliphatic epoxies tend to react more slowly with aliphatic amines than do conventional glycidyl ethers. They do, however, harden and the rate at which they harden depends on the structure of epoxy resins. When hardened, they exhibit different properties than that of hardened glycidyl-ether epoxy resin. To some extent these differences can be predicted from their structures the righ structures and short side chains suggest that these materials should give rigid structures of high deflection temperatures but at the same time be rather brittle. The resins tend, therefore, to be used in applications such as glass fabric reinforced laminates. In these applications, their low viscosity facilitates the manufacture of the laminates.

ACYCLIC ALIPHATIC EPOXY RESINS

These are epoxy resins which are essentially aliphatic but which, unlike cyclo-aliphatic epoxy resins described earlier, do not contain a ring structure and can be classified in the groups, (a) Epoxidised polyolefins and (b) Epoxidised oils.

Epoxidised Polyolefins

These compounds are made by epoxidising a polyclefin such as butadien. A schematic representation of one such compound is shown below.

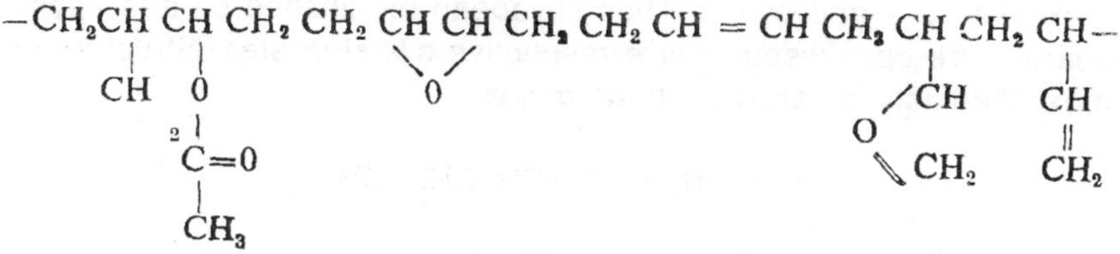

Interesting points in this structure are (1) the potentially high functionality of the molecule, i.e. its large number of reactive points. Thus depending on the value of n, there may be and usually are, considerably more than two epoxy groups per molecule. In addition, there are some residual double bonds capable of reaction, not to mention hydroxyl groups. (2) the high molecular weight, hence high vicosity of the resins (3) the fact that epoxy groups present are not activated by ether links, as in the glycidyl resins.

Typical physical properties of three basic epoxidised polybutadiene resins are given in Table 7.5.

TABLE 7.5

TYPICAL PHYSICAL PROPERTIES OF EPOXIDISED POLYBUTADIENE RESINS

Appearance	*Type A* amber	*Type B* light yellow	*Type C* light yellow
	liquid	liquid	liquid
Viscosity at 25°C	18000	16000	1500
Epoxy equivalent	177	145	232
Non-volatile matter present	99.1	94.2	77.1
Sp. gr. at 25°C	1.01	1.014	0.985

Most notable points about these resins are (1) the lower viscosity ones contain a volatile constituent, presumably some kind of diluent and (2) they have a specific gravity than that of glycidyl-ether resins.

Only epoxy resin A is suitable for use as a casting resin because the other two resins contain volatile materials which would prove troublesome during vacuum degassing operations. Epoxy resin C is used as a laminating resin because of its low viscosity.

Epoxydised Oils

Double bonds in certain oils and esters can be epoxidised to give epoxidised oils and esters. Thus soyabean oil, linseed oil and epoxy stearate are epoxidised to give respective oils stearates. Structure of epoxidised actyl stearate is shown below.

$$C_8H_{17}(CH_2)_7\,\underset{\backslash\;O\;/}{CH\,CH}\,(CH_2)_7\,CH_3$$

The epoxidised oils are liquids of rather low viscosity than the diglycidyl ether of bisphenol A resin. These react toward hardners in a manner similar to that of the other non-glycidyl-ethers discussed earlier. Thus they react rather slowly with amines but at a reasonable rate with anhydrides. These materials hardened give rather leathery products which have so far not found widespread application in their own right. However, the more lightly epoxidised linseed is showing promise, particularly in adhesive applications.

GLYCIDYL ETHERS OF BISPHENOL F AND EPOXY NOVOLAK RESINS

Bisphenol F is a condensation product of phenol and formaldehyde. It can be reacted with ECH to give a series of glycidyl ethers. The resins derived from bisphenol F are more expensive than the bisphenol A resins but have a much lower viscosity and hence are particularly suitable for use in solvent-free coatings. They are manufactured by Ciba-Geigy, Dow Chemical Co; and Dai Nippon. The condensation of phenol and formaldehyde can be made to yield a phenol novolak resin instead of bisphenol novolak resin. In the same way. epoxy cresol novolak resins can also be obtained. Epoxy novolak are not normally used alone for coattings but can replace 5-15 per cent of the DGEBA resins used in order to obtain increased reactivity and better resistance against organic acids. The simplast novolak is bispenol F in which n=O but novolaks with 10-12 phenolic hydroxyl groups can be synthesized.

A typical epoxy phenol novolak novolak resin used in the manufacture of composites has the following properties.

Form	semi solid
Epoxy value	5.5-5.7 ep/kg.
Viscosity at 52° C	35,000-70,000 CP
Density	1.20-1.25 g/cm^3

MANUFACTURE

LABORATORY PREPARATION OF DGEBA (mol. wt. 380)

The apparatus employed is a heated reaction vessel with thermometer mechanical stirrer, dropping device for admitting apueous NaOH, and a vapour take-off to which is fitted a water cooled condenser with a thermometer and a condensate collection and a separative chamber provided with a return to convey the lower ECH layer to the reaction vessel. The separative chamber also has a draw-off and collector for the upper water layer.

The reaction vessel is charged with 1388 parts (15 moles) of ECH and 342 parts (1.5 moles) of bisphenol A. The stirrer is started and the solution of bisphenol A in ECH is heated to 119° C, whereupon ECH begins refluxing at a temperature of 112° C. During a period of 3.5 hours 304 parts of 40 per cent aqueous NaOH (3 moles) is added to the boiling reaction mixture. Heating is continued for an additional 15 minutes. After all the caustic is added. The reaction mixture is then subjected to distillation for removal of unreacted ECH.

In order to separate salt from crude product, approximate 550 parts of toluene is added with stirring and mixture is filtered, the salt cake being washed with additional toluene and washing combined with filterate. The mixture is then subjected to distillation for removal of toluene, the mixture being heated to temperature of 120° C at mm pressure. The resulting viscous products in amount of 509 parts, have a Durran's Mecurry method softenting point of 6° C epoxy value of 0.519 epoxy equivalents per 100 grams and contains 0.52 per cent chlorine.

COMMERCIAL PREPARATION

Epoxy resins are produced commercially by a batch process; regardless of whether a one-stage or a two-stage process is used.

A batch process of resin preparation is described below.
Basis : 300 kg epoxy resin

MATERIAL REQUIREMENTS

Epichlorohydrin	495 kg	1.65	100	165
Bisphenol A	307 kg	1.02	70	70
Caustic soda	110 kg	.35	10	-

Epichlorohydrin is charged to a stainless steel kettle equipped with an agitator and reflux condenser. Bisphenol A is then added and contents are mixed. The temperature is raised to 50° C. Caustic soda is then added. Exothermic reaction starts by addition of caustic soda. External steam heating is stopped at this stage. Reaction temperature is maintained in between 55-65° C. If necessary, cooling water can be circulated in the jacket to maintain this temperature. The contents of the reactor are constantly stirred during caustic soda addition which should take 2-3 minutes. The reaction mixture is then held at 60-65° C for a further 30 minutes. The caustic soda is added as a 30 per cent solution. The total reaction time is 3.5 hours and the yield is 66 per cent of theory. At the end of the reaction, the mixture is allowed to separate into an aqueous and an organic phase.

The organic layer is then charged to a distillation still to recover excess epichlorohydrin. The distillate forms two layers, the bottom being principally epichlorohydrin and the top a mixture of epichlorohydrin and water. The residue is the still.

APPLICATIONS

Epoxy resins have a wide range of applications. It is, however, not possible to discuss all these applications in detail in this book. Major applications of epoxies are in the following fields.

1. Adhesives
2. Surface coatings
3. Lamination
4. Potting

5. Reinforced plastics
6. Civil engineering consturction
7. Tooling and moulding industry
8. Miscellaneous industries.

Largest amount of epoxy resin is used in surface coatings. Other applications which consume large amounts of resin include adhesive and the electrical industry.

ADHESIVES

Epoxy adhesives in commercial practice are based on DGEBA, the diglycidyl ether of bisphenol A. These resins are characterised by the following.

(1) Low shrinkage during curing
(2) Low viscosity at high solid content (or even 100 per cent solids)
(3) Absence of volatile compounds.
(4) Low initial tack
(5) High brittleness when cured, which results in low adhesive peel strength of adhered joint.

The low initial tack and brittleness of cured resin can be overcome by suitable formulation. Also control of physical form (e.g. liquid, paste or film) is also made. Aliphatic amines, e.g. diethylenetriamine and triethylene tetramine are most common hardeners for these adhesives. Although the aliphatic amines are generally effective curing agents at room temperature, bend strengths are higher if heat is used, possibly because of increased polymer chain flexibility at elevated temperatures.

MODIFIERS FOR EPOXY ADHESIVES

As described above, cured epoxy resins are fairly brittle. Although flexibility can be achieved by incorporating plasticizers of ester type, but they result in loss of shear strength. So epoxy resins are modified for increased toughness by addition of other polymeric materials. The line between resinous modifiers and curing agents, in this context, is not sharp, since the modifying agents often have functional groups capable of reacting with the epoxy. Important modifiers are listed below.

1. Polyamides

Textile and moulding nylons (such as nylon 66,6 and 610) are highly crystalline polymers incompatible with epoxy resins. The polyamide modifiers used are based on dimer acids, for example, dimerized linoleic acid and ethylenediamine. These polymers are complex molecules containing primary, secondary amine groups as well as amide groups. They have relatively high amine equivalent weights and are therefore used in large proportions in epoxy resins. They give adhesives which are characterised by unusual flexibility and toughness. Another class of nylons used as modifiers are "soluble nylons". They are either copolymers or alkony methylated derivatives of nylon 6 or 66. In either case the products are clear, amorphous and soluble in aqueous alcohol, chlorinated aliphatic hydrocarbons, and other common solvents. Adhesives from epoxy nylon combinations have toughness, high lap shear strength and extremely high peel strength at ambient and slightly elevated temperatures. These modifiers are room temperature adhesives.

2. Phenolics

Phenolic resins, preferably resols react with bisphenol A epoxy resins to give adhesives that are widely used today in moderately high temperature applications. In practice the amount of resol used is considerably greater than required to cross-link the epoxy, so that the overall effect is principally one of using the epoxy resin to toughen the phenolic and improve adhesion to metal.

Fillers

Fillers are often incorported in epoxy adhesives to obtain one or more of the following advantages.

(1) Lower cost

(2) Less shrinkage

(3) Lower coefficient of thermal expansion

(4) Greater heat resistance.

Titanium dioxide, lead oxide, ferric oxide, alumine etc. are the common fillers that impart superior strength at 180° F. At room temperature, however, the unfilled system is stronger than the filled compositions.

On curing, epoxy resins possess excellent bonding characteristics and the reaction takes place without the evolution of volatiles and, often, even without heat or pressure. They may be used to bond various metals, rubbers, and glass with satisfactory results although contain plastics such as P.V.C. and on polyethylene the bond is usually poor.

The relatively high price of epoxy resins has limited their widespread use for bonding processes in the wood or allied industries. Urea, melamine and phenol-formaldehyde are normally used for plywood and the many other furniture applications, although for certain structual applications where wood laminates of high strength are required the epoxies are generally to be preferred. Metal bonding is very successful with epoxy resins which are now used extensively in the aircraft industry where, in addition to good bond requirements, good thermal resistance is also required.

Some of the epoxy resins are used not only for their good adhesive properties alone but also combined with toughness especially for floor-surfacing compounds in the construction of new floors and in refluxing old ones. These compounds may be laid on concrete, metal or wood substracts, and by suitable formulation a range of colours, surface finishes and thicknesses can be made to suit various industrial and domestic requirements. For this type of application there are normally three-component systems consisting of resin, curing agent and aggregate.

Epoxy resins are also used as adhesives in the bonding of microscopic hollow spheres of phenol formaldehyde resin, and known as synthetic foams. These foams are used extensively for replacing rotton wood in old buildings. They are supplied in putty form and can be travelled into cavities where, eventually, they set to a tough hard mass.

Typical formulations of various types of epoxy adhesives are given below.

(1) GENERAL PURPOSE PASTE ADHESIVE

PART A

Ingredients	*Parts by wt.*
Epoxy resin	10.0
Bentone (optional)	0.7
Methyl alcohol	0.2
Titanium dioxide	1.0
Calcium carbonate	2.8

PART B

Polyamide curing agent	6 parts
(liquid resin)	0.4
Bentone	0.1
Methyl alcohol	10.5
Calcium carbonate	0.3

Mix part A (white) with equal volume of part B (dark grey) until a uniform light grey colour. White or dark streaks indicate poor mixing.

Properties

(1) Pot life	1 to 2 hr.
(2) Cure time	24 to 36 hr at 75° F

It is used for bonding metals, ceramics, plastics and rubbers. It is a commonly used epoxy-resin adhesive.

(2) FAST ROOM TEMPERATURE CURING GENERAL PURPOSE ADHESIVE

PART A

Ingredients	*Parts by wt.*
Epoxy resin	1.0
Asbestos shorts	1.0
Alumina	1.0

PART B

Modified amine adduct	2.5
Asbestos shorts	1.0
Alumina	1.0

Mix part A and part B until a smooth adhesive is obtained.

Properties

Pot life	30 min.
Cure time	4 hr.

It is used for bonding metals and other metals of constructions.

(3) TOUGH GENERAL PURPOSE ADHESIVE

For resilient bonds and good low temperature characteristics, Ciba has investigated blends of liquid epoxy resin and a liquid polysulphide resin cured with a liquid amine hardener. An example of such an adhesive is given below.

Ingredients	Parts by wt. (1)	Parts by wt. (2)
"Araldite" 6020	100	100
"Thiokol" LP-3	50	50
Dimethylaminopropylene	10	-
"DMP" 30	-	6

After a cure of 1 hr. at 100° C, the tensile shear strengths were as follows.

Test temperature, °C	*Tensile shear strength, ps* (1)	(2)
-40	870-1885	2180-2470
20	1740-3200	2470-3200
70	145-290	580-725

4. AIRCRAFT ADHESIVE

Ingredients	*Parts by wt.*
"Epon" 1001 (Solid at room temperature)	33
"Polyophen" 5023	67
Dicyandiamide (101 mesh)	6
Aluminium dust (64 per cent through 325 mesh)	100

This adhesive is used in impregnating glass tape used in binding structural members of jet aircraft.

The "polyophen" is a low molecular weight phenolic made with excess formaldehyde, containing 15 per cent water.

The glass tape acts as a carrier for the adhesive and permits a heavier glue line. The prepag is stable for several months at room temperature, or infinitely when refrigerated.

PATCHING, CANKING AND SEALING COMPOUNDS

Every formulator has his own recipes for epoxy patches and sealing compounds, of which the following are some of those popularly used.

5. STICK SOLDER ADHESIVE

Ingredients	*Parts by wt.*
Epoxy resin	100
Aluminium powder	60
"Santocel" 54	5-10
Methylenedianiline	28.5

The hot melt mix is cast in 0.5 in. diameter tubes and allowed to harden at room temperature. The sticks remain usable for more than 5 week at room temperature, or much longer when refrigerated.

The part to be soldered must first be heated sufficiently to melt the end of the stick under slight pressure; then additional heat is applied continuously to effect cure.

6. CANKING AND GLAZING COMPOUND

PART A

Ingredients	*Parts by wt.*
Epoxy resin	100
Aluminium stearate	20
Titanium diamide	80
Calcium carbonate	65

PART B

"Epi-cure" (viscous flexibilizer hardener)	150
Aluminium stearate	20
Calcium carbonate	225

Parts A and B are mixed mechanically and applied to clean surfaces with a junking gum, putty knife or high pressure gum. This compound is suggested for bending sash metal to wood, steel to concrete, steel to wood.

7. CONCRETE FLOOR PATCH

Liquid epoxy resin	100
Salt free sand	300
"Lancast A"	70
Bisphenol A	5

The surface to be repaired must be free of loose spaltings, dirt and oil. If the surrounding concrete is weak, it is best to break it up and clean it. After the patch has been trowelod on and smoothened over, additional sand may be sprinkled on top to provide a nonskid surface. At ordinary temperatures, gelatin occurs in 1 to 2 hours but it is best to wait overnight before submitting the floor to severe usages.

8. BOAT PATCH COMPOUND AND SEALER

Ingredients	*Parts by wt.*
Liquid epoxy resin	100
"Lancast" A	80
Triphenyl phosphite	10
Calcium carbonate	50
"Cab-o-sil"	5

The boat must be thoroughly dry and clean. Rotted wood should be scraped away. The patch will cure overnight at moderate room temperature, or in 1 hour under infrared lamps. Both wooden and polyester boats may be repaired. Unlike other resinous patches, the epoxies fanction satisfactorily with all common keel woods.

9. ORGANIC BODY SOLDER

Epoxy based solders for repairing automobile bodies have excellent adhesion to the base metal, negligible shrinkage during cure, superior impact resistance, and good machinibility.

PART A

Ingredients	*Parts by wt.*
"Araldite" 6005	65
"Araldite" RD-2 (reactive diluent)	8
Glass fibres	7

"cab-o-sil"	10
Kaolin	15
Titanium dioxide	2

PART B

"Lancast" A	35
DMP 30	5
Halo black	0.15
"cab-o-sil"	5
Asbestine 3-X	50
Kaolin	5

The ingredients of parts A and B are mixed in numerical sequence at room temperature, then passed through a three-roll mill. The two are mixed in equal proportion by weight and applied by putty knife. The potlife is 1 hr. at room temperature, but the materials will cure in 20 min. at 100° C e.g. under a heat lamp.

SURFACE COATINGS

The epoxy resins are well known for their outstanding chemical resistance but they have the drawback of limited exterior durability and high price. They find wide applications in storing finishes e.g. undercoats for refrigerators; washing machines etc.

In the building industry epoxy finishes are used in chemical factories to give protection against acidic vapours, oxidising and reducing gases such as chlorine and sulphur dioxide and spillage of aggressive chemicals. In such cases they are mainly used as two component paint i.e. the base component and the hardener which are mixed prior to use and have a limited pot life. The inherent nature of the resin is such that it continues to cure after conventional drying and so it is recommended to give one week's interval between applications and exposure to corrosive conditions.

For the sake of simplicity epoxy coatings may be divided into two broad categories.

1. Solvent based system

(a) Room temperature curing-This groups includes solid or liquid resins which are cured by polyamides, polyamines etc. Air-dry esters are also included in this category.

(b) Heat curing finishes-This group includes solutions of solid resins, liquid resins, or epoxy esters cured by urea-or melamine, or phenol formaldehyde resins.

2. Solventless (100% solid) system

These are coatings based on liquid resins which are either room temperature cured or heat cured, depending on the choice of hardener.

AMINE CURED COATINGS

One of the most common types of solvent based epoxy coatings are based on the lower molecular weight solid epoxy resins cured with aliphaic polyamines at polyamides. System of this type offers chemical and solvent resistance normally associated with competitive type heat cured system.

Since the curing reaction takes place at ambient temperatures, systems of this type are necessary two component systems. After addition of the hardener, the working life (pot life) varies from 8-26 hours, depending on the formulations.

Epoxy/polyamine systems give excellent coatings over ferrous and non-ferrious metals, concrete and wood. Typical applications are around oil refineries, petro chemicals plants, and marine installations. Normally the coatings are applied by conventional means (spray or brush) in multicoats consisting of primers and top coats. Polyamide cured epoxy systems are widely used where conditions of water immersion are encountered, particularly in marine applications. Both the amine cured and polyamide cured epoxy systems exhibit excellent chemical resistance, and find wide use in maintenance applications where resistance to corrosion or chemical attach must be considered.

ESTER TYPE COATINGS

Epoxy resin ester coatings are used widely. They are produced in formulations similar to the alkyd contings. Epoxy esters are available in short, medium and long oil lengths. The long oil epoxy resins have limited chemical resistance whereas the short oil lengths esters exhibit good chemical resistance.

Epoxy esters, like drying oils, promote surface wetting and are often used where optimum surface preparation is not possible. Because of their limited chemical resistance, epoxy esters find their maximum use in mild, chemical corrosive areas and in marine environments too severe for the use of alkyd type coatings.

HEAT CURING FINISHES

Heat curing finishes are one of the most sizable markets for epoxy resins in combination with other resins. Generally, these systems include the higher molecular weight epoxy resins cured with aldehyde condensation products such as urea-melamine and phenol formaldehyde resins.

Resins of the 4000-5000 molecular weight range are used primarily for this type of coating. The phenolic resin is generally one of a low degree of condensation, and part of the methylol groups may be etherified with butanol. Generally, the ratio of epoxy phenolic ranges from 70:30 to 80:20, depending on the properties desired.

Acid catalysts such as phosphoric acid or the morpholine salt of p-toluene sulphonic acid may be added to accelerate the cure.

Epoxy phenolic systems are used for coatings on process equipment, tank and drum linings, can coatings, pipe linings, and similar applications where excellent chemical resistance is required.

Epoxy-amino resin combinations have slightly less chemical resistance than epoxy-phenolic systems, but exhibit better initial colour and colour retention. There are almost limitless possibilities in variation of the epoxy resin with urea melamine; the proportions in the epoxy amino resin can vary from 90:10 to 60:50.

System of this type are used in appliance finishes and primers, protective coatings for the food industry, can and drum coatings.

SOLVENTLESS COATINGS

Solventless coatings or high solids epoxy coatings have become quite popular in last few years. These systems make possible the application of hard, highly resistant films in one coat which has stimulated their use in a growing number of applications.

Advantage of solventles coatings are (1) high built in a single application (2) minimisation of pin holes and other surface defects due to the absence of solvents (3) excellent heat and chemical resistance, and (4) lower application cost per mil of coating applied.

Two other categories of epoxy coatings are recognised. They are:

1. Powdered coatings
2. Solution coatings

POWDERED COATINGS

These coatings are generally useful for small parts and have been used for coating small motor stacks to replace conventional slot paper insulation. They provide good edge coverage but are unsuitable for large pieces.

Epoxy thermosetting powder coatings usually contain a mixture of pigments, one or more, solid epoxy resinous binder, flow control agent, curing agent and in some instances a catalyst. System ranging from generally fusion to dry blending in used produce these powders.

A typical formulation based on azelaic acid is given below.

Ingredients	*Parts by wt.*
Epoxy resin (first part)	32.20
Azelaic acid	9.80
Potassium acetate	0.03
Lamp black	0.91
Colloidal silica	3.49
Epoxy resin (2nd part)	45.45
Stannous acetate	4.45
Flow control agent	5.52
Total	100.0

Charge the initial part of the epoxy resin (mol. wt. 1060) to the kettle equipped with a heat source and mechanical agitator. Raise temperature to 292° F and add curing agent and then decrease the temperature to 240° F and add potassium acetate and lamp black. Raise the temperature to 290° F. Add the colloidal silica. Then add second part of epoxy resin (mol. wt. 1060) and stannous acetate and flow control agent and raise temperature to 294° F.

SOLUTION COATINGS

The epoxy resin coatings are used for coating laboratory furniture, lawn furniture appliances, hardwares; for can and drum lining, military aircarft, floor and masonary coatings, swimming pool paints etc. The largest single market for epoxy resin coatings is in specialised formulations used for automotive finishes. The majority of the remaining market is broadly described as the maintenance field.

The typical applications of the maintenance field is in oil refineries, linings for transmission pipe line and paper mills.

Industrial maintenance coatings are cold-cured epoxy resin coatings. These coatings consist of primer coat, undercoat and a top coat. Typical formulations for such coats is given below. The paint system is brushed or sprayed to a film thickness of 2 to 3 mils per coat.

FORMULATION

Ingredients	primer kgs	Undercoat kgs	Topcoat kgs
Basic lead silico chromate	430	296	129
Iron oxide	17	68	-
Titanium dioxide (rutile)	-	-	45
Chromium oxide	-	-	63
Asbestos	85	68	58
Mica	28	23	18
Bentone in 95.5 methanol water	3	3	3
Epoxy resin	199	201	212
Methyl isobutyl ketone	43	44	56
Lenolling agent	10	24	25
Xylene	23	65	69
Oxitol glycol ether	67	65	69
Gyclosol 53 solvent	103	126	86
	1016	836	842
Curing agent system			
Polyamide resin	107	108	114
Xylene	46	63	93
Solvent	58	46	49
	211	217	256

Some other formulations based on epoxy resins are given below.

1. EPOXY-AMINE COATING COMPOSITION

Ingredients	% by wt. solid basis (a)	(b)
Epox 1001 (epoxy resin)	9.15	80.1
Beetle 216-8	2.9	2.5
Diethylene triamino	5.6	-
Curing agent C-111	-	17.4
	100.0	100.0

Solvent composition	% by wt.
Methyl isobutyl ketone	33.0
Cellosolve solvent	33.0
Xylene	34.0

Beetle 216-8 is the trade name of American cyanamid company for a urea formaldehyde resin. Curing agent C-111 is a proprietary amine compound available from shell chemical corporation.

The amine or curing agent is packaged separately usually as a 50 per cent solution in the coating solvent. The solvent mentioned above produces good flow and may be used for brush application. For spray application the following solvent application is preferred.

Ingredients	% by wt.
Methyl isobutyl ketone	45
Butyl cellsolve	5
Toluene	50

The above coating is dust free and hardens overnight but it requires about 6 days to develop its maximum resistance to chemicals. It can be used on metal or primers which are not affected by the solvent. The amine cured epoxies can be used in mastics which permit application of coatings up to 25 mils thick.

In general, a total thickness of about 5 mils, applied as one coat of primer and two coats of finish, gives coat protection. Such systems are used for industrial maintenance, farm equipment, handling corrosive fertilizers, and pipelines carrying gas, oil, water and mild chemicals.

2. EPOXY-PHENOLIC RESIN GRAY FINISH

Ingredients	Parts by wt.
Titanium dioxides, rutile	10.3
Lamp black	0.1
Epoxy resin (Epox 1009)	25.8
Phenolic resin (Durez 15956)	13.9
Cellosolve acetate	19.3
Toluene	19.3
Solicylic acid (25 per cent in Neosol)	10.6
Silicone resin (SR-82)	0.4
	100.0
Total solids	53.0%
Pigment : binder ratio by wt.	1:4
Epoxy : phenolic resin ratio	65.35

3. EPOXY-PHENOLIC RESIN GRAY PRIMERS

Ingredients	% by wt. (a)	(b)
Titanium dioxide, rutile	45.1	43.9
Lamp black	0.9	0.9
Epoxy resin (Epox 1009)	11.8	13.3
Phenolic resin (Methylon 75108)	-	4.5
Cellosolve acetate	15.9	16.8
Toluene	15.9	16.8
Salicylic acid (5 per cent in Neosol)	3.7	3.6
Silicone resin (SR-82)	2.3	3.6
	100.0	100.0
Total solids	65.3	63.5
Pigment : binder ratio by wt.	2.4:1	2.4:1
Epoxy : phenolic ratio by wt.	65.35	75.25

Formulation 3 (a) is a typical finish coat for use over the primers. This finish may be used directly on passicated steel or even the primers. It should be sprayed to give dry film thickness of 1.0-1.5 mils and baked at 15 min at 400° F to 30 min at 350° F.

4. 100% REACTIVE EPOXY COATINGS

Ingredients	Parts by wt. (a)	(b)	(c)
Base composition			
Red iron oxide	25.0	-	-
Titanium dioxide	-	2.0	2.0
Cab-o-sil*	4.0	4.5	4.5
Epoxy resin ERL- 2774	100.0	89.3	89.3
Epoxy resin ERL- 0810	-	10.7	10.7
Linde R-64 silicone	0.8	0.8	0.8
Hardener portion			
Epoxy hardener ZZI-0814	25.0	25.0	-
Thiokol LP-3**	-	-	50.0
DMP-10	-	-	5.0
Glycorol	2.5	2.5	3.2
Lampblack	-	0.25	0.6

*Gdofrey L, Gabot, Inc,
**Thikol chemical corp.

The suggested manufacturing procedure is to disperse the iron oxide or a titanium dioxide as a three-roll mill in part of the base vehicle. Mix the cap-o-sil and silicone resin with the paste

on a high-shear mixer and add the remainder of the base vehicle. Prepare the hardener separately by blending in a mixer. The base and hardener should be pressure filtered through a 100-mesh screen and then packaged separately.

For spray application with the cusmer equipment, the base and hardenser ar placed in separate pressure pots. The proportioning machine delivers the two components in the correct ratio to the spray gun where they are mixed and atonized for spraying.

The above compositions may be used as maintenance coatings for the inside or outside of metal and concrete tanks and other structures where filling is desired on every surface or where skid resistant coatings are desired on floors or sample sand or other grit may be blown into the spray stream so that it will become bound by the composition. 4 (c) is designed to have good flow and flexibility, and is suggested for repairing concrete surfaces.

5. EPOXY-POLAMIDE WHITE ENAMEL

Pigment base	Pounds	Gallons
Titanium dioxide, rutile	809	23.1
Epoxy resin	900	90.0
Xylene	450	62.3
Methyl isobutyl ketone	450	67.5
Add to base when ready to use		
Versamid 125	300	37.0
Xylene	180	25.1
Cellosolve	20	2.6
	3109	307.6

Total solids	64.5%
PVC	15.4%
Pigment : binder ratio by wt.	0.9:1.0%
Epoxy polyamide ratio	75:25

The two components as given above are packaged separately and mixed before using. The enamel may be air-dried or baked at 300° F for about 10 minutes to produce very tough chemical-resistant coatings.

6. EPOXY-PHENOLIC PRIMER VEHICLE

Ingredients	Pounds	Gallons
Bakelite phenolic resin CKR-2400	75.0	8.32
Bakelite epoxy resin EKR-2053	25.0	2.51
Tung oil	97.7	13.40
Linseed oil	97.7	12.57
Mineral spirits	241.6	27.20
Theoretical yield	537.0	73.0

Cooking Procedure

Heat resins to 450° F in, 30 min, hold for 30 min. Add linseed oil and heat to 565° F in 15 min, hold for 30 min. Add tung oil and boil at 465° F to obtain viscosity at 55% non-volatile in mineral spirits and a colour of 10.

7. EPOXY-PHENOLIC PRIMER

Ingredients	*Pounds*	*Gallons*	*% by wt.*
Iron oxide red	254.0	6.49	45.0
Zinc oxide	28.2	0.60	5.0
Barytes	282.0	7.61	50.0
Vehicle (Formula 6)	436.0	58.80	69.7
Butanol	6.80	1.01	1.1
Xylene	180.2	25.17	28.8
Pb drier (24 %)	2.0	0.22	0.3
Co drier (6%)	0.8	0.10	0.1
	1190.0	100.0	

Total solids	67.8%
PVC	33.8%
Consistency	64 KU

Drier: 0.3% Pb+0.03% Co as metal to oil in vehicle.

LAMINATION

Epoxy resins are used in the manufacture of both low and high pressures laminates. As laminating resins they are used with a variety of reinforcing agents such as glassfibre, asbestos and certain synthetic fibres. As noted earlier, they cure without water of condensation, which makes them ideally suitable for this application. Epoxies also exhibit excellent mechanical, thermal and electrical insulating properties. Such laminates also possess excellent chemical resistance.

The use of epoxy laminates has been restricted in all but some of the highly specialized industrial fields due to the relatively high price of the base resin in comparison with some of the more common resins. Very few used have been foundin the domestic consumer field, although they are used in industry where their superior mechanical strength and good heat and chemical resistance are required. Typical applications include structural components for aircraft and missiles, chemical resistant tanks, and laminated tubes and pipes for conveying oil.

During the last few years, its use in filament winding has grown rapidly. The rapid growth of filament winding as method of producing reinforced plastics was primarily due to military interest in producing light weight high strength missile cases, but filament winding for commercial uses already represents an extremely large and attractive market.

Laminating covers wet lay up as well as dry lay up or 'prepag' uses. The prepag method is most popular where it is advantageous to apply the resin to the reinforcing material for later use. Wet lay up is used for on the job applications. For the majority of applications, the wet lay up process shows definte economic advantages. For this process, liquid resins are generally used either with liquid aromatic amines or with liquid acid anhydride curing agents. For the dry lay up or prepeg process, generally solid resins are used, usually with an aromatic amine curing agents that will form a suitable 'B' stage with the resin so that the preimpregnated glass curing has some storage stability.

POTTING

Epoxy compounds are used for potting and encaptulating many electrical parts because of ease with which they produce noisefree castings. This condition is essential to prevent breakdown or electrical deteriorations. These epoxy systems exhibit high dielectric strength, high resistivity, good moisture resistance, good chemical resistance. Some of the applications include electric motor parts, automotive coils, cable splices, relays, commutators,and selenium rectifiers.

The use of pre-impregnated glass cloth in the electrical industry is increasing. This is used for tapes, slot linings in electrical machines and the like.

• Chapter 4 •

ION-EXCHANGE RESINS

INTRODUCTION

Ion exchange resins been described as elastic three dimensional hydrocarbon networks to which ionisable groups are attached (suspension polymerization, sulphonation alkylation and amination). Although the manufacture of ion exchange resins involves well known unit processes but a great deal of ingenuity and care is needed for the synthesis of these resins, particularly in controlling the rate of reaction and extent of various reactions and in maintaining within a specified range the particle size distribution of the resin.

ION EXCHANGE PROCESS: The process of ion exchange may be defined as the reversible interchange of ions between a liquid phase in which there is no permanent change in the solid structure. The solid is the ion exchange material. "Reversible" and no permanent change are the key points in this definition of ion exchange. Ion exchange has important applications is water conditioning, such as softening and deionization.

It provides a method of separation useful in many chemical processes and in analysis. It has special utility in chemicals purification, medical research, food processing, mining, agriculture, and a variety of other areas.

With few exceptions, the ability of ion exchange rests with the ability to use and re-use the ion-exchange materials. For example, in water softening;

$$2R\text{-}Na^{+}+Ca^{2}+ \rightleftharpoons R\text{-}_{2}Ca^{2+}+2Na^{+}$$

The exchanger R+ in exchange for calcium and thus remove calcium from hard water and to replace it with an equivalent quantity of sodium.

Subsequently the calcium loaded resin may be treated with a sodium chloride solution, bringing it back to the sodium form, ready for another cycle of operation. This conversion step is commonly called regeneration. Millions of gallons of water may be softened per cubic foot resin during an operating period of many years.

Ion exchange has been found to occur in a wide variety of substances such as silicates, phosphates, flourides, humus, cellulose, wood, proteins, alumina, resins, lignin, living cells, glass, barium sulphate, and silver chloride.

The first significant contributions to ion exchange are largely due to Thomson and Way in 1850, prior to the postulation, by Arhemious in 1885, to the concept of ionization. These investigators showed an elution of calcium proportional to the ammonia used in elution. Ion exchange has been used on an industrial scale since about 1910 with the introduction of water softening using natural and, later, synthetic zeolites. Sulfonated coal, developed for industrial water treatment, was the first ion exchange material stable at low pH. The introduction of synthetic organic ionexchange resins in 1935 resulted from the synthesis and description by Adams and Holmes of phenolic condensation products containing another phenolic or amine groups which could be used for the reversible exchange of cations or anions. The period 1940-45 has been marked by a rapidly increasing degree of sophostication in the design of ion-exchange materials. The future holds promise of many new and unexpected used and further product sophistication. Ion-exchange resins have now, however, reached a considerable degree of maturity and the rapid changes of last twenty five years are not likely to continue at anything approaching the earlier pace.

To be generally useful, an ion exchange must meet a certain number of basic requirements, many of which are closely interrelated, so that the modification in one may not be possible without some change in another. Conventional ion-exchange materials contain ion-active sites throughout their entire structure with a grossly uniform distribution of activity.

FUNCTION GROUPS: Ion exchange resins consits of the principal parts, a structural portion (polymer matrix) and a functional portion (ion-active group). The wide variety of ion-exchange resins formulations and properties derives from various combinations of these parts.

TYPES OF ION-EXCHANGE RESINS :

Ion-exchange resins can be divided into time categories e.g., (1) Strong acid, (2) Weak acid, (3) Strong base, (4) Weak base, (5) a broad miscellaneous category of ion-specific structures.

STRONG ACID RESINS

They are best exemplified by the principal sulfonaterd styrene divinylbenzene copolymer products. All are spherical products prepared by sulfonation of styrene-divinyl-benzene copolymer heads with the sulfonating agent of choice.

WEAK ACID RESINS

Weak-acid resins have been prepared by a wide variety of procedures and encompass a large number of functional groups and structures. Functional groups may include phenolic, phosphorus, RP $(OH)_2$ or carboxylic entities of a rather wide range of acid strength. The most common weak acids are those prepared by crosslinking an unsaturated carboxylic acid such as acrylic or methacrylic, or maleic with a cross linking agent such as divinyl benzene or ethylene dimethacrylate. An important family of weak acid exchangers is based on phenolic condensation reaction which incorporate the carboxylic acid group.

STRONG-BASE RESINS

Prior to the advent of strong-base anion-exchange resins in about 1950, there was no ion exchange process for the complete deionization of water. The older weak base resins were not ionized at a pH high enough to remove weak acids such as silicic acid. All of the strong base resins of present commercial importance contain quaternary ammonium groups fixed to a poly (styrene divinyl benzene) matrix to eliminate this earlier deficiency.

Synthesis involves choromethylation of the copolymer head using chloromethyl methyl ether and a Friedol-Crafts condensation catalyst such as $AlCl_3$, $SnCl_4$ or $2nCl_2$. The beads become fully swollen in the ether.

WEAK BASE ANION EXCHANGE RESINS

These resins contain without exception primary, secondary, and/or tertiary amine groups, or generally a mixture of these. A wide variety of products are available, generally condensation products of aliphatic polyamines with formaldehyde or with alkyl dihalides, such as ethylene dichlorides, or with epichlordydin. Another group of weak-base anion exchange resins is that prepared by the reaction of an amine or polyamide with the chloromethylated styrene-divinyl benzene copolymer head.

In the miscellaneous category of ion-exchange resins are the chelating resins.

PROPERTIES

The performance of an ion-exchange resin is determined by its properties and by the operating conditions. The properties are strongly interrelated and it is not possible to consider a single property independently of several others.

CAPACITY

Ion-exchange capacity may be expressed in a number of significant ways. Total capacity, i.e., the total number of sites available for exchange, is normally determined by one of two general methods, in either case after first converting the resin by chemical regeneration techniques to a given ionic form. The ion may then be chemically removed from a measured quantity of the resin and quantitatively determined in solution by only one of several conventional analytical methods, for example, a cation exchanger in the hydrogen form may be stripped of hydrogen ion with a NaCl solution collecting all the elurate and titrating with strand and base.

Alternatively hydrogen ion may be titrated with directly in the presence of the resin and a neutral salt solution. Total capacity may be expressed on a dry-weight, net-weight or net-volume basis. The dry-weight capacity, miliequivalents per gram, dry weight, of the resin is the most precise measure of the extent of chemical substitution during synthesis, as may be mathematically determined by comparison with a theoretical 1:1 reaction. For example, one sulfonic acid group per benzene ring on a styrene 8 per cent DVB resin would show a dry-weight capacity of about 5.35 mg/g. The net-weight capacity includes consideration of the solvent (water) uptake, and is expressed in milliequivalents per gram of the water resin. Net volume capacity, milliequivalent per mm. of the net resin has particular significance in the end use.

SWELLING EQUILIBRIA

The solvent retention capacity of an ionexchanger is reproducible, equilibrium quantity depends on the ion exchange capacity, ionic form, the kind of solvent, the compositionof the solution, the extent of cross-linkage, relative humidity, and temperature. Water swelling of an ion exchanger is primarily a hydration of the fixed ionic groups and thus, increases with an increase in capacity to the limits of the restraints imposed by the net work.

IONIC EQUILIBRIUM

Ion-exchange reactions are reversible; by washing a resin with an excess of electrolyte, it can be entirely converted to the desired salt form.

$$\bar{R}\,A^{+} + B^{+} \rightleftharpoons \bar{R}\,B + A^{+}$$

KINETICS

The speed with which ion exchange takes place determines the portion of the equilibrium capacity which may be utilized in a practical dynamic situation. Overall exchange rates may be influenced by a change in solvent nature and content, the particle size, the temperature, and the functional group (kind and concentration). Exchange rates are most rapid in water systems, and become increasingly show with less polar solvents.

CHEMICAL STABILITY

Ion exchange materials have chemical stability limitations beyond which it is not practical to operate with cation exchangers attacking first on the more susceptible functional groups. More highly cross-linked structures have a longer useful life because of the greater number of sites which must be attacked before swelling reduces the useful capacity and produces unacceptable physical properties. The quaternary ammonium salts are the least stable, with a temperature limitation of 50° C often recommended for hydroxide cycle operations. The tertiary amines are most stable.

PARTICLE FORM AND SIZE

Ion-exchange materials are sold as granules or spheres of the proper size and uniformity to meet the needs of a particular application. The majority of ion-exchange resin products are prepared and sold in spherical form. Bead size is controlled by the conditions of suspension polymerisation; in addition, size classifying operations may be carried out afterwards, generally by screening. Products are sold in standard particle sizes, from 400 mesh to 16 mesh.

PHYSICAL STABILITY

To be capable of useful life, ion-exchange material structures should resist physical degradation by forces they encounter. Quality control tests have been designed to evaluate stability to attrition and osmatic shock; microscopic examination for internal cracks and broken particles has also proved useful.

DENSITY

Ion-exchange resins in the water-swollen state typically show a specific gravity in the range 1.1-1.5. Density as normally reported is a bulk density as installed in a column, including a normal 35-40 per cent voids volume for a spherical product.

BED EXPANSION

Backwashing of an ion-exchange column for removal of fine partiles of exchanger and dirt impurities and to reduce the pressure drop across the column is a standard operating practice. Backwashing above a certain minimum rate causes a partial fluidisation of the resin bed and increase in the void volume between the resin particles, and an increase in the bulk volume now occupied by the resin. This increase is called expansion. The measure of the expansion at a specified cross-sectional flow rate and temperature is called bed expansion.

APPLICATIONS

WATER SOFTENING

The treatment of water has always been the dominant area of ion-exchange applications and in this area, water softening accounts for the major tunnage of resin sales. Hard water which contains principally calcium and magnesium ions cause scale in powerplant boilers, water pipes and elomestic cooking utensils. Hard waters also cause soap precipitation producing an undesirable grey curd and a waste of soap, water softening involves the interchange of one hard ion (calcium) for another soft ion of like charge on the resin. Typically, hard water is passed through a bed of a sodium form cation exchange resin and softened.

WATER DEIONIZATION

Water softening at best provides only a partial removal of solids. Industrial boilers require increasingly soft water as boiler temperatures and pressures are increased to prevent both sealing and corrosion of the boiler tubes and turbine blades. Deionization by ion exchange provides the most common solution to the problem. Deionization of water for drinking purposes is practised to a limited degree in regions of high salinity water. Deionized water is of general use in the laboratory. It is used in the garage or service station for battery water, it is used in the home for steam irons.

Deionization generally requires the successive steps of strong acid cation and strong base anion exchange or vice versa.

$$R\text{-}H+ + NaCl \longrightarrow RNa + HCl$$
$$R\,OH- + HCl \longrightarrow R+Cl- + H_2O$$

Resin generation is accomplished with a mineral acid solution, HCl or H_2SO_4, for the cation exchanger and a base, such as NaOH for the anion exchanger.

Mixed-bed resins containing near equivalent quantities of regenerated cation and anion resins give very high quality water, a resistance in excess of 10 per cent attainable. Such water quality is required when removing radioactive contaminants as are encountered in nuclear power plants. Also in washing highly specialised electronic parts, as TV tubes, or in highly critical laboratory experiments, this quality of water is required. Throwaway units used in the home or laboratory are often mixed bed for convenience rather than for quality.

MISCELLANEOUS APPLICATIONS

In additions to the principal processes of softening and deionization already discussed, there are a great number of other applications which are also used in commmercial practice. Dealkalization by chloride ion exchange is a process in which such anions as sulfate, bicarbonate, and carbonate, which tend to from insoluble salts with polyvalent metal ions are replaced with chloride ions.

$$2R^+Cl^- + CO_32^- \longrightarrow R_2\text{-}CO_3 + 2Cl^-$$

Simultaneous softening and partial deionization may be accomplished by contacting a portion of the raw water with an acid form cation exchanger and the balance with the sodium form of the same exchanger.

CHEMICAL CONVERSION

One example is the spent phosphoric or acetic acid liquors from the pickling of aluminium and magnesium sheet. Ion exchange enables more efficient use of the acid by substituting the lower cost H_2SO_4 as a source of hydrogen ions, and providing better plant control for uniform pickling operations.

CHEMICAL PURIFICATION

Purification of water soluble non-electrolytes such as glycerole glycols, sugar, and formaldehyde is accomplished by deionization methods analogus to those used in water treatment. Iron removal in the purification of hydrochloric acid may be accomplished by the use of an anion-exchange resin which extracts the negatively charged iron chloride complex.

CHEMICAL CONCENTRATION

Metals may be concentrated in solution by extraction at a low concentration level and stripping at a high concentration. Uranium is extracted from leach liquors by anion exchange, then concentrated as well as purified by elution with a solution such as HNO_3,-NH_4NO_3, in which the uranium has a greatly reduced tendency to form an anionic complex.

ION RETARDATION

A usual ion-exchange phenomenon involves the use of amphoteric ion-exchange resins, containing both anion and cation groups molecularly intermixed. With these resins it is possible to obtain via column operations, a separation of an electrolytic impurity from a liquid such as ethylene glycol by water elution. The process of ion retardation is particularly promising for the deionization of known solutes. Similarly operated, these resins may be used for separations of electrolytes from one another and for ion materials.

ACID RETARDATION

Conventional strong base anion exchangers have the property of sorbing strong mineral acids from solution by a non-exchange process. By operations, analogus to ion retardation, salts or water soluble non-ionic species may be separated from strong acids by water elution.

CATALYSIS

By direct analogy with classical chemisitry, either the functional group or the mobile ions of an ion-exchanger may serve as catalyst for a chemical reaction. In general, a strong acid resin in its acid form may be substituted for hydrochloric or sulfuric acid with the added advantage of being easily filtered from the reaction mixture for reuse. Most promising large-scale applications are in olefin epoxydation, hydrolysis, and eserification reactions. Some of the newer macroporous resins greatly extend catalytic possibilities especially into non-aqueous systems such as alkylation.

ION EXCLUSION

Ion exclusion is an elution process for separating ionized mateials from the preferentially sorbed non or slightly ionized materials when both are present in aqueous solution.

ANALYTICAL APPLICATIONS

The use of ion exchange resins in chemical analysis has become extremely widespread in recent years. All of the various applications previously described may be employed on an analytical basis.

DRYING

Ion-exchange materials have been found to be excellent dessicants particularly useful in the column drying of non-polar liquids such as the hydrocarbons. With modification of the supporting media they may be used in conventional drying columns.

PLANT NUTRITION

Ion exchanger formulations containing nitrogen, phosphorus, and potassium in addition to the minor elements that may be deficient have been found to be useful in fortifying a wide variety of putting soils. Such a fortified soil may retain a large supply of nutrient without injury to the plant. The need for frequent fertilization is eliminated, nutrition is continuous and self regulating.

MANUFACTURE

BASIC PRINCIPLES

From a synthetic point of view there are two methods of synthesizing an ion exchange resin. The first method consists of building the ionic groups into the resin structure, during the resin polymerization. In other words, the ionic groups are an integra constituent of the monomer, prior to the polymerization. The second consists of first forming a polymer unit and then subsequently introducing the ionic groups into the hard polymer structure. The chief advantage of first method is that the resulting resin is a true homogenous mass of high mechanical strength.

POLYMER FORMATION

Since the ion exchange resins are polymers containing ionic groups, their synthesis is governed by the well known principles of polymerization. The first method of polymerization involves reactions in which a product of the reaction of phenol and formaldehyde may be represented as.

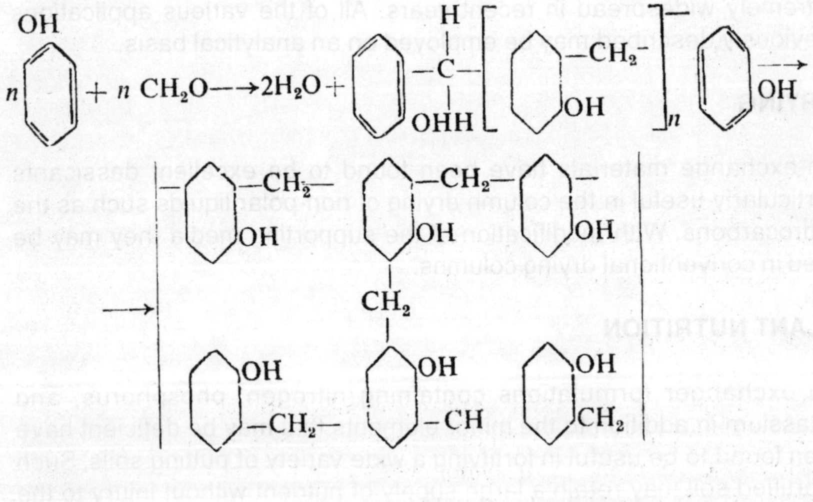

Vinyl polymerization, involves polymerization of monomer molecules without the formation of any by-products.

MANUFACTURE OF POLYSTYRENE BASED ION-EXCHANGE RESINS POLYMERISATION

The first step in the synthesis of an ion-exchange resin consists in building up a three dimensional cross-linked matrix hydrocarbon chains.

This is achieved by polymerising styrene or its derivatives with a suitable monomer like divinyl benzene by suspension polymerisation. The two monomers, both an liquid form are charged into a large glass lined reactor where they are stirred with water and dispersed into small globules. Small amounts of organic peroxide catalyst like benzoyl peroxide are added to the suspension. The peroxide decomposes into free redicals and initiates the polymerisation at the unsaturated ends of the monomers. When the inhibition period is overcome, copolymer begins to form very rapidly and at this stage there is a tendency for the globules to collapse into sticky larger particles.

In order to control the particle size and prevent globules from agglomerating into big lumps, small amounts of suspension stabilisers are introduced into the reactor. Gelatin, starch, polyvinyl alcohol etc. are some of the common suspension stabilisers used.

Polymerisation is carried out below 200°F for approximately 3 hours followed by refluxing till the beads harden. Any excessive heat evolved during the process is suitable controlled by circulating water. At the end of the reaction the beads are filtered, washed and dried for two hours. The desired size of the beads can be obtained by controlling such variables as speed of mixing, temperature, concentration of catalyst, ratio of monomers to water, pH etc. Usually the diameter of a bead is in the range of 1-0.3 mm. However faster and much efficient ion-exchange reactions can be achieved with smaller sized beads because the diffusion rate of a contacting solution within the resin particle is inversely proportional to the cubs of the particle size.

SULPHONATION

The copolymer beads provide the basic matrix into which ionic groups are introduced to enable the material to function as an ion-exchanger. For the synthesis of a cationexchange resin, the cured copolymer beads are charged into a sulphonation kettle with concentrated sulphuric acid. the slurry is heated with stirring for several hours. Sulphonation takes place at the para position of the styrene component of the copolymer. To facilitate a smooth and uniform degree of sulphonation, the beads are

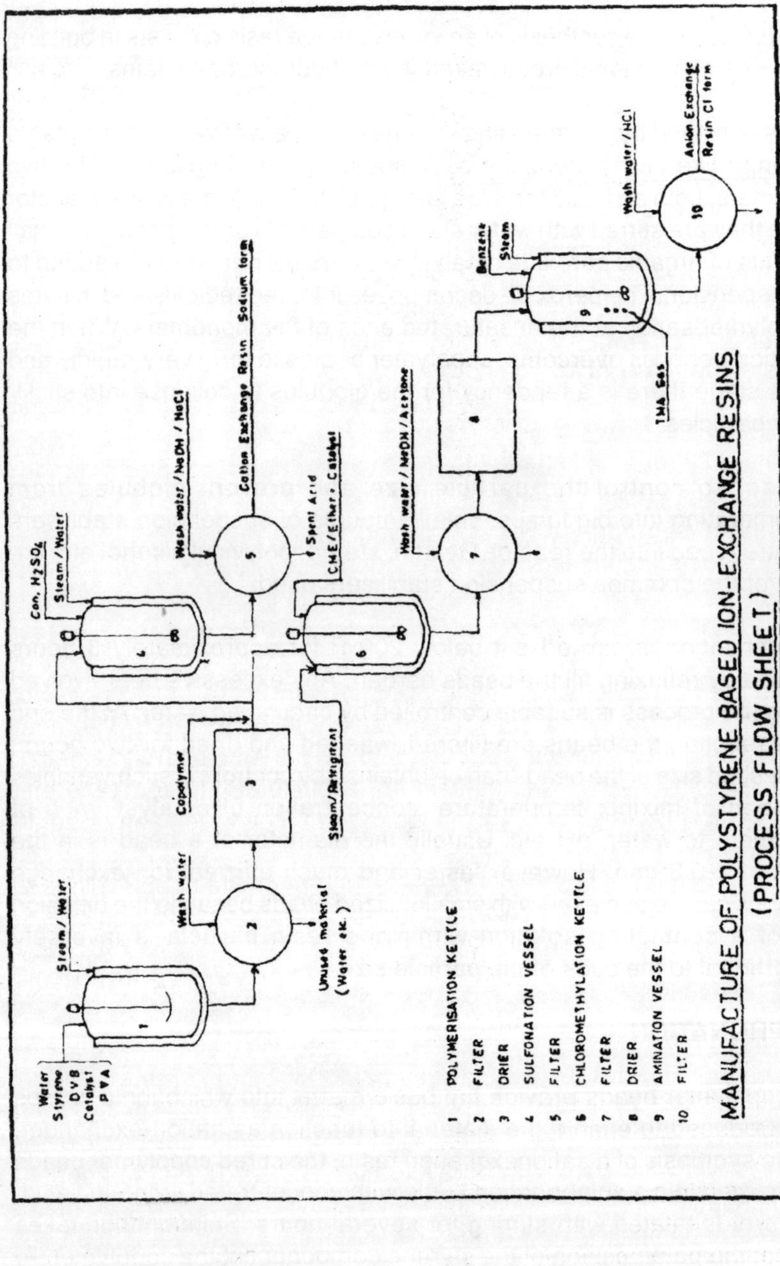

Fig. 13.0 Flow Sheet for manufacture of polystyrene based ion-exchange resins

preswollen in solvent like toluene, ethylene dichloride, nitrobenzene etc. and then sulphonated. The sulphonated beads are filtered and washed. The washing process needs a lot of ingenuity and skill. Care should be taken to avoid any thermal and cosmatic shock being imparted to the beads. The resin so obtained is usually converted to the sodium form to stabilise against degradation and pick up of impurities during packaging and transport.

CHLORINATION AND AMINATION

Chloromethylation and amination are the two steps necessary to introduce basic groups into the polymer matrix. In this process dry copolymer beads are charged into a reactor and chloromethyl ether is added. They are left undisturbed until all the beads are swollen completely. Chloromethylation is an alkylation reaction that preferentially introduces - CH_2Cl groups at the para position of the styrene ring in the copolymear. Ethylene dichloride or diethyl ether which dissolves anhydrous aluminium chloride is charged into the reactor and stirred with the swollen beads. The system is cooled by circulating cold water externally and when the temperature is sufficiently low, required amount of anhydrous aluminium chloride is added and the mixture is allowed to react by stirring. The chloromethylated product is then filtered, washed and dried. The fully chloromethylated beads become brown or greyish brown in colour.

The beads are then transferred into an amination reactor where they are swollen in solvents like benzene, dioxane etc. and are cooled to room temperature. A steady stream of trimethylamine gas is passed into the reactor and the temperature is also gradually increased. After several hours the reaction is completed and the strongly basic quaternary ammonium resin is filtered and washed. It is usually supplied in chloride form.

Different types of anion exchange resins can be prepared by eminating the chloromethylated beads with amines like dimethyl amine hydroxy ethyl dimethyl amine.

ALTERNATIVE METHOD OF SYNTHESIS OF AN ANION EXCHANGE RESIN

The literature contains many references to the synthesis of anion exchange resins. Most of the methods involve the formation of a resin by the polymerisation of an aromatic amine and formaldehyde or a polymerine, a phenol, and formaldehyde. Nitration and subsequent reduction of various insoluble polymers have been investigated to a lesser extent.

An early anion exchanger, Wolfatit M, has been prepared from m-phenylene diamine, polyethylene diamine, and formaldehyde water to the extent of 0.5 kg, of m-phenylene diamine, 0.225 kg. of hydrochloric acid, and, 0.21 kg. of ice are stirred until the m-phenylene diamine dissolves. Polyethylene diamine to the amount of 0.06 kg, 0.15 kg. hydrochloric acid and 0.15 kg. of ice are then added. By further addition for water (0.15 kg.) the temperature is brought to 8-11°C. 30 per cent of formaldehyde (0.825 kg). is added and the temperature is dropped to 2-3 C by addition of 0.15 kg. of ice. The temperature quickly rises to 65° C and the resin is removed after several hours and dried at 80-90° C. The resin is crushed and washed.

D'Alelio has synthesized an anion exchange resin by means of nitration and subsequent reduction of a styrene-divinyl benzene copolymer. 12 parts of a copolymer containing 90 parts of styrene and and 10 parts of divinyl benzene are nitrated (reflex for 2 hours) with a mixture of 20 parts of nitric and 30 parts of sulphuric acid. The resin is then washed and nitration repeated. The nitrated products is dried and reduced with 23 parts of stannous chloride and 100 parts of hydrochloric acid at the reflux temperature. After being washed with sodium hydroxide, the product exhibits an anion exchange capacity of approximately one milliequivalent per gram.

PROCESS OF MANUFACTURE

The raw materials required to produce 400 kg. anion exchange resin are:

m-phenylene diamine	241 kg.
Poly ethylene diamine	37 kg.
Formaldehyde (30%)	496 kg.
Hydrochloric acid (30%)	226 kg.
Ice	250 kg.

Water, m-phenylene-diamine, hydrochloric acid are added to an agitated vessel. Ice is then added with stirring until m-phenylene diamine dissolves. Polyethylene diamine, hydrochloric acid, and ice are then added. By the further addition of water,the temperature is brought down to 8-11° C. 30 per cent formaldehyde is then added and the temperature is brought down to 2-3 per cent by addition of ice or by circulating cold water through the jacket. The temperature at this stage quickly rises to 65° C. The resin is removed after several hours, filtered and dried in a dryer. The dried product is packed for sale.

• *Chapter 5* •

MELAMINE FORMALDEHYDE RESIN

INTRODUCTION

The chemical melamine (2,4,6-triamino-1,3,5 triazine) was first prepared shortly after the discovery of urea, in 1943, by Liebig. It was first neglected as commercial material and it was not until a century later that Henkel, in 1935, patented its resinous condensations with formaldehydde. Melamine when reacted with formaldehyde produces resins similar in appearance to those of urea but superior in respect of water resistance.

The advantages of melamine resins in plastics and other applications emerge particularly from such properties as their initial water solubility and ease of application from acueous systems, stepwise control and advancement of polymerization, freedom from colour, high degree of hardness, good thermal properties, non-flammability, and are resistance.

Major application of melamine formaldehyde resin is in the quality table water. Other applications include those in paper, electrical industry.

RAW MATERIALS

MELAMINE

Melamine is a white crystalline solid, sparingly soluble in water, and melts just above 350° C; sp. gr.1.573. It is produced on a commercial scale by heating dicyanamide under pressure with ammonia or by fusion with guanidine salts. Chemically it is the triamine of cyanuric acid and may also be considered as the trimer of cynamide. The reaction between lime and coke has also formed the basis of the commercial production of melamine.

In India, there is no unit at present for the production of melamine but one or two units are expected to come into production in the near future.

Other raw materials i.e. formaldehyde and thio urea, required for resin production have already been described in the previous chapters.

CHEMISTRY OF RESINIFICATION

Melamine reacts with formaldehyde to yield methylol melamines. Three reactive amine groups can be reacted with as many as 6 moles of formaldehyde. By reacting 1 mole of melamine with 3 moles of warm formalin until solution is obtained and quickly cooling, crystalline trimethylol melamine may be obtained. The reaction can be represented as below.

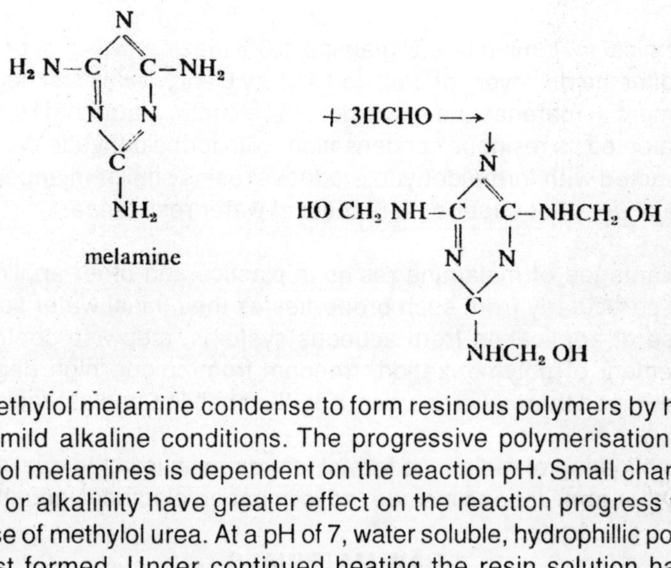

The methylol melamine condense to form resinous polymers by heating under mild alkaline conditions. The progressive polymerisation of the methylol melamines is dependent on the reaction pH. Small changes in acidity or alkalinity have greater effect on the reaction progress than in the case of methylol urea. At a pH of 7, water soluble, hydrophillic polymers are first formed. Under continued heating the resin solution has less tolerance for dilution with but is readily diluted with water alcohol mixtures. With still further heating, some resin may be preecipitated from solution by alcohol and the solution will separate into layers on cooling.

Curings of the melamine resins may be accomplished by simple heating. The presence of small amounts of acid will accelerate the heat cure, especially for butylated products. Unlike urea resins, however, melamines do not cure satisfactorily at room temperature even in the presence of an acid catalyst.

LABORATORY PREPARATION

The apparatus required for melamine formaldehyde resin preparation consists of (1) 1 litre bolthead flask with reflux condenser (2) vacuum distillation apparatus with air bubbling tube and screw clip (3) Thermometer (110° C),(4) Hot water bath.

(a) Procedure

45 cc. 40 per cent formalin are put into a 1 litre bolthead flask and adjusted with N/1 sodium hydroxide solution to pH 7.0-7.5, using B.D.H. universal indicator. 252 g. melamine and 6 cc. 0.880 ammonia are then added, and the flask is heated under reflux until the first bubbles of the slightly exothermic reaction appear. The flame is taken away and is applied later as required. The liquor is boiled gently under reflux for 30 minutes from the start of the exothermic reaction. Care should be taken to see that flask is agitated whilst the liquor is refluxing. The liquor is then vacuum distilled from a water bath maintained at 65-75° C at a pressure of about 25 mm mercury, i.e. 1 inch, to give a thickish syrup. The pH of the resin syrup is adjusted to 7.5-8.5.

The solids content of the resin syrup is determined as described below.

25 g. of acid-washed silver sand of about 50 mesh size is contained in a flat bottom dish about 3 inch in diameter, 1 inch deep, and made of glass. The dish alongwith the sand, rod and cover glass are weighed to the nearest 0.001 g. Then about 0.5 g. of the resin solution is put in the dish, the covered glass put on and the covered dish, with the glass rod on top,is quickly weighed to the nearest 0.001 g. The object of using the cover glass is to prevent the loss of solvent during weighing. 7 cc. of acetone or other solvent are then thoroughly mixed with the weighed sand and resin solutions, using the rod which is left in te mixture. The dish is put in warm place, such as on top of the oven, to allow most of the solvent to dry off and then without any further mixing the dish is put in an electric oven at 135° C for two hours. The dish is removed from the oven, put in the dessicator to cool and reweighed with, of course, its cover glass.

Then from the three weights solids content of the solution is calculated.

(b) FORMULATION

A formulation for melamine formaldehyde resin preparation is given below.

Ingredients	*Parts by wt.*
Melamine	175
Formaldehyde (37%)	450
Butyl alcohol	600

(c) PROCEDURE

Reflux the ingredients on a steam bath for 30 minutes with constant stirring. Transfer to a distilling unit and remove the water. When no more water distills off, cool and adjust to 50 per cent non-volatile content.

This type of resin can be modified in a number of ways. Combinations of urea and melamine may be used. Part of urea and melamine can be replaced by substituted phenols, thioourea etc. The aldehyde portion of the resin may be changed to acetaldehyde, coroton aldehyde etc.

Longer-chain alcohols can be used in place of the butyl alcohol. Soluble resins are produced with hexyl or octyl alcohol. Polyhydric alcohol can be used as well as partially reacted polybasic acids.

APPLICATIONS

Typical applications of melamine formaldehyde resin are in the following field.

1. Moulding powders
2. Adhesives
3. Laminating resins
4. Surface coatings
5. Paper industry
6. Textile finishes.

The individual application and the type of resin used for that application is described below.

MOULDING POWDERS

The base melamine resin is produced in a fairly low state of condensation. Melamine-formaldehyde molecular ratios vary from 1:1.5 to 1:3.0. The condensation is carried out under faintly alkaline conditions, and although the actual process of resin manufacture is quite simple, rigid control of the pH is essential.

There are two general methods for converting the resin into a moulding powder. One, which is termed as the wet process, consists of kneading the filler (wood flour and bleached wood pulp) with the aqueous resin until the filler becomes thoroughly impregnated. The resultant mix is then broken up into the fine crumbs and dried to the required plasticity. At this stage the material is in a form similar to coarse dessicated coconut and is placed in a ballmill together with catalyst (acidic, e.g. hexamine), lubricants (stearates) and pigments. It is then ground to a fine powder and finally stucked to remove any coarse particles. The resultant moulding powder may be too bulky for certain applications and can be densified by granulating either on heated mixing rolls or in Banbury mixer.

The other method, termed as the dry process, merely consists of mixing the condensed resin with fillers, catalyst, lubricants, and pigments on heated mixing rolls. At the correct temperature the mix resinifies and can then be sheeted off and finally granulated.

The moulding of melamine formaldehyde powders are superior to the urea formaldehyde plastics in a number of respects. These include

1. Lower water absorption, especially with mineral-filled resins.
2. Better resistance to staining by aqueous solutions such as fruit juices, and beverages. Further improvement in this respect is still desirable and somewhat better results have been detained with benzoguanamine along with melamine.
3. Electrical properties, which are initially similar to urea formaldehyde resins are maintained better in damp conditions.
4. Better heat resistance.
5. Greater hardness.

The properties of melamine type plastic stem from those of melamine itself. Thus this plastic is superior to the urea type in heat and boiling water resistance. The extension of amino plastics by melamine into the tableware field has been made possible by the performance, in these properties combined with outstanding hardness and impact resistance. Melamine plastic is the hardest known plastic. The first large scale use was in heavy duty tableware for cafeterias and institutions but soon extended to home and general dining use. Its appeal in the home first arose because of simplified and highly functional design, later from embossed patterns and currently from colour treatments introduced through the method of moulding or moulding in of foils or overlays. The base resin is water-white and transparent. With cellulose filler the light transmission is reduced and the plastic becomes highly translncent. Thus a wide range of effects is possible by pigmenting the moulding composition in various degrees. A clear, unfilled melamine plastic is also available and is used chiefly for launderable buttons. In addition to the extensive application of decorative melamine plastic in tableware, its uses extend to bottle closures, buttons, razor housings, jewellery and lock case, kitchen accessories, and housewares of all types as well as washing machine agitators and telephone hand sets.

In typical moulding practice, preforms of uniform weight are charged to the cavities of heated multi count compression type die. As the die is closed upon the material under pressure, it softens and flows, taking the form of the die. Within 30-45 sec, as polymerization is initiated, the charge becomes rigid. When polymerization is sufficiently advanced, "cure" has taken place and the moulded pieces are then discharged from the hot die. Moulding temperatures are generally 310-340° F for melamine moulding resins, and pressure 1500 to 1600 lb/in^2. For small objects. such as buttons which are moulded in automatic presses, a rapid curing formulation is prepferred and here the cure may be 20-30 sec. For tableware items which have a thicker cross section, cure is longer, and depending on other conditions, the cure may be 2-5 min. Not only is cure shortened by preheating the charge but improved uniformity and appearance of the moulded part are realized. For large items and particularly those which are intricate and have metal inserts, preforming is a necessity. Prewarming serves to soften the charge and decreases the pressure needed to close the die.

Melamine moulding resins with fillers other than collulose serve industrial and military purposes. An asbestos filled composition is used widely for moulding distributors and other parts of nitrogen systems of aircarft and tractors. Exceptional are and heat resistance are required here. A glass fibre filled plastic additionally offers high strength and the best dimensional stability of the melamine plastics which meets requirements of heavy duty electrical switch and cicuit breaker gear.

The physical properties of moulded melamine resins, determined in most cases by ASTM methods are given in Table 4.0.

TABLE 4.0

Properties of Melamine Moulding Powders

Property	*Melamine formaldehyde*	
	Cellulose	*Mineral*
Specific gravity	1.5	1.8
Compression ratio	2	2
Moulding ratio	310-340	270-340
Impact strength, ft-lb (rotched Izod)	0.24-0.28	0.30-0.40
Compressive strength, lb/in^2	40-45000	25-30,000
Tensile strength, lb/in^2	7-8000	5.5-6500
Dielectric constant		
60 cycles	8.4-9.4	10.2
10^6 cycles	7.6-8.0	6.1
Dielectric loss factor		
60 cycles	0.44-0.78	1.0
10^6 cycles	0.26-0.34	0.3

The properties of moulded melamine resins vary with the degree of cure. The rate of urea also varies with the thickness of the part. These are important considerations for optimum properties in the mould product and therefore mould design also has a definite bearing on ultimate properties.

ADHESIVES

Melamine resins and melamine urea resins are normally used without catalyst and are hot pressed to obtain a cured glue line. The melamine resins are more expensive than the urea resins and are therefore customarily restricted to applications requiring improved water resistance. Water proof exterior-grade plywood, marino-grade, and heavy timber marine laminations are good examples of melamine adhesive applications. In addition, melamine resins can be used advantageously in wood particle boards, moulded wood waste products, sporting goods and quality applications requiring light coloured, non staining glue lines.

Melamine resin is frequently added to urea resin to provide improved water resistance. Because of the beneficial effect of even modest amounts of melamine resin, improved glue lines can be obtained at a moderate increase in cost. Unmodified melamine resin adhesives give bonds comparable in durability to those obtained with phenolic and resorcinol resin adhesives.

The melamine resin adhesives are superior to urea adhesives in the following properties.

1. Boil resistant
2. Long working life and assembly time
3. High bonding strength
4. Heat and chemical resistance
5. Neutral glue line pH

Sources

Melamine resin adhesives are supplied mostly as dry, stable powders without catalyst or filler, combinatios of urea and melamine which contain fillers or filler catalyst systems are also available for tapeless splicing and boil resistant plywood.

POWDERED MELAMINE ADHESIVES

Powdered melamine and melamine-urea copolymer resins for adhesive usage are maufactured in the same equipment as spary-dried amino resins. The resins are essentially the same as those prepared for making industrial moulding compounds or for use in laminating, but are polymerized to a more advanced stage in the primary liquid stage of manufacture. The products still retain water solubility, but only in highly concentrated solutions.

Melamine resins can be cured to an insoluble glue line without catalyst by application of heat, and therefore are sold as neat resin or mixed with ligneous filler copolymers of melamine and urea may or may not require a separate catalyst to achieve complete cure depending on the proportion of melamine to urea in the formulation. When the melemine content is equal or greater than the urea content, no catalyst is uesd.

Blending of powdered resins with filler and other additives is accomplished by physical mixing in the dry state in a cone or ribbon blender. At times anti-caking agents are added to the blender to aid in retaining their free flowing properties during storage.

Formulation

1. *Uncatalyzed Mix-Long Working Life*

"Cymel 401"	80 lb
Shell flour	20 lb.
Water	60 lb.
Viscosity	10-12 poises
Working life @ 80° F	12-18 hr.
Gelation time @ 80° F	24 hr.

2. *Catalyzed Mix-Influence of Catalyst on Working Life*

"Bauxite MF-300"	100	100 lb.
Shell flour	20	7.5 lb.
Water	55	40-50 lb.
"Catalyst Y"	0.25	2.5 lb.
Working Life @ 75° F	8	2-3 hr.

3. *Melamine Resin Fortified Urea Adhesive*

"Cymel 401" fortifier	0	5	10	15	20 lb.
"Urac 180 or 186"	150	150	150	150	150 lb.
Shell flour	10	10	10	10	10 lb.
"Hardener M-325"	2	2	2	2	2lb.
Viscosity	7-10	7-10	7-10	8-12	10-15 lb.
Mix life @ 80° F	-	8-10	8-10	8-10	8-10lb.
Gelation time @ 80° F	-	20-24	20-24	20-24	20-24lb.
Maximum assembly @ 80° F	2-3	12-15	15-20	20-24	20-24lb.

LAMINATING RESINS

For this application the resin is taken to a fairly advanced stage of condensation. Melamine formaldehyde laminating resins are more popular and are retained in the form of dry powder by spray-drying the resultant condensation resin. The subsequent powders have a relatively long shelf life and can be used as and when required by dissolving in water or water alcohol mixtures, and heating to 60° C to give a solid content of 40-50 per cent. The resin used in paper treatment is in the solution form and contains 50-60 solids. The resin can be applied to paper or fabric or by direct immersion or by roller coating. The resultant sheets are cut into appropriate sizes and the laminates can then be built up from numerous sheets. The resultant laminate can be cured by pressing at 120-150° C under a pressure of 500-2000 lb./in^2. In the preparation of many of the well-known decorative laminates the printed pattern layer is impregnated either with a urea-melamine co-condensate or as is more common, a phenolic resin, and a protective translucent overlay sheet, treated with melamine resin super imposed.

The common type of melamine resin laminate for a counter top is 50-60 mils. in thickness. In the construction of such a laminate phenolic-resin-impregnated kraft paper sheets make up the core with the melamine resin being used in the surface sheets. One of these, the print sheet, is a resin impregnated alpha cellulose paper which carries the printed design, for example, simulated wood grain or linen fabric. On top of the print sheet is a protective, transparent overlay in the form of a resin treated paper of high rayon content.

Today, the largest use of melamine laminates is for decorative, combined with utilitarian, purposes for dining table and counter tops, wall panelling, schoolroom desk tops, and home, business, hotel furniture surfacing. Excellent resistance to cleansing agent, and alcohol and food staining, in addition to the properties already mentioned, is responsible for the extensive acceptance of melamine resin laminates.

SURFACE COATINGS

Many of the advantages of melamine resins are derived from their solubility in water and ease of application from this medium. Melamine resins are easy to cure and less hard than urea resins made in a similar manner. These resins offer better alkali resistance and are able to sustain higher baking temperatures.

For use in surface coatings, melamine formaldehyde resins are also modified by condensation in an alcoholic medium. The properties of alkylated melamine formaldehyde resins very with the alcohol used methylated methylol melamines are soluble in water. The water solubility decreases as the length of the alcohol chain increases. Butyl alcohol with methylol melamines yields resins which are insoluble in water, but completely soluble in a mixture of xylol and butyl alcohol.

Melamine formaldehyde condensation products can also be modified by reaction with polyhydric alcohols in place of monohydric alcohols and they may also be reacted with poly basic acid-polyhydric alcohol reaction products. Other modified resins can be made by reacting melamine and formaldehyde with other substances which can combine with formaldehyde, such as urea, thirourea, and phenols.

The advantages of melamine formaldehyde resins over the urea formaldehyde are listed below.

(1) The baking schedule of melamine formaldehyde resin formulated coatings can be lowered as much as 100 F without a decrease in the hardness of the film as compared to a similar urea-formaldehyde resin formulation.

(2) If the same baking temperature is used, the baking time can be materially reduced.

(3) More alkyd resin can be used with melamine formaldehyde resins to attain the same degree of hardness of film as compared to the urea formaldehydes.

(4) The heat resistance of the melamine resin is superior to that of the urea type. Melamine formaldehyde resins are capable of withstanding a temperature of 450° F to the same degree as urea formaldehyde will withstand 300° F.

(5) The chemical resistance of the malamine resins is equal and in some cases superior to that of urea resins.

Formulations

1. *Warpproof refrigerator finish*

Ingredient	Parts by weight
Titanium dioxide	285
Medium-oil-length nonoxidizing alkyd (60 per cent nonvolatile)	365
Urea-melamine formaldehyde resin (60 per cent nonvolatile)	190
Xylol	60

The point may be reduced with xylol or with the previously listed high strength solvent mixture to spraying viscosity. The enamel is sprayed on, air-dried for 20 minutes, and baked at 300° F for minutes.

2. Red automobile finishing enamel (Sunfared Baking)

Ingredients	Parts by weight
Toluidine toner	50
Medium-oil-length oxidizing type alkyd (50 per cent nonvolatile)	320
Melamine-modified alkyd resin (50 per cent nonvolatile)	40
Xylol	35
6 per cent manganese naphthenate	0.25

Reduce with xylol to spraying viscosity. Bake for 15 to 30 minutes under infrared lamps. The curing time will depend on the size, number, and arrangement of the infrated lamps.

3. Heat resistant white baking enamel

Primer

Titanium dioxide	88
Titanium calcium pigment	150
China clay	50
Short-oil oxidizing-type alkyd resin (55 per cent non volatile)	400
Urea formaldehyde resin (50 per cent nonvolatile)	150
Hi-flash naphtha	150
Butyl alcohol	25

Finish coat

Titanium dioxide	275
Medium-oil-length nonoxidizing alkyd (60 per cent nonvolatile)	175
Alkyd-modified melamine formaldehyde resin (55 per cent nonvolatile)	375
Xylol	150

Reduce to spraying viscosity with xylol or a high strength solvent mixture. The drying schedule for the system is as follows.

The primer after application is air-dried for 45 minutes whereas the finish coat is air-dried for 20 minutes. Bake at 300° F for 30 minutes.

PAPER INDUSTRY

In the treatment of paper, urea resins were first used on a limited scale by so-called tub application to impart wet strength to the fibre and as an adhesive in corrugated boxboard making. What the paper industry needed was resins adapted to the papermaking process which could impart the special properties sought.

The first such resin to reach commercial importance was a melamine resin. This was incorporated into the paper sheet by way of the slush stock in the paper beater as melamine resin acid colloid. Such a colloid develops upon dissolving a soluble type melamine resin or intermediate in a suitable acid. As an example, trimethylolmelamine may be dissolved as the hydrochloride using one equivalent of hydrochloric acid. With further reaction this solution gradually assumes a Tyndal blue haze and other properties including electrophorasis. When the colloid was added to the fibrillated stock in the beater, the cation was selectively absorbed by the fibre; the property of wet strength was developed as the paper sheet progressed through the fourdrinier machine. The effect may be interpreted as involving orientation of the resin, as it is taken up by the fibre, at the points of fibre contact since this is conducive to lowering the surface free energy. Curing at these sites, it achieves its maximum effect by uniting the fibres through new forces both chemical and physical. By the beater addition of 1-3 per cent of resin based on the fibre marked improvement in wet strength occurs along with improvement in dry strength, folding endurance, and wet rub resistance. Tear resistance generally falls off slightly. The degree of improvement of paper depends on many factors such as degree of resin reaction or age, foreign ions in the white water, quantity of alum used, as well as the type of stock furnished to the beater.

Today there are a large number of amino resins, cationic and anionic, available commercially, which have been specially formulated for beater.

The patent literature describes modifications of melamine formaldehyde with sulfur dioxide, sodium sulfite, hydroxy acids, amino acids and various amines; numerous other polymeric formulations for introducing hydrophillic groups have been directed to this end use.

Untreated commercial papers as a rule have wet tensile strength equivalent to 10 per cent and less of their dry strength. By resin treatment this propertion can be readily altered. Depending on type of paper, wet strength may then vary from 33.3 to 100 per cent of the original dry strength. This gain plus the improvement in other properties mentioned is the basis for its extensive use in blueprint uses, shopping ad shipping bags, military maps, certian paper currencies and food wrapping papers. With the currently expanding operations in knitting and weaving of paper yarns, application of wet strength paper can be expected to grow.

Such resins are also used to some extent as binding agents for paper coatings. A relatively new development is the use of polymeric agents in the beater for improvement of dry strength of various fiber stocks. Acrylamide-acrylic acid copolymers, for example, are effective for this purpose.

TEXTILE FINISHES

Melamine resins are widely used ir the resin finishing of textiles. Several grades of the resin are used. Its superior qualities over urea resins have out weighted the increased cost. Generally when 10 per cent urea resin solids on the fabric were used an equivalent effect could be achieved with 5 per cent melamine resin. When applied to wool and wool mixed goods for shrinkage control during laundering, at 6-10 per cent resin solids, the melamine resin offered a large margin of superiority, the urea resin producing a relatively poor effect. The durability of the melamine finish through laundering and use in all cases is one of its chief advantages. In addition to the improvement in properties mentioned, resin treatment made possible durable glazed chintz and embossed effects and both resin types are now used for these purposes.

In a typical treatment of a fabric for wrinkle resistance, cotton, for example, the fabric is bleached and scoured free of size and preferably mercerized. From the suitably catalyzed resin solution the fabric passes through a pad mangle, then into a tenter drier where curing takes place, and finally into a washer. Curing conditions vary from 4-15 min. at 280° F to 2-6 min. at 320° F. In order to secure good penetration into the fibre the treating must be monomeric or nearly monomeric. Melamine resins, in the form in which they are made, dissolve more readily in water than the ureas. Alcohol modified types in addition to unmodified types are used. Melamine acid colloids are particularly effective in the treatment of wools. Resin treatment results in a fuller hand to the fabric and a softening agent may be used accordingly in the resin treatment bath. Modified resins are also used obtain permanent water repellency.

It is common practice in laundering to use chlorine bleaches particularly with white cottons. Urea resins tend to hydrolyze with such treatment and chlorine reaction results in some tendering of the fabric and loss in tensile-strength. Melamine resins are more resistant to hydrolysis and to tensile strength loss with chlorine bleach. The first melamine resin finishes tended to yellow slightly due to chlorine. The extent of after yellowing of amino resin varies, depending on the severity of the laundering treatment. In order to block the positions of attack by chlorine in the polymer structure other materials have been proposed, at least one of which is available commercially. These include dimethylolethylene urea, uron-formaldehyde, and triazone-formaldehyde types. Dimethylol-ethyleneurea does not polymerize very well and it is one of a group of alkyl substituted ureas whose effectiveness on cotton has been attributed to reaction with the cellulose.

• *Chapter 6* •

PHENOL FORMALDEHYDE RESINS

INTRODUCTION

It is probably true to say that resins based on the reaction between phenol and formaldehyde have been used for far longer than any others with the exception of the 'mother of plastics', cellulose nitrate. They were the first truly synthetic materials to be used in producing plastics and since their initial production, around 1912, they have developed quickly and have reached industrial importance for a diverse number of applications in many countries.

The history of the phenolic resins dates back to the 1870's. Many scientists had been interested in the reaction of phenols with various aldehydes but no great success was achieved until the chemical work of L.H. Backland, which was made known in a series of papers and patents. His initial work was mainly carried out in the period 1905-1910 and its significance lay in his discoveries of how to control the phenol aldehyde reaction by adjusting the ratio of the two reactants. The reaction could thus be controlled and stopped at an intermediate stage.

"Phenolic resin" is a term that describes a wide variety of products resulting from the reaction of phenols and aldehydes. Although phenol itself is the dominant phenol, resorcinol and alkyl-substituted phenols such as cresols, xylenols, and p-tert-butyl phenol, and p-phenyl phenol are used in substantial volume.The aldehyde used is almost exclusively formaldehyde, but small amounts of acetaldehyde and furfur aldehyde are also used. Formaldehyde is sometimes used in the form of its dry powder polymer.

The phenol-aldehyde reaction products may be a liquid or a solution, a solid or a powder, and it may be pure resin or modified with fillers or polymeric compounds.Most phenolic resins are heat-hardening or thermosetting. The resin may be delivered to the user ready to be cured or it may be in the temporarily thermoplastic "novolvak" form to which a hardener, hexamine, will be added.

The major use categories for phenolics are moulding compounds, coatings, and industrial bonding resins. The latter include resins for grinding wheels, created abrasives, brake lining, clutch facing, laminates,plywood, adhesives, glass-wool, thermal insulation, bonded organic-fibre padding, foundry sand, bonding wool-waste bonding, and other miscellaneous applications.

RAW MATERIALS

PHENOL

In its pure form phenol consists of white crystals that melt at about 41° C. For the manufacture of synthetic resins the phenol in the form of 90 per cent phenol and 10 per cent ortho-cresol or in the ratio of 80/20. The phenol can be obtained either in the natural state or by synthetic means. The so called natural phenol is obtained from coaltar by distillation, extraction of the middle oil cut by caustic soda, then acidification and finally distilling. The basic raw materials for synthetic production is benzene, which may be converted to phenol by the sulphonation, Rosching or cremene process. In India, phenol is produced and sold by Herdillia Chamicals. Bombay; Hindustan Steel Ltd. Bhilai etc.

FORMALDEHYDE

Formaldehyde is a gas which, on chilling, will condense to give a liquid boiling at 19 C. This aliphatic aldehyde is prepared by the controlled catalytic oxidation of methyl alcohol. The procedure normally adopted is to pass a mixture of the alcoholic vapour and air over a heated catalyst, usually copper, the probable reaction being one of the dehydrogenation. Vapours of water and formaldehyde condense to yield formalin. There are several grades marketed although for resinification purposes it is normal to use solutions containing between 35-40 per cent by weight of formaldehyde, and formic acid and methanol as impurities. The latter material is to some extent advatageous as it will impart stability during storage. In India, commercial grade formaldehyde is produced by Nuchem Plastics, Faridabed; Allied Resins & Chemicals, Kolkata; Atul Drug House Ltd. Mumbai and some other units.

HEXAMINE

This materials is a derivative of formaldehyde and is obtained by passing ammonia gas into 30 per cent formalin at room temperature. Hexamine is almost universally used for curing of novolak resins; the amount used varies from 6-14%.

It is a white crystalline powder, or colourless lustrous crystals in pure form. It is practically odourless.

In India it is made and sold by Allied Resins and Chemicals Ltd. Kolkata; Atul Drug House Ltd. Mumbai etc.

CHEMISTRY OF RESINIFICATION

The reactions of phenol and formaldehyde are based on the facts that formaldehyde has a functionally of two and that phenol has a functionality of three, for it will react at the position para to the hydroxyl and at the two positions ortho-to the hydroxyl. The two meta positions will react only under severe conditions not generally found in resin reactions, and can be considered inactive. Thus, phenol and formaldehyde can react to a three-dimensional crosslinked structure. Since a substituted phenol such as o-or p-cresol is only bifunctional, the reaction can proceed only to linear form without crosslinks under usual conditions, m-cresol on the other hand, is tri-functional and can react to a crosslinked form.

Since both phenol and formaldehyde are relatively small molecules and the polymerization results in a rather tightly bunched structure, the physical properties of the crude resin include a low degree of flexibility and good high-temperature strength.

TYPES OF PHENOLIC RESINS

There are a great many factors which may be varied to introduce special characteristics to phenol-aldehyde reaction products. The factors which divide phenolic resins into two great classes are the pH of catalyst-specifically whether there is more or less than one mole of formaldehyde per mole of phenol.

When aqueous formaldehyde at the commercial concentrations of 37-40% (by wt) and pure phenol are mixed, no measureable reaction occurs within a period of days or weeks. A catalyst which will raise or lower the pH from the 3.0-3.1 of the initial mixture is needed to start the reaction.

Acids are used in appropriate strengths to give pH readings in the range between 0.5. and 1.5. When bases are used two ranges are recognized; an intermediate zone from 4 to 7, and the truly alkaline zone from 7 to 11.

Two types of phenolic resins are generally recognized.

(1) Resols or one step resin
(2) Novolaks or two step resin.

RESOLS

If a catalyzed mixture of phenol and formaldehyde contains one or more than one mole of formaldehyde per mole or phenol, it will have the ingredients and functionality to be thermosetting. When such a mixture is catalyzed with a base, resol or one step resin is formed. In commercial practice, 1.5 to 2.0 moles of formaldehyde per mole of phenol are used. Resols are physically liquid or solid brittle products depending on the catalyst and conditions of manufacture. Resols form the raw materials for adhesives, mattings, casting and laminating resins etc.

NOVOLAK

This phenolic resin made from an aldehyde and phenol, has no reactive methylol groups in the molecule and therefore incapable of condensing with other novolak molecules on heating with addition of hardening agents.

A novolak is produced when the molar ratio of formaldehyde to phenol is less than one and the reaction is catalyzed by an acid. In commercial practice, 0.75 to 0.90 mole of formaldehyde per mole of phenol is used. These resins are thermo-plastic and do not set on heating but melt and flow. They are pale-coloured brittle solid products having a melting point between 65-90° C. They are also called two-stage resin. The major application of novolaks is in the moulding materials.

EQUIPMENT FOR PHENOLIC RESINS MANUFACTURE

The major items of equipment required are:

(1) Reactor,
(2) Shell and tube condenser,
(3) Vacuum pump,
(4) Heating equipment etc.

Figure 2.0 shows diagramatically a type of arrangement of the process equipment used for manufacture of phenolic resins.

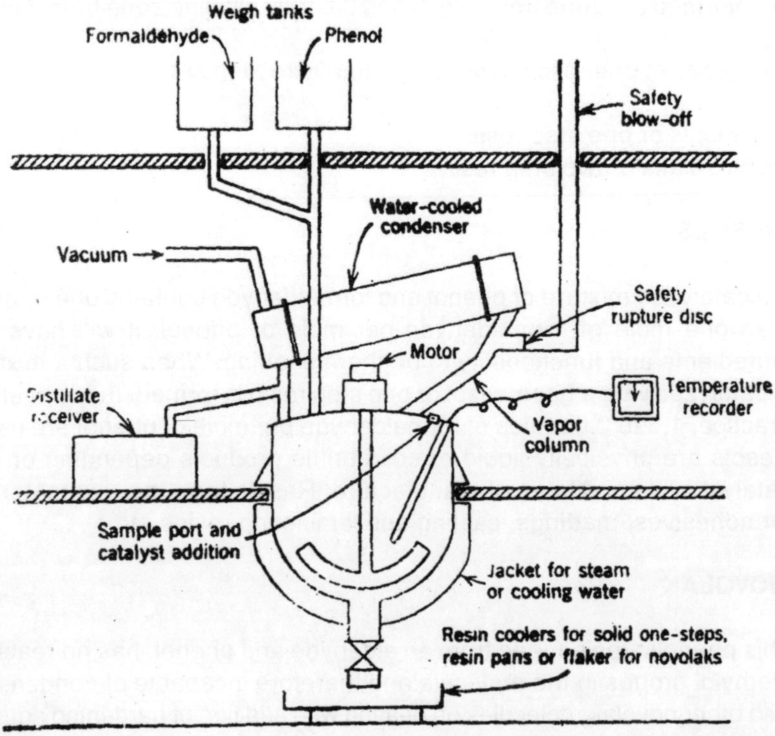

The various equipments used for phenolic resin production are described below.

REACTION KETTLE

It is a cylindrical vessel with dished top and bottom and provided with a jacket for steam-heating and water cooling.

One of the several metals may be used for kettle construction, the device depending on the type of resin to be made. For most type of resins, stainless steel is a suitable material of construction.

The size of the kettle may vary considerably from a small pot size about 20 litres to 10,000 litres of production vessels.

The kettle is fitted with a number of services and other connections for enabling the process of resin-manufacture to be carried out smoothly. Through an air-tight gland in the centre of the top there passes the vertical shaft of the stirrer, the latter is usually of the anchor type, fitting closely to the wall of the vessel. Other connections provided at the top are feed inlet line, sight glasses, manhole, vapour outlet, and condensate return lines, measuring instruments etc.

In large kettle of over 2,500 gallon capacity, internal coils are necessary to obtain adequate heating and cooling capacity.

CONDENSER

The condenser used is usually of the shell and tube type and is laid in an almost horizontal position with a wide vapour inlet to the top end of the condenser. It is generally of the same metal as that of the kettle. A pipe from the lower end leads back to a U-type bend. However, by altering the setting of two valves, the distillate can be led into a distillate receiving tank.

For the manufacture of many resin it is necessary to operate under reduced pressure. Therefore, a vacuum pump is connected to the receiver.

HEATING SYSTEMS

For normal phenolic resins manufacture, steam heating is adequate and for this purpose a boiler of the suitable capacity can be used. But where high temperatures are required, as in resin-modified phenolic resins, it is usual to heat the still by other means than steam. Several methods are in use, one of which is to circulate high boiling liquid or its vapour through the jacket or limpet coils, the liquid being heated in a second boiler called thermopack boiler. One system uses a mixture of diphenyl and diphenyl oxide (e.g. Domtherm) as the heat exchange liquid.

As already pointed out, stainless steel is the preferred material of construction for the phenolic resin plant; other metals like copper and nickel can be used for novolak resins while mild steel or copper can be used for resols. With some variations, the same equipment can be used for novolak as well as resols.

MANUFACTURE OF RESOLS

LABORATORY PREPARATION

(a) Ammonia catalyzed

The apparatus required for the preparation consists of:

(1) 1 litre bolthead flask with reflux condenser,

(2) Bowl of cold water,

(3) Vacuum distillation apparatus with air bubbling tube and screw clip,

(4) Thermometer,

(5) Hot water bath,

(6) Flat tray.

PROCEDURE

250 g, phenol, 250 c.c. 40 per cent formalin, and 25 c.c. 0.880 density ammonia are mixed together in the bolthead flask, the ammonia being added last with careful shaking. The liquor is then warmed continuously under reflux by means of a low bunsen flame applied by hand direct to the flask, the flame being moved about to prevent local heating. As soon as bubbles start to rise, showing that the exothermic reaction has begun, the burner is taken away and the liquor allowed to come to the boil on its own. If the reaction starts to get out of hand the bowl of water should be held up and the flask immersed in the water. After the reaction has settled down, heating should be continued over a tripod and gauge until the liquor becomes cloudy. The precautions taken during the preliminary heating are necessary because the reaction is strongly exothermic. After the cloud point is reached, the liquor is given ten minutes further boiling and then transferred to the distillation apparatus. By this time, the liquor would have separated into two layers.

Vacuum distillation is started, the distillation flask being heated by means of a water bath maintained at approximately 80° C. The distilling liquor is agitated occasionally by slightly opening and closing the screw clip to admit a little air. Distillation is continued at a pressure of about 25 mm. mercury, i.e. 1 in, until the rubber tube connecting the receiving flask with the vacuum pump is carefully taken off. A sample of resin is obtained by dipping with a glass rod. At the brittle bead stage a small portion of the resin is poured into a flat tray to cool. This is used for testing for melting point, staring time and gel time.

To the remaining resin, which is still hot, about 200 cc. of industrial methylated spirit are added to give a resin syrup of about 60 per resin content. The spirit should be added at the start in amounts of about 30 c.c. the resin being allowed to mix in before further additions. When a comparatively mobile syrup is obtained the bulk of the spirit may be added.

The P:F ratio used here is 1:1.25. The theoretical molecular ratio is 1:1.5. The syrup formed by this method can be used to prepare a laminated material.

(b) Soda Catalysed

The apparatus required for this preparation is similar to that of the ammonia catalyzed process.

PROCEDURE

188 g. phenol, 188 c.c. 40 per cent formation and 11.25 c.c. 33.3 per cent sodium hydroxide solution are mixed together and warmed carefully under reflux. Care must be taken during this initial warming as the reaction is exothermic and may become vigorous. It may become vigorous. It may require cooling in a bowl of cold water.The mix is heated under reflux for 45 minutes.

The liquor is then vacuum distilled from a water bath heated to approximately 80° C at a pressure of about 25 mm. mercury, i.e. 1 in, to give a resin syrup.

The resin syrup is used to prepare a medium shock moulding material.

COMMERCIAL PREPARATION

The type of production equipment for one-step resins or resols depends on whether the product is to be solid and grindable or is to be finished as a liquid. For the solid resins the agitator must scrape the jacketed area of the kettle bottom to prevent over-reaction at the surface, and the discharge cock must be quite large so as to drain the contents rapidly as possible.

The phenol and formaldehyde are charged to the kettle. The alkaline catalyst is added and the pH of the batch is checked. It is generally kept above 0.8. The alkaline catalyzed reaction is milder than the acid type because of the difference in chemistry and because the larger ratio of formaldehyde introduces more water into the batch. Water moderates the temperature rise because its specific heat is higher than phenol and it dilutes the reaction. Nevertheless, there is sufficient exothermic reaction so that steam heat is stopped when the temperature reaches 60-70° C. The reaction temperature varies with the particular product being made. It is common to conduct reflux under low vacuum in the range of 80-100° C for 1-3 hrs.

Dehydration differs from novolak practice in that it is desirable to finish it as quickly as possible at a much lower temperature to prevent over-reaction or gelation. Vacuum is ordinarily used throughout the dehydration and the temperature of the batch is not allowed to go much over 100° C. When the temperature has reached 90-95° C the resin is tested for gel time which is a measure of its advancement. Samples are taken periodically and progress of shorter and shorter gel times is followed until the desired range is reached. This may be from 60 to 90 sec. at 150° C. The resin is then considered finished and it is discharged. In order to stop the reaction as quickly as possible the solid one step resins are discharged into resin coolers. These are assemblies of water-cooled bottle plates spaced about 1.5 in. apart so that the resin is chilled quickly in layers beteeen the plates.

Lower-molecular-weight one-step resin may be manufactured in the same reaction kettles used for novolak resins. The reaction cycle, however, is more nearly like that of the solid one-step resins. The reaction temperature may be as low as 60° C under vacuum reflux or 102° C at atmospheric pressure. Time at reflux temperature will vary from 1-3 hrs. followed by vacuum dehydration to hold finishing temperature below 100° C. For the very low molecular weight, highly methylolated, highly water soluble liquid resins the finishing temperature must be held as low as possible, preferably below 50° C. This is possible because the very low molecular weight results in low viscosity which can be handled at this low temperature.

A typical formulation for making a resol is as follows.

Cresylic acid (40 per cent m-cresol)	100 parts
Formalin (37 per cent w/w)	90
Catalyst, ammonia	9

ADVANCES IN MANUFACTURE

Much engineering effort has been devoted to lower the cost of resin manufacture. In the case of novolaks, the long atmospheric reflux reaction can be speeded up by using the pressure to raise the batch temperature, and this method is used to a limited extent. Continuous methods have great appeal and a variety of them have been patented. Their limitation is that they produce a great volume of a single product or very minor variations of it. For markets exist for this quantity of such a narrow specification range. On the contrary, the phenolic industry is characterized by a large variety of products to which batch production is ideally suited.

In general, the continuous process passes a mix of phenol, formaldehyde, and catalyst through coils or tubes in a heat exchanger which travel sufficiently long to give appropriate residence time. On emerging, the polymer is continuously evaporated and cooled to liquid form or, if a solid, delivered molten to resin flakes for chilling and packing. One technical problem is that the long reaction coils may become fouled and they are difficult and expensive to clean. A continuous process has been developed for non-step resin for the manufacture of Novolak.

LABORATORY PREPARATION

The apparatus required for the preparation is same as for ammonia catalyzed resol.

PROCEDURE:

250 g. phenol, 160 c.c. 40 per cent formalin (1:0.8 molecular ratio) and 3.15 g. oxalic acid are mixed together in the bolthead flask. The liquor is then warmed continuously under reflux by means of a low bunsen flame applied by hand direct to the flask, the flame being moved about to prevent local heating. As soon as bubbles start to rise, showing that the exothermic reaction has begun, the burner is taken away and the liquor allowed to come to the boil on its own. If the reaction starts to get out of hand the bowl of cold water is held up and the flask immersed in the water. After the reaction has settled down, heating is continued. with the flask on a tripod and gauge, until the liquor becomes cloudy.

After the cloud point is reached, the liquor is boiled for a further 10 min, and then transferred to the distillation apparatus. By this time the liquor will have separated into two layers.

Vacuum distillation is started, the distillation flask being heated by means of a boiling water bath. The distilling liquor is agitated by slightly opening and closing the screw dip to admit a little air. Distillation is continued at a pressure of about 25 mm. mercury i.e. 1 in, until a withdrawn sample gives a brittle bead on cooling in water. To withdraw a sample the rubber tube connecting the receiving flask with the vacuum pump is carefully taken off, then the cork in the distilling flask is removed and a sample of resin obtained by dipping with a glass rod. At the brittle bead stage the resin is poured into a flat tray to cool and is kept for making moulding materials.

COMMERCIAL PREPARATION

In a typical reaction cycle molten phenol at 60-65° C and warm 37-40% formaldehyde at about 40° C are charged to the kettle. Agitation is started and is continued throughout the cycle. The acid catalyst is then added and the batch is tested for pH. Steam heat is applied to raise the temperature until the exothermic reaction becomes strong enough to cause the batch to heat without further steam. This point will vary with the acidity of the particular formula within a range of 60-85° C. Mild reactions may be allowed to heat up to atmospheric reflux whereas more strongly exothermic reactions (at lower pH) will be held at 85-90° by vacuum reflux until the atmospheric pressure has subsided. Reflux at atmospheric pressure is continued with steam heating as necessary for periods of 3-6 hrs. depending on the catalyst and amount of formaldehyde that has to be reacted. At the end of the reflux period the condensate is distilled from the kettle. When a large part of the water has been removed and the batch temperature has increased to 120-150° C, vacuum may be applied to remove remaining moisture and some of the unreacted phenol. The final dehydration temperature will range from 140-160° C and the final vacuum will be up to 25-27 in. Hg. The exact point at which the distillation should be stopped is gauged by a control test made on a sample taken from the kettle. Melting point or solution viscosity may be used.

When the resin is completed, it is discharged through a quick opening bottom cock to cool in shallow pans or on specially cleaned floor areas, or it may be fed to a resin flaker. For those novolaks which are made to be used in solution, solvent is added while the batch is still molten in the kettle and with the condenser set for atomospheric reflux. Solvent is added slowly at first and then more rapidly as the batch cools. The completed solution is discharged from the kettle to drums, or tank as desired.

The cycle for manufacturing high-ortho-content novolaks differs primarily in that after the water has been removed, a second reaction period at 150-160° C is necessary before removing unreacted phenol. Due to the high pH of 5-7, the resin contains methylol groups which must be condensed with phenol otherwise gelation will result.

A typical formulation for making a novolak is as follows.

Ingredients	Parts by wt.
Phenol	100
Formaldehyde (37% w/w)	70
Catalyst, 5N HCl	0.3

WORKS CONTROL TESTS FOR PHENOLIC RESINS

There are a number of tests carried out for determination of the various properties of the resins. These tests can be divided into two classes.

(1) Works Control Test,
(2) Quality Control Test,

Works control teste are those tests which are made by the production technologists. They give an indication to the production technologist about the processing of the preparation of resins. These tests are generally simple and used as quick works control tests for such matter as the control of degree of polymerisation etc. They are given below.

(1) Melting Point.
(2) Viscosity of Resin Solution.

(1) MELTING POINT:

This test is carried out both in case of novolaks and solid resols. A small amount of resin is ground finely in a mortar and then a little of it is introduced into a melting point capillary tube. The tube is attached by means of rubber band to the bulb of a 250° C thermometer and then immersed in a breaker of a liquid having high boiling liquid, for example, liquid paraffin. The temperature of the bath is then raised by means of a small bunsen flame at a rate of 2° C rise in temperature per minute and the temperature is noted from the moment meeting of resin starts until it is complete. The meeting point is expressed as this temperature range.

(2) VISCOSITY OF RESIN SOLUTION:

This test is used as a works control for alcoholic solution of novolak or one-stage phenol-formaldehyde resins. For works control meticulous degree of accuracy is not required nor is it necessary to express the result in terms of absolute viscosity. For this purpose either Gardner Stand and viscosity tubes or B.S. flow cup or Ford cup 4 are used. Choice is made according to the viscosity range.

B.S. flow cup is a simple type of outflow viscometer and is used for rapid assessment of the viscosity of the resin solutions in terms of flow-time. The general basis of the test is to measure the time at 25±0.5° C. for 50 c.c. of solution to flow out of a standard cup. The flow time should be between 30 and 120 seconds, so with a given test solution a rough preliminary test should be carried out to determine which of the range of standard cups is approximate. The B.S. flow cup A 10 is suitable for the viscosity range of 1-5 stokes, A 13 cup for 3.5-10 stokes, and A 15 cup for 7-25 stokes. The cup is put in stand and levelled with the aid of spirit level placed across the top of the cup. A 50 c.c. graduated cylinder is put under the hole at the bottom of the cup. The temperature of the test sample is adjusted to 25°C±0.5 . The hole in the cup is closed by a finger and the cup is filled just to overflowing the test sample. Then the excess liquid in the cup is scrapped off with the straight edge so that it falls into the over-flow gallery in the cup. Next, at the same time finger is removed and the stop watch started. When 50 c.c. of liquid has run into the cylinder the watch is stopped and the flow time in seconds is noted. The result is expressed as so many seconds British Standard flow cup A 10, A 13 or A 15 at 20° C. The flow cup must be cleaned immediately after use and great care exercised not to damage the cup.

QUALITY CONTROL TESTS FOR PHENOLIC RESINS

There are many quality control tests that can be done to determine the properties of novolak resin, most important of which are:

(1) Flow,

(2) Curing time,

(3) Free phenol,

(1) DETERMINATION OF FLOW

Pellets of standard density are made from the resin sample by means of a simple constant volume pelleting mould. A convenient sample weight is 0.3 grams, which provide a pellet in the shape of a cylinder of quarter inch in dia (1/4") and quarter an inch (1/4") high. Several pellets should be made from the sample under test, and stuck near the edge of a 3" x 4" glass-plate. It is preferableto include in each test at least two pellets prepared from the standard resin of known characteristics. The resin used as a standard can be slow indefinitely provided that it is kept in air-tight container, and stored in cool place. An aqueous solution of gum tragacanth will be found suitable for sticking the pellets to the glass plate.

The plate containing the pellets is supported in a stand which will incline the plate at angle of 45 and assembly is placed in an over at 100° C for 2 hrs. The resin melts, and runs down the plate, curing as it does so. The length of resin track produced is an indication of flow properties of the resin and it is customary to express the flow in mms. Accurate temp. control is essential and the oven used should of air-circulating type in which temp. can be maintained at 100±5° C.

(2) THE CURING TIME

The apparatus required for this test consists simply of a metal plate of substantial weight provided with a no. of the saucer shaped depressions, each of about half an inch in diameter in its upper surface. The plate should be fitted with electric heating elements, and also be drilled with a noze to serve as a thermometer jacket. A thermostat control should be fitted and the apparatus thoroughly shielded from all draughts.

The plate is raised to a temp. of 150°-160°C. A sample of resin then placed in one of the depressions by means of a slit wire and the time recorded at which the resin reaches distinctly rubbery state. Several determinations should be carried out in each resin and the mean cure time recorded. Practices required before cure time can be accurately judged but once experience has been gained, no trouble should arise.

(3) FREE PHENOL

The resin is finely ground and 5 gms, are placed in a 1 litre flask with an approximately equal volume of silver sand. About 350 ml, of distilled water are added and the mixture steam-distilled into flask containing 20 ml. of 20 per cent sodium hydroxide solution. At the end of the distillation the distillate mixture is transferred to 1 litre graduated flask and made up to the mark with distilled water. A measured amount of bromide-bromate solution and 10 mls. of 50 per cent (V/V) hydrochloric acid added. A stopper is placed in the flask. After 10 min, 10 ml of 10 per cent potassium iodide solution are added and the liberated iodine titrated with N\10 sodium thiosulphate in the normal way, using starch as indicator. The free phenol may then by calculated from the titration figures.

For resols, following quality control tests are done.

(1) Loss of weight in stoving on 135° C,

(2) Stoving time,

(3) Free phenol.

(4) LOSS OF WEIGHT ON STOVING AT 135° C

This test is also sometimes performed for novolaks. The test is carried out in flat-bottomed dishes, 7 cms. in diameter and 2-3 cms. deep. made of nickel, stainless steel or tinplate. About 0.5 gms. of resin or resin solution. accurately weighted, is distributed over 10 gms. of acid-washed silver sand of 44-85 B.S. mesh no. fineners by adding a small quantity of solvent such as acetate, and stirring with a metal rod 2 mm. in diameter. The dish containing the resin and the sand is heated in a ventilated oven maintained at 135 ± 2°C for 2 hours. After cooling in a desicator, the dish and contents are reweighed and the loss in weight of the resion is calculated as a percentage of the original weight.

(5) STOVING TIME

A 10 gms. sample of one-stage resin is heated in a dish in an oil-bath at 135° C. The dish is held on the oil surface with toungs. The molten resin is moved about in dish with the spatula. The time is noted between melting and hardening of the resin.

PROCEDURE

To a mixture of 100 parts of phenol and 240 parts of 30 per cent aqueous formalin (2,4 moles) is added 3 parts of NaOH in 20 per cent aqueous solution. The mixture is heated for 2-4 hours at the temperature of 60-65° C. The resulting material is concentrated under vacuum of 30 mm. mercury until a temperature of 65° C is reached. Sufficient lactic acid is added to the syrup to neutralise the alkaline. This is followed by addition of 15 gms. of glycerine. Vacuum concentration is continued until the dehydration is complete.

PROPERTIES

The phenolic resins may be transparent or nearly transluscent, ranging in colour from very pale amber to dark brown. They may exist in a solid or liquid form depending upon the molar ratio of the initial reactants and the type of catalyst used. Novolaks are of the solid type and are brittle resin like substances which may be crushed to a very fine powder for use in moulding compositions or dissolved in organic solvent for certain bonding applications. The liquid resins of the resol type vary in viscosity from that of thick thread.

The phenol novolak has a specific gravity of approximately 1.25, the cast resin (unfilled) 1.34 and wood-flour or cellulose filled mouldings 1.35 to 1.4. The physical properties will vary according to the fillers as given in Table 2.0. The cured resins are practically insoluble in common solvents, hot oils, aqueous acids and salts, but are, however, slighlty soluble by alcohols, water and dilute acids and alkalies. They decompose in concentrated oxidizing acids and hot alkalies.

PHENOLIC MOULDING POWDERS

Moulding compositions or powders may be defined as moulding materials which flow readily under the influence of heat and pressure and assume the shape of the canty. Under this definition comes a wide range of compositions that differ chiefly by the type of the filler they contain. Althrough it is possible to mould the resin itself without an addition of the other ingredients, the articles so produced have limited applications and the addition of fillers increases the range of usefulness by modifying the properties of the product. So tensile, impact, electrical, heat-resistance and other properties can be improved and it is often only of secondary importance that the filler also reduces the cost of moulding compositions. The ingredients which are commonly found in moulding compositions are noted below.

(1) Resin,
(2) Filler,
(3) Mould lubricant,
(4) Accelerator,
(5) Plasticizer,
(6) Colourants,
(7) Hardening agents.

TABLE 2.0

PHYSICAL PROPERTIES OF PHENOLIC RESINS

	Cast resin	Moulding resin			Laminating resins		
	Unfilled	*Wood flour filled*	*Chopped cotton fabric*	*Mineral filled*	*Paper*	*Fabric*	*Asbestos*
Specific gravity	1.34	1.35–1.4	1.34–1.38	1.9–2.0	1.24–1.38	1.34–1.138	1.6–18
Tensile strength, lb/m²	4–10,000	5–8000	5–8000	3–20000	8–20000	8–20000	6–12000
Shear strength lb/m²	6–8000	8–10000	10–15000	4–15000	5–12000	5–12000	4–8000
Compressive strength lb/m²	10–25000	15–35000	20–32000	20–40000	25–40000	20–40000	20–32000
Impact strength ft. lb/notch	0.2–0.6	0.1–0.5	0.3–3.5	0.25–1.5	0.3–1.5	1–4	0.5–1.5
Specific heat	0.4	0.35	0.34	0.3	0.35	0.35	0.3
Coefficient of thermal expansion/(°C)	3–8	3–6	2–6	2–4	2–3	2–3	2–3
Dielectric constant (10^3 c/s)	4 plus	5–15	5–10	5–10	4–8	6–12	10–18
Chemical resistance							
Weak acids	R	FR	FR	R	FR	FR	R
Strong acids	Decomposed by oxidising acids resistants to reducing organic acids						
Weak alkalies	R	R	R	R	R	R	R
Strong alkalies	A	A	A	A	A	A	A
Solvents	R	R	R	R	R	R	R

R————Resistant
A————Attacked
FR————Fairly resistant

Resin part has aiready been discussed in the preceding pages. It is now proposed to deal with rest of them and their role in the moulding compositions separately.

FILLERS

The idea of adding a filler to a phenoplast resin in order to produce a combination which could be moulded satisfactorily originated by Dr. Bakeland. Filler is any substance rather organic or inorganic, which is mixed with a resin to produce a homogeneous mixture which can subsequently be moulded. The filler facilitates the moulding process, which is usually very difficult with pure resin, and also improves the physical properties of the moulded article.

The selection of the proper filler for a moulding powder has an importance which is secondary only to the selection of the phenoplast resin. The filler is most important for controlling mechanical and strength properties of the moulded articles; to a lesser extent it affects the electrical properties and heat resistance. The resin is important because it must give the proper flow and the proper bond, and must also permit curing to a well-finished piece in a reasonable length of time. The exact nature of the resin is important in securing the most desirabie electrical properties.

The general requirements for a satisfactory filler have been classified into two groups.

(1) Primary requirements,

(2) Secondary requirements.

The primary requirements are essential for satisfactory moulding, while some compromise is possible for certain uses in the case of secondary requirements.

PRIMARY REQUIREMENTS

1. Good impact and tensile strength in the moulded component,
2. Low mositure absorption,
3. Low specific gravity in the moulded piece,
4. Easy wetting by resins and dyes.
5. No chemical or physical effects on steel dies and particularly on abrasive effects,

6. Low cost and adequate supply.
7. Non-flammability or low burning rate,
8. Freedom from odour,
9. Supplies must be readily obtainable and of uniform quality.

SECONDARY REQUIREMENTS

1. Good electrical characteristics in the moulded piece.
2. Light colour which is retained at elevated temperature and in presence of chemical materials such as in preparation of moulding powder.
3. Inertness to acids, alkalies etc.
4. Easy machineability.
5. Heat resistance,
6. Availability.

TYPE OF FILLERS

Fillers are usually classified primarily according to their general chemical nature-organic or mineral-and they are further subdivided according to their chemical composition and physical structure.

Most commonly used fillers for manufacture of different grades of phenolic moulding powders are as under:

(I) Wood flour,
(II) Walnut shell flour,
(III) Cotton flock,
(IV) Chopped fabrics,
(V) Twisted cotton cords,
(VI) Mica,
(VII) Slate dust,
(VIII) Diatomceous silica,
(IX) Asbestos.

(I) Wood Flour

Wood flour is by far the most widely used filler for phenoplast moulding powders. According to one estimate probably 70 per cent of the phenolic moulding powder used today is filled with this material. The reason for this lies partily in the low cost of the filler and partly because wood flour is easily incorporated into the resin. The resulting combination can be easily moulded and gives a finished product with excellent surface finish and strength which is satisfactory for most uses.

Wood flour for use in plastics is nealy always obtained from the softer woods such as varieties of pine, fir, sprice etc. It is important that the wood the selected to ensure the minimum contamination with knots, and resin spots. The grinding of the wood flour is an important part of its preparation. A type of attrition grinding is used; this has the advantage that the wood structure is not entirely destroyed and a certain portion of its fibrous nature is retained despite these precautions, the fact remains that in wood flour a large part of the fibre structure is almost completely removed. The wood flour is usually so ground, so that nearly all of it passes through a 60 or 80 mesh screen. The average length of the individual wood fibre is from 0.002 to 0.007 inch. The use of coarser material results in a poor finish of the moulded article. Experiments have been made in the use of more finely ground wood flour, but no advantage has been demonstrated.

(II) Walnut-shell Flour

Walnut-shell flour is a cellulosic type of filler which is used in place of wood flour when some special properties are desired. As compared to wood flour, walnut-shell flour gives a more lustrous finish to a moulded pheno-plast,and slightly better water resistance. The physical properties of a moulded phenoplast containing walnut-shell flour are in general quite similar to a general purpose product filled with wood flour. The impact strength is about 10 per cent lower, due to less fibrous nature of the walnut shell flour.

(III) Cotton Flock

This is a popular filler which is used when improved shock-resistance properties are desired. The shock resistance is about 3 to 10 times that of WF filled compositions depending upon the proportion,length of the filler and processing method. A basic specification for cotton flocks is given in

Modern Plastics Encyclopedia

Moisture max. per cent	4.0
Ash max. per cent	0.5
Bulk, c.c./10 g.	40-50
Oil absorption, c.c./10 g.	20-30
Acetone soluble matter, per cent	3.00
Residue on 40 mesh screen, per cent	10-20
Residue on 60 mesh screen, per cent	5-15
Residue on para, per cent	60-100

The cotton flock should be uniform in bulk and fibre length and absolutely free from tough matter, such as oils, starch, rayon and metallics.

(IV) Chopped Fabric

Chopped fabric improves impact length quite considerably more than cotton flock. The nuture of the fabric varies from a light cotton base to a heavy conves base and the chopped fabric may come from various sources. The av. size of the particle size is 1/4" to 1/2" in any one direction. Whereas the increasing particle size improves impact strength the surface of the resulting moulding is poorer.

(V) Twisted Cotton Cords or Strings

Twisted cotton cords or strings cut into short length surpass cotton flock or chopped fabric in their reinforcing quarters, but this is accompanied by reduction in flow and mouldability. The average thickness of cords is about 10 to 80 thousandth and length 1/4 to 3/4".

The named cotton fillers consist of nearly pure cellulose and show an affinity for the phenolic resin. It is probable that when fluid resins are used, the resin may penetrate into the central tabular canal of the cotton fibre.

(VI) Mica

Mica usually in the form of dust, is the prepared filler when exceptional electrical properties are required, but because of its poor wetting and strength properties when compound with phenolics, it is often desirable to add a rein for cing filler, forexample asbestos. Mica is a complex potassium and aluminium silicate with an approximate formula: $K_2O.3Al_2O_3.6Si_2O.\ 2H_2O$. For optimum electrical properties, it should be free form iron impurities.

(VII) Diatomceous Silica

Diatomaceous silica is pure silica forming the skelons of microscopic marine chemicals called diatomacea. Silica fillers are exceptionally heat and acid resistant. The mechanical properties imparted to the mouldings are poor and silica fillers show a distinct abrasive action on the mould surface.

Its Sp. gravity is 2-2.3 as compared with 2.45-2.80 for asbestos.

(IX) Asbestos

It is fibrous mineral filler which imparts heat and chemical resistance, whilst maintaining good electrical and mechanical properties. The Sp. gravity f commercial grade varies from 2.45 to 2.80 and the dry density is between 12.40 lbs/ft^3. Grades with long fibres, for example, 1/2 in. or longer should be used where good mechanical properties, especially impact aimed at heat resistance is good up to 400° C, this temperature being well above decomposition of temperature of the resin.

2. MOULD LUBRICANT

The function of the mould lubricant is to prevent adhesion between the moulding and the mould surface. Earlier it was applied to the mould surface, but presently it is incorporated in the composition. The mould lubricant under heat melts and being largely incompatible with the moulding composition, it migrates to the surfaces where it spreads over as a thin layer bet ween mould and moulding. The most commonly used substances are given below.

(1) Zinc stearate

(2) Stearic acid

(3) Carnauba wax

(4) Calcium, magnesium & aluminium stearate.

3. ACCELERATORS

Accelerators are invariably basic; they increase the rate of hardening. Lime and magnesium oxide are most-commonly used, but their inclusion is not recommended when good electrical properties are desired. Apart from accelerating the resin basis serves to neutralise any free acidic bodies present in the moulding composition. This factor is of some importance as acidic substance like free phenol cause sticking of the mouldings to the mould surface.

A further interesting property of the basic oxides is their ability to gel syrups one-stage resins without affacting their thermoplasticity. This characteristic can be made use of in the preparation of moulding composition.

4. PLASTICIZER

Although it is possible by using large amounts of plasticizer to produce soft, flexible products, it is not usually derived to reduce rigidity and hardness of the product.

Among these, furfural is most prominent, although its use is limited by its tendency to darken and it is thus only used for black mouldings. Furfural is a mobile liquid of characteristic odour, boiling at 162° C. Being an unsaturated aldehyde it is capable of entering into combination with the resin-constituents and it is found that furfural improves curing rate. If high boiling plasticizers are to be used, their properties is lower than that of the low boiling plasticizer. Tricresyl phosphates are such plasticizer.

5. COLOURANTS

Colouring of the phenolic moulding composition is complicated by the progressively darkening colour of the resin, which turns yellow to reddish-brown on moulding as well as by the possible discolouration of the filler. If it is desired to obtain lighter shades and improve brilliancy, white pigments, for example titanium dioxide pigments, lithopone and zinc oxide are usually added. Pigment or dyes may be used for colouring but there is now a tendency to use dyes whenever possible as their colouring power for a given cost is generally greater and quantity required considerably smaller.

Black : Nigrosine spirit soluble, carbon black

Brown : Sudan brown, iron oxides

Blue : Victoria blue R and 4R methyl violet 10B

Green : Malachite green, chromium oxide green

Red : Sudan red 6 and 3 B rhodamine B,

Orange : Sudan orange E & R benzidine orange.

For the reason already mentioned, white and light colours are difficult to achieve and, as these colours are not stable, manufacture of light-coloured mouldings is not considered to be sound. Best colour range and stability can be achieved by using one-stage resin and liberal use of white pigments.

PRINCIPLES OF COMPOUNDING

The properties of the various ingredients used in formulating a moulding compound are governed by the properties of the compound desired. The amount of resin used should be sufficient to coat and waterproof the filler particles and fuse them in a solid mechanically sound mass. In case a cellulosic filler like wood flour or cotton is used, the resin content of the moulding composition varies from 40-60 per cent by weight. When heavier fillers, such as asbestos or mica is used, the weight proporation of the resin is 30-50 per cent.

Accelerators are usually added in the amount of 0.5 to 5 parts by weight of the resin. An increase in propertion acts beneficially on curing time but adversely on the electrical properties. The proportion of lubricant used varies from 1 to 3 per cent.

Nigrosine, for black, is added in the proportion of 1 to 3 per cent. For light colours, white pigment 5 to 10 per cent on the weight of the resin may be used.

Since the wood flours differ appreciably in colours, sometimes it becomes necessary to cover up the colour of the filler than that of the resin. For white colouration; titanium dioxide, lithopone or zinc oxide are the most commonly used pigments.

Some formulations of moulding compounds are given below.

1. P.F- WOOD FLOUR MIXTURE :

Phenol-formaldehyde resin (novolak)	400 gm.
Hexamethylene tetramine	60 gm.
Wood flour	550 gm.
Total	1,010 gm.

2. FORMULATION FOR A BLACK COMPOUND

Ingredient	*Parts by wt.*
Phenol-formaldehyde resin (P/F ratio =1/0.9)	100
Wood flour (anhydrous)	110

Stearic acid or zinc stearate	2
Lime	2
Nigrosine (spirit-soluble)	2
Furfural	5
Hexaamine	12.5

MANUFACTURE

The manufacture of moulding compounds can be understood by following flow diagram.

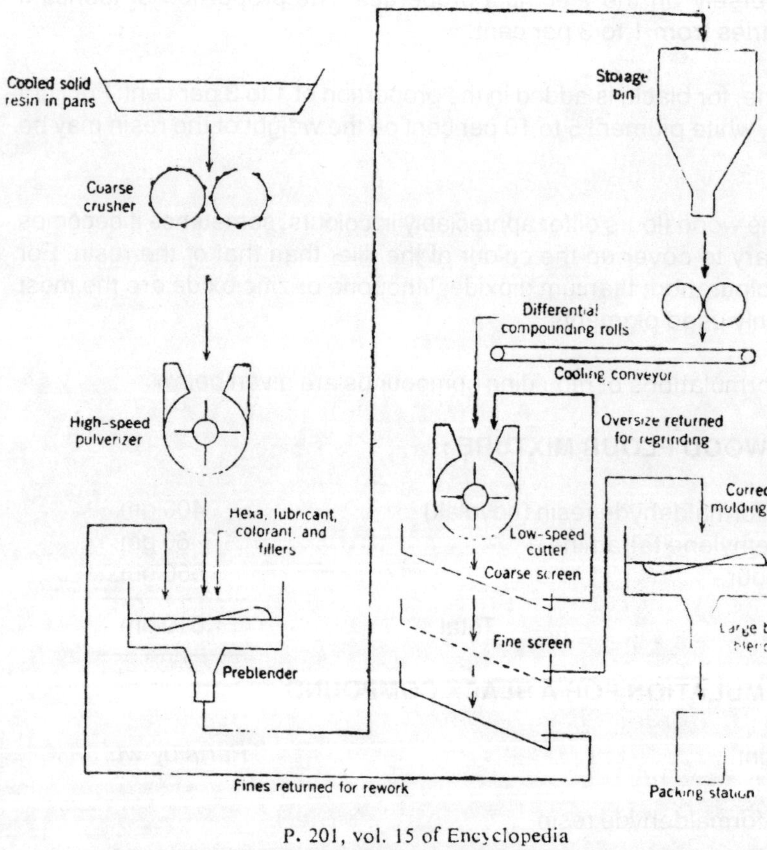

P. 201, vol. 15 of Encyclopedia

Fig. 2.1 Flow diagram for manufacture of phenolic moulding compounds

The manufacture of moulding compounds from resins can very in different ways. Usually, the manufacture of phenolic moulding compounds is a hot compounding operation in which the resin is fluxed and intimately mixed with the dry ingredients.

The solid resin is used where rolling and kneading operation is permisible. But where it results in the disintegration of the filler, as in the case of fibrous materials such as cotton and asbestos, the resin is introduced in the form of a syrup and hot mining can be avoided.

When the solid resin is in the form of lumps, it is crushed and then ground in a pulverizer. The ground resin is then mixed with other ingedients like filler, lubricant, curing agent, colours etc Before mixing on rollers, it is usually necessary to blend the intimately in a preblender so that the resulting mix is homogeneous. When the filler is wood flour, which is in fact most usual, the mixing is done on rollers.

When the pre-mix from the preblender is passed through rollers, the filler gets evenly distributed into the resin. In this process the resin, premixed with the filler, is brought to its melting point on the heated rollers (110° C), thus enveloping and impregnating the compounding ingredients. It is found that it is better to bering wood filler to a predetermined moisture content. High moisture content, above 10 per cent, reduces mechanical and electrical strength of the moulding. The loss in strength is attributed to the insufficient penetration of fillers into the resin due to high moisture content. Whereas very low moisture content, although gives good mechanical and electrical properties, but increases processing difficulties.

The charge of the feed material to the mixer may vary considerably, being usually determined by the size of the mixer. The length of the mining operation is determined by the degree of impregnation required. While designing a mixing machine, it is important to take into consideration some changes occurring during mixing. These include evaporation of moisture and hardening of resin due to curing which gradually stiffens the mass and power requirements for mining is thus increased.

Ingredients	*Parts by wt.*
Phenol	29
Formaldehyde (40%)	72
Dilute ammonium hydroxide (density 0.9)	12
Water	800
Finely-divided wood	100

Finely-divided wood is digested with phenol or a homologue thereof, dilute ammonium hydroxide and water for 4 hours at 200-300 pounds per square inch. Then 72 parts of 40% formaldehyde (or other aldehyde) are added and the mixture is refluxed for 1 hour. The resulting product when dried and moulded under heat (150° C) and pressure (1000 pounds per square inch) is strong, water resistant, and resembles lignum vitae in many respects.

The use of resin is determined by the types of fillers being added into the resin. A kneader type machine has been most common in use. But these days internal mixers like Banbury used extensively in rubber industry has been gaining popularity because of the rapid, forceful and thorough impregnation.

If the hexa has not been added at the preblending stage, it should be added just prior to the completion of the mixing. This procedure permits longer mixing periods since danger of hardening in the initial mixing period is removed.

The material leaves the rolls in the form of a sheet or, in the case of coarse fillers, in crumbs, and for the majority of purpose has to be ground. For this purpose, in the case of wood-flour mixtures, high speed distintegrators are used. The sheet is commonly referred to as a "blanket" and the thickness of the sheet is usually in the range of 1/8 to 1/4 inch. It is allowed to cool before disintegration.

It is then broken up and the pieces are fed to a grinder where the comminution to its final size takes place. The resulting moulding powder is fed to a blender where member of batches are blended to ensure uniformity of delivery. Magnetic separator is generally included in the flow-sheet to remove any piece of iron which may have incidentally been introduced into remove any piece of iron which may have incidentally been introduced into the moulding composition. For the blender the materials are introduced into airtight containers, normally steel drums, and ready for despatch.

In the cold mixing process, the mixer used is a simpler machine like a tumbling barrel or ribbon blender. The main objective of mixing at this stage is to interdispense the solid resin and the filler particles. The impregnation and polymerization process is carried out on the rolling mill. The rolling operation takes somewhat longer time than in the hot mixing process.

For smooth running of the operation it is essential that the material should adhere to one definite roller and form a smooth blanket. The adhesion is controlled by the temperature differential and speed differential of the rolls. As the rolling proceeds the melting point of the composition increases and consequently its adhesion characteristics shift towards higher temperatures. Predominant practice is to find out the adhesion by fuel i.e. by noting the softness of the blanket where the desired flow is reached.

APPLICATIONS

The applications of phenolic resins for moulding powders may be classified according to their final end-use, i.e. general purpose, heat and impact resistance and also resistance to cold flow. They are low cost materials, possessing good dimensional stability, heat resistance and also resistance to cold flow. The resultant moulded articles are normally black to brown in colour. The general-purpose compounds are usually wood-flour filler and possess a popular balance of properties/price for a wide variety of applications. Typical applications include telephone hand-sets, steering wheels and facing panels although the former application is being replaced quite extensively by thermoplastics. The impact resistant grades contain chopped fabric and can be used for pump impellers, washing machine agitators, lavotory seats and electrical switches. Heat-resistant grades containing asbestos fillers are used in aircraft and missile applications. The electrical resistant grades are used for automobile ignition parts, cool formers, etc. Phenolic moulding powders can be used in electrical equipment where insulation requirements are not too stringent, such as plugs, switches, switch-gear cases and covers.

ADHESIVES

LABORATORY PREPARATION

The apparatus for a cold setting phenol-formaldehyde adhesive consists of :

(1) 250 c.c. bolthead flask with reflux condenser.
(2) Vacuum distillation apparatus with air bubbling tube and screw clip.
(3) Thermometer (110° C)
(4) Hot water bath,
(5) 10 c.c. measuring cylinder,
(6) Several pieces of wood about 6 in. x 2 in. x 1/2 in.
(7) 6 clamps.

PROCEDURE

50 g. phenol, 92 c.c. 40 per cent formalin (molecular ratio 1:2:3) and 2.2 c.c. 33.3 per cent sodium hydroxide solution are placed in a 250 c.c. bolthead flask. The mixture is boiled under a reflux condenser for 60 minutes. The pH is adjusted to 7-7.5 in m using B.D.H. universal indicator, by adding N/1 lactic acid, and the resin is vacuum distilled at a pressure of about 25 mm mercury, i.e. 1 in. from a water bath at about 75° C until a thickish syrup is obtained.

To make the hardening catalyst.

(a) 5 c.c. concentrated hydrochloric acid are diluted with 7.5 c.c. industrial methylated spirit.

(b) 2.5 c.c. water are added to 7.5 g. toluene pare-sulphonic acid.

20 g resin syrup are weighed and 1 c.c. hardening catalyst either (a) or (b) is mixed with it to give a glue which should be used within an hour.

Two pieces of smooth wood are lightly coated with catalysed syrup clamped together with an end to end overlap and allowed to stand overnight.

The adhesion is empirically tested by putting one end of the assembly in a vice and breaking the joint open with a hammer. A good joint should show wood failure when breaking, that is there should be splinters of wood torn away with the adhesive.

COMMERCIAL PREPARATION

The phenolic resins normally used for adhesive applications are the liquid resol types with an alkaline catalyst.

These are produced by reacting phenol and formaldehyde in a molar ratio of 1:2. The initial pH of the reaction medium is usually neutral or slightly alkaline to allow the formation of methylol grougs, and then raised to a mildly acid medium (pH=5) to ensure a steady rate of condensation. The reaction can be followed by viscosity measurements and the tendency of the resin to be hydrophobic. At a predetermined stage the process is stopped by neutralization and the resin is then either dehydrated under vacuum, to give a viscous product of 1-10 poise and 60-70 per cent solids content, or spray dried to give a resin powder. The resin syrup can then be stabilized by the addition of weak bases or by protective colloids such as starch. The liquid product has a life up to 6 months.

The phenolic plywood glues can either be cured by heat alone at 135° C or by adding small amounts of paraformaldehyde at temperatures as low as 115° C.

Curings time is 5 min. at 270-300° F and 200-500 psi. The resin glues are usually extended with a filler such as wood flour and often with dried animal blood products. The spray dried powder while to be used as an adhesive is dissolved in water to produce an aqueous solution. Before the solution is spread on the wood, the filler is added to the resin solution.

The amount of filler used in the resin glue varies from 10-20 per cent on the dry resin content. The fillers prevent too rapid absorption of the resin solution by the wood fibres of the ply.

APPLICATIONS

The largest usage of phenol formaldehyde resin adhesives is in the manufacture of exterior grade Douglas for plywood. Some hardwood plywood for special purposes is also made with these adhesives such as for example, in the manufacture of hardwood plywood for use out-of doods, fir-resistant plywood, and certain types of composite fibre doors involving wood vaneers. Doors for exterior openings also make use of phenolic resin adhesives.

The newest use for phenol-formaldehyde resins, and one predicted to grow fastest in the near future, is as a binder for wood particles in the particle board industry. The bending of glass-fibre mats, particularly for insulation work, is another important use of phenolic resins. Asbestos fibre is used as reinforcing agent in this application. It is also used in the bending of abrasive grits in the manufacture of grinding wheels. For some marine applications involving complex moulded shapes and room-temperature cure, resorcinol formaldehyde reins are used. Phenolic resins bond well to some metals such as iron, bronze and aluminium.

Applications include bonding of brake linings to shoes and phenolic laminated sheet to aluminium.

FORMULATIONS

Some formulation of phenolic resins for different applications are given below.

1.	Uformite 430	1000 parts
	Flour	70
	Water	60
	Catalyst	10

Uformite 430 is a water soluble phenolic resin glue which may be used either as a cold bending adhesive, i.e. at a temperature of 70° F, or for hot pressing. It has a sp. gr. 1.32, and contains 68-72 per cent solids in water.

The method of preparing the mix is simple. The catalyst is added slowly to the glue accompanied by constant stirring. The flour is then added and the mass thoroughly mixed. The working life of the made-up glue is approximately 6 hours and should be put into work without delay.

2. PHENOLIC BAKING CEMENTS

Phenolic resin cements are now extensively employed in the manufacture of various kinds of electrical apparatus, such as resistors, commutators, transformers etc. Their best known application is probably for basing electrical light bulbs and radio tubes as well as brushes. The resins are usually available as granular powders which require mixing industrial alcohol to secure a cement of the required viscosity and also as highly vicous or parts-like cements with a resin content of 75-85 per cent and a viscosity at 25° C of about 4,000 centipoises.

3. PHENOLIC RESIN PUTTY

Mixtures of phenolic resin and asbestos can be mixed in situ with 30 per cent alcoholic solution of sulphuric acid (the catalyst) and made into a cement for applying to rough wood, dried silicate cement and rubber coated metal surfaces. The liquid resin is mixed with the filler to form a putty like mass of the required consistancy and prior to use needs thorough mixing with the alcoholic acid solution. It is usually applied to the surface to be protected with a hardwood trawel.

4. PHENOLIC RESIN RUBBER CEMENT

Commercial phenolic resin rubber cements may have a composition of 15 per cent total solids and 85 per cent volatile solvents and an acid value, expressed in terms of m. gms KOH per gm. of resinous base, of 8.5. These cements are air-drying and find many applications where quick drying and flexible film is required. They will stick ordinarily incompatible materials such as phenolic laminated paper and even plywood.

COATINGS

Phenolic resins are used in coatings both as the solefilm former and to fortify drying oils. Resins used as the sole reactive ingredient are alkalinecatalyzed one-step phenol-formaldehyde resins. A typical example would involve two moles of formaldehyde to one mole of phenol and would be reacted to high molecular weight before being dissolved in alcohol. The coating baked at 325-450° F, has excellent solvent and chemical resistance to all but alkalies and strong acids, adheres well, and has good heat resistance. This type of coating is widely used in drum and can linings, milk and beer processing equipment, water tanks, and air conditioning equipment.

The resins used with drying oils are made with para-substituted phenols to obtain the necessary solubility or compatibility. Ortho-substitution gives solubillity but poor colour stability. The phenols of major commercial value are p-cresol, p-phenylphenol, p-tert-amyl phenol. These oil-soluble resins may be alkaline or acid-catalyzed. Resins based on bisphenol A are widely used in combination with resin and ester gums make modified phenolic resins.

The acid-catalyzed resins, of which those based on p-phenyl and p-tert-butyl-phneol are the most important, are used by being cooked with vegetable drying oils to make oleoresinous varnishes. P-phenylphenol resins give varnishes with excellent colour, fast cooking, and fast drying. The butyl phenol resins are more widely used, however, because of lower cost, better adhesion, and better tolerance for low cost solvents. One promising new development in phenolic resins for coatings involves the formations of a diglyceride of the one of the less-soluble, slower-drying, low-cost oils such as soyabean oil. This product is reacted with an equivalent of toluene di-isocyanate and then with an oil-soluble phenolic resins are often used in combination with resin or ester gum varnishes. In this application, the alkaline-catalyzed heat-reaction resins are most commonly used.

The phenol-formaldehyde resins as such can be used as lacquers. For this use, either liquid resols or solid resols, dissolved in alcohol, are applied. In special cases the hardening is effected with the aid of acids.

Resols soluble in alcohol are also used in manufacturing of storing varnishes. On heating, these resins change to insoluble and infusible compounds and are notable for their resistance to chemical action. Varnishes from these are used in electrical industry.

A typical procedure for making a varnish from p-phenyl phenol novolak and tung oil utilizes the following components.

Ingredients	*Parts by weight*
p-Phenyl novolak resin	100
Tung oil	100
Xylene	200
Lead cobalt naphthenate drier	0.25

PROCEDURE

The resin and tung oil are heated together to a temperature of 230° C for about 30 minutes and are maintained at this temperature for further 15-20 minutes to reach the required viscosity. The batch is then cooled and the xylene added followed by the driers dissolved in some of the xylene.

A varnish made by the above method will dry very quickly to give a tough, durable film resistant to weathering, weaker acids and caustic soda solution. It is particularly useful as the basis of chemical resistant coatings.

As stated earlier, the modified oil-soluble phenolic resins are made by dispensing a phenol formaldehyde condensation product in a natural resins, such as resin, the principal constituent of which is abietic acid. The phenolaldehyde product may be added gradually to the hot resin, or the condensation may be gradually accomplished in situ by adding the phenol and formaldehyde to hot resin. Complete esterification is usually accomplished at the same time by adding glycerol, penta-erythritol, or ethylene glycol. A typical formulation for preparation of resin-modified phenolic is given below.

FORMULATION FOR RESIN-MODIFIED PHENOLIC RESIN COATING

Ingredients	*Parts by weight*
Glycerol	260
Cresol	400
Formalin (30 per cent)	600
Resin	2600

PROCEDURE

Cresol and formalin are charged and pH is made alkaline with aqueous caustic solution. Reactants are heated for 4-6 hours at 60° C. Thereafter, resin is dehydrated under vacuum until a sample taken becomes clear. Now resin is charged to a kettle of suitable capacity and 500 parts of the cresol-formaldehyde resin syrup is added and temperature is raised to 250° C. Steam distillation is done for 3 hours and then glycerol is added and little magnesia is added. Esterificatino is done at 260° C. Thereafter it is discharged and stored. Esterification should be stopped when the acid value is 15-20.

BONDING RESINS

This market area includes the use of phenolic resins to bond friction materials, abrasives, wood particles, and inorganic fibres for insulation.

FRICTION MATERIALS

Phenolic resins are the principal bonding agents for the asbestos used in friction materials.

Resins for friction materials may be made insolvent for extruded linings or for the saturating of woven asbestos fabric. They may also be made as dry powders for moulded dry mines. Types of phenolic resins to be used depend on the specific properties desired in the friction material. Two-step phenol-formaldehyde resins have fair-to-good friction and excellent mear. Mixed phenol-alkylphenol resins are modified with 10-20 per cent of vegetable drying oils such as tung, linseed, or soyabean-oil to give solid grindable two-step resins that can be used in dry mix processes to obtain a softer braker-pedal action. Resin solutions for extrusion are usually modified with a high level of oil, the result being a viscous, talky binder that holds wet asbestos mix together during extrusion, drying, and even cure.

The phenolic resins provide the bending strength and the basic friction and wear characteristic but many other ingredients are added to modify or improve certain performance factors. Common fillers employed in formuations include finely powdered burite for higher density and better wear, and cured cashew-nut shell liquid resin particles for more uniform friction performance. A typical formulation for a general purpose friction material is given below.

FORMULATION

Ingredients	*Parts by wt.*
Phenolic resin	15
Asbestos	55
Fillers	30

The end uses of these resin bonded friction materials are in automotive brake linings, clutch facings, and automotive-transmission discs, but a wide variety of other products are made and include brakes for oil-mill drilling rigs, power derricks, and railroad cars.

BRAKE-LININGS

Brake linings and centre facings are the principal items in this group. Several types of linings are recognized. In one type a fabric of asbestos fibre, cotton fibre and compressed or laminated type are included. In other type an asbestos fibre-liquid composition is extruded. The extruded material is then dried and partially cured. It is then compressed by calendering or pressing and baked to complete the cure. For manufacture of brake linings, the composition is press-moulded in sheets and partially cured. The sheet is then cut as desired, and the segments are shaped and given a final cure at 300 to 400° F.

The specifications of phenolic resins for friction materials are given below.

1. Very thick liquid resin is suitable for the manufacture of woven linings. The resin should have a solid content of approx. 80 per cent, and a viscosity of approx. 40 poise at 40° C.

2. Powdered phenol formaldehyde two-stage resin is suitable for the production of moulded brake linings and particularly disc pads.

Melting point (capillary)	85° C
Volatile content	2 per cent approx.
Cure time @ 140° C	2 min.
Particle size	less than 20 per cent on 200 mesh

A typical composition for making brake linings empolying powdered resins is given below.

Ingredients	*Parts by wt.*
Powdered phenolic resin	22
Asbestos fibre	48
Burytes	30

It should be moulded to shape at a pressure of 1 ton/m^2 for 30 minutes at 150° C. Fast curing at temperature up to 200° C is sometimes necessary to obtain optimum properties.

GRINDING WHEELS AND COATED ABRASIVES

In this category of use are included the grinding wheels, sand-paper, abrasive coated discs, sheets and bolts. The basic ingredients of these abrasive tools are suitable abrasive grains and a binder to hold them. Fillers and reinforcements are usually added. Carborundum, diamonds, aluminium oxide and silicone carbide are the major abrasive materials and are used in grit from 12 to 325 mesh.

Binders are usually made up two parts; a liquid which is used to wet the surface of abrasive grains and a powdered resin which is anchored to the abrasive by the liquid film until the mass can be pressed and heat cured. During the curing process the liquid and powdered resins merge into one binder.

Alkali-catalyzed phenolic resols are extensively used as the wetting agent, even though they have a limited storage life and can be more nonuniform in compositions. The amount varies with the material and conditions. As little as 5 per cent of the powdered resin frequently suffices. Quality of the binder is judged best for preparing and testing bars of abrasives.

POWDERED RESIN

The powdered resin employed is commonly novolak phenolic resins. These resins have desired percentage of hexamine hardener.

There are three grades of two-stage phenolic resins which are used for grinding wheels. They are tabulated below.

Property	*Short flow grade*	*Medium flow grade*	*Long flow grade*
1. Melting point, ^oC	85/95	85/95	80/90
2. Cure time @ 120°C	90 secs	110 secs	190 secs
3. Hexamine content	9 per cent	6 per cent	6 per cent

Standardization of particle size of the powdered resin is important. Many grades shall pass through 250 mesh screen.

A typical formulation for making two-stage phenolic resin suitable for grinding wheels may be as follows.

Ingredients	*Parts by wt.*
Phenol	440 kgs
Formaldehyde (30 per cent)	430 kgs
Catalyst (Conc. H_2SO_4)	0.3 per cent on the wt. of phenol

PROCEDURE

Solid grindable novolak resin is prepared by the usual procedure as described before. The resin is tested for melting point and hot plate gel time. It is many times necessary to correct or adjust formulation according to one's own plant variable. The solid resin is broken in coarse powder either manually or by means of coarsers in grinder. The hexamine is weighed and mixed with coarse resin. The thoroughly mixed resin hexamine is then fed to impact type swing hammer mill and mix is then pulverised to desired fineness. Fine pulverised resin powder is very securely paced to check the change in mixture content.

PROCESSING

In this application the grit is first wetted with a low-viscosity liquid one-step phenolic resin or furfural, 1-3 per cent of the weight of the grit Next, a dry mixture of phenolic resin and fillers is added and combination of wet grit and powder is tumbled until each particle of grit has a coating powder. The mix is temporarily dry and free-flaming. The amount of powdered phenolic resin varies from about 6 to 10 per cent of the weight of the grit. The quantity and type of fillers will vary with the intended use of the wheel. Two-step phenolic resins are used almost exclusively because the moisture given off during cure of one step resins results in undesirable porosity, and the two-step resins have better heat resistance.

The free-flowing grit-resin mix is charged by weight to a mould. Pressing may be done at room temperature for 1-2 min at 2000 to 5000 psi. The dense preform which results is removed from the mould and cured in an oven. Relatively long cycles are used with temperatures being increased gradually to a maximum temperature of 365° F where it is held for 12 hours. The pressing may be done for higher-density structures; the mould is at 300-320° F and 2000-3000 psi; curing takes an hour. Usually hot-pressed wheels are given an oven posture also.

COATED ABRASIVES

This term is applied to sandpaper, discs, sheets, and belts to the surface of which abrasive grains have been bonded. They are rapidly coming into use. Bachings for coated abrasives are paper, fabric, vulcanized fibre, and some other materials.

Phenolic resins used in coated abresives are the alkali catalyzed. They are available in many viscosity range and solids content vary from 65 to 75 per cent.

Phenolic resins have replaced hide glue for industrial grades of "sandpaper" where heat is generated in dry grinding or where water-cooling is required.

Industrial coated abrasives are manufactured from cloth or tough paper base. First a "making" coat of medium-viscosty liquid one-step resin is laid down on a continuous web of the backing. Next, the loose grit is adhered electrostatically, the web passing wet-side down over a pan of grit. An electrostatic field causes the grit to jump up to the paper and remain embedded in the resin layer. After the incured coated sheet has been partially dried in a low-temperature-oven cycle at 140° F, a second, thinner coating of lower-viscosity liquid one-step resin is applied as a top-size to anchor the grit thoroughly. The coated web is taken off in rolls to be cured at 225-250° F for 3-4 hours.

WOOD PARTICLE BOARD OR WALL BOARD

Products have evolved from a attempt to make profitable use of the large volumes of sawdust that is available in plenty as a cheap material, various blends of wood particles are used.

In one applications, coarse particles of the sawdust are blended with 10-15 per cent powdered phenolic resin. The blend is then surfaced with a finer wood flour. The resulting blend is moulded into toilet seats at 500-1200 psi and 320-350° F for 5-10 min. Flat panel boards are made from wood shavings sprayed with 5 per cent of liquid one-step phenolic resin and pressed at 200 psi and 340° F for 10 min. Such boards may be used as it is, or may be surfaced with a decorative wood vaneer or phenolic laminate for furniture or wall-panel uses.

INSULATION

Phenolic resins are used to bond glass-and rock-wool fibres for thermal and acoustical insulation.

In one process, the low-molecular-weight highly water-soluble resin is diluted to 10-15 per cent and sprayed on glass fibres as they are being steam blown from a molten state. The heat of the glass evaporates the excess water and the fitted fibres collected at the bottom of the blow chember are carried on a belt through an oven to cure.

In another process chopped glass fibres are mixed with powdered resin in a chember and the mat collected at the bottom is cured in the same way. Organic fibres are also bonded with powdered phenolic resin. Usually the powder is shifted into a loose web of the fibres as it comes off as a standard cotton batting garnet.
Specifications for the low viscosity liquid one-step resins require dilutability with 15-20 volume of water of ensure that resin will not precipitate or clog spray equipment. The powdered resins are also one-step phenolics. To keep the low cost of these materials, plain phenol-formaldehyde resins are used.

FOUNDRY RESINS

Phenolic resins are employed in several metal-casting applications. These include foundry core and shell.

Two-step phenolic resins are used for this process. Liquid phenolic resins modified with some urea formaldehyde resin are used in core blowing process. A lubricant such as calcium stearate is added during the coating cycle to improve the flexibility of the composition. Solids content of the liquid resin used vary from 65-70 per cent.

Typical formulation for making shell moulding phenolic resin suitable for pre-coating process is given below.

Ingredients	*Parts by wt.*
Phenol	440 kg.
Formaldehyde (37 per cent)	305 kg.
Catalyst (Conc. H_2SO_4)	0.32% of the weight of phenol.

SHELL MOULDING PROCESS FOR METAL CASTING

This process is also known as 'corning process'. In this process a mixture of sand and resin or pre-coated sand is dumped on to a hot pattern, where it is allowed to rest for a given period, then shell is stripped off from the pattern. But in the case of dry process the shell along with the pattern is passed through an oven where curing is carried out in 2-3 minutes at a temperature of about 200° C. On emergence from the oven the shell is stripped off the pattern and pattern is taken into dump box for production of another shell.

The two shells, whilst hot, are glued together with an adhesive to form a complete mould. So there are two processes in the shell moulding process.

Sand Pre-coating Process

To produce the pre-coated sands, the sand is first heated, generally at 140-110° C and dropped into 'Z' blade mixer. 140° C temperature is used when solid resin in used and 110° C when liquid resins are used.

After addition of resin the mixing is carried out for a suitable period of time, usually for about 3 or 4 minutes, and a solution of hexamine into water and lubricant like calcium stearate are added. The water boils off from the sand, and the hexamine is equally distributed throughout the resin coated sand. Contents of mixer are then dumped into a mill to grind down any lumps which may have been formed and the coated sand is discharged into a cooling area.

Precoating resins can be supplied as a coarse powder, in form of flakes, chips or as a solution in industrial alcohol.

A pure phenol novolak resin supplied as a coarse ground powder should have the following properties.

1. Capillary melting point	70-80° C
2. Volatiles	Less than 6 per cent
3. Moisture	Less than 0.5 per cent

Dry Mix Process

Instead of using a precoated sand foundries use a mixture of resin and sand which they prepare themselves. For this process it is only necessary to mix the required quantity of resin and sand, usually 4 per cent to 8 per cent of resin on the sand, and proceed as described before.

Properties of resin powder suitable for this process are given below.

	Grade I	*Grade II*
1. Capillary melting point	89° C	85° C
2. Hot plate wire @ 120° C-secs	127	127
3. Button flow @ 130° C-min	41	30
4. Particle size on 200 mesh	<2%	<2%

Where shell moulding is applicable the process has shown definite advantages such as.

1. Excellent surface finish on castings.
2. Close dimensional tolerance in castins.
3. Greater detail in castings.
4. Permeability of the shell permits moulding of thinner sections.
5. Consistant pattern production.

6. Production is adaptable to automatic operations.
7. There is less scrap metal and more good castings per ton.
8. Less sand and resin is required.
9. Moulded parts require less machinery,
10. Unskilled labour can be used.

• *Chapter 7* •

POLYESTERS

INTRODUCTION

The name polyester is used to describe a diverse group of materials formed as a result of a condensation reaction between a polyhydric alcohol and a polybasic acid. The history of these materials can be traced back to as early as 1847, when a Swedish scientist obtained a white amorphous solid of a resinous nature on heating glycerol with tartaric acid. The reactions was subsequently modified later, in England, by replacing the tartaric acid with phthalic anhydride (acid). This particular work was carried out by Watson Smith who, in 1962 obtained a wide range of resinous products from such reactions, which he named 'glyptal'. The name was in use until made virtually obsolets by the introduction of 'alkyd'. The term 'alkyd' was originally coined by R.H. Kienle who carried out many classical polymerization studies on polyesters used for surface coatings and moulding powders.

A great advance was considered to have been made in 1937 when Carlton Ellis, in America, discovered that by adding unsaturated monomers to unsaturated polyesters the setting (curing) time was substantially reduced. This made the polyester resins attractive for use on a commercial basis, in addition to stimulating further interest.

The industry founded on polyester resins has been relatively slow in growing although, from the period 1919-1926, there was considerably industrial development of these resins in varnishes and paints. The use of polyesters for purposes other than surface coatings can be considered to have started at the outbreak of the second world war when the first industrial uses of polyesters as laminating resins were seen in the U.S.A.

The major applications of polyester resins are in the field of surface coatings, lamination and casting, moulding powders etc. By varying the nature and combinations of the base raw materials, fillers, reinforcement and cure time, it is possible to obtain polyester resins exhibiting a wide range of properties. The base resins may be tailored to give certain specific characteristics, for instance, resistance to solvents, alkalies, acids or bleaching agents may be required, or possibly high heat distortion temperatures, flexural of compressive strengths.

CLASSIFICATION

Polyesters can be broadly classified into unsaturated and saturated polymers. These two broad divisions can then be further subdivided as follows.

1. UNSATURATED

(a) Laminating and casting resins

These are based on dibasic acids and dihydric alcohols. The polyester unit formed must be capable of copolymerizing with vinyl-type monomer, thereby yielding a vinyl-polyester copolymer or simply a cured polyester having a thermoset structure.

(b) Alkyds

These are, in general, of the same type as (a) although the 'glyptal' (surface coatings) types are modified with oils or fatty acids. This term is also used to describe a group of thermosetting moulding materials based on the reaction of a dehydric alcohol with an unsaturated acid such as moleic in place of the conventional phthalic acid. A vinyl-type of monomer is also necessary to effect speedy cross-linking and curing. These meterials, when suitably modified with certain fillers, are used as moulding powders for compression and transfer-moulding techniques similar to those used for phenol and aminoplasts.

2. SATURATED

Saturated polyesters include fibres and films, plasticizers, polyurethane foams.

In this chapter, only unsaturated polyester will be discussed.

RAW MATERIALS

A polyester, as the term is used here, refers to an unsaturated polyester base resin dissolved in a polymerizable monomer such as styrene. When catalyste are added to cause the points of unsaturation in the polyestei chain and monomer to cross link or thermoset the finally cured product becomes a copolymer of the polyester and monomer.

Innumerable variations can be made in the composition of the base polyester and the type and amount of cross-linking monomer to yield resin with a wide range of properties before, during and after polymerization. The main variables which control these properties are:

1. The kind and amount of dibasic acid used.
2. The kind of alcohol used.
3. The type and amount of cross linking monomer.
4. The molecular weight of the polyester resin.
5. The inhibitor system.

Some understanding of the effects of these variables on the resulting polyesters is essential if the chemist is to tailor make polyester rsins to meet certain requirements for the cured polymer, whether it will be in the form of a casting or high reinforcement with fillers.

ACID CONSTITUENTS

A large number of dibasic acids, which could as used in the synthesis of a polyester molecule, are available on a commercial basis. The types of acids selected, with respect to the molecular weight, configuration, pendant groups and presence of unsaturated bonds available for cross linking contribute to the properties of the final product. Since unsaturated dihydric alcohols are not available on a commercial basis, the majority of the commercial resins have their unsaturated groups in the acid component of the polyester chain. Most resins are made up of at least two dibasic acids except in some cases where the high degree of cross linking is required and a single unsaturated acid such as maleic or fumaric acid, ic the only acid component. In a mixed acid composition the lower the ratio of unsaturated acid, the less closely linked the copolymer obtained in the cross linking reaction. Such copolymer will be more flexible (lower modulus of elasticity), more heat and solvent sensitive and slower in curing.

The molecular weight of the constituents used will determine the frequency of ester linkages in a polyester chain. These ester linkages are highly polar and exhibit strong attracting forces (vander walls forces) between the adjacent polyester chains which tend to rigidity the three dimensional copolymer structure inceasing its physical strength and chemical resistance in much the same fashion that additional cross-linking would accomplish.

A. Phthalic acids

The most commonly used unsaturated acid in commercial resin is phthalic acid. This is used in anhydride form since it is readily available than other acids. Commercial resins, having zero to 60 mole per cent of phthalic acid for the acid phase of the polyester resin, are typical of the resin structures synthesized from phthalic anhydride. Higher percentage of phthalic anhydride would yield more flexible, less reactive resins. This is not generally the method of preparing flexible resins on a commercial basis.

B. Isothalic acids

It is made by oxidation of meta-xylene and assumed commercial importance as an alternate modifier to phthalic anhydride. It is a white solid melting at 330° C. It reacts slowly with glycols than the phthalic anhydride but using correct experimental techniques, it is possible to obtain polyesters of high molecular weight, which give cured products having high heat distortion temperature and other improved properties. It is insoluble in water but soluble in ethanol. It does not boil but just sublimates.

The isothalic polyester resins, as they are generally called, have superior strength, toughness, increased heat and chemical resistance and higher molecular weights. The higher viscosity of these resins allows higher concentration of styrene than normally used with phthalic anhydride.

In addition to phthalic and its isomeric acid, there are a number of saturated acids available commercially and can be used in synthesizing polyesters. Some of such important acids are discussed below.

(a) Adipic Acid

It is obtained from phenol by first reducing it catalytically to cycloexanol acid thereafter obtaining cyclohexane ring by vigorous oxidation with nitric acid.

Adipic acid is white solid material with melting point of 153° C. It is slightly soluble in water. Its structural formula is

$$HOOC\text{-}(CH_2)_4\text{-}COOH$$

(b) Sebacic Acid

It is obtained commercially by treating castor oil with sodium hydroxide under pressure at temperature above 200° C. The Sebacic acid melts at 133° C.

Modification of an unsaturated polyester resin with a long chain dibasic acid of the type $HOOC\text{-}(CH_2)_n\text{-}COOH$ results in a degree of flexibility depending upon the number of 'n'.

(c) Tetrachloro endic acid

It is sometimes used in preparation of polyester with self-extinguishing properties . Other more effective acids for self-extinguishing properties are:

(1) Chloro endic acid
(2) HET acid

C. Saturated dibasic acids

The most important from the viewpoint of cost, availability and the end properties of the polymer are given as under.

(1) Maleic anhydride or Maleic acid
(2) Fumaric acid

These two acids have some chemical formula but different special configuration.

Maleic acid	*Maleic Anhydride*	*Fumaric acid*
H-C-COOH ‖ H-C-COOH	H-C-CO╲ ‖ O H-C-CO╱	HOOC-C-H ‖ H- C-COOH

In maleic acid (Ci & form) two carboxylic groups are adjacent and acid forms an anhydride. Fumaric acid has transformed and does not form anhydride.

Property	*Maleic acid*	*Fumaric acid*
Melting point	130° C	284° C
Solubility (gins/100 parts)		
(i) Water at 40° C	112.5	1.07
(ii) Ethanol at 30° C	69.9° C	5.75

Maleic and its anhydride are obtained commerically by the catalytic oxidation of benzene. Fumaric acid is obtained by heating maleic acid and as a by-product of the manufacture of phthalic acid.

Commonly used other unsaturated dibasic acids are given below.

(1) Chloromaleic acid $HOOC\text{-}C(Cl)=C(Cl)\text{-}COOH$

(2) Itaconic acid $CH_2=C\text{ - }COOH\text{-}CH_2\text{-}COOH$

B. ALCOHOLIC COMPONENTS

The alcohol component of the polyester structure has an important influence on the properties of the cross linked polymers as any one of acids. Flexibility, crystallinity, water and heat sensitivity are the properties which are mainly affected by the choice of alcohol. The principal alcohols used in polyester synthesis are:

(1) Glycols (two hydroxyl groups)
(2) Monohydric alcohols
(3) Polyhydric alcohol

As the chain length of the glycol is increased, so is the flexibility of the resulting copolymer by the increased spacing of the polyester linkages and acid constituents some of which will contain bonds for subsequent crosslinking. Better strength properties and lower cost favour the use of longer chain saturated acids, such as adipic in the manufacture of flexible polyesters.

The simplest acid most readily available is glycol of symmetrical structure as ethylene glycol. However, polyesters based on ethylene glycol and varying ratio of saturated and unsaturated acids tend to becomes hazy and crystallize upon standing. Longer chain polymethylene glycols and symmetrical branched glycols are also products of crystalline polyesters with fumaric acid.

As regards choice of the glycols, a few generalisations can be made.

(1) The longer chain length of glycol used in the polyester, the greater is the degree of flexibility in the cured polymer.

(2) The effect of having oxygen bridges in glycol is to increase the water sensitivity of the polyester.

(3) When trihydric alcohols or higher alcohols have been used as partial replacement for the glycols, it is necessary to employ a total hydroxyl content that is in excess of that required for dibasic acids alternatively to balance the high functionality of these higher alcohols with mono hydroxyl alcohols such as decyl alcohol or mono basic acids.

In table the more readily available glycols which may be used are listed below. Their important properties are also given.

Glycol	*Structure*	*Ml. pt.*	*Boiling point*	*Sp.gravity*
Ethylene	$HO—(CH_2)_2—OH$	62	197.6	1.11
Propylene	$CH_3—CHOH—CH_2$		187.4	1.038
Butylene	$CH_3.CHOH.CH_2.CH_2OH$	90	207.5	1.0059
Diethylene	$HO—CH_2—CH_2—O—CH_2—CH_2—OH$	106	245	1.1184
Triethylene	$HO—CH_2—CH_2—O—CH_2—CH_2—o—CH_2—CH_2—On$	150	287	1.7254

PROPYLENE GLYCOL

The propylene gas obtained from cracking of petroleum is passed in chlorine water to give propylene chlorohydrin.

$$Cl_2 + H_2O \longrightarrow HOCl + HCl$$

$$C_3H_6 + HOCl \longrightarrow CH_2 = \overset{OH}{CH} - CH_2Cl$$

The propylene chlorohydrin is heated with lime slurry and converted to propylene oxide. The propylene oxide is purified and treated with a little mineral acid to give propylene glycol. Likewise ethylene glycol is also prepared and diethylene glycols are obtained as the by-product in the manufacture of ethylene glycol. Polyhydroxyl alcohols with more than two hydroxyl groups (glycerol, pentacrythritol etc) are seldom used in the manufacture of polyester chain.

C. CROSSLINKING MONOMERS

Monomers are used to copolymerise with the points of unsaturation the linear polyester and thus develop the cross linked or thermoset structure. Since cross linking reaction occurs at the time of application of polyester resins, the process should have knowledge of forming a moulding operation. Monomer serves as a solvent for the viscous polyester polymer prior to occurrence of cross linking reaction.

(a) Styrene monomer

A number of considerations that have been responsible for most frequent use of styrene as a diluent monomer are as under.

(1) Low cost

(2) Good strength of cured resins

(3) Good compatibility

(4) Availability

(5) Volatility

For most applications styrene is used in range of 1-2 moles to each mole of unsaturated acid in the polyester. To determine exact ratio it is necessary to determine moles of unsaturated acid per 100 gms of polyester and weight per polyester in solution in the styrene. On the basis of above information 104 grams of styrene would be combining with each gm mole of unsaturation to give one styrene link between unsaturated groups. From a practical stand point, however, a total ratio of stryene to unsaturated acid would undoubtedly leave some unreacted acid groups. There will be some cross-linking chains which will contain two or perhaps more molecules of styrene. There may also be some acid group which will react with no styrene linkage. It is also theoretically possible to have some formation of polystyrene which is not likely to occur to any significant extent, since the reactivity potential indicates that the additional reactions between styrene and unsaturated acids are much likely to occur than the reaction of an acid to an acid or of styrene monomer to styrene monomer.

There is generally an optimum range of styrene content for maximum physical properties; this will vary with the type of polyester structure being used in respect of acid and glycol consititutents, per cent of unsaturated acid and the molecular weight ofthe polyester chain. Flexible polyester resin with a very low unsaturated acid content generally requires a rather high styrene dilution to develop optimum tensile strength and eliminate the otherwise cheesy character. Polyester with higher ratios of unsaturated acids generally requires low styrene content (20 to 40 per cent styrene on weight basis) for maximum physical strengths. Beyond a certain point additional styrene increases the brittleness (lower tensile elongation) and gives lower heat distortion temperature. Table No. 5.0 shows the effect of styrene dilution on the physical properties of three polyesters based on the same raw materials with different ratios of unsaturated and saturated acids.

(b) Diallyl phthalate monomer: C_6H_4 $(CO.O.CH_2{=}CH_2)$ can be prepared by reacting phthalic anhydride with excess of allyl alcohol at about 80-100 C in presence of an esterification catalyst such as sulfuric acid and a polymerization inhibitor such as bronze. It has following properties.

B.P.	= 150° C at 1 mm pressure
	= 290° C at normal atmospheric pressure
Sp. gravity	= 1.12

Solubility in alcohol, ketones, aromatic hydrocarbons but insoluble in water.

(c) *Special diluents*

(i) Triallyl cyanurate : It imparts remarkable improvement in heat resistance. It is made by reacting cyanuric chloride with excess of allyl alcohol in presence of sodium hydroxide at 15-20° C.

TABLE 5.0

EFFECT OF STYRENE DILUTION

Per cent styrene	Exotherm °F	Strength Psi	Modulus X 10^5	Strength Psi	Modulus X 10^5	Elongation per cent	Heat distortion	H_2O absorption 24 hr. at 17°F per cent
Propylene glycol maleate/Phthalate-40/60								
30	347	16,100	5.9	7,900	7.8	1.31	158	0.21
40	349	14,100	5.9	9,100	6.8	1.73	172	0.17
50	340	15,700	5.3	9,500	7.5	1.85	176	0.17
Propylene glycol maleate/phthalate-50/50								
30	380	19,000	5.8	8,300	8.1	1.32	194	0.23
40	392	17,700	6.3	9,200	7.9	1.70	201	0.21
50	396	15,700	5.2	8,000	7.2	1.70	199	0.20
Propylene glycol maleate/phthalate-60/40								
30	400	17,200	5.7	8,600	7.9	1.38	219	0.25
40	407	17,800	6.0	7,200	7.6	1.46	226	0.25
50	404	17,700	5.1	6,600	7.0	1.23	225	0.28

(ii) Methyl Methacrylate: Use of methyl metacrylate results in considerable improvement in the weathering characteristics of polyesters. But it is costly monomer.

CHEMISTRY OF CONDENSATION

The unsaturated polyesters is essentially formed by condensation of the acid and alcohol to form a soluble resin, and then the addition of crosslinking agent to form the thermosetting resin. A typical reaction may be represented as follows.

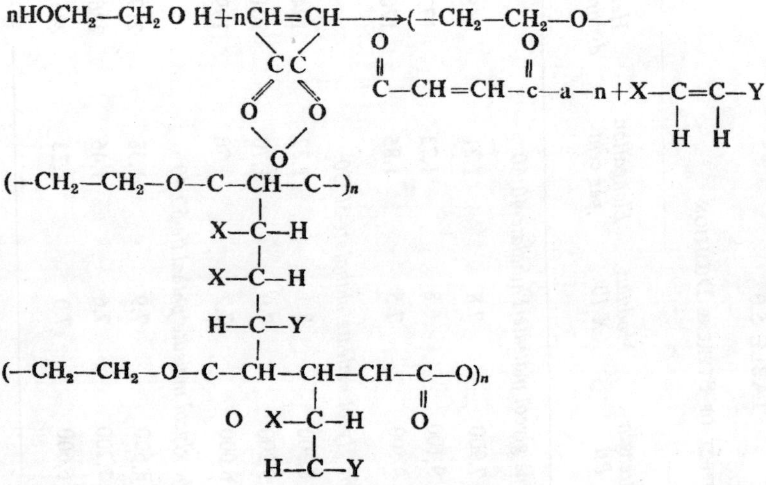

(Cross-linked structure)

The preparation of unsaturated polyester resins essentially requires the following components.

(i) POLYESTER COMPONENT

This part of the resin is prepared first and is sometimes called the alkyd portion. The starting materials are glycols and unsaturated dibasic acids or anhydrides.

Ethylene maleate, however, is seldom used because of limited compatibility in the commonly used monomers. Propylene glycol is used most often in commercial rigid resins, while diethylene and dipropylene glycols are used to impart flexibility.

TABLE 5.1

CROSS LINKING MONOMERS

Monomer	*Molecular weight*	*Equivalent weight*	*Boiling point °F*	*Formula*	*Primary characteristics*
1. Methylmetacrylate	100	100	212	$CH_2 = C(CH_3) - C(=O) - OCH_3$	Weathering
2. Styrene	104	104	293	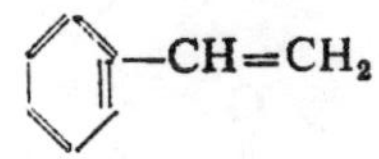	(Cost, strength properties reactivity compatibility)
3. Vinyl toluene	118	118	342	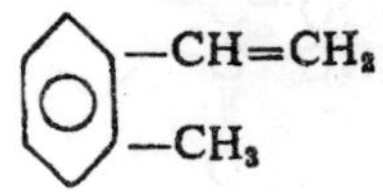	Low volatility
4. —methyl styrene	118	118	—	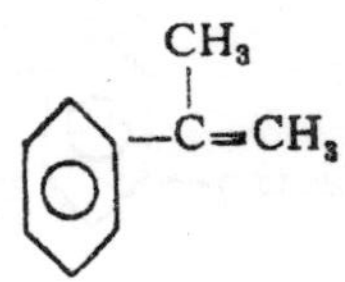	Reduced reactivity
5. Divinyl benzene	130	65	—	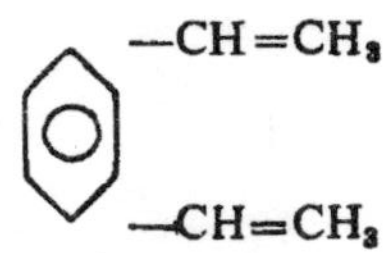	—

TABLE 5.1—(*Contd.*)

6. Dichloro styrene	170	170	—	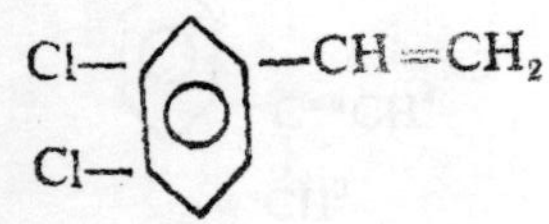	Fire and heat resistant
7. Diallyl Phthalate	246	123	SS4	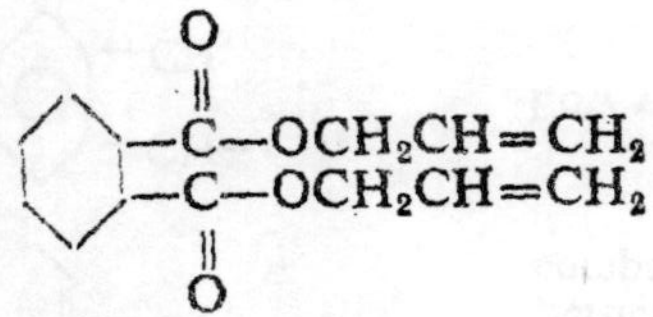	Low volatile
8. Triallyl cyanurate	249	83	324 @ 2 mm	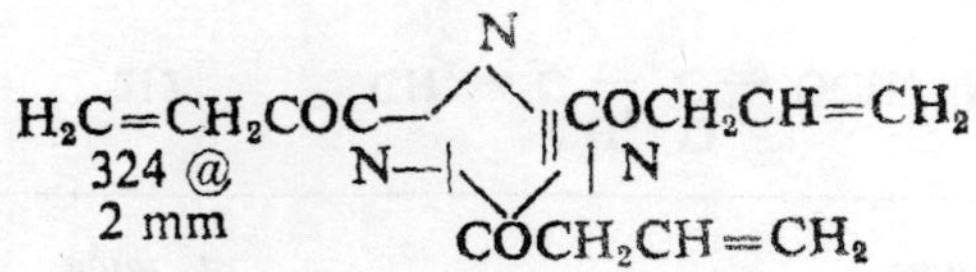	Heat resistance

The unsaturated acids used are almost exclusively meleic or fumaric: maleic being cheapest and available as its anhydride. However many of the commercial polyesters also contain saturated dibasic acids such as phthalic, adipic, and succinic. Phthalic acid is a more common component because of the price and the properties imparted. Isophthalic acid is also sometimes used.

(ii) MONOMER COMPONENT

General polymerizable monomers are available for use. Krope and Bradley have reported the use of methyl methacrylate and vinyl acetate. Styrene has, however, proved to be a cheap monomer with nearly ideal properties. Other vinyl compounds are also sometimes used. The monomer must have the property to copolymerize much faster with the polyester double bonds than with itself. Otherwise a mixture of copolymer and polymeris obtained which usually is incompatible. Allylic type monomers copolymerize with polyesters but usually at a slow rate. Styrene probably constitutes 85 per cent of the total amount of monomer used commercially in this field. Besides being available at a low cost, it also has an advantage of ability to copolymerize rapidly. Its boiling point is sufficiently high so that it can be added to the hot polyester without volatilization. This same property prevents excessive evaporation at room temperature during commercial use. In addition, its solvency is high so that a large amount of polyester can be dissolved in it. The product of commerce contains 20-45 per cent by weight of styrene.

(iii) MINOR COMPONENTS

Besides the two major components commercial considerations necessitate a third type of compound. If an unsaturated polyester and pure styrene are mixed together, copolymerization may take place quickly. This is particularly true if the polyester is warm or hot at the time of addition. However, commercial styrene contains 10 ppm of t-butyl catechol as a storage stabilizer, and some storage stability is thus imparted to the polyester resin. This amount is usually inadequate. One of the first major problems in the industry was to find an inhibitor which would provide sufficient time for ordinary shipping and consumption. Several types of compounds are now in use which provide adequate stability for 6 months to a year. Hydroquinone and some of its derivatives provide adequate stability for 6 months to a year.

Catechol and some of its derivatives behave similarly. For example, t-butyl catechol has been widely used. Resorcinol and its derivatives have been found to be much less effective. Quaternary ammonium salts and tertiary amine salts are found to be quite effective in preventing copolymerization. Aryl and alkyl phosphites have limited stabilizing activity. Many other compounds have strong stabilizing effects, such as phenols, nitropheols, copper compounds, sulfur and some of its compounds, carbon black and certain other pigments. However, the compounds are not used because they usually prolong or practically stop the cure of the resins.

Other minor constituents include 'light stabilizers' which are added to some resins to prevent yellowing during outdoor exposure. Salicylates and dihydroxy benzophenone derivatives are employed for this purpose.

MANUFACTURE

The major operations involved in the manufacture of polyester resins are esterification and blending which are carried out in their respective kettles. The selection of proper raw material is important from the point of view of economics of the process, availability of raw material and the desired properties of the final product. The most common raw materials used, however, are propylene glycol, maleic anhydride (or sometimes phthalic anhydride) and styrene monomer. In addition small quantities of inhibitors and other additives are required for the process. Hydroquinone and t=butyl catechol are the most common inhibitors employed for this purpose.

The method employed for the manufacture of polyester resins essentially involves a batch process which is carried out in two basic steps as mentioned above, namely the poly condensation reaction (or polyesterification) and blending the polyester resin with the monomer. Due to the sensitivity of the polyester resin to contamination bath in the course of the condensation reaction and during subsequent handling, the material of construction rnust be carefully selected. Most equipment for processing polyester resin is constructed of various stainless steel alloys. Type 304,316 and 347 are more popular. Owing to the wide variety of ingredients used in the manufacture of resin the chemical corrosion resistance of stainless steel is a distinct advantage over most other alternative metals.

The esterification kettle is charged through a manhole with required amount of glycol, and the solid anhydride. The kettle is equipped with efficient agitators. The kettle is closed and swept with inert gas such as nitrogen. Heat is applied and the charge is heated to 175-200° C, depending on the type of product produced. The vapours formed are carried away by a slow strenm of intert gas through a partial condenser which returns glycol but passes the water to total condenser. The esterification is continued until a predetermined acid number is reached, usually in the 10-15 range. The glycol is employed in slight excess in the charge. The inert gas flow is then increased, and the batch is blown at full heat until the alkyd reaches a predetermined viscosity. When this is reached, the heat is turned off and the inert gas flow reduced. The batch is now dropped into blending kettle. the blending kettle is provided with coils through which hot or cold water may be circulated. This kettle is purged with inert gas. The alkyd is cooled to 100-102° C and any inhibitor may be added at this stage. Styrene is pumped into the blending kettle in required amount. Agitation and cooling must be efficient at this time to prevent any further copolymerization. The cooling is continued to room temperature and final adjustment to specified viscosity is done by styrene addition. The batch is then pumped, through a filter press, to storage tanks into drums.

REACTION KETTLE

The reaction kettle used in polyesterification reaction is designed along the same lines as the standard batch reactors widely used in the chemical industry. The kettle is provided with a manhole used for access to the kettle for repairs, cleaning and for charging the reactants. Thorough agitation is required to provide intimate contact immiscible materials during the early phases of the reaction and to provide a homogeneous blend during the later stages. Mechanical agitaion is generally supplied through a motor driven propeller, paddle or turibines. The pitched blade from type turbine which creates mixing through a high degree of turbulence is widely used. The agitator is fitted is fitted with a sprayer for the administration of the inert gas. The overall result of mechanical agitation and inert gas spraying are more rapid reaction, more uniform moleculor weight distribution and fewer side reactions.

HEATING SYSTEM

Direct heating system may be employed using oil, gas or electricity. However, indirect heating system using dowtherm as the heating medium is considered to be a better alternative. This involves higher construction costs but also has advantages such as automatic temperature control, flexibility, cooling provisions and a high degree of safety. The direct heating system based on oil, gas and electricity are the simpler and often the least expensive from the stand point of original construction cost. This, however, may give a product of poor colour due to local overheating, poor temperature control, inaphility to rapidly and loss of thermal efficiency due to accumulation of carbonaceous scales. Although electerical heating is the most expensive, it has the highest thermal efficiency.

PARTIAL CONDENSDER (REFLUX CONDENSER)

The basic function of the partial condenser is to avoid the excessive loss of volatile reactants, particularly glycol. This condenser operates between the boiling point of water and that of glycol to allow water to pass over and to recover the uncreacted glycol. This condenser may be a packed column for more efficient separation of affluent vapours fractionating column or a packed column approximately 1 ft. in dia and 7 ft. high is considered adequate for a 1000 gallons kettle. The column may preferably be fitted with a heating or cooling coil in the top section to create more reflux if necessary to prevent undue water condensation near the end of the esterification cycle. This heating coil can be made of a double helix of 1/2" stainless steel tubing with enough length to give a surface area of the order of 20 ft^3 for 1000 gallons kettle. A temperature controller to adjust the supply of steam or water, automatic rasching ring ring packing is found to be quite satisfactory and economical.

TOTAL CONDENSER

The total condenser consists of a bundle of single pass tubes in which the vapours go through the tubes and cooling water is in the shell. Around 200 sq. ft. of condensing area is considered adequate for a 1000 gallons kettle. The mixture of water and glycol after being condensed in the total condenser will separate in the decanter and the glycol is returned through the loop to the kettle and the water is sent to caliberated receivers. The condensate collected in receivers is checked by the refractive index to the amount of glycol carried over. The quantity of water collected is a guide to the progress of polyesterification.

BLENDING OR THINNING TANKS

When the polyesterification reaction is completed the resin is cooled to a suitable temperature from blending with the cross-linking monomer. This operation is usually carried out in a separate vessel large enough to handle or total condenser that is properly vented to atmosphere. The kettle is provided with internal coils through which hot or cold water may be circulated. The blending kettle should be provided with direct reading scales and placed in a room separated from reaction kettle by fire proof walls.

PACKAGING OF THE PRODUCT

The resin detained after blending is held for final adjustment in viscosity and inhibitor or any special modification which occurs at this point in operation. The final product is packaged directly into lined drums or other containers. The blended resin is usually filtered through a filter press.

In all phases of handling the finished resin, it is important not to place it in contact with metals such as as iron or tin, copper or other substances which may be picked up to contribute catalytic, acclerating characteristics to the resin.

Bulk shipments of polyester resins are carried out regularly in stainless steel or suitably lined tanks. If the resin is to be held in bulk storage, the tanks should be fabricated with metals or linings the effect of which on storage life has been established. If the resin is to be held for a prolonged period, a continued record of the storage temperature should be maintained and samples should be taken out at regular intervals to check the inhibitor content. This is accomplished by observing for drift in gel time with catalyst added or change in ucatalyzed stability at elevated temperatures.

PROCESS CONTROLS

As in any chemical process, the quality and uniformity of the finished product is a direct function of the procedures used in all phases of the process. To obtain quality products consistently it is essential to maintain rigid control on raw materials, the manufacturing process itself and the final product.

(A) RAW MATERIALS CONTROL

The major raw materials used in manufacture of polyester resins are fairly common organic chemicals which are produced in large volume to standard specifications. The constants on any particular lot are generally available from the manufacturer and most applications require only the minimum checking by the user.

The cross-linking monomer requires close checking for possible polymer formation, fairly simple tests such as refracture index or precipitations in certain solvents can be made to determine polymer formation. One part of styrene diluted with five parts of methyl alcohol will show cloudy precipitates if polymer is present. It is good practice to evaluate thoroughly the new grades and sources of raw materials for any adverse effects they may have on processing characteristics and final properties.

(B) MANUFACTURING CONTROLS

Exact operating procedures from charging raw materials, duplicating the reaction conditions and terminating the reaction at the same point all contribute to the quality and uniformity of the final product. The proper raw materials charge is calculated on the basis of stiochiometric balance between the acid and glycol phases. An exact molar balance is not always added at the start of the reaction because of such factors as,

(1) In some procedures low-boiling components may be carried off in the water distillate and thus require proportional excess charge.

(2) In some cases certain components are added after a part of condensation reaction has been completed in order to build certain type of polymer structures.

Control procedures used during the course of reaction to keep track of its process includes.

(i) Amount of water removed : One mole of water is removed for every glycol-acid linkage; one half mole for every glycol anhydride linkage.

(ii) Acid number: A measure of unreacted acid groups and is therefore related to the number of average molecular weight. This is the test most frequently used to follow and terminate the condensation reaction.

(iii) Viscosity : It increases directly with average molecular weight. Viscosity is generally used as a double check on acid number near the end of the reaction; it is generally adjusted within a narrow range in final ester monomer mixture.

Other factors which are critical during the reaction are the reaction temperature and the inert gas.

(C) FINAL PRODUCT CONTROL

When the polyesterification reaction has reached an end point, generally determined by the acid number or a combination of acid number and viscosity, it is cooled to and blended with monomer. Any special additions, such as light stabilizers or room temperature accelerators, are generally are generally added at this time.

A number of other tests are run to characterize the final product with respect to physical constants important in certain fabrication procedures. Adjustments can be made in the polyester monomer ratio, inhibitor content, accelerators etc. to bring the respective characteristics into specified ranges. Tests run on the final product generally include most of the following.

(1) Acid number

(2) Viscosity

(3) Specific gravity

(4) SPI gel time or room temperature gel time in a preaccelerated system.

(5) Uncatalyzed stability.

(6) Refractive colour.

Other special tests may be run on resins formulated for special properties such as weather resistance, chemical resistance, flame resistance, heat resistance etc.

APPLICATIONS

The major applications of polyester resins are in the following fields.

(1) Reinforcing applications

(2) Laminating

(3) Moulding powders

REINFORCING APPLICATIONS

Glass reinforced polyester resins are now widely used in such applications as helmets, vehicles and boats. Boat building is one of the most successful applications of reinforced polyester resins. Boats made almost entirely by the wet lay-up process are becoming widely used throughout the world, their main attraction being their resistance to salt water, sunlight, termites and rot. While the initial cost is equivalent to wood and other conventional materials, maintenance costs are lower, repairs are easier and the boats have longer life. Helmets are another important application of polyester resins. Their demand is nowadays on the increase as the wearing of helmets has been made compulsory by legislation.

The polyester resins used in reinforced plastics are mostly syrup liquids with vicosities varying from 200 to 2000 centi-stokes and with the colour varying from pale straw to almost colourless clarity.

The formulation of a general purpose polyester resin is given below.

FORMULATION FOR A GENERAL PURPOSE POLYESTER RESIN

Ingredient	*Quantity in kgs.*
Phthalic anhydride	295
Maleic anhydride	98
Propylene glycol	250
Styrene monomer	290
Inhibitor (0.01 per cent hydroquinone)	0.0852

This is the most common polyester resin used in glass reinforced mouldings. The typical and most common applications of such a resin are in helmets, tubs and bathroom accessories, large structural layers, can and automobile bodies, television cabinets etc.

Properties

The specific properties of general purpose grade are given below.

1. Acid value (mg KOH/gm.)	25
2. Specific gravity 25° C/25° C 1.	12-1.4
3. Viscosity at 25° C	200-400 cps.
4. Stability (in the dark)	
at 25° C	6-12 months
at 65° C	3-20 days
5. Monomer content	25-30 per cent

ISOPHTHALIC GRADE

As the name implies, it is another grade of polyester having isophthalic acid in place of phthalic acid. Incorporation of isophthalic acid increases molecular weight of the polymer, induces superior chemical resistance and gives better strength and toughness.

Formulations

Ingredients	*Quantity in kgs.*
Propylene glycol	150
Isophthalic acid	128
Ethylene glycol	104
Fumaric acid	290
Styrene	395
Inhibitor (hydroquinone)	0.285

Applications of this grade are in the lining of glass-reinforced plastics for chemical plants, ducts and hoods, storage tanks etc.

Properties

1. Viscosity	500-1000 cps
2. Specific gravity	1.1
3. Acid value	15 ± 5
4. Appearance	Straw
5. Stability (in dark) at 25° C	3-6 months

The reinforced plastics are made by various moulding techniques which include matched die or bag moulding, mat or preform moulding, pre-preg moulding etc. These processes are described below.

MATCHED-DIE MOULDING

Matched die moulding includes all moulding processes involving the use of rigid moulds which match or conform to the dimensions of all surfaces of the finished piece. This generally involves two dies-the male plug or force and the female or cavity. Some more complex mouldings may involve dies containing can activated inerts or split sections to mould under out sections which could be formed from plaster, plastics, low melting alloys. The production on tools which can be internally heated and used to mould reinforced polyester resins by three distinct processes. (a) Mat or preform moulding: where the reinforcement is impregnated in the mould. (b) Premix moulding: In this process, the reinforcing fibres are premixed with the resin pigments type extenders and other modifying agents to give a moulding compound which is charged as a wad at bulky mass.

(a) Mat or preform moulding

This moulding process is the most widely used method of producing reinforced plastics. It generally involves the use of random pattern chopped glass strands shaped to the contour of the part. When the part is virtually a flat shape, blanks of reinforcement can be cut from continuous rolls of glass mat available in various weights. A single ply or multiple plies of mat are used to give the reinforcement required for particular part. Glass mat can also be used for the simplest three dimensional parts where a blanket cut from a flat mat can be shaped to the contour of the piece.

(b) Premix moulding

A technique widely used for the manufacture of lower cost polyester products is to premix resin, reinforcement and fillers to produce a single charge of material which is compression moulded in matched metal dies. For small parts of larger shaped sections which do not require maximum physical properties, premix moulding gives high production rates with relatively low cost moulding materials.

APPLICATION OF MOULDING TECHNIQUE TO MANUFACTURE OF HELMETS

Helmets are manufactured by matched die or bag moulding processes. The moulds for this purpose are made of either aluminium, wood or some other sheet metal. The mould consists of two halves-male plug or force and female or cavity. First of all mould release agent is applied to the female or cavity. It is generally the practice to wax the mould and polish slightly before applying the uniform coat of polyvinyl alcohol with a piece of cloth or sponge. Now gel coat is applied by brushing on to the prepared mould surface an even layer 0.25 mm to 0.50 mm thick. The gel coat is layer of resin usually coloured and containing no fibrous reinforcing material and is applied to give a smooth, glossy and weather resistant finish. When gel coat reaches an almost tack-free condition, laying up of resin and glass fibre is started. Now successive layers of glass fibre rein forcement saturated with a prepared resin system are laid. A typical resin formulation is given below.

Resin	100 parts
Accelerator	2 parts
Catalyst	

The reinforcement consisting normally of chopped strand glass mat, should be coated roughly to shape and should extend beyond the mould about 2.5 cms. to enable a satisfactory edge to be obtained on trimming.

When the gel coat has reached the required condition, a liberal coat of the laminating resin mix should be brushed on the top of the gel coat. One layer of mat is placed on the top of the resin through the mat. Condensation is achieved by rolling thoroughly and methodically with a washer roll to bring through the mats as much resin as possible. Further resin mix is added to starved areas. Rolling is to be done well so that bubbles are eliminated. Likewise second and third layers are laid up in similar manner. Lastly a resin layer is applied. Polished male is sometimes brought to exert pressure to give compactness and smoothness. On completion of laying up, the moulding is allowed to gel at room temperature that shall take about one hour. Then the moulding is transferred to a warm room and left for several hours. For crushing effect, expanded polyestyrene foam backed jute fabric is glued to the moulding. It is now trimmed to the required size.

LAMINATING APPLICATIONS

Polyester laminates are used in storage tanks for oil water and certain chemicals. A wide variety of household applications and other articles are now produced from polyester laminates. Furniture, luggage, ornaments, sinks, trays and handles, washing machines and toys are among the extensive range. In office and industry similar applications are found, including machine housings, guards and cabinets, although some of them are now being replaced by thermoplastics.

Another use for polyester resin which is growing rapidly is in roof sheeting. For such applications these laminates have the advantage of ease of handlings, good strength and weathering properties, a wide range of colours and a high degree of transparency.

The manufacture of laminating resin is carried out in a similar manner as described earlier. The liquid resin obtained is converted into the solid state by a further chemical reaction termed copolymerization. The copolymerization is effected by dissolving the resin in a reactive solvent which reacts with the unsaturated groups to form a three-dimensional polymers. The crosslinking that occurs is activated by a free radical mechanism which causes opening of double bonds. Materials used for this reaction are sometimes called catalysts or initiators. They are usually organic peroxides; two very popular materials are benzoyl peroxide and methyl ethyl ketone peroxide. The speed of dissociation of these peroxides can be accelerated by the use of certain metallic salts or amines. The most popular accelerator for general use is cobalt naphthenate, which is normaly used in conjunction with methyl ethyl ketone peroxide.

The polyesters can be cured either by hot or cold techniques, and for the former, benzyl peroxide or tertiary butyl hydroperoxide are preferred while, for the cold-cure, methyl ethyl peroxide or cyclohexanone peroxide are more commonly used.

1. FIRE RESISTANT GRADE

Fire retarding or flame resistance is defined as slow rate of burning while in contact with a source of heat or the ability to extinguish itself when source is removed. This property in the polyester resins is introduced by any one of the following methods.

1. Incorporation of antimony oxide up to 20 per cen by weight in polyester resins before use. But it results in loss of transparency.

2. Best fire resistance is obtained by replacing 50 per cent of phthalic acid by hexachloro endomethylene tetrahydro phthalic anhydride (HET acid) and replacement of 15 per cent of styrene by triallyl phosphate. Other formulation vairables are same as for general purpose polyester resin.

Fire resistant grade is used to manufacture laminated matched die moulding, moulding compositions for electrical and decorative purposes, impregnating and casting.

Properties

1. Viscosity at 25° C (CST)	850
2. Specific gravity (25° C)	1.11
3. Acid value (mg KoH/gm)	25
4. Monomer content	36

2. GENERAL PURPOSE GRADE

A formulation for general purpose polyester resin is given below.

Ingredients	*Parts by weight*
Propylene glycol	160
Maleic anhydride	115
Phthalic anhydride	85
Xylene	20
Hydroquinone	0.5
Quinone inhibitors	0.005
Styrene monomer	150

PROCESSING TECHNIQUE

Polyester resin laminates are produced by impregnating the base material with the resin and then consolidating by applying heat and/or pressure. The degree of impregnation will affect the characteristics of the final laminate, which is dependent upon such variables as the type of base material and resin solvent (if any), resin characteristics (e.g. solids content and viscosity) or impregnation time. The production techniques can be conveniently classified as either (a) high pressure (b) low pressure. The fact that no by products are evolved on curing polyester resins, as with epoxy resins, means that the low-pressure process is more commonly used. The high pressure process is used with polyesters for dough or gunk mouldings.

LOW-PRESSURE PROCESS

The moulding of polyester resins with glass fibre by this process is made simpler by virtue of the facts that no volatiles are evolved or curing needed, and that the reaction can be effected without heat. Pressures from zero to 500 lb/in^2 are all that is normally required to consolidate these low-pressure (contact) resins. The term reinforced plastics has now become virtually synonymous with low-pressure or contact laminates.

MOULDING POWDERS

As it is evident that glyptals (alkyds) are thermosetting resins, but the time required to effect a final cure for certain applications is far too long to be practical. To obtain resins suitable for moulding powders it has therefore been found necessary to replace the phthalic acid with an unsaturated material such as maleic acid. The resultant unsaturated polyester can then be made to cross-link rapidly via the ethylene linkages at temperatures in the region of 150° C or even lower by using initiators such as benzyl peroxide, as already mentioned. The curing action is also effected with an unsaturated monomer. Moulding powders have also been produced by using an unsaturated alcohol instead of the more conventional saturated type. For example, phthalic anhydride may be esterified with allyl alcohol to produce the ester diallyl phthalates which is cross-linked by using an organic peroxide and opening up the double bonds in the vinyl groupings.

Typical applications of alkyl moulding powders include valve holers, insulating sleeves, parts for television assemblies, capacitor and commutator parts. They have also found limited uses as oven door housings and housings for business machines.

Alkyd mouldings are resistant to water, salt solutions, detergents and common organic solvents. In general they are resistant to acids but have poor resistance to alkalies. They are vary similar in this respect to general purpose phenolic moulding materials and in direct contrast with the aminoplast mouldings which resist alkalies but not acids. Some general properties of moulding materials are listed in Table 5.2.

TABLE 5.2

GENERAL PROPERTIES OF ALKYL MOULDING MATERIALS

Moulding Properties	*Standard cure*	*Fast cure*
Shelf life	Good	Fair
Pelleting properties	Fair	Good
Bulk factor	3-4.3	2.0-2.2
Hot strength	Poor	Fair
Specific gravity	1.6-1.8	2.0-2.2
Import strength (ft. lb/in notch)	0.1-0.2	0.1-0.2
Electrical properties	Good	Good
Electric strength	250-350 V/mil	250-350 V/mil
Resistance to insert cracking	Good	Good

• Chapter 8 •

POLYVINYL ACETATE

Polyvinyl acetate has been available commercially since the 1930's. Growth was slow until the 1940's when polyvinyl acetate dispersions were introduced.

The adhesives industry is currently the most important outlet for polyvinyl acetate. Other major applications are in the field of paints and coatings, textile finishes, paper coatings, printing inks, starches etc.

Polyvinyl acetate came into widespread use in adhesives in the 1940's as a synthetic resin substitute for hide glue. Superior properties of the synthetic resin offset their higher price. Polyvinyl acetate adhesives were adaptable to new high speed machinery in the paper converting and packaging fields and were enthusiastically received they found a place in wood adhesives and later were introduced in the familiar household "white glue"

Mention of polyvinyl acetate for use in the adhesives industry alone gives a rather confining picture of the resin. Its use in other industries actually depends on its adhesive, binding and film properties as much as it does in the adhesives industry. In surface coatings dynamic growth of polyvinyl acetate has continued since 1950. The early technology produced emulsion paints for exterior masonry and subsequently for interior prime sealers and flat well paints, exteriro wood paints and industrial primers and finishes. The textile industry uses polyvinyl acetate mostly in the emulsion form, for finishes that impart durability, strength and "hand" to woven cotton and other fabrics. Now uses as binders for "non-woven" or 'bonded" fabrics may exceed those on woven fabrics. Paper coating and manufacturing offers an excellent potential for new polyvinyl acetate copolymers. The potential new markets of polyvinyl acetate are in the fields of paints, textiles and paper coatings. It depends on expansion of relatively new uses such as hot melts, redispersible powders, cement additives, etc. in the adhesives and building products industries.

CHEMISTRY OF POLYMERIZATION

Early studies of the polymerization of vinyl acetate and the structure and properties of the polymer were made during the first quarter of the century. The first patents on polymerization were also issued during that period; the first real commercial development began in 1925. Commercial polymerization was underway of 1929. Since then, numerous technical articles have been published dealing with polyvinyl acetate.

Vinyl acetate polymerizes by the free-radical addition reaction. Free radicals generated by the decomposition of organic peromides such as benzoyl or hydorgen peroxide or of inorganic "per" salts such as potassium or ammonium persulfate are commonly used to initiate polymerization conventional methods of bulk, solution, suspension and emulsion polymerisation are used. Reactions ordinarily are accomplished at temperatures above room temperature. Recent studies on polymerization at room temperature or below, on irradiation techniques and on the use of ionic catalysts foreshadow the preparation of newer modifications. Longer and straighter molecules, finer particle size in the case of emulsions and even spatially regulated structures are visualized.

MANUFACTURE

Generally monomers can be polymerized by one of the four methods; polymerization in bulk, in solution, dispersed as large particles in water and as emulsion polymerisation. Vinyl acetate has been polymerised industrially in bulk in solution and in suspension and in emulsion. About 90% of the polyvinyl acetate is manufactured by emulsion techniques.

While in most laboratory experiments, polymerisation can be performed in undiluted or in controlled dilution with solvents, which do not affect the process seriously, these mentioned processes of polymerisation pose difficulties in large scale production.

Bulk polymerisation is used as a process for obtaining polyvinyl acetate. But there are several causes of difficulty in bulk polymerisation, the prominent is the removal of heat of polymerisation. Generally the heat of polymerisation is of the order of 20 kcal/gm-mole. The problem of heat transfer becomes more vital on larger scale of production, partly because the conducting surface becomes relatively less as the mass increases, being proportional to the surface of the reactor; which is normally a cylindrical kettle equipped with a stirrer. Moreover as the process proceeds, the mass becomes more and more viscous thus rendering stirring more difficult.

Reports from Germany, describing the bulk polymerisation process, give details of production in 800 litres reactions based on the fact that the hot polymer is sufficiently liquid to be discharged directly or by a continuous process in which the polymerizing monomer is passed down a polymerising tower. The upper part of the tower is stirred and final resin is passed on a continuous band over a breaking darn before discharging.

Suspension polymerisation is confined to the production of polymers in conditions which amount to a water cooled bulk polymerisation, depending on the addition of a dispersing agent. The dispersing agent forms an envelope around the heads and prevents their coagulation and fusion during polymerisation. Of old German formulations, Mowilith 70 pearls (polyvinyl acetate) were prepared by using 1.2 kg. benzoyl peroxide for 600 kg. vinyl acetate monomer. The aqueous phase was 0.8 kg. of 0-toluene peroxide with 1-2 kg. of dispersing agents.

LABORATORY PREPARATION OF POLYVINYL ACETATE

The apparatus required for emulsion polymerisation consists of (1) 500 cc. bolthead flask, (2) electric stirrer, (3) water (4) thermometer (110° C), (5) buchner vacuum filteration apparatus, (6) temperature controlled oven.

PROCEDURE

A solution is prepared in a 500 cc bolthead flask from 150 cc. distilled water and 0.75 g sodium bicarbonate, 0.5 g sodium bisulphite, 1.0 g ammonium persulphate. To this solution is added 50 cc. of a 5 per cent (w/v) aqueous solution of high viscosity polyvinyl alcohol as emulsifying agent and 50 g redistilled vinyl acetate monomer. The liquid is stirred vigorously to give an emulsion. The flask and contents are placed in a water bath at about 25° C and the stirring is continued for 1-1.5 hours to give an emulsion containing 25 per cent of polymer.

A portion of this emulsion is poured on to a glass plate which has been levelled with spirit level. The emulsion is levelled off with a straight edge, the projecting points of which ride on the glass plate and ensure a 35/1000 in gap between the straight edge and the plate.

The remainder of the emulsion may be diluted with an equal amount of water and saturated salt solution added with stirring. The precipitated polyvinyl acetate is then filtered off at the pump, washed well with water and dried in an oven at 40° C.

COMMERCIAL PREPARATION

Polyvinyl acetate emulsion may be made with a surfactant alone or with protective colloid but the usual practice is to use a combination of the two. The more commonly used surfactants are the well known anionic sulphates but catonic emulsifiers and nonionics are also suitable. The most commonly used protective colloids are synthetic materials. The polyvinyl acetate emulsions of commerce are made with higher ratios of protective colloids in the recipes and usually contain 50 per cent solids. The function of a colloid which may be a natural one such as gum acacia or strach, a semi-synthetic such as hydroxyethyl cellulose or a synthetic such as polyvinyl alcohol or the sodium salt of polymethacrylic acid, may be used partially to increase the viscosity of the medium and so act as a co-stabliliser, particularly in increasing mechanical satbility of a polymerised product.

Nonionics when used alone do not normally give very fine particle size emulsion, probably due to their lack of charge. However, even a fractional percentage of an anionic surfactant will greatly reduce particle size in conjunction with a nonionic emulsifier. While the presence of colloids and polyelectrolytes is optional, they may account for the equivalent of up to 4 per cent of the monomers, or even higher if desired, especially of polyvinyl alcohol, although a normal quantity of polymeric stabiliser would be about 1-2.5 per cent depending on the overall stabiliser balance.

The initiators or catalysts used in vinyl acetate polymerisations are the familiar free radical types such as hydrogenperoxides, peroxy sulphate, benzoyl peroxide etc. Emulsion polymerisation is conducted with water soluble catalysts, especially where monomer has been added continuously. Hydrogen peroxide, H_2O_2, is of comparatively mixer interest, except in vinyl acetate and copolymer systems, particularly where polyvinyl alcohol is a stabiliser. The persulphates including those of sodium, potassium and ammonium, are the most general for this purpose. While potassium persulphate is most readily available, its restricted solubility can be a disadvantage, particularly where excess initiator has to be fed into a polymerising system.

It is sometimes desirable to feed in continuously during a reaction, particularly so with a persulphate initiator. The rate of hydrolysis of vinyl acetate is pH. sensitive and it is desirable to minimise hydrolysis of monomer since it produces acetic acid (which can affect the catalyst) and aldehyde (which may lower the molecular weight of the polymer undesirably).

When a redox system is employed th emulsion should be blanketed with an inert gas such as nitrogen when polymerisation is performed under reflux. The nitrogen should be of a high purity grade of the order of 99.9 + per cent, since the commercial cylinder nitrogen may increase inhibition because of the appreciable quantity of oxygen, of the order of 1 per cent, which is forced into the polymerising liquid. Once polymerisation has begun, the nitrogen current may be discontinued since the emulsion effectively blanked with the monomer vapour.

In a direct persulphate initiated system under reflux, it is not normally necessary to employ an inert gas blanket, although some controversy has arisen on this matter. In the experience of the author the use of nitrogen has no other effect than to cause some monomer loss by vaporisation in a large scale process with vinyl acetate.

Where a reaction is performed under autogenous pressure no degasification of oxygen is normally necessary for monomers which are added under pressure. With other monomers, it is only desirable to deoxygenate when using redox systems, to reduce the inhibition time at the start.

Organic peroxides such as benzoyl peroxide is used in emulsion polymerisation. Benzoyl peroxide is first dissolved in monomer, but it is included rather exceptionally in formulations. Azodi isobutyro-t-butyl hydroperoxide is occasionally used as an alternative initiator. t-Butyl hydroperoxide can be a part of the water or monomer phases, depending on solubility and whether it is a part of the redox system.

In the actual process, the emulsified solution of vinyl acetate is prepared first separately and then this being transferred to a specially designed (for efficient temperature control) reactor for polymerisation, automatic temperature control is used then all other ingredients (catalysts) chain transfer agents), are added to this reaction vessel.

With this reactor, reflux condensing arrangement is provided so that vapour can be condensed and again passed to the reactor. Thus the temperature of the reaction is maintained at about 72° C by efficient temperature control and this reaction mixture is well stirred for the complete period of about 5 hours. In this period the mixture boils and the vapour forms which is condensed in the condenser (reflux) and returned to the kettle.

Thus after about 5 hours, about 88% polymer form is obtained and then the final product is transferred to the still and by fractional distillation, the solvents and unchanged vinyl acetate are separated out by steam distillation process and this will give about 99% polyvinyl acetate which is run into drums.

But in other way only a small portion of monomer and catalyst are charged and the remainder is added during the course of reaction of polymerisation. Better control of rate of polymerisation may be maintained in this way and this is particularly important on industrial scale operations where large quantitites of materials are involved and heat of dissipation is limited. This also leads to the small particles size and a more separable dispersion. On the molecular level delayed monomer feed leads to more branches in the polymer chain. Emulsifier may also be added as an ingredient. Another common practice, after the polymerisation had been run at a given temperature is to raise the temperature and finish the reaction in that fashion, in order to assure the absence of unreacted monomer. Thus polymerisation may be carried out to over 99% conversion and there is no requirement to strip unreacted monomer.

The design of plant must take into account problems such as heat transfer and adequate cooling. The agitation is a fairly complex problem and different agitators may be desirable depending on the maximum viscosity of the product under manufacture. The mixing is improved by putting baffles (vertical) in the reaction vessel.

The use of baffles is recommended in case of reactors of capacity 15000 litres or more. As the surface only increases in proportion of 2/3 of the increase in volume for constant shape. The heat transfer problems increase with the size of te reactor and to overcome this it is possible to include a heat exchanger in the plant through which the reaction mixture is pumped several times. Anciliary vessels such as heat tanks for mixing water phases, and separate cooling are also included in the plant. The accurate instrumentation is necessary in large plants and the thermometers values and gauges are sited properly.

At the end of polymerisation usually done in 2 to 5 hours, there should be only small traces of monomer present. Excess monomer is therefore sometimes removed from the final emulsion by blowing air or nitrogen through the heated product, and it has been practised that vacuum has been applied to a polyvinyl acetate emulsion stabilised with a modified polyvinyl alcohol merely to remove the last traces of monomer along a considerable amount of vats. The problem of removing excess monomer is sometimes difficult as it is often absorbed strongly by the polymer particles. this problem is sometimes avoided by addition of a second less objectionable monomer at the end of polymerisation.

A diagram of a typical reaction kettle used for polyvinyl acetate emulsion preparation is shown on the following page.

SPECIAL TECHNIQUES CONTINUOUS PROCESSES

The batch process which has become standard for emulsion polymerisation has the usual disadvantages associated with this type of process. Although it is strongly exothermic, heat is required to start the reaction, except for certain redox processes operating at ambient temperature. Heat is also required during the completion phase, which in a batch system is often unduly long. Moreover, the time required to charge and empty vessels is not inconsiderable, and for a reaction which lasts 6 hours, it would be difficult to operate a plant turn round in less than about 10 hours.

Formidable difficulties arise in the design of a suitable reactor for continuous polymerisation. It would be necessary to emulsify a stream of monomers at one end of the reactor, and this would be followed by the emulsion slowly proceeding through an appropriate reactor maintained at suitable temperatures to obtain a steady reaction, presumably in several sections, while the final product must, if necessary, be stripped of surplus monomer and passed through a suitable cooling arrangement. It would seem fairly obvious that some form of tube reactor be needed for this purpose. It would, also the necessary to prevent the formation of solid polymer on the side of the vessel.

Some possible designs for continuous reactors are described in the patent literature. In a process described the outflow of emulsion is restricted so that the process operates under pressure. A small-scale continuous polymeriser is described having a length of 1.5 m, and overall capacity of 100 l. and could deliver 240 kg per day of polyvinyl acetate. After 1000 hr operation no precipitate had formed on the sides of the reactor. A suggested example is an emulsion of vinyl acetate, stabilised with about 5.5 per cent of polyvinyl alcohol of saponification value 140, and at overall solids content of about 51.5 per cent. The initiator system is t-butyl hydroperoxide with sodium formaldehyde sulphoxylate, a solution of which is fed into the tube a short distance from the start, the reactor being heated in two sections, the lower half at 80°, and the upper at 70°. The emulsion is pumped against gravity.

In a modification of this continuous process, the product after removal

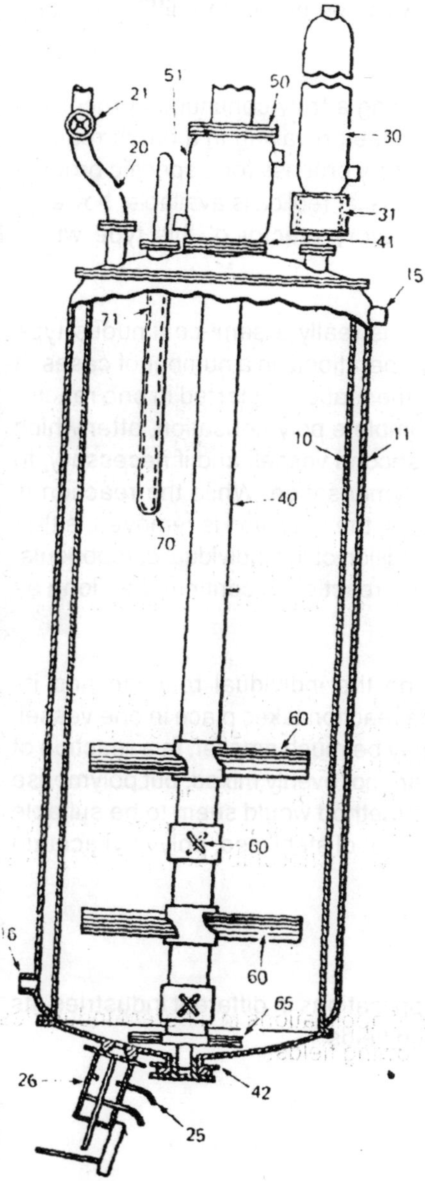

Emulsion Polymerisation Kettle[23]

Key:

(10) *cylindrical aluminium kettle*
(11) *jacket*
(15) *jacket inlet*
(16) *jacket outlet*
(20) *charge line*
(21) *valve*
(25) *discharge line*
(26) *valve*
(30) *reflux condenser*
(31) *sight glass*
(40) *agitator shaft.*
(41) *top bearing*
(42) *bottom bearing*
(50) *stuffing box*
(51) *shaft condenser*
(60) *agitator blades (main)*
(65) *small agitator*
(70) *thermometer pocket*
(71) *thermometer*

Fig. 9.0 Emulsion Polymerisation Kettle

from the reactor tube is subjected to a sudden cooling, which has the effect of removing entrained air, shown to be one of the difficulties of a truly continuous process.

One of the further difficulties of operating a truly continuous process is that conditions differ markedly from those prevailing in a batch reactor, so that it is difficult to design a satisfactory process for a specific product other than on the plant itself, unless a smaller replica is available; however it would be difficult to design a laboratory reactor of this type which would give significant results.

An alternative type of process, which is really a semi-continuous type has been suggested, and is probably operational in a number of cases. It is a 'cascade' system, in which a polymerisation is started in one reactor to a level of, say 80-90 per cent of complete polymerisation, after which the reaction mixture is pumped to a second vessel, and if necessary, to a third for substantially complete polymerisation. While the reaction is liquid being pumped to a second vessel, the emulsion is removed, either by a pre-emulsion addition, or by the addition of the individual components, or possibly by the mixture of both. The reaction is continued as long as necessary.

The actual conditions will depend on the individual reaction and its behavious. Where the main part of the reaction takes place in one vessel, the second or subsequent vessels may be much smaller. In a reaction of this type the contents of the reactors are not evenly mixed, but polymerise as they pass through the vessel. The method would seem to be suitable for the production of some polyvinyl alcohol stabilised, polyvinyl acetate emulsions.

APPLICATIIONS

Polyvinyl acetate has a number of applications in different industries. Its major applications are in the following fields.

1. Paints & coatings
2. Adhesives
3. Textiles
4. Binders
5. Miscellaneous industries

These applications alongwith formulations are discussed inthe following pages.

PAINTS & COATINGS

Most polyvinyl acetate emulsions suitable as bases for emulsion paints are available technically at about 55 per cent solids. If plasticiser can be stirred in directly, the solids content can be increased to 57-58 per cent. The final paint normally has a solids content of about 55 per cent, hence there is some latitude in formulation. A polymer with a relatively high intrinsic viscosity, say above 0.45, is desirable.

The pigment binding power of polyvinyl acetate is moderate only. To have very high ratios of pigment, binder should be avoided except in the manufacture of cheap products, simulating 'distempers', which are unlikely to require frequent washing down, e.g. ceiling paints. With the normal balance of pigments, most paints are formulated at pigment: binder ratio of 1:1 to about 2.5:1, corresponding to PVC of approximately 27 to 45 per cent.

As the 'natural' pH of a polyvinyl acetate emulsion is on the acid side, between about 4.5 and 6.0, care should be taken in using calcium carbonate in any form as a pigment, since the liberation of carbon dioxide might cause gassing of the paint, possibly causing the containers to burst. If it is desired to use a pigment with slight basic properties, the mineral wollastenite, a calcium metasilicate, has been suggested.

The major pigment used with polyvinyl acetate homopolymers is rutile titanium dioxide. This is about 60-70 per cent of the total pigment in a typical part. Extenders can be selected from wollastenite talc, china clay, barytes and mica, inter alia.

The preparation of a mechanically stable emulsion paint presents comparatively little difficulty. The surface tensions of the emulsions are invariably low, between about 35 and 40 dynes, and there is a considerable quantity of 'surplus' surfactant which is not actually stabilising the resin particles. In addition most technical emulsions contain a colloid; hydroxyethyl cellulose and gum acacia are amongst the most popular, although the inclusion of various polyacrylate and polymethacrylate salts is well known. In consequence there is rarely a paint stability problem which might otherwise be caused by stabiliser being described from the resin particles on to the pigment particles.

For compounding into polyvinyl acetate emulsion paints pigments may be made into a paste with the aid of a wetting agent such as sodium hexamotaphosphate at about 0.1 per cent of overall pigment weight, together with about 1 per cent of a nonionic colloid such as hydroxyethyl cellulose, methyl cellulose, or ethyl hydroxyethyl cellulose. As an alternative a nonionic surfactant is employed with carboxymethyl cellulose although in some cases the latter has been reported to have a destabilising action. Various polyelectrolytes such as a salt of maleic anhydride-di isobutylene copolymer, or polyacrylate and polymethacrylate salte may also be utilised. For high temperature stability ionic type dispersants are preferred in the pigment paste, whether of the sodium hexametaphosphate, anionic dispersant or inoised colloid type, e.g. sodium carboxylate at about 0.15-0.5 per cent on pigment weight is also suggested as an additive for high temperature storage in above formulations.

In the final mixing of the paint, defoamers and microbiocidal agents may be added. Care should be taken in the addition of mercurials both because of temicity and also because of the danger of discolouration due to the bleaching out of coloured mercury compounds from the paint film by condensation.

Some formulations on paints and coatings are given here:

Ingredients	*Interior/Exterior*		*Interior/Exterior*	
	Semigloss	*Eggshell*	*Flat*	*& Low Cost*
Rutile titanium dioxide	240	300	300	200
30% lithopone	-	-	-	250
China clay	-	30	50	-
Barytes	-	30	50	-
Methyl cellulose	50	72	-	-
Sodium carboxyethyl cellulose	-	-	80	-
Sodium hexametaphosphate	5	8	-	9
Polyexythelene oxide fatty ether	-	-	16	-
Water	147	125	140	180

Polyvinyl acetate emulsion (10% plasticised)	445	-	-	-
Polyvinyl acetate emulsion (14% plasticsed)	-	436	365	-
Polyvinyl acetate emulsion (20% plasticised)	-	-	-	275
Pigment/binder ratio	0.8/1	1.5/1	2/1	3/1
Pigment/volume concentration (%)	18.3	30.2	38.0	44.7
Non-volatiles (3)	55	60	60	60
SG-25° C	1.22	1.36	1.22	1.37
Viscosity at 25° C (poises)	1.40	4.0	1.6	1.8

Polyvinyl acetate based paints are unsuitable on highly alkaline surfaces such as fresh plaster or asbestos cement. It will be found that the life of a paint under these conditions will only be a matter of months. This is due to hydrolysis of the resin and the bleaching away of the resulting polyvinyl alcohol. Most vinyl acetate copolymer based on paints suffer to some extent from the same defect.

The preparation of a typical emulsion paint is best illustrated by the formulation given below. This formulation is based on gum acacia.

EMULSION PAINT FORMULATION (GUM ACACIA BASED)

Ingredients	Semigloss	Egg shell finish 1	2	Matt
Rutile tianium dioxide	100	100	113	100
Lithopone	-	34	7	-
Mica	-	20	45	-
Blanc fixe	-	-	-	40
China clay	-	10	113	30
Talc	10	-	-	-
Polyoxyethylene fatty ether	0.1-0.25	-	0.3	-
Sodium hexamet-aphosphate	2	3	-	4
Sodium carboxymethyl cellulose				

(2.5-5% aqueous)	32	60	135	35
Polyvinyl acatete emulsion (16.7% plasticised, 54% solids)	100	200	-	-
Polyvinyl acetate emulsion (16.7% plasticised, 54% solids)	-	-	-	92
Water	50	78	43	127
Pigment/binder ratio	1.1/1.0	1.65/1	1.5/1	3/1
Solids content (%)	54	53	57	60

Luthopone, which is included in some of the formulae previously is comparatively rarely used at present time because of the reactivity of pigments containing sulphides. It may be replaced by barytes or another filler.

ADHESIVES

Polyvinyl acetate is among the most universal of synthetic resin adhesives, and by far the major part is in form of a water based composition. It has the advantage of low cost, which is tending to diminish against the rising costs of other goods. The major application is with callulosic substractes e.g. wood and paper. Most emulsions in use are based on a polyvinyl alcohol stabiliser. It is usual to utilise as stabiliser about 4-5 per cent of a polyvinyl alcohol containing about 10% residual weights is preferred since high molecular weight polymer alcohols tend to give excessively high viscosities. The nature of the polymerisation process can also cause a major variation in viscosity of polyvinyl emulsion where polyvinyl alcohol is the main emulsifier. Most of the emulsions required for adhesive purposes have a somewhat coarse particle size, from about 0.5 u to l u. The tendency to creep is the major disadvantage of polyvinyl acetate in adhesives and it is sometimes overcome by a cross-linking procedure.

Some formulations of adhesives based on polyvinyl acetate emulsion are given below.

General purpose Adhesive

Ingredients	*Parts by weight*
Polyvinyl acetate emulsion (65% solids, Polyvinyl alcohol based)	100
Plasticiser	10-15
Clay filler	0-30
Cooked starch or dextrin	0-1000
Preservative	0-2
Stabiliser	0-2
Wetting agent	0-0.2
Secondary water	0-100
Defoamer	0-2
Deodorant	0-1

Fillers such as china clay or calcium carbonate are added in some cases particularly where the emulsion is used on exceptionally porous substrate and its purpose is to retain the adhesive on the surface, otherwise, the 'strike' in may be complete, and there will not be enough to form a bend. Ultrafine low density amorphous silica gels have a reinforcing effect on many polymer emulsion adhesives, there being an optimum addition which may be about 2% on emulsion weight. Another way of preventing this penetration is to use a high viscosity penetration with minimum wetting agents, or also to add a solvent, which often causes a very sharp rise in viscosity.

The emulsion with high polyvinyl alcohol stabiliser content is to be applied in case an emulsion with low change in viscosity on dilution is desired, about 10-15 per cent on the wt. of monomer be of this type. This modification is of course accompanied by increased water sensitivity, but this can be overcome to some extent by adding an agent such as glyoxal.

It is sometimes desirable to obtain emulsions which are hot hot "cold water dispersible for removal of stains". In this case the emulsion can be prepared containing a relatively high concentration of anticoalescing agent conveniently. Polyvinyl alcohols or various other cellulose ethers and at least 35 per cent by weight of this or a water-soluble plasticiser such as glyoxal. In order to increase the open time of the adhesive either polyvinyl alcohol is included in the formulation, or else a cellulosic thickner. The setting rate of the adhesive is increased by the use of polyvinyl alcohol as stabiliser in preference to other colloids or surfactants by copolymerisation in order to soften the polymer, and by addition of solvents. Setting time is increased of solids contents are reduced especially below 45 per cent by the inorganic fillers. In other way, a fast setting composition is obtained by blending the emulsions, one based on polyvinyl alcohol and about half to an equal weight of a second which has a different stabiliser system e.g. hydroxyethyl cellulose. In general, these two colloid systems although not incompatible with each other have a slight mutual destabilising action, resulting in earlier inversion during drying and hence a faster setting speed. Among thickners which may be added to polyvinyl acetate emulsions when used for adhesive purposes, polyacrylic acid salts, starches, dextrin (other than borax modified) even in large quantities and cellulosic thickners such as methyl cellulose or hydroxethyl cellulose, may be included. These also affect the rheological properties by presenting the marked thickening under high shear. Gum has been quoted as additive, as in casein, although in latter case, the addition of a preservative is essential.

QuickTack Polyvinyl Acetate Emulsion Adhesive

Ingredients	*Parts by wt.*	
	(1)	(2)
Polyvinyl acetate emulsion (55% solids)	100	100
Butyl benzyl phthalate	12	-
Sulphonamide	12	-
Chorinated biphenyl	-	11
Water	9	-

The flexibility of a polyvinyl acetate adhesive can be increased either by copolymerisation or by external plasticisation usually by dibutyl phthalate, tritolyl phosphate, or mixtures, although a wide variety of plasticisers are available. These are normally directly stirred stirred up into the hot emulsion and they are absorbed, either rapidly or slowly into the emulsion particles. Plasticisation, by increasing the solid content, tends to increase the viscosity slightly. The addition of plasticiser often increases the apparent strength of wood or other adhesive. It will also increase creeps, although this can be avoided to some extent by increasing molecular weight as high as possible. Most standard plasticisers for polyvinyl acetate are found useful in various adhesive compositions. Dibutyl phthalate is a general plasticiser, imparting flexibility and softening with relatively low volatility. Diethyl phthalate is another alternative where fast tack is required. Benzyl butyl phthalate is considered as a good, if slightly more expensive, alternative to dibutyl phthalate in most applications, because of lower volatility, improved mositure resistance and film toughness.

Formulation for Highly Branched Polyvinyl Acetate Emulsion

Phase I	*Wt. in gms.*
Polyvinyl acetate emulsion stabilised with polyvinyl alcohol (55% solids 900-1200 cps.) base emulsion	600
Distillate water	37
Sodium formaldehyde sulphoxylate	0.5

The above is placed in a 3 litre flask with stirrer, thermometer, two dropping funnels, burette, condenser, the flask is immersed in a water bath, which is heated so that modified heat is at 70° C.

Phase II	
(67-69%) partially hydrolysed polyvinyl alcohol 6% viscosity of aqueous solution at 10° C average 25 cps (13.6 aq.)	145
Partially hydrolysed polyvinyl alcohol medium molecular wt. (67-69%)	55
Hydrogen peroxide (3%)	25
Distilled water	87
Sodium bicarbonate	0.9

Phase III	
Vinyl acetate	425
Nonionic surfactant containing acetylonic units	2

Phase IV	
Sodium formaldehyde sulphoxylate	1.5
Distilled water	35

Phase 2,3, and 4 are added in independent streams to the polymerising mixture which is allowed to rise to 80° C over 3 to 3.5 hrs. being finally retained for 1 hour at 80° C by which time free monomer should be reduced below 0.5 N. Final solids content is 545%.

Another group of plasticisers, consisting of a group of chlorinated biphenyls of varying viscosities, density and boiling point increasing with chlorine content respectively are also in consideration. The products of increasing chlorine content respectively, are considered suitable as compatible plasticisers at a 20% addition based on resin content, although plasticisation efficiency as mesasured by low temperature flexibility is less than dibutyl phthalate. These plasticisers are low in cost, impart quick tack and have good adhesion to many surfaces. Oil resistance and low volatility are required in addition to normal adhesion properties. They include 3-ethyl-hexyldiphenyl phosphate which is non-ionic, cresyl diphenyl phosphate triphenyl phosphate, the plasticising efficiency of the first named being slightly superior. Solid plasticisers, which include diphenyl-phthalates,dicyclohexyl phthalate and p-toluene sulphonamide have special interest in delayed tank adhesive. The plasticisers can be emulsified into standard polyvinyl acetate products without loss of stability and give plasticising efficiency equal to that of dibutyl phthalate and superior to addition. Polyethylene glycol ethers monohydric phenolics with only short chain alkyl groups attacked to phenol may also be used be used as plasticisers for polyvinyl acetate. These products are water soluble and surface active and the plasticised films exhibit permanent tack. A typical example is the monophenyl polyvinyl acetate if the plasticised state if used as an adhesive for a plastic film may embrittle and fall due to plasticiser into the substrate.

Special Formulation of Polyvinyl Acetate Adhesive

The addition of 5 per cent thiourea or an alkali metal cyanate, and up to 5 per cent polyvinyl alcohol and a small quantity of boric acid to polyvinyl acetate emulsion makes it suitable for adhesive purposes. It is also able to form a continuous film at low temperature. The rapid setting of polyvinyl acetate adhesive can be obtained, on inclusion of ungelatinised starch and by heating the wet film above gelation points of the mixture. A similar composition, comprising a mixture of gelatinised and ungelatinised starch with a polyvinyl acetate emulsion proves very suitable as an adhesive composition for the laminated paper products.

Suitable compositions are given below.

	Polyvinyl Acetate	*Dibutyl Phthalate*
	% by wt. of composition	*% by wt. of polyvinyl acetate*
A. Adhesive bonded wet high tack not required	22-50	20-40
B. Adhesive bonded dry strong bond and duration of tack requird	15-45	35-60
C. Adhesive bonded wet high tack required bond may be weak	11-40	60-180
D. Adhesive bonded dry by heat sealing	22-50	20-40

Class A compositions are effective for padding paper and for bonding cloth. Class B compositions are suitable as cements used in shoe manufacture as are class C, suitable as seal and lining cements. Class D compositions are useful for applying labels by automatic machinery.

There are also various other additives used in polyvinyl acetate emulsions aimed for adhesion.

Polyvinyl Acetate Adhesive including Crosslinking Agents

Glyoxal is the crosslinking agent which is generally used. It is available as a 30 per cent solution. It is necessitated where water resistance of composition is to be increased and 'creep' is to be reduced.

Glyoxal is stable below pH 8, and should preferably be kept below pH 7. Glyoxal is specially recommended for emulsions based on polyvinyl alcohol, and is added at 10-20 per cent of the weight of alcohol. Sometimes it is seen to have weakened adhesion presumably by reacting with all the polar groups in the molecule. The use of various crosslinking agents in adhesive compositions on a polyvinyl acetate basis has been recommended the used of a phenol aldehyde condensation product in ratios varying from 0.3 to 4.0 vinyl acetate polymer per unit of phenol condensate e.g. trimethylol phenol. An acid catalyst is present and partially hydrolysed polyvinyl acetate is recommended. The products can be used in bonding of laminiation of porous substrates such as wood, textiles, leather, paper and asbestos cement board. Chromic acetate and acid salts such as chromic nitrate or aluminium nitrate may be used as curing agents and vinyl acetate copolymers may be included in the composition.

Copolymers of vinyl acetate and glycidyl acrylate or methacrylate, together with trimethylolphenol set rapidly at ambient temperatures to give water proof bonds in presence of an acid catalysts, the products suitable for laminating. Another product an acetone formaldehyde condensate with polyvinyl acetate over a range of concentrations, the mixture is thermosetting.

OTHER SYNTHETIC ADHESIVES

Butadiene Copolymers

Synthetic polymers in particular styrene butadiene copolymers are used in latex form for many purposes as a substitute for natural adhesives, sometimes special modifiers are included in styrene butadiene latices. Carboxylic acid like methacrylic acid or itanoic acid and 2-vinylpyridine is added in the copolymerisation to give adequate binding to polar substrates. This type of terpolymer emulsion is used in the tyres and allied industries in formulations which bind reinforcing textiles to rubber. Latices including heterocyclic nitrogen bases have been precipitated and after redissolving in benzene used as an adhesive with a boric acid dispersion.

A typical latex formulation which in this case is polymerised at 5° C for 1.5 hours, and short stopped at 60 per cent conversion is given below.

Latex Containing 2-Methyl-5-Vinylpyridine

Ingredients	*Parts by wt.*	
	1	**2**
1,3-Butadiene	75	75
Styrene	-	15
2-Vinyl pyridine	-	10
2-Vinyl-5-pyridine	25	-
Potassium chloride	0.1	-
Sodium salt of condensed alkyl aryl sulphuric acid	9.3	-
Potassium pyrosulphate	-	-
Ferrous sulphate	0.096	-
Potassium persulphate	0.083	-
Cumene hydroperoxide	-	0.3
Tertiary dodecyl mercapton	0.27	0.4
Potassium Fatty acid soap	6	5

ADHESIVE COMPOSITION CONTAINING CARBOXYLATED LATEX

Ingredients	*Parts by wt.*
Maize starch (equivalent of 995 lb. dry)	1170 lb.
Carboxylated latex (44 per cent butadiene, 51 per cent styrene, 5 per cent itanoic acid, 40 per cent solids)	30 gallons
Dimethylol urea (added at 6 per cent solids)	50 lbs.

The above makes 550 gallons of adhesive.

A rather unusual adhesive, specifically claimed as useful in joining a sealing liner in a metal bottle closure shell with automatic machinery consists of a butadiene styrene latex blended with a borax solution of egg albumen is about 2 : 1 and overall solids can be about 52 per cent. Heat is essential for activation.

ADHESIVE WITH SPECIFIC FUNCTIONS

Pressure Sensitive Adhesive

Pressure sensitive adhesives can be defined as adhesive materials which when dry and completely free from solvent or other carrier possess a lasting and aggressive tack which enables them to adhere to a wide variety of substrates upon contact.

The two major types of pressure-sensitive adhesives are those which are intended to be permanent, and in which any attempt to separate the two components will cause to tear of the paper or other substrate and types which are only intended to be temporary such as destination labels on railway carriage windows. In between them, there may be some application e.g. certain desirable to remove the adhesive covered coating for repositioning where required but, which will develop a firm bond later possibly by a more conventional diffusion process.

Formulation of Spontaneous Resin Emulsion

Ingredients	*Parts by wt.*			
	1		2	
	A	B	A	B
Resin solution	0.65	-	50.65	-
Resin	-	40.0	-	40.0
Solvent	-	10.0	-	10.0
Oleic acid	-	0.65	-	0.25
KoH solution (2.5 per cent)	6.15	-	10.25	-
Water	-	6.0	-	10. 0
KOH (100 per cent)	43.2	-	30.50	-
Diluents and modifiers	-	43.20	-	24.50
Ammonium caseinate solution 10 per cent solids	As required			
	100.0	100.0	100.0	100.0

This resin should have a viscosity of 25 to 30 poises. If the viscosity of the solution resulting from the proportions of resin and solvent specified falls outside the 25 to 30 poise range, it should be adjusted by adding more resin, or solvent as needed.

The resin may be pentalyn A, pentalyn H, a blend of pentalyn A and Hercolyn, poly pale ester 10, stabilite ester 10 or other suitable resin.

The solvent may be toluene, xylene, or other equivalent water immiscible solvent.

Emulsion for Pressure-sensitive Adhesive

Ingredients	*Parts by wt.*
Nonphenol-ethylene condensate (97 per cent by wt. of ethylene units)	22.4
Sodium acetate	1.0
Water	465.0
Sodium meta-bisulphite (in 10 parts water)	0.9
Ammonium persulphate (in 10 parts water)	0.45
2-Ethylexyl acrylate	352
Acrylic acid	6.4

The polymerisation follows a conventional procedure for 3 hours at 60-70° C after which the following is added and heating continued for an hour further.

Ammonium persulphate (in parts water)	0.45

The final emulsion is stable containing 46 per cent by wt. solids.

Terpolymers of vinyl acetate, di-2-ethyl hexyl-maleate and alkyl acrylates produce permanently tacky adhesives which enable untreated polyethylene, polypropylene and other very strongly hydrophobic polymers to adhere to themselves and other materials without pretreatment. Terpolymers containing vinyl acetate, an acrylate ester which is at least 50 per cent of monomers and 1-5 per cent of an unsaturated acids have been disclosed for the purpose.

Pressure sensitivity may be developed by heating (in absence of crosslinking agents) a copolymer which includes at least 50 per cent by weight of a simple acrylic ester as part of one component, whilst the other component is based on a monoester of glycol e.g. hydroxypropyl acrylate.

A typical emulsion copolymer contains monomersd with the following composition.

Ingredients	*Parts by wt.*
2-Ethyl acrylate	1386
Vinyl acetate	900
Hydroxypropyl methacrylate	250

The monomers are polymerised by a typical anionic menionic emulsifier system, using a redexilator system of ammonium persulphate and a sodium metabisulphite adding part of the initiator and part of the monomer by gradual addition the final product being of 46 per cent solids and 300 cps. It could be thickened by a post addition of hydroxyethyl cellulose.

While if dried at 52° C coating on polyethylene phthalate tape the coating dissolved completely when immersed in acetone,if dried at 150° C for 3 minutes it showed only slight swelling after 15 minutes immersion.

Formulation for Pressure Sensitive Adhesive

Monomer	1	2	3	4	5	6	7	8
2-Ethylexyl acrylate	58	80	90	90	90	77	77	78
Vinyl acetate	42	20	10	-	-	-	20	20
Methyacrylic acid	-	-	-	10	5	3	3	-
Acrylic acid	-	-	-	-	5	-	-	-
Styrene	-	-	-	-	-	20	-	2

Copolymers of which the principal component is an acrylate ester, especially 2-ethyl hexyl acrylate and preferably prepared in emulsion are useful for coating bioxially oriented polypropylene film which has been activated electrostatically. Typical monomers are shown in the above table. The coatings are dried below 99° C to avoid softening of the film.

An alternative resin ratio, especially recommended for quick stick is 78 parts of 2-ethylhexyl acrylate, 20 of vinyl acetate and 2 parts of acrylic acid. It may be thickened by a solution of sodium polyacrylate for application purposes; with the addition of 20 to 80 per cent of a non crosslinked acrylic latex on a styrene copolymer or homopolymer is considered to be a pressure sensitive adhesive for polypropylene or polystyrene substrates including oxially oriented polypropylene polyropylene film. The acrylic polymer is capable of keeping to the substrate but is non-tacky and compatible with natural rubber. Suitable copolymers are ethyl methyl methacrylate/styrene and polybutyl acrylate. This type of adhesiveis useful where a package has to be opened and resealed using finger pressure only. The acrylic or styrene polymer is present from 20-30 per cent of solid material present.

Pressure Sensitive and contact Adhesive

Ingredients	*Parts by wt.*	
	1	2
Ethyl acrylate	87	87
Methyl methacrylate	10.5	3
Itaconic acid	2.5	-
Methyacrylic acid	-	10
Bromotrichloromethane	0.5	0.5
Tert-octylphenoxy polyoxyethylene with 30 per cent ethylene oxide	6.0	6.0
Ammonium persulphate	0.2	0.2
Sodium hydrosulphite	0.25	0.25
Water	100	100
	170.0	170.0

The above composition adhesive is prepared by a conventional redox method, raised to pH 6.0 with potassium hydroxide adjusted to 30 per cent solids and may be compounded with titanium dioxide Tio2 (rutile) which has been previously dispersed.

The composition may be neutralised and used fillers, one of the best being rutile titanium dioxide.

The fillers have a reinforcing effect on the composition, and may be used up to 125 per cent of the polymer weight. Besides pressure sensitive application they are suitable for use as contact adhesives e.g. they may be coated on porous surfaces and substrates assembled without clamps while the adhesive is either still wet or allowed to dry. The surface to be adhered should be coated if they are both impervious, or the impervious one if one surface is porous. About 5 minutes drying time is required. The surfaces should be coated, and contacted immediately after application.

Pressure Sensitive Acrylic Composition

Monomer phase	*Parts by wt*
2-Ethyl hexyl acrylate	170
Vinyl acetate	75
N-butoxymethyl acrylamide	5
Aqueous Phase	
Hydroxyethyl cellulose, low viscosity	
(8 per cent solution)	31.12
Water	250
Sodium borate	1.7
Potassium persulphate	1.0
Alkyl aryl polyether alcohol (surfactant)	5.0
Dioctyl ester of sodium sulphosuccinic acid	1.25

PREPARATION

The water phase is prepared cold and 25 parts of monomer mixture added, the temperature being raised to 75° C and the remainder added over 2 hours between 75° C and 80.5° C. A further 0.25 parts of potassium persulphate in 10 parts of water is added and the reaction is continued for a further hour. The fine emulsion has the following characteristics.

Total solids	46.5%
Viscosity	1600 cps.
pH	4.6

This composition is an excellent pressure sensitive adhesive for vinyl acetate, baked at between 130° C and 150° C. The cohesive strengths of these polymers may be increased by the simultaneous copolymerisation of an acidic monomer such as acrylic or methacrylic acids together with a monomer of a glycol which is capable of polymerisation. About 3 per cent of a product such as the hydroxyethyl or hydroxypropyl esters of acrylic methacrylic acid are used conveniently in polymerisation, all monomers dissolved together. The addition of about 10 per cent of total monomers of methyl acrylate assists in maintaining a high strength bond.

TEXTILES

Polyvinyl acetate and its copolymers in emulsion form tend to be used as finishes. Polyvinyl acetate emulsions may, however, be used to coat interlinings so as to impart heat seal properties. If a plasticised homopolymer is used, then the plasticiser should be of a non-migratory type to avoid subsequent straining. Allied to this, similarly plasticised emulsions may be applied to cause the formation of bondages, although the standard internally plasticised resins are preferred.

BINDERS

Binder in Incediary Composition

Polyvinyl acetate has been used as a binder for match heads in conjunction with polyvinyl alcohol. Precaution is taken not to experiment with incediary composition except under expert supervision.

As Resin Binder

The process of bonding fibres to form a fabric in current practice includes certain solution type bonding agents, polymer emulsions etc. Emulsion binders quoted in the industry include polyvinyl acetate among others. With regard to the various resin types, polyvinyl acetate and its copolymers are generally lacking in resilience and have a tendency to creep, but could be used for dispersable products. The polyvinyl acetate is used as a binder for laminates in which one sheet consists of a non-woven organic fibre, and the other a net of thermoplastic fibre such as high density polyethylene.

As Binder (Casts and Moulds)

This dispersion of plasticised polyvinyl acetate is used to bind materials such as clay, kaolin and cork dust; a heavy paste of the viscous emulsion and filler is pressed into solids and dried. It is claimed that the products are stronger than plaster of paris and they are used to make toys and dolls. This type of binding application is of industrial interest and polyvinyl acetate and allied copolymers are still highly binding the fillers and cellulosics. The coarser types of polyvinyl acetate or emulsifiable powders are best employed as polyvinyl alcohol stabiliser basis.

As Hydraulic Binding Agent

Polyvinyl acetate emulsion is able to function as hydraulic binding agent in many compositions, particularly where chemical reaction is involved in the setting or drying process i.e. in cementitious compositions. The composition used is a high proportion of polyvinyl acetate to plaster of parts in a proportion not exceeding 1:1.9 preferably with the addition of about 1% hydroxyl cellulose solution.

Additive to Prevent Lime Staining

The phenomenon of 'lime staining' is most noticeable on alkaline plaster and takes the form of a bloom on the surface of the paint film which is found to consist wholly or substantially of crystals of calcium acetate. It appears to be formed by alkaline hydrolysis of polyvinyl acetate by a high lime plaster. Calcium acetate seems to be sufficiently soluble in the polymer to be blanched through and to appear on the surface.

Additive to Cement

Polyvinyl acetate is used in some typical flooring compositions with cement as ingredient. The formulation is given below.

Ingredients	*Parts by wt.*		
	Heavy duty floor	*Office floor*	*Matt floor*
Portland cement	100	100	100
Sand	100	150	200
Graphite chips	150	100	-
Asbestos fibre	-	25	-
Cork granules	-	-	100
Pigment	5	5	5
Polyvinyl acetate emulsion (55% solids, 20% plasticised)	13-14	13-14	20-22
Water	26-30	25-30	20-22

The emulsion diluted with 2 parts water is gauging liquid for (i) and (ii). The emulsion diluted with 2% part of water is gauging liquid for (iii).

The direct addition of polyvinyl acetate emulsion to mortars plays a very profound part both physical and chemical. One of the functions of the polymer is that it fills the gap whichsoever if the atmosphere is too dry. It can be shown that the cement resin ratio rises above 2:1, the resin gradually becomes the continuous phase. The compressive strength of polyvinyl acetate cement mixes decrease very sharply as does the tensile strength. Maximum mechanical strength is attained when the ratio of polyvinyl acetate: portland cement is 0.8:1, the maximum ratio at which the polyvinyl acetate can be regarded as a filler for the mortar. The wear resistance is considered to be up to 30 times that of plain concrete floors.

MISCELLANEOUS APPLICATIONS

IN GLASS FIBRE TREATMENT

Polyvinyl acetate in emulsion form is one of the most satisfactory resins used in conjunction with coupling agents. Properly applied, the size should not be visible through the thermoset polyester.

COMPOSITION FOR GLASS FIBRES

Ingredients	*% by weight*			
	1	**2**	**3**	**4**
Vinyltris B-methoxy ethoxy silane	0.62	0.90	-	-
Ammonium allyl silameate	-	-	0.40	-
Potassium allyl polysiloxeate	-	-	-	0.2-0.5
Polyvinyl acetate in emulsion form	5.14	5.14	4.5	-
Dibutyl phthalate	-	-	0.4	-
Butadiene-ethalate (60:40 ratio) emulsion	-	-	-	1-5.0
Amine lubricant	0.15	0.06	0.25	-
Hydrochloric acid	0.9	0.06	H_2SO_4 adjust pH 5 & 8	to pH_6
Wate r	90.0	93.6	Balance	Balance

The silane should be added to the water with strong agitation. It should then be followed by polyvinyl acetate, as available, in a 50-55 per cent emulsion, and the lubricant. The 700 g.m. of the lubricant formed by the reaction product of tetraethylene pentamine and pelagoric acid, solubilised with acetic acid is mixed 50-60°C with 300 ml. of conc. HCl, and added immediately after the polymer, a final adjustment with HCl being made to bring the pH to 3.8.

IN COATING OF FOODSTUFFS

The coating of foodstuffs directly with polyvinyl acetate layer probably persists for 40 years. Polyvinyl acetate seems to be the only polymer in use for this purpose. Bread, in particular, has been the subject of treatment. Modern work has been directed to the use of modified polyvinyl acetate emulsions into which they can sprayed. If a coating is applied to cheese so that it is reasonably permeable to air, then the cheese may be cooled immediately on and allowed to ripen on standing.

The formulation for a foodstuff coating is given below.

Ingredients	*Parts by wt.*
Polyvinyl acetate emulsion (55% solids)	64
Carboxymethyl cellulose (60% aq.)	16
Starch	8
Plasticiser as (below)	12
Citrus pectin, grade 400	3
Glycerol triacetate	45
Glycerol (84-87%) aq.	20
Sodium carboxy methyl cellulose 6% aq.	2
Castor oil	5
Water	25

IN WALL PAPER COATING

The problem of obtaining truly net washable paper is a serious one since almost all emulsion polymer top coats produce a slight sheen. If sufficient silica or other filler is added to obtain the desiree of wetness, transparency is seriously reduced. These difficulties are overcome if a composition is prepared from an emulsion e.g. polyvinyl acetate polyvinyldene chloride to which is added in slurry form a polysaccharide which is partially soluble in cold water e.g. starch etc.

A formulation for wall paper coating is given below.

Ingredient	*Parts by wt.*	
	1	**2**
Water	45	45
Plain wheat flour	15	-
Modified potato starch (hot soluble)	-	15
Vinylidene chloride copolymer emulsion	120	-
Polyvinyl acetate emulsion including 10 per cent on polymer wt. of di-isobutyl phthalate	-	120
Diatomaceous silica (particle size 6u)	10	10
Silica particle size (about 7u)	-	10
Water	to 40% solids	30
Drying temperature	min. 60° C	min 40° C
Drying film coating weight g/m²	15	20
Gloss (per cent)	10	10

In (1) the wheat flour is slurried with water, heated to 65° C, then cooled and polymer emulsion is added, followed by silica and water. In (2) the starch is slurried directly and the silica is slurried with water before addition.

IN MISCELLANEOUS PAPER ADHESIVES

It is possible for an adhesive system for bonding paper to substrate to be arranged in two layers consisting of adhesive e.g. polyvinyl acetate emulsion which may be applied to the base, and above it a layer of polyvinyl alcohol and a wetting agent. The system is activated by water and is suitable for wall paper, label posters etc.

AS ADHESIVE IN THE BUILDING INDUSTRY

Polyvinyl acetate has wide application, but should be avoided under conditions of continuous high humidity, otherwise there is little restriction to its use. In all cases a 20-25 per cent plasticised polyvinyl alcohol based polyvinyl acetate is recommended except in the case of concrete to ceramic where a 10 per cent internally plasticised dibutyl maleate copolymer is suggested or alternately a spray-dried polyvinyl acetate emulsion powder. In a test application involving concrete or wood or tiles, the adhesive is stronger than the components.

A number of adhesives may be mentioned here.

Wood to PVC
Cork to aluminium
Concrete to concrete
Concrete to paraquet
Concrete to ceramic
Concrete or wood to tiles

IN FIREPROOF AND WATER PROOF COATINGS

Compositions which are suitable for both fireproof and waterproof coatings are formed from a polyvinyl acetate emulsion, plasticised with dibutyl phthalate to about 10 per cent and blended with bitumen, cement and other agrregates. A thin coating composition can be applied to a textile web, and used on interior partitions including those in mines. A coating may also be applied to steel, glass and wood, and in thicker coatings for repairs to roads and pavements.

AS SESAME SEALANT

Ingredients	*Parts by wt.*
White	212.5
Hydrated lime	25
Titanium dioxide	12.5
Spray dried polyvinyl acetate	50.4
Water	97

IN TYPEWRITER BOND

Polyvinyl acetate emulsion size about 2/1 can be included in a rather interesting composition suitable for typewriter bond. The composition comprises the emulsion, hydroxyethylated starch and colloidal silica in a ratio of about 14.5:1. The finished paper has the advantage that type material can be readily erased without successive surface abrasion.

IN SHOE FINISHES

Compositions for bonding the plies at the heel end of shoes may be obtained by mixing a synthetic polymer emulsion, preferably one of the polyvinyl acetate in concentrated form i.e. up to 60 per cent solids with a solvent with some water solubility. Suitable solvents are ethyl acetates, methyl acetate, acetone and methyl ethyl ketones, the latter being the most useful. Suitable proportions are 1 to 3 parts of solvent to 11 of emulsion, 2 parts being the most all-round useful ratio. This mixture will penetrate and stiffen most fabrics e.g. those with a cellulose nitrate impregnant.

AS CRACK FILLER

Polyvinyl acetate has been used as a suitable base especially in areas where dampness is natural during application in kitchen and bathroom fittings and more modest as a crack filler.

IN WOOD COATING

Polyvinyl acetate and melamine formaldehyde resins as a mixture are applied on paper to saturation. This saturated paper may be used in wood coating by drying and pressing at 5-20 kg/m^2 at 120-200° C.

• Chapter 9 •

POLYVINYL ALCOHOL

Polyvinyl alcohol is believed to have been first prepared by the German chemist Willie Hermann. Its first commercial application was undertaken in the year 1920 in Germany and it was commercially introduced into the U.S.A. in 1939 by Du-Pont company. Chemically polyvinyl alcohol can be broadly classified as a polyhydric alcohol with secondary hydroxyl groups on alternate carbon atoms. It must be remembered that the theoretical vinyl alcohol monomer does not exist, since it rearranges to acetaldehyde. The polymer vinyl alcohol can only be obtained by hydrolysis of some other vinyl polymer. Commercially this term includes all resins made by the hydrolysis of polyvinyl acetate.

The variations of these two major factors during processing markedly affect the properties of the final product. The properties vary according to the molecular weight of the parent polyvinyl acetate and the extent of hydrolysis. The stucture of polyvinyl alcohol obtained by complete hydrolysis may be represented by $CH_3CHOH\text{-}(CH_2\text{-}CHOH)n\text{-}$, where n is related to the molecular weight of the parent resin. Although the formula for ordinary polyvinyl alcohol is commonly written in this manner it must be remembered that this is an idealised structure and in practice some heat-to-heat polymerisation occurs, resulting in a (1,2-glycol) structure ($CH_2\text{-}CH\text{-}CHOH\text{-}CH_2\text{-}CH\text{-}OH\text{-}CHOH\text{-}CH_2\text{-}CHOH\text{-}CH_2$).

On partial hydrolysis, proportional amounts of residual (CH_3 Ceo-) group are distributed along the chain in place of (OH) and the amount of such acetate groups is expressed as a percentage of the acetate content, thus in a polyvinyl alcohol of (70%) containing (30%) of acetate group of the original polyvinyl acetate were hydrolysed to hydroxyl groups and 70% remains acetate group. The hydroxyl group content of the polyvinyl alcohol is of the primary group concern for commercial application, a sample where 87-89 per cent of the acetoxy group is replaced by alcohol groups and in the acetylated fully hydrolysed grades, a minimum of 98 per cent of acetoxy group is replaced by alcohol groups and in the super hydrolysed grade, more than 99.7 per cent of the polymer is hydrolysed to polyvinyl alcohol.

The term polyvinyl alcohol means a material composed of linear molecules with the structure (A-(CH_2 OH) P-B) in which the distribution of degrees of polymerisation (P) and the average steresochemistry of the (CH_2 CHOH) segment with respect to each other (tacticity) are both specified and the end groups (A & B) are small and chemically inert. Methods are available for the determination of these two physical and chemical properties of this composition of matter in all its possible variation. It would seem in principale relatively straight forward. To a substantial extent these main features of chemical structures can indeed be controlled. The distribution of molecular weight can be controlled if not only by the method of preparation then through the fairly arduous task of fraction and selection. The tacticity has recently come under reasonable control through the discovery of reliable methods for its measurement through the exploration of novel preparative routes to PVA.

Vinylesters are almost certainly polymerised only by free radical catalysts. Reports of the use of leisler type and "polar" catalyst rarely occur mostly in lubious patent literature and probably involves free radical catalyst derived from the system. The presence of non-polar solvents compatible with free radical catalysts is permissible but the facility of the polymer is restricted by the mechanisms of propagation of polymerisation, characteristics of addition of a free radical to arinyl compound. This type of propagation gives a fairly random arrangement of stereosequences which for common polyvinyl esters is not affected much by variations in the temperature and permissible conditions of polymerisation. On the other hand, vinyl ether can be polymerised by polar catalysts such as boron trifluoride which probably act through the formation of reaction addition complexes between the catalyst and the other groups. Moreover these catalysts can tolerate both polar and non-polar solvents and show specifically in the average orientation of the added monomer units that is markedly dependent on the polarity of the solvent. This effect can be used to obtain samples of PVA that differ widely tactically.

Some attempt has been made to obtain polyvinyl alcohol directly by the polymerisation of acetaldehyde with a variety of catalysts and reaction conditions. But the molecular weights of the product are severally limited or their chemical structure is questionable. Further possible research in this area may eventually lead to success.

Polyvinyl alcohol is a water soluble synthetic polymer. It is white to green coloured powder. Its properties depend on the degree of polymerisation and percentage of alcoholysis both of which are controllable in processing. Its water solubility increases as molecular weight decreases. With the increase in its molecular weights its elongation strength, tear resistance and flexibility improve. PVA has high impermeability to gases. It is unaffected by oils, greases and petroleum hydrocarbons. It is attacked by acids and alkalies. It forms films by evaporation from water solution.

Two grades (viz. FH and PA) of polyvinyl alcohol are available commercially. The FH grade contains about 3 per cent acetate while PA grade contains about 30 per cent acetate on weight basis. It is available in three viscosity grades viz. low, medium and high. The viscosities of solution of different grades of polyvinyl alcohol are shown in the following table. The maximum concentrations of polyvinyl alcohol generally used in the pastes are 17 per cent for the high viscosity grade and 22 per cent for the medium grade.

VISCOSITIES OF POLYVINYL ALCOHOL SOLUTIONS

Concentration %	*Temperature °F*	*Viscosity in cps.*		
		High	*Medium*	*Low*
4	68	50-70	20-40	4-6
	160	10-20	4-5	1-2
8	68	10 00-1400	200-300	1-2
	160	100-200	50-70	4-6
12	68	12000-14000	2600-2800	80-90
	160	1100-1500	300-450	15-20

Both completely and partially alcoholised polyvinyl alcohols have many characteristics in common which make the polymer valuable to a number of industries. Among the most important properties are:

1. Water solubility
2. Ease of film formation
3. Grease oil and solvent resistance
4. High tensile strength
5. Excellent adhesive and binder qualities and
6. Ability to function as a disperser stabilizer.

The major applications of polyvinyl alcohol are in the fields of adhesives, binders, paper sizing, textile sizing and finishing, containers, bags, grease paints, ceramics, cosmetics, stencil screens, steel quenching etc.

In many instance manufacturers now find that although polyvinyl alcohol may be more expensive than other materials, overall economics favours polyvinyl alcohol. For example, one pound of polyvinyl alcohol is capable of replacing about three pounds of casein in paper coating formulations. On a straight cost comparison, this replacement ratio readily justifies replacement of casein as a pigment binder. The use of polyvinyl alcohol for paper coating has continued to grow not only for these economics considerations but also because polyvinyl alcohol can be tailored to satisfy specified end use.

Polyvinyl alcohol is currently experiensing extensive growth in the textile warp sizing field. The unique performance properties referred earlier have permitted polyvinyl alcohol to replace other sizing materials in many applications.

Polyvinyl alcohol films have achieved new importance as the demand for gas barrier properties grows. The bulk of the film used now is in low pressure vacuum by moulding where the property of low adhesion to most plastic and metal materials allows the film to be stripped readily from the article. PVA film may find utility in film laminate structures designed for long term food packaging where where advantage can be taken of impermeability of polyvinyl alcohol to oxygen, fats and oils.

The use of PVA in adhesives and emulsifiers has continued to expand as the use of synthetic adhesive system has increased. the need for more demanding adhesive properties, as in paper bound laminates, has stimulated the use of PVA based adhesives. Polyvinyl alcohol provides increased production efficiency, greater binding versatility and more water resistance.

MANUFACTURE

Production of polyvinyl alcohol resin is a multistep process, since vinyl alcohol monomer is a nonexistent entity, rapidly rearranging itself into acetaldehyde. Thus, it is first necessary to produce polyvinyl acetate resin from vinyl acetate monomer, and follow with alcoholysis of the polyvinyl acetate to the polyvinyl alcohol.

These reactions are illustrated as follows:

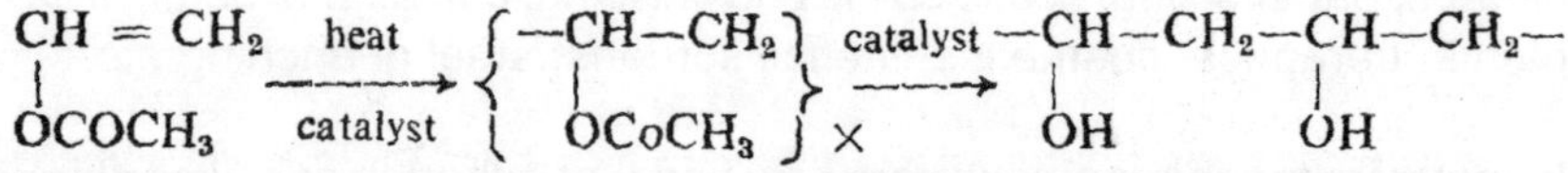

Vinyl acetate Polyvinyl alcohol

Polymerisation of the acetate resin is carried out by conventional processing techniques using either bulk or bead polymerisation. The resulting polyvinyl acetate resin is then dissovled in a solvent, usually methanol, and alcoholized by use of either an acid or alkaline catalyst. Polyvinyl alcohol, insoluble in the methanol and by product methyl acetate precipitates out and is then filtered, washed, dried and packaged. The polyvinyl alcohol is characterized by the viscosity or degree of polymerisation and the per cent hydrolysis or degree of saponification.

Both viscosity and alcoholysis are controlled in the manufacturing process and are important in determining end-product characteristics and commercial utility. The molecular weight, or measure of polymer viscosity, is a direct function of the molecular weight of the precursive polyvinyl acetate resin fed to the alcoholysis reaction. This is normally controlled by use of "chain-breakers" during the polyvinyl acetate polymerisation.

Polyvinyl alcohol can be plasticised with water, glycols. It has a rubbery consistency if enough plasticiser is incorporated and can be used for the production of oil and grease proof sheets and houses.

Generally speaking, polyvinyl alcohol is commercially available in four molecular weight ranges. For simplicity in discussing molecular weight or degree of polymerisation, the four types are referred to as super-high, medium-, and low viscosity polyvinyl alcohols. The average molecular weights of the four types are: super-high viscosity, 250,000 to 300,000; high viscosity 170,000 to 2,20,000; medium viscosity 120,000 to 150,000; and low-viscosity 25,000 to 35,000.

As the molecular weight of polyvinyl alcohol decreases, the water sensitivity or ease of water solubility increases. Higher values for tensile strength, tear resistance, elongation, and flexibility are obtained with increasing molecular weight.

The per cent alcoholysis is controlled by either allowing the alcoholysis reaction to go to completion or stopping it at a desired level. Commercially polyvinyl alcohols at two alcoholsis levels are considered important. These are the so-called partially hydrolysed grades which represent products alcoholized 87 to 89 per cent and the completely hydrolysed grades which are alcoholized 99 to 100 per cent. Changes in per cent alcoholysis also affect product properties. As the per cent alcoholysis increases, tensile strength, tear resistance, and elongation increases. Water sensitivity is anomalous in that maximum sensitivity occurs at about 88 per cent alcoholysis. One would expect water sensitivity to increase further as complete alcoholysis is approached. However, as more hydroxyl groups replace acetyl groups from the polyvinyl acetate polymer, hydrogen bonding beings and water molecules find it increasingly difficult to envelop the polymer chain and effect solubility. Heat is therefore required to dissolve the completely alcoholized grades of polyvinyl alcohol. Use of heat also promotes solubility of the partially alcoholized grades.

By combining the variables of alcoholysis and viscosity, a range of polyvinyl alcohol types can be produced. For example, Du Pont produces eleven grades of Elvanol polyvinyl alcohol which find commercial utility in large volume. End-use requirements govern selection of the grade used in any specific application.

PROCESS OF MANUFACTURE

The hydrolysis of polyvinyl acetate is carried out with methanol using sodium hydroxide or sodium metal or sodium methoxide as catalyst. This may be carried out batchwise.

Polyvinyl acetate (as dry powder) is taken in the reactor properly arranged for stirring and jacketted for heating or cooling. The reaction is made of stainless steel and equipped for automatic temperature control. Sufficient quantity of methanol with small amount of methyl acetate is added to the reaction vessel and a uniform solution of polyvinyl acetate in methanol is prepared. Normally excess of methanol is taken to avoid the incomplete reaction (a mixture of methyl acetate and methanol is taken to avoid the incomplete reaction). The mixture is then heated by supplying outside heat so that the whole charge completes into a solution form. Then it is again cooled down to room temperature (about 20° C) and a specified amount catelyst along with methanol is fed into this reactor. This mixture is again stirred well for a period of about 5 to 6 hours depending upon the required degree of hydrolysis.

Due to hydrolysis polyvinyl alcohol separates out into the fine powder form which settles down in the bottom of the reactor on standing. Thus, the whole mass is taken out of the reactor and filtered and washed with methanol and remove unreacted polyvinyl acetate from the products. The filtered product is then dried in a vacuum drier to give white crystals of polyvinyl alcohol.

The mixture of methanol and acids are passed on to the reactor and then sent to a distillation column. There the top product from distillation column contains around 60 to 85 per cent of alcohol and the balance optimum amount of methanol.

COMPOUNDING & MODIFYING POLYVINYL ALCOHOL

Polyvinyl alcohol solutions are generally modified prior to use to change or control characteristics of the end product. Typical modifications include addition of plasticisers, insolubilisers, extenders, defoamers etc.

PLASTICISERS

Plasticisers which have been found to be most effective in imparting softness or flexibility to polyvinyl alcohol are some of the high boiling point water soluble organic compounds containing hydroxyl amide or amine groups. The ester type water immiscible plasticisers commonly used with plastics are not compatile with polyvinyl alcohol.

At present the most widely used plasticiser for polyvinyl alcohol is glycerine. It is compatible in substantial proportions with both the partially and completely hydrolysed types and has good stability, resistance to extraction by organic solvent and high softening effect.

EXTENDERS

The addition of materials such as starch, dextrin, gelatin, casein and urea to PVA compositions lower the cost and is advantageous in some cases. In other cases the advantage of a lower cost per pound is lost because the desired results cannot be obtained with the extended polyvinyl alcohol.

Compatibility with starch varies with both the grade of starch and the type of polyvinyl alcohol. In general, the compatibility increases with the per cent hydrolysis of and viscosity of the polyvinyl alcohol. Several of the low viscosity oxidized starches have been found suitable for use with polyvinyl alcohol as a size for paper. Starches have also been used in combination with polyvinyl alcohol as a size for warp sizing.

Only small proportions of most grades of dextrin are compatible with polyvinyl alcohol. Solution compatibility is favoured by low total solids. The dextrin which has been found to be most compatible with polyvinyl alcohol is a 100 per cent cold-water-soluble type of yellow potato dextrin.

This dextrin usually can be mixed in all proportions, provided the total solids are less than 15 per cent.

Stable mixture of solutions of some photographic and pharmaceutical grades of gelatins and polyvinyl alcohol can be made, but most low-quality gelatins and glues are not compatible.

When used as an extender, casein should be dissolved in an alkaline material, such as ammonium hydroxide, which does not precipitate the polyvinyl alcohol. The polyvinyl alcohol solution should also be made alkaline before adding to the casein solution. Borax and sodium carbonate should not be used to dissolve the casein since only very small amounts of these salts are required to gel or precipitate polyvinyl alcohol.

Low-cost waste sulfite liquor products can be used as extenders. However, these materials increase the viscosity and, since they are highly coloured, impart considerable colour to solutions.

INSOLUBILIZERS

Polyvinyl alcohol is generally not recommended where moisture proofness or a high degree of water resistance is required. For maximum water resistance, completely hydrolysed grades of polyvinyl alcohol are chosen. Methods of increasing the water resistance of polyvinyl alcohol include heat treatment and the addition of inorganic acids, dibasic organic acids, various metal salts, titanium organic, aldehydes or water-soluble formaldehyde derivatives. Insolubilized films of polyvinyl alcohol can be dissolved in hot 3 per cent solution of hydrogen peroxide.

PRECIPITANTS AND GELLING AGENTS

A number of organic and inorganic compounds, precipitate polyvinyl alcohol from water solutions or cause gelling. Such agents are sometimes useful in applications where it is advantageous to control the penetration of polyvinyl alcohol solution into porous surfaces.

Only small amounts of some salts are required to precipitate polyvinyl alcohol from water solutions, whereas others are tolerated in large proportions. Salts illustrating the latter class are potassium iodide, sodium nitrate, zinc chloride, potassium thiocyanate, and calcium chloride. Salts typical of the former class are sodium carbonate, potassium sulfate, and sulfate. These salts will cause polyvinyl alcohol to precipitate from solutions if the salt content of the solution exceeds 4 per cent.

One of the most effective gelling agents for polyvinyl alcohol is borax. As little as 0.1 per cent borax, based on weight of solution, causes a 5 per cent solution of completely hydrolyzed polyvinyl alcohol to gel. Ammonium hydroxide, mineral acids, congo red etc. are some of the other gelling agents used.

PIGMENTS AND DYES

Care should be taken in the selection of pigments and dyes as some cause gelling or thickening of polyvinyl alcohol solutions. This may result from the presence of large proportions of soluble salts or from the action of the colouring agents themselves. Only a small proporation of the soluble salts should be permitted in pigments and dyes to be used with polyvinyl alcohol.

WETTING AGENTS

Practically any of the common wetting agents can be used with polyvinyl alcohol solutions. The amount required varies with the conditions but is usually 0.05 to 0.20 per cent, based on the weight of the solution.

ANTI-FOAMING AGENTS

Foaming of polyvinyl alcohol can be reduced by raising the temperature, reducing the amount of agitation, or adding a defoamer. Lorol 20 fatty alcohol technical, bubble breaker 259, and Antifoam A silicone compound are amoung the defoamers which have proved to be suitable for use with polyvinyl alcohol. If a defoamer is necessary, about 0.1 per cent based on the weight of the solution, should be added during the preparation of the solution. If foam develops later, additional defoamer can be added as required.

APPLICATIONS

Industrial applications for polyvinyl alcohol that are dependent on one or more of the previously discussed properties of the resin are adhesives, binders, paper coating and sizing, textile sizing and finishing, emulsifying, dispersing, chemical intermediate, and unsupported film.

These applications are described below in a descriptive way.

ADHESIVES

The high tensile strength and adhesive characteristics of polyvinyl alcohol have resulted in extensive use in adhesive manufacture. The types are widely diversified-from high-wet-strength for paper to remoistenable adhesives.

Polyvinyl alcohol alone or combined with extenders, pigments, and insolubilizers, is used extensively in the preparation of high-wet strength adhesives for paper. Combinations of polyvinyl alcohol with starch or clay are especially effective and economical. Small proportions of polyvinyl alcohol substantially increase the strength and water resistance of starch and dextrin adhesives. When maximum water resistance is required, completely alcoholized grades of polyvinyl alcohol should be used.

Some adhesives made by the Du Pont company have outstanding water resistance. These adhesive, essentially mixtures of polyvinyl and starch extended with an acid-type clay have the advantage of better machinibility than the urea-formaldehyde resins. Applications of water-resistant adhesives based on polyvinyl alcohol include use in boxboard, wallboard, and paper bags.

The partially hydrolyzed grades polyvinyl alcohol are usually selected for use in remoistenable adhesives. The curl tendencies of the coated paper are reduced, and blocking at high humidities occurs.

The use of polyvinyl alcohol in adhesives is in conjunction with polyvinyl acetate emulsion and formulations of these adhesives have already been included in the previous chapter on polyvinyl acetate emulsion.

BINDERS

Polyvinyl alcohol is a highly efficient binder for a wide variety of materials including textile fibres. It is also used as a binder for catalyst pellets, cork, plaster, and waste products. As a binder in ceramics, polyvinyl alcohol imparts high green strength and good extrusion properties, thereby reducing breakage.

Polyvinyl alcohols are used as binders for nonwoven fabric and ribbon, showing excellent adhesion to both cotton and rayon fibres. In most applications where polyvinyl alcohol acts as a binder, excellent results can be obtained by using as little as 2 to 5 per cent polyvinyl alcohol solids.

PAPER SIZING

Polyvinyl alcohol offers paper manufacturers a water soluble resin which is useful in strengthening, transparentizing, greaseproofing, gasproofing, and otherwise improving the printing qualities of paper products. Conventional sizing and coating equipment can be used to apply the water solutions to paper.

For most paper-sizing applications, the completely hydrolyzed grades of polyvinyl alcohol are used in order to obtain maximum strength and water resistance. These grades have less tendency to stick to calender rolls and drying cylinders than do the partially hydrolyzed grades. Polyvinyl alcohol solutions can be conveniently applied to paper at the size press or calender stacks.

When sizing at the calender stack, the polyvinyl alcohol solution should be applied from water boxes on unheated rolls, and it may be necessary to add paraffin wax to prevent sticking to the rolls. If paraffin wax is needed, 25 to 50 per cent (based on the dry weight of the resin) of an emulsion such as Alwax 251° C size or paracol 600 water-dispersible wax emulsion is suggested.

The solution concentration varies with the absorbency of the paper and the viscosity of the polyvinyl alcohol. A 3 per cent solution of a high viscosity resin is generally applied at the calender stack, although higher concentrations of lower viscosity grades can also be handled with no difficulty.

Grease-resistant papers can be produced by surface sizing with polyvinyl alcohol. If absolute grease-resistance is required, a continuous coating must be applied. Printing areas on paper sized with polyvinyl alcohol show higher gloss as a result of reduced ink penetration, as well as a smoother finish due to more even distribution of the ink. For some time this has been popular in boxboard applications.

Surprisingly small amounts of polyvinyl alcohol are required to increase substantially the strength and flexibility of bond, ledger, index, blueprint, and many other high-quality papers. For example, a 2.5 per cent solution of a high viscosity, completely hydrolyzed type of polyvinyl alcohol applied by means of a size press to 24-pound, 100 per cent rage paper stock increased the Mullen burst strength 52 per cent and the schopper fold test value 78 per cent in the machine direction and 126 per cent in the cross direction.

Glassine paper sized with polyvinyl alcohol has improved strength, a transparency, gloss, grease resistance, and dimensional stability. It is affected less by humidity and aging as polyvinyl alcohol is less hydroscopic than some transparentizing agents and does not volatilize.

If polyvinyl alcohol is properly applied to paper surfaces producing a continuous film without inholes or breaks, the paper is absolutely grease proof and highly impervious to oxygen and many other gases. Such papers are useful in the manufacture of containers for oils, greases, and chemicals. Some polyvinyl alcohol does not adhere well to such materials as asphalt and resins, it can be used as a coating on paper intended for packaging these materials.

PAPER COATINGS

Polyvinyl alcohol is well suited as a binder in pigmented coatings for paper. The ratio of binder to pigment is unusually low, and the aqueous dispersions flow on smoothly, producing together, whiter coatings with improved printing qualities. Good results can be obtained with as little as 2 to 4 parts of polyvinyl alcohol to 100 parts of clay.

High-viscosity or medium-viscosity grades are generally used as binders for pigmented coatings. Where economic limits are severe,combinations of starch and polyvinyl trials, 1 part of polyvinyl alcohol to 9 parts of a low-viscosity, oxidized starch is suggested. Even in smaller proportions, polyvinyl mixed with starch produces a noticeable improvement over the starch alone. The water resistance of pigmented coatings in which polyvinyl alcohol alone or in combination with starch is used as a binder can be increased by use of insolubilizers, such as dimethylolurea or trimethylol melamine.

Pigmented coatings coataining polyvinyl alcohol can be applied with the various types of coating equipment in general use.

TEXTILE SIZING AND FINISHING

High tensile strength, flexibility, good abrasion resistance, and adhesion, combined with water solubility, clearly indicates the usefulness of polyvinyl alcohol as a textile size. The size can be applied by the customary sleshing, skein, and single-thread methods to warp, filling and knitting wears.

Good results are being obtained with all types of filament and spun yarns including the hard to size synthetics. Readily soluble in water, polyvinyl alcohol can be easily removed from the grey goods. In some cases it can be removed in the dyebath without a desizing operation.

One of the most important advantages of using polyvinyl alcohol as a warp size is its low biochemical oxygen demand (B.O.D.). Test results indicate that polyvinyl alcohol has 5-day B.O.D. of only 200 parts per million, compared with a 5 day value of 5,000 for starch.

Polyvinyl alcohol also finds wide use as a textile finish, particularly in combination with thermosetting.

EMULSIFYING AGENT

An important property of polyvinyl alcohol is its ability to function as a nonionic emulsifying agent. As such it exhibits certain advantages over a variety of other emulsifiers. It behaves primarily as a protective colloid and tolerates substantial concentrations of electrolytes, particularly acids.

Moreover, it forms synergistic emulsifying combinations with certain surface active agents. Enhanced, emulsifying action and less thickening often result with such combinations.

Polyvinyl alcohol can be used to emulsify or disperse a large number of materials including vegetable oils, mineral oils, solvents, plasticizers, waxes, and resins. Although it functions both as a surface active agent and protective colloid, and is a good emulsifying agent when used alone, results are sometimes improved by the addition of a small amount of a product such as Duponol ME dry surface active agent-powder, which is particularly effective in lowering the interfacial tension. Stable emulsions can be made with polyvinyl alcohol in both acid and alkaline media. In some applications, it serves as a binder and thickener as on emulsifying agent.

In general, the partially hydrolyzed grades, with the high viscosity grades are more effective than the low viscosity grades.

Generally 2 to 5 per cent polyvinyl alcohol, based on the total weight of the emulsion, should be used for oil-in-water type emulsions containing 30 to 50 per cent of the dispersed phase. For initial tests, 3 per cent polyvinyl alcohol alone and 0.5 per cent of a surface active agent is suggested.

POLYVINYL ALCOHOL FILMS

Many uses in the manufacture of containers, including bags and paper container liners for oils, greases and paints, and chemicals, have been suggested for polyvinyl alcohol films. The packaging of unit quantities of materials such as soap, dry bleaches, bluing bath salts, insecticide, and disinfectants in water-soluble containers facilitates their use.

Preweighted quantities can be added to the water without breaking the packages or removing the wrappers, thereby saving time and reducing material losses. Sealed bags made from this film can be used for vacuum or gas packaging of materials which need protection from oxygen to preserve their properties.

Polyvinyl alcohol film has been used for making oxygen tents; in vacuum or bag moulding; as a wrapping for polished metal requiring protection from gases, such as oxygen and hydrogen sulfide; and as a water soluble backing for embroidered lace during its manufacture with Schiffi equipment. When oriented by stretching, the film polarizes light. This unique property is advantageous in the manufacture of sunglasses, desk lamps, automobile headlights and windshields, and in certain photographic techniques. Because of its low degree of adhesion to several other plastic materials, polyvinyl alcohol film prevents sticking to moulds.

Where maximum film strength and solvent resistance are desired, completely hydrolyzed grades of high or medium viscosity are suggested. For cold water soluble film, partially hydrolyzed grades are used.

CERAMICS

Several ceramic applications have been found for polyvinyl alcohol. One such use is in the manufacture of china flatware. As little as 0.1 per cent polyvinyl alcohol, based on the dry weight of the clay, when added to a "short" casting slip improves the working characteristics.

Another ceramic use is as a temporary binder. For example, 2 to 3 per cent polyvinyl alcohol, based on the dry weight of the ceramic body, gives good results in the manufacture of steatite tubing. Solubility assures uniform distribution of the binder.

Using polyvinyl alcohol as the binder, low pressure is required for extruding steatite; and tubing with smoother walls is produced. The extra strength derived from the binder reduces losses due to handling and machining.

Reports indicate that a small amount of polyvinyl alcohol added to steatite produces soft granules that handle easily in the automatic machines for dry moulding, and gives usually good moulding characteristics. Polyvinyl alcohol has also given good results as a binder for glaze compositions. For this application, per cent polyvinyl alcohol based on dry weight of glaze composition is recommended.

MOULDED PRODUCTS

Plasticized polyvinyl alcohol can be moulded into rubber-like articles ranging in durometer hardness from 10 to 100. High strength, flexibility, resistance to grease and organic solvents, imperviousness to gases, and good ageing ability characterize these articles. They are not suitable for applications requiring a high degree of water resistance. Polyvinyl alcohol is available in the form of tubing, red sheeting, and a variety of moulded articles.

PROTECTIVE COATINGS

Polyvinyl alcohol has been used as a temporary protective coating to prevent scratching of highly polished metals and plastic materials during fabrication and shipment. Having very little adhesion to these materials and being water soluble, coating can be stripped or washed off earily with water when no longer required. Polyvinyl alcohol is also useful for protecting metals from the tarnishing effect of gases. Coatings based on polyvinyl alcohol are used to protect white sidewall tiles from dirt and scuffing during stripping. The coating is removed by stripping or washing off.

COSMETICS

The emulsifying, binding, film forming, and thickening properties of polyvinyl alcohol have all found use in cosmetic preparations. Highly stable emulsions of natural fats can be prepared with partially hydrolyzed grades of polyvinyl alcohol. Cold creams, cleansing creams, shaving creams, and facial masks based on polyvinyl alcohol have been formulated.

• Chapter 10 •

PVC RESINS & PLASTISOLS

INTRODUCTION

The vast majority or PVC homopolymer and copolymer resins are polymerised in a suspension system and hence are referred to as suspension or general purpose resins. Suspension resins are used in the calender and extrusion processing of vinyl plastics. Suspension resins will vary in particle size but the most common type, the hot dry blend variety, falls between 75 and 200 m in diameter. Speciality types fall in the 200-350 m range. Other speciality types fall between 30 and 125 m. In any event, such resins are granular in nature with a porous surface. The intermediate and larger particle types are free flowing powders by virtue of their size.

Suspension resins are mixed and milled with plasticizer and other components of a vinyl compound with heat and pressure, then formed into a useful shape, be it a calendered film for shower curtains, or calender sheeting for pool linings, or an extruded insulation coating over wire. The equipment used for processing suspension resins, such as high speed miners, Banburry mills, calenders and extruders, are capable of bringing the vinyl plastic mix to the required processing temperature and are massive enough to exert the force necessary to form this thermoplastic mass of plastic material.

Dispersion grade vinyl resins are a fine particle size by comparison with the suspension type. Dispersion grade resin is talc-like in quality i.e. not grainy, and has a no-flow quality because of its fine particle size. This type of resin is also known as a stir-in type or plastisol or organosol type.

A plasticol is, therefore, a dispersion of this fine particle, size type PVC resin in plasticizer. A stable paste is formed whose viscosity properties will depend upon the particular properties of the resin used and the plasticizer level and type. This paste is formed by simply mixing the resin into the plasticizer with sufficient shearing shearing action to ensure a reasonable dispersion of the resin particles in the plasticizer. The ability to form a stable paste is dependent upon the particle size of the resin and emulsifier coating on the resin, as will be discussed.

After preparation this liquid vinyl system may be spread onto a cloth, paper or metal substrate, or otherwise cast or slushed into a mould. In all cases the liquid nature of the plastisol system is the key to its ready applications.

After coating or moulding, heat is applied. This causes the PVC resin particles to dissolve in the plasticizer. Upon cooling, this solution of PVC polymer in plasticizer possesses all the excellent properties of vinyl plastics. The various changes a plastisol system goes through from its initial liquid state to its fused condition are schematically shown in Fig. 12.0.

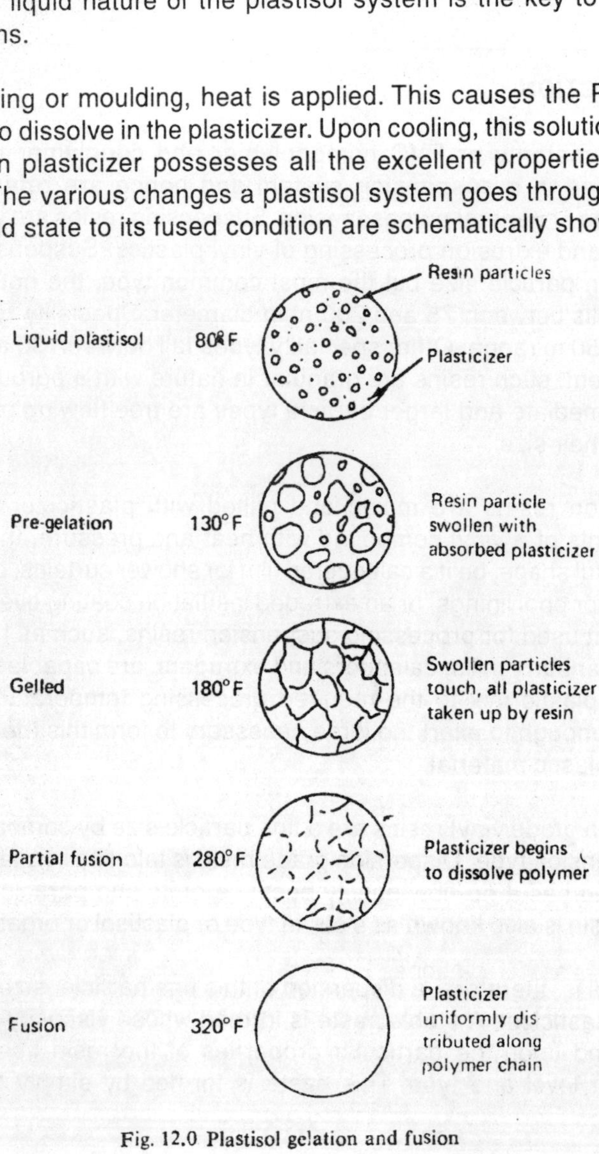

Fig. 12.0 Plastisol gelation and fusion

The top circle in the above figure depicts the tiny particles of a dispersion grade or plastisol resin uniformally dispersed throughout the continuous phase, i.e. the plasticizer. It is in this stage that the plastisol is coated, dipped, moulded or sprayed. As soon as the coating process is accomplished, heat is applied to the vinyl. The initial response of the system to this heat is for the plasticizer to begin solvating the resin particles. This rapid migration of plasticizer inot the resin particle causes it to swell until the plasticizer is absorbed by the particle. The plastisol loses its fluidity, since the external phase, the plasticizer, having been imbibed by the resin, is no longer available to fluidize the system. At this point the physical state of plastic is not unlike swiss cheese, i.e. dry, crumbly, with no cohesive strength. The plastisol enters the gel state when its temperature reaches approximately 180° F, but this will vary up or down depending upon resin type and plasticizer type and level.

As heating continues, at 280° F the molecules of plasticizer begin to work their way between the polymer units and fusion begins. If the plastic were cooled after being brought to the temperature and no more, there would be cohesive mass, but with a minimum of physical strength. Full fusion, i.e. full strength, is accomplished when the plastic mass is brought to approximately 325° F before cooling. Here too, the optimum fusion temperature will again depend on the resin type and plasticizer type. It is interesting to note that in the calendering and extrusion processes the vinyl compound is brought to its fluming of fusion temperature by both adding heat from an external source and by mechanically working the compound. In the plastisol system the plastic mass is not worked. All the fusion heat comes from an external source.

DISPERSION RESIN MANUFACTURE

Plastisol resins are polymerized in latex form, First, vinyl chloride monomer (VCM) is added to the water phase, in which it disperses as droplets. Some monomer dissolves in the water and migrates to a polymerization site where the VCM adds onto other VCM units to form a polymer. This polymer grows to a molecular weight controlled by the temperature of the reaction. A high polymerization temperature causes the reaction to proceed rapidly, resulting in many low molecular weight polymer units. Low temperatures allow the polymerization to span a longer time period, hence providing time for the polymer to grow a higher molecular weight. Catalyst is required to initiate the reaction and keep it going. Emulsifier is necessary to product the tiny emulsion sized particles from coagulating after they form.

There are other processes. One of these involves the homogenization of monomer droplets in the water phase prior to polymerization. Here the emulsifier acts to protect these monomer droplets as they polymerize in situ. In this case the catalyst must be soluble in monomer droplet to work effectively.

In any case, a latex of polymer particles is formed and to render this into a useful form, the resin must now be separated from the water plase. This drying step in generally accomplished by drying the latex in a spray dryer, where under considerable pressure the latex stream is broken up into fine spray droplets, then mixed with volumes of hot air which flash away the water. Now the virtually dry resin drops to the bottom of the dryer where it is conducted on a stream of air to a grinder. The grinder acts to reduce any resin dusters that may have developed in the latex or in the dryer. In this way latex at 35 per cent PVC-65 per cent water, for example, is dried to its dry powder form with approximately 3 per cent moisture. This 3 per cent moisture level will subsequently reduce to less than 1 per cent if the resin is stored under relatively dry ambient conditions.

Polymerization of VCM with a comonomer such as vinyl acetate produces a copolymer material. Its properties are similar to those of a homopolymer resin, and the essential differences will be discussed. Generally, the level of comonomer falls between 5-10 per cent of the resin by weight.

PROPERTIES OF THE DISPERSION RESIN

A plastisol resin may be characterized by a number of basic properties associated directly with the resin itself. These include.

1. polymer, i.e. homopolymer of vinyl chloride or a copolymer of vinyl chlorided with a smaller amount of comonomer generally vinyl acetate.

2. molecular weight of the homopolymer or copolymer.

3. particle size distribution of the finished resin, including presence of agglomerates of resin particles.

4. type and level of emulsifier present as a coating on each resin particle.

It is well to note that the particle size distribution and the emulsifier content of the resin in its finished or dry form may not be what it was in latex form during its manufacture. This is so since the effective particle size may be altered through particle agglomeration in the latex or in spray drying with subsequent agglomerate breakdown in the grinder. Likewise, emulsifiers and other additives not present nor needed for polymerization may be added to the latex or to the dried and ground resin. Such materials are added to enhance plastisol properties.

PASTE FORMING PROPERTIES

The case with which virtually all plastisol resins mix with plasticizer to form a smooth stable paste is due to the fine particle size and the emulsifier coating on the resin particles. The emulsifier coating encapsulating each resin particle aids the wetting of each particle by the plasticizer phase.

Plastisol resin is vacuum compacted into its bag container. This is usually the commercial form of the resin. The densification of the resin in this way can lead to a minor increase in mixing effort in terms of torque and/or time to effect a complete dispersion of polymer particle in plasticizer. In any event, the plaste so formed is generally quite stable and will, if kept at or near room temperature remain so indefinitely. Resins with coarse agglomerates and for wetting properties may show evidence of agglomerate settling, particularly in low viscosity compounds. This shows up as a sludge at the bottom of the storage vessel. This sludge will generally redisperse with agitation. Some resins increase in viscosity over a period of time. A portion of this increase is thixotropic in nature and with agitation the compound will revert to a lower viscosity state. A portion of this viscosity increase is permanent. The reversible portion of this viscosity increase is atributed to the resin particles flocculating into a loose network. If plasticizer penetrates into the particle we have the irreversible effect, or permanent viscosity increase.

Resins vary in their ability to form fluid pastes at low plasticizer levels without the benefit of diluents. This is function of their particle size distribution. Resins exhibiting an optimum distribution of large and small particles,such that maximum packing of the small particles in the voids between the large particles is achieved, possess paste-forming properties at the lowest plasticizer levels. At all plasticizer levels the particle size distribution of the resin plays an important role in shaping the general rhological properties of plastisol compounds based on these resins.

AIR RELEASE

Vast quantities of air bubbles are entrained in the compound during its preparation. The air release properties of a plastisol refer to the ease with which these air bubbles are released by the compound. These may be subsequently removed in a vacuum deaerator and in some cases this deaeration may be accomplised during the mixing operation itself. This latter procedure involves the use of special mixers that will pull a vacuum whole mixing.

Subsequently, during the coating, moulding or otherwise processing of the compound, additional quantities of air may be entrained. For example, the rolling bank, behind the knife in a knife coater or in a coating through of a reverse roll coater, will gulp in air bubbles. These bubbles if not sheared out as the compound is coated under the knife or through the rolls, may show up as defects in the coating. Pigmented coatings and embossed coatings tend to be less sensitive in this respect, but clear organsol coatings, on the other hand, cannot tolerate poor air release since the bubbles trapped in the film are quite visible. If enough are present, they will observe the printed pattern the organsol is coated over to protect.

There is the possibility that the spread out compound will spontaneously release these air bubbles while it is still fluid, between the coating machine and its gelation point in the oven. However, high coating speeds reduce this interval of time for spontaneous bubbles break to occur. Likewise, the excess compound drained out of the mould in the slush moulding process may trap air bubbles, which, on the next moulding cycle, will show up as defects unless spontaneously burst or are mechanically removed from the compound. Mechanically deaerating a compound overcomes to some extent any inherent deficiencies the compound has in this respect. Here the general viscosity level of this compound correlates with its ability to process through the deaeration equipment, but the amount of frothing the compound will do under a vacuum is related to the inherent ability of the compound to release air. Heavy frothing under vacuum may slow the deaeration process or otherwise complicate it, as will a high compound viscosity.

GELATION PROPERTIES

The rate at which a plastisol compound proceeds from its fluid to its gelled state is a matter of considerable importance in many applications. This is particularly true where gelation is used to control the thickness of plastisizer deposited on the surface of a mould, as is the case in slush moulding and hot dipping. Although the gelation characteristics of a plastisol are controlled to a major extent by plasticizer selection, the most practical means by which to achieve gelation control is again through resin selection. In general, resins with a low-shear viscosity tend to be higher in gelation temperature and the reverse is true. This is so because it simply takes longer for a compound based on a low-shear viscosity resin to get to its gelation point, thereby reflecting itself in a higher gel temperature.

In a homologus series of resins where the only variable is molecular weight, it is found that the lower molecular weight resins provide lower gelation temperatures. However, different resins with equivalent low shear viscosity and equivalent molecular weights may have widely different gelation characteristics. This is attributed to the emulsifier on the resin particle and the speed with which it is dissolved by the plasticizer penetrates into the resin particle.

In summary, then, the gelation property of a resin is a function of its general low shear viscosity level and its molecular weight. Although a resin may vary in viscosity from lot to lot, this is not necessarily picked up as a variation in gelation temperature. In a homologus series, decreasing molecular weight results in a decrease in gelation temperature as does the use of a copolymer resin.

FUSION

With the application of fusion heat, molecules of plasticizer are driven between the polymer chains in such a way that upon cooling the plastic has useful physical strength. We have, in effect a solid solution of polymer in plasticizer. Establishing the oven temperature/time conditions needed to effect optimum fusion for a vinyl plastisol is best done by the pragmatic method of preparing films on glass or metel plates and fusing them in an oven under various temperatures/time conditions.

It has been found that once a vinyl film has been left in the oven long enough for it to come to the temperature of the air in the oven, it will, when cooled, assume the tensile strength associated with that temperature. Prolonged exposure of the film beyond that time needed to bring it to the oven temperature does not increase the physical strength of the film.

GLOSS AND CLARITY

Many plastisol products are embossed, for example, when coated cloth is used for upholstery and garment applications. Other products require a dull finish, and here plastisol blending resins are used to good advantage.

On the other hand, some clothing and boot applications on the cloth known as the "wet look". Similarly, products used in highly styled ladies' shoes require a high gloss, as so many plastisol and evganesol flooring products.

Plastisol resins are inherently glossy and the degree to which they are fused certainly has a bearing on their gloss, i.e. higher fusion temperatures result in improved gloss. However, as a practical matter, extra fusion is not feasible since most substrates cannot tolerate an exposure to high temperature, nor do modern processing speeds allow for anything but a minimal exposure to heat. Another approach to high gloss is to reduce the molecular weight of the resin used, but here the resulting loss in physical strength may not make this a practical approach either.

The basic dispersion resin particle is in the micron range. More specifically, dispersion resin particles generally fall between 2-2M. With the latter size as a maximum, the development of high gloss would not be a problem since a 2M particle when plasticizer, as occurs during fusion, will melt down to form a continuous and smooth surface. However, the agglomeration of resin particles that may occur in the resin manufacturing process provides the source of large particles that do not completely flux out in the film during fusion, resulting in a loss of both gloss and clarity.

These agglomerates may form while the resin is still in latex form, during and after polymerization. Next, the spray drying process itself may be the source of agglmoerates. Finally, if the grinding step does not reduce the agglomerates formed in the latex or dryer back to, or near, their original particle size, agglomerates find their way into the plastisol mix. These agglomerates are generally tight enough to resist any size reduction through the usual compound mixing operation. In those cases where a plastisol is passed through a paint mill, some improvement may result, but this step is not too frequently practised for plastisols,and almost never in the case of organsols. The presence of these agglomerates will interefere with the continuity of the film and consequently reduce both clarity and gloss.

HEAT STABILITY

The PVC polymer is not particularly heat stable, and unless protected, decomposes when exposed to the elevated temperatures associated with fusion. The decomposition product is HCI, and the eveolved HCI acts to further decompose the vinyl, i.e. vinyl decomposition is autocatalytic. In virtually all formulations, it is necessary, therefore, to prodect the vinyl from this heat degradation effect. This is accomplished by including in the formulation certain chemicals which function as heat stabilizers. These stabilizers act to chemically absorb the evolving HCl, thereby reducing its catalytic influence to the extent that vinyls may be processed at temperatures in the 300°-400° F range without any significant loss in properties, principally colour, due to thermal degradation.

Vinyl stabilizers are based on matallic compounds of barium, cadmium, zinc, lead, and tin. In chemically blown vinyl foam work, lead and zinc are most applicable since they also act as a catalyst for the chemical blowing agent. The conventional stabilizer system based on barium, cadmium and zinc is designed to provide maximum heat stability with a minimum of yellowing during the fusion process. Barium is most effective in protecting the compound from the harmful effect of high fusion temperatures and extended periods at these temperatures. But with barium used alone, the vinyl would quickly develop a yellow cast. Cadmium and zinc are not effective for long term heat exposure during fusion, but are very effective stabilisers during the early stage of fusion and thereby minimize yellowing.

COMPOUNDING OF PLASTISOLS

The multitude of applications in which vinyl plastisols are used today has triggred development of a vast number of materials such as new plasticizers, stabilizers, fillers, viscosity modifiers, etc. Through proper combination of these ingredients a wide range of properties can be formulated into a vinyl compound, e.g. low temperature flexibility, low fogging, non-toxicity, good viscosity ageing characteristics. A given ingredients will affect a variety of plastisol's characteristics. For example, a compound containing resin and DOP can be modified for more rapid or lower fusion through use of a higher solvating plasticizer, e.g. butyl benzyl phthalate in place of DOP. As a result fusion time and temperature are decreased, but simultaneously the viscosity of the plastisol will be increased due to the higher solvating power of the BBP. This may or may not be desirable, but it illustrates the point. The compounds must recognise that any compound additive for improvement of one property may alter others.

The constantly increasing number of available compounding ingredients plus many variables which exist in compounding make it impossible to include sufficient information to cover all the aspects of this field.

COMPOUNDING INGREDIENTS

RESINS

The basic ingredient in every plastisol or organosol is, naturally the resin. Dispersion resins are generally classified by the following three criteria.

Polymer type (Homopolymer or copolymer)
Molecular weight
Size and shape of particles

A copolymer may be necessary in place of a homopolymer in processes which require a low fusion temperature. Oven conditions, processing rates or the heat sensitivity of the substrate to be coated may dictate this choice. Fusion temperature decreases with increasing vinyl acetate content. A 7 per cent acetate copolymer will reach ultimate physical strength at 270°-280° F, whereas a 3 per cent copolymer requires a 310-320° F for complete fusion. In general, copolymers, regardless of the molecular weight, will not reach complete fusion at temperatures below 350° F. Other reasons for employing copolymers over homopolymers are improved adhesion to certain substrates and higher elongation at a given plasticizer level.

Resins of a given molecular weight are usually chosen according to the physical requirements of the finished product. Higher molecular weight resins field higher physicals but require more heat and longer fusion time than lower molecular weight resins. Therefore processing requirements must be considered before making a choice of resin molecular weight.

A factor contributing to the viscosity stability of a plastisol is the size and shape of the resin particles. Dispension resins usually range in particle size between 0.5-2 m The finer particles have a larger total surface area and therefore, higher plasticizer absorption. This will generally result in higher viscosity and poorer viscosity stability. The same principle holds true for particle shape. Irregular shapes have a larger surface area than spherical shapes and therefore higher viscosities are obtained.

BLENDING OR EXTENDING RESINS

Blending resins are frequently used in plastisol compounds. They have a particle size range of 10-150 m and are primarily used to lower the cost of the formulation. Blending resins are available both as copolymers and homopolymers.

Stabilizers are improved through the addition of epoxidised oils and phosphites (chelators)

THICKENERS

For certain applications, a compound must have a low, high shear viscosity, as well as a high yield. In spray coating, for example, the plastisol must flow readily through a nozzle at high shear but must not sag after deposition on the surface. This type of rheological behaviour is referred to as a high pseudoplastic ratio, or more commonly, as thixotropic. High viscosities can generally be obtained by decreasing the plasticizer level, but if flexibility is to be retained and pseudoplasticity is required, special thickeners or fillers may be added.

SURFACTANTS

The addition of a surfactant contributes long term heat stability; cadmium and zinc help maintain light colours. Frequently, these examples of other properties are listed in Table 12.0.

TABLE 12.0

PLASTISOLS - EFFECTS OF PLASTICIZER SELECTION

Property	Plasticizer
Low Fusion temperature	BBP, BOP, TCP
Low viscosity	NODP, DCP, DIDA
High viscosity	BBP,TCP, polymerics
Flame retardance	Phosphates, chlorinated waxes
Good electricals	Trimellitatos, electrical grades of phthalate plasticizers
Low temperature flexibility	Adipates, azelates sabacetes
Stain resistance	BBP, high efficiency primaries
Low volatility	Polymerics, trimellitates, DTDP, DIDP, NODP
Low migration	Polymerics, trimellitates, DTDP, DIDP, NODP
Non-fogging	Polymerics, trimellitates, DTDP, DIDP

In a range of molecular weights and particle sizes, they usually have low oil absorption, which reduces the viscosity of the plastisol at a given plasticizer level. They also produce a grassy surface in coatings and mouldings, reducing surface gloss.

PLASTICIZERS

Plasticizers are categorised either by function or structure. Structurally, they may be classed as monomeric or polymeric, and functionally, as secondary.

Simple monoesters are diesters of monobasic and dibasic acids or dihydric alcohols. Due to their molecular weight, polymeric plasticizers are higher in viscosity. In plastisol compounding this is generally a disadvantage which limits usage.

Plasticizers which have good permanance, compatibility and plasticizing efficiency are considered primary. Conversely, less compatible plasticizers with low plasticizing efficiency are considered primary.

The quantity of plasticizer required to produce a specific elongation or softness is a measure of its efficiency. With few exceptions, the most efficient plasticizers are fastest fusing.

HEAT STABILIZERS

Since vinyl chloride polymers degrade from the heat required for processing, a stabilizer must be added to the system.

Stabilizers have the ability to accept the Hol which is released from the polymer as a result of degradation, The stabiliser also prevents discoloration from this degradation process. The stabilizer selected must be compatible with the other ingredients in a system and should disperse readily.

In plastisols, the most commonly used stabilizers are the barium cadmium-zinc types. In those synergistic systems barium generally improves outdoor weathering, but the latter should be used with caution since the increased absorption of heat with dark coloured materials may adversely affect aging. Whereas organic pigments may be affected by changes in pH, the cadmium-selemide pigments are quite insensitive. They also have good heat and light stability but are rather poor in colour intensity.

FILLERS

Another ingredient frequently used in non-clear formulations is filler. Ground whitings, precipitated and activated chalks, clays, ground silica, precipitated calcium carbonates, calcium silicates, asbestos etc. are commonly used in formulations. Although these materials are primarily used for cost reduction, they do impart certain desirable qualities, e.g. better electrical properties, reduced tackiness, and better scuff resistance.

Another disadvantage of high filler loadings is the increase in active agent which serves to lower viscosity and improve viscosity stability and air release. Polyethylene glycol derivatives and other surfactants are known to be effective. Depending on the formulation, 0.5-1.5 of a surfactant will generally lower the viscosity by 30-40 per cent.

PIGMENTS

When pigments are incorporated in a plastisol formulation, care must be taken that complete disperion of these pigments will occur. This is best achieved by predispersing the powdered pigments with plasticizer on a ball mill or three rose paint mill, followed by addition to the plastisol during the mixing cycle.

Among the most commonly used pigments are titanium dioxide, carbon black, iron and coloured red salts. A number of organic pigments may also be used.

Titanium dioxide viscosity which results in high oil absorption as well as small particle size, reduces the amount of plasticizer in the plastisol, causing an increase in viscosity.

BLOWING AGENTS

The most commonly used chemical blowing agent is azodicarbonamide which produces foam with a high closed cell content. Through selection of the heat stabilizer-activator, the temperature at which expansion will occur can be adjusted. Depending on the characteristics of the resin and other ingredients in a formulation, a blowing agent will be chosen which will yield the desired cell structure and foam density at the required temperature. For example with a resin that fuses at 320° F, a blowing system would be chosen which decomposes at 340° F. This assures retention of the gas bubbles within the plastisol and produces lowest possible foam density.

Another method that is used involves the mechanical whipping of plastisols. A silicone surfactant is added to control the cell size, foam density and cell stability. In this method, the plastisol formulation contains no blowing agent. This type of foam is applied by knife and neither expands nor contracts during the fusing cycle. A fine uniform cell structure is produced. A wide range of foam types and desnities can be obtained with this process. Foam densities as low as 12-14 lb/ft^3 are possible.

SOLVENTS AND DILUENTS

Volatile additives are used to lower the viscosity of a plastisol, extending their usefulness to many coating applications. These solvents known as dispersants and diluents affect the organosol in a somewhat different manner.

Diluents have somewhat low solvating power and may be used alone or in combination with the higher solvating dispersants. Lowest viscosity is obtained with a correct balance of these two materials. The more commonly used diluents are generally inexpensive aliphatic hydrocarbon solvents which are available in a broad range of boiling points. Typical dispersants, such as the ketones and aromatic solvents, are more polar and generally more volatile, (e.g. MIBK). Toluene and xylene-solvents may be added directly to the plastisol during preparation or just prior to use.

COMPOUNDING FOR SPECIFIC PLASTISOL PROPERTIES

VISCOSITY

The viscosity of a plastisol is influenced by factors such as:

1. Particle size and type of resin
2. Type and amount of plasticizer
3. Surfactants
4. Amount and type of filler
5. Amount and type of blending resin
6. Mixing procedure

To lower the viscosity of a plastisol, one or more of the following modifications can be employed.

1. Change from copolymer to homopolymer; change to coarser particles size resin.

2. Change from higher to lower solvating plasticizer, increase level of plasticizer, add low solvating secondaries.

3. Add surfactant or increase amount already present.

4. Decrease to filler level or change to filler with lower oil absorption.

HARDNESS

The hardness of a fused plastisol is primarily a function of the amount and efficiency of the plasticizer present in the formulation. Thus, to decrease hardness one can supply; (1) increase plasticizer, (2) use a more efficient plastisizer.

Step (1) usually decreases viscosity, whereas step (2) will cause the viscosity to increase, due to the higher solvating power of the more efficient plasticizer.

FUSION AND GELATION TEMPERATURE

A plastisol with a low gelation temperature also has a low fusion temperature. Fusion temperature is a function of the type of resin, molecular weight and choice of plasticizer.

PREPARATION OF PLASTISOLS

In order to properly discuss the preparation of plastisols and organosols or non-aqueous vinyl dispersions all of the steps involved from the handling of incoming raw materials through the storage of the finished dispersion must be considered. These areas are discussed in the same sequence as they occur in the plant, e.g. raw material handling, mixing (equipment and procedures), deaeration, and, finally handling of the finished product.

Formulations of vinyl dispersions vary over a wide range. For the purposes of this discussion, the following tabulation covers the range of ingredients most commonly employed, together with a typical formulation.

Ingredients	*Normal Range*	*Typical Value*
Dispersion resin	60-100	90
Extender resin	0-40	10
Plasticizer	30-100	50
Stabilizer	1-5	3
Filler	0-50	10
Pigment	0-5	1
Volatile diluent	0-10	3
Miscellaneous additives	0-5	0.5

Homopolymers can be fused at 300° F. Those with higher molecular weight require higher temperatures. Copolymers containin g approximately 7% vinyl acetate will fuse at 380° F and the temperature increases with decreasing acetate content. The table below lists some of the commonly used in order to fusion temperatures :

BBP	Lowest	fusion
TCP		
BOP		
DOP		
DIOP		
DIDP		
DOA		
DOZ		
DDA	Higher	fusion

To summarize the followinց steps can be taken to lower the temperature.

1. Use lower molecular weight resin
2. Substitute copolymer for homopolymer
3. Substitute monomeric for polymeric

PHYSICAL PROPERTIES

Physical strength properties of a compound are primarily a function of the molecular weight of the resin, the amount used and filler content and fusion conditions.

Therefore, ultimate tensile and tear strength is obtained by :

1. Use of highest molecular weight resin.
2. Use of sufficient processing time and temperature for complete fusion.

LOW TEMPERATURE FLEXIBILITY

Resistance to low temperature brittleness can be improved with apliphatic ester plasticizers such as the adipates, sebacates and azeleates.

GLOSS

The gloss of a fused plastisol is a function of the degree of fusion, the particle size of the resins and solid fillers, and the smoothness of the mould surface. High gloss surfaces can be produced as follows.

1. Pure more completely
2. Use finest particle size dispersion resins and fillers
3. Eliminate coarse blending resins and fillers
4. Polish mould surfaces.

To reduce gloss, steps (1) through (4) can be reversed or an embossing roll can be used on the coating line.

CLARITY

Clarity or present light transmission of a fused plastisol is controlled by a variety of factors, such as the degree of fusion, the type of plasticizers and the amount and type of resins and fillers in the plastisol. Manufacturers of resins, plasticizers and stabilizers usually have recommendations available and should be consulted for such informations.

HEAT STABILITY

Heat stability depends on the processing conditions of the plastisol and colour requirements for the finished article. Liquid barium-cadmium-zinc types are the most commonly used in plastisol applications. Suitable stabilizers for light coloured products, as well as for severe conditions, can be obtained for most processing conditions, 2-3 part of stabiliser per hundred parts of resin are sufficient. Mild processing conditions such as short fusion cycles and low fusion temperatures may require less.

Low fusing copolymer plastisols used as adhesives for lamination may not be required.

FLAME RETARDANCE

PVC, with its high chlorine content, is salt extinguishing but the commonly used plasticizers are flammable.

Therefore, additives are required for compounds which contain more than 30 parts of plasticizer for self-extinguishing properties. Incorporation of 1-3 phr. of antimony trioxide or the addition or phosphate or chlorinated paraffin plasticizers gives good results; combinations of these materials can also be used.

NON-FOGGING

With the increased usage of vinyls in automotive applications and growing interest in safety, non-fogging properties have become increasingly important. Fogging is the condensation of volatiles from the vinyl compound onto interior vindow surfaces, reducing visibility.

Volatile plasticizers and volatile components in resins and stabilizers are the most serious offendres. Higher boiling plasticizers, e.g. NDOP, trimelliates and polymerics are frequently suitable. With special gradeds of resins, satisfactory fogging results are available.

FORMULATIONS

General starting point formulations for the various applications are listed below.

COATING

One of the most important application areas is the coating of fabrics and other flat continuous substrates using a knife or roll coating technique. Some general requirements for a plastisol and suggested formulations are shown below.

APPLICATIONS	SOME GENERAL REQUIREMENTS
Loose weave substrate; knife coating; shear	Medium viscosity at low and high rates; high yield.

Tight weave or continuous substrate; roller coating	Low viscosity at both low and high shear; high yield.
Tight weave or continuous substrate	Low viscosity at both low and high shear.
Strand coating	Low viscosity at both low and high shear, high yield; rapid gelation rate.

Suggested starting point formulations for these applications are as follows.

KNIFE COATING

Ingredients	*Parts*
Plastisol resin hompolymer	100
DOP	36
DOA or DOS	20
Epoxy plasticizer	5
$CaCO_3$	10-30
Ba-Cd-Zn stabilizer	3
Tio_2	5
Mineral spirits	10 or as required
Toluene or MIBK	5 or as required

STRAND COATING

Plastisol resin homopolymer	100
DOP	40
DOA	25
Antimony oxide dispersion	6-8
Epoxy plasticizer	5
$CaCO_3$	0-15
Ba-Cd stabilizer	2-3

SPRAY COATING

This coating technique is often used when irregular shapes or large objects are to be coated. The basic properties of a plastisol for this purpose are low viscosity and high yield.

FORMULATIONS

Ingredients	*Parts*
Plastisol resin homopolymer	80
Extender resin	20
DOP	35
DOA or DOS	15
Epoxy plasticizer	5
TiO_2 paste	5
Filler (high oil absorption)	1-3
$CaCO_3$	10-20
Dibasic lead phosphite	4
VM and P naphtha	10-15 (as required)

CASTING

It is important to maintain a low to medium plastisol viscosity with little or no yield, to permit the flow required for the moulding process. The use of secondary or extender plasticizers helps reduce viscosity. For this type of application, the plastisol should be deaerated before use and should have good air release properties.

A starting formulation for a mould casting application would be as follows.

MOULD CASTING

Plastisol resin homopolymer	60
Blending resin	40
DIDP	25
DIDA	20
Extender plasticizer	10
Epoxy plasticizer	5
Ba-Cd-Zn stabilizer	3
Pigment dispersion	as required

SLUSH AND ROTATIONAL MOULDING

The two methods of moulding are quite similar and require similar plastisol properties.

Blending resins and low solvating plasticizers are effective for producing the low viscosity and low yield. This also tends to increase the gelation temperature, which prevents lip formation or runs on the interior of the moulded articles.

Another requirement of both applications is deaeration prior to use and good air release properties. This is of particular importance in a slush moulding compounds where excess plastisol is poured from the mould and collected in a reservoir for reuse during subsequent moulding steps.

ROTATIONAL MOULDING

Ingredients	*Parts by wt.*
Plastisol resin homopolymer	70
Blending resin	30
DIDP	40
DOA	25
BBP	15
Epoxy plasticizer	5-10
$CaCO_3$	5-20
Ba-Cd-Zn stabilizer (low paste out)	3
Pigment dispersion as required	

SLUSH MOULDING

Plastisol resin homopolymer	70
Blending resin	30
DIOP	30-35
BOP	20
Medium MW polymeric plasticizer	10-15
Epoxy plasticizer	5

$CaCO_3$	5-20
Ba-Cd-Zn stabilizer (low paste out)	3
Pigment dispersion	as required

DIP COATING (HOT AND COLD)

Although these processes both involve the immersion of the mould into the liquid plastisol medium, the basic difference is that in the first process the mould is preheated and in the second it is dipped cold. Each requires a special formulation to prevent the compound from dripping and sagging from the coated part after removal from the plastisol bath.

HOT DIP COATING

Ingredients	*Parts*
Plastisol resin homopolymer	100
DOP	40
DINP	25
Extender plasticizer	10
Gelling agent dispersion	4-5
Epoxy plasticizer	5
Ba-Cd-Zn stabilizer	3
Pigment disperion	as required

A cold dip plastisol is required when the object being coated is thin or is very irregular in thickness. In some applications lower viscosity may be required for dispersion of thin coating. The formulation can be adjusted for this purpose by incorporating a small amount of solvent. Since cold dip formulations generally must predoplastic values for non-sag and high oil absorption filler is recommended. In applications where thick coatings are required, a thirotropic additive may be used. A typical cold dip formulation is as follows.

COLD DIP COATING

Plastisol resin homopolymer	100
DOP	50
DOA or DOS	25

Thickener dispersion	2-4
Precipitated $CaCO_3$	10-20
Epoxy plasticizer	5
Dibasic lead phosphite	4-5
Pigment dispersion	as required
Aliphatic solvent	0-5 (as needed)

FOAMS

Several starting point formulations with brief descriptions of each are as follows.

CHEMICALLY BLOWN FILMS (Basically closed cell structure)

Ingredients	*Soft form*	*Filled Soft form*	*Hard form*
PVC emulsion plastisol resin homo polymer	70	70	70
Extender resin	30	30	30
DOP	20	60	50
BBP	70	10	14
Epoxy plasticizer	5	5	5
Blowing paste azocarbonamide	6	6	6
Zinc blowing catalyst	3	-	-
Dibasic lead phosphite	-	-	6
Ba-Cd-Zn stabilizer	-	3	-
$CaCO_3$	-	20-25	-
Surfactant	1.5	-	-
Approximate foam density lb/ft3	19	21.5	20
Moulding temperature	360° F	360° F	360° F

CHEMICALLY BLOWN OPEN CELL FOAM

Ingredients	*Parts by wt.*
Plastisol resin copolymers	100
DOP or DIDP	50
DDTP	30
Polymeric plasticizer	20
Dupanol ME	2
Neutral calcium petronate	4
Ba-Cd-Zn phosphite	3
Nitrogen & blowing agent	5
Approximate foam density lb/ft^3	17
Moulding temperature	300^0 F

MECHANICALLY FROTHED FOAM OPEN CELL STRUCTURE

Ingredients	*Unfilled*	*Filled*	*General purpose*
Plastisol resin copolymer	80	80	-
Plastisol resin homopoymer	-	-	80
Blending resin	20	20	20
DOP	35-40	35-40	35-40
DIDP	20-25	25-30	30-40
BBP	15-20	15-20	-
Silicone vinyl foam surfactant	4-8	4-8	4-8
$CaCO_3$	-	10-40	10-30
Pigment dispersion	as required		
Foam density lb/ft^3	variable depends on plasticizer levels, as well as frothing equipment and operation.		
	280-300° F 280-300° F		

RAW MATERIALS

As usage of vinyl dispersions continues to grow, several applications have developed where considerable attention to the most efficient handing of the raw materials must be used. These materials divide naturally into two main categories. These are the liquid components, consisting of plasticizers, volatile diluents, wetting agents and most stabilizers, and the dry ingredients, which include resin, filler, pigments and a few stabilizers.

BULK HANDLING

Of the liquid ingredients, only one, the plasticizer, is used in sufficient quantity to warrant special handling consideration. Plasticizers are quite easily handled in bulk and, since they are used in very large volume throughout the vinyl industry, bulk shipping and storage is quite common. Such bulk storage and handling systems consist of standard elements for storing and handling liquids. Since corrosion is not a problem with most plasticizers, common steel can be used in most instances. Vertical steel tanks of from 5000-25,000 gal. capacity are usually recommended. Where usage does not warrant such large storage facilities, 550 gal horizontal be placed either below or above ground. The charging line (usually 2 in. pipe) should be extended to the bottom of the tank to prevent generation of static electricity from the free-falling liquid.

While viscous plasticizers are not widely used in vinyl dispersions, occasionally situations are encountered where low outdoor temperatures are sufficient to increase viscosity to the point where it is necessary to heat the storage tank with external steam coils.

Centrifugal pumps, steel bronze lined, are normally used. The pump should be located and installed so that it can both unload the bulk vehicle to the storage tank and subsequently transfer the plasticizer from storage to production units. A cartridge filter should be installed on the discharge side to remove dirt or other extraneous matter.

STORAGE

The precaution to observe in the storage of raw materials is to avoid conditions which would enable them to pick up moisture. Some fillers, pigments and resins, for instance, will pick up measurable quantities of water when stored under conditions of high temperature and relative humidity. Liquids stored in partially filled containers, open to the atmosphere are liable to pick up moisture through condensation during periods of sudden temperature range. This moisture, if carried into the vinyl dispersion, can create problems in some applications. In such cases, it must be removed by techniques described later in the section on deaeration, or special ingredients, such as calcium oxide, must be added to the formula to counteract its presence.

MIXING EQUIPMENT

Vinyl dispersion resins currently used in the preparation of plastisols and organosols are characterized as "stir-in" resins. The description was originally coined differentiate between these resins and earlier products. These precurser products required grinding type mixing, such as normally used with colour pigments, in order to achieve adequate dispersion. While relatively simple stirring techniques are indeed now used for making vinyl dispersions, considerable care in the choice of mixing equipment is needed to achieve satisfactory results.

The principal function which must be perfomed in the mixing of simpler forms of vinyl dispersion is to reduce the degree of agglomeration persent in the dry resin particles as they are dispersed throughout the liquid medium. To do this adequately the resin particles must be subjected to at least moderate shearing action in a fashion which will minimize any heat build up in the overall batch during the mixing cycle. If the temperature of the dispersion is not kept under control during mixing, premature solvation of the resin may begin to occur. The solvation results in a generally undesirable increase in viscosity or even gelation of the dispersion. While safe mixing temperatures will vary considerably with different types of formulations, normal, good practice will keep mixing temperatures below 90 F throughout a conventional mixing cycle.

To achieve good shearing action with little attendant temperature build up, two basic types of mixing actions are in general use.

HIGH SPEED MIXERS

This utilizes a specially desipned agitator, blade operating at very high rpm to create extreme turbulence in the area of the mix immediately surrounding the mixing blade. In a mixer setup, particles being dispersed are deagglomerated by high velocity impact with one another and also by shearing forces. Excessive heat buildup is avoided by doing intensive shearing on only a small percentage of the total mix at any given moment. The heat generated in the intensive zone is thus dissipated throughout the mix. Complete dispersion can usually be achieved rapidly before the total mix becomes overheated. A normal mixing cycle is about 15-30 min. Materials mixed in this matter must be sufficiently fluid in nature to permit generation of the necessary high turbulence in the primary mixing area. While no precise upper viscosity limit can be given, since different materials require varying amounts of shear to effect dipersion, commercial practice for mixers employing this principle is for materials generally below 20,000 cps in batches from 2-2000 gal in size. Impeller speeds used range from 600-6000 rpm depending on batch size and viscosity.

PASTE & DOUGH MIXERS

The second major category of mixer in preparing vinyl dispersions utilizes the shearing forces developed in continuous kneading of a dough like mass to achieve particle deagglomeration. Indeed, at least one popular mixer of this type has been designed primarily for use by the baking industry. Since there are many ways in which the necessary kneading action can be imparted to a mix, equipment in this general category includes a rather wide variety of designs.

Most are variations of one sort or another in pony or change can type mixers. Both single and double designs are common. In most instances a motion or planetary type mixing action is used. By utilizing relativley low mixing speeds, excessive heat build up is avoided. Mixing cycles are generally in the 30-60 min. range. Depending on specific design, mixers of this type can handle extremely viscous putty-like materials but can be used to prepare low viscosity dispersions. In the latter instance, dispersion is accomplished by withholding a portion of the liquid ingredients in the system and thus dispersing the solid materials in a heavy paste. The mix is then let down to the desired final viscosity by adding the balance of the liquids. Mixers of this type are necessarily of somewhat limited capacity, ranging from 1 gal. or less to a practical maximum of about 300 gal.

OTHER TYPE MIXERS

One unique type of mixer which has recently obtained a high degree of industrial acceptance is shaped like an inverted cone. It employs a screw flight agitator which rotates on its oven axis while arbiting the periphery of the conical tank.

This principle effects a useful compromise between the two classes of mixers previously described. Viscosities of the heaviest materials which cna be handled satisfactorily are at least double of those which can be processed in heavier duty dough mixers. Capacities of the new design mixer are quite broad, ranging from under 10 to over 5000 gal.

In addition to the principal types described above, a wide variety of other types of equipment are used to a lesser extent, either for special processing needs or where less demanding requirements permit their use.

For lighter viscosity plastisols where degree of dispersion is not critical, simple slow speed paddle mixers and ribbon blenders are sometimes used.

Where very good dispersion of resin and other solid ingredients such as fillers and pigments is required, equipment typical of the paint industry is still employed, such as ball or pebble mills for lighter viscosity dispersions and three roll mills for heavier, more viscous ones.

Other types of pigment dispersing equipment, such as colloid mills, are generally unsatisfactory, however, they generate too much heat during mixing.

MIXING PROCEDURES

Mixing procedures used in preparation of vinyl dispersions are influenced principally by the type of mixing equipment used.

HIGH SPEED - LOW VISCOSITY

With high speed agitation mixers, which operate best at low viscosity, the general practice is to add all of the liquid ingredients ot the mixer first and to blend these briefly. Resin and other dry ingredients are then added. These are generally not added all at once, but in relatively large increments over a short period of time. Mixing is then continued until the desired degree of dispersion is achieved. Total mixing time is short, rarely exceeding 30 min. If longer mixing cycles are used, care must be taken to ensure that the mix does not overheat.

The same basic procedure is used with other low viscosity oriented types of mixers, such as paddle mixers and ribbon blenders. Since these mixers are less efficient, however, much longer cycles are normally required, commonly in the 1-2 hr. range. Heat build up is seldom a problem.

After all of the dry ingredients are charged, mixing of the stiff paste is continued as in first procedure. Likewise, after complete dispersion is achieved, the batch is let down with the balance of the liquids and mixed until uniform.

ORGANOSOLS

Organsols are a dispersion of solid particles in an organic liquid, generally consisting of a mixture of plasticizers and solvents. Upon addition of the resin to the liquid, the viscosity of the mixture is very high, but then as dispersion and break down of the agglomerates proceeds, the viscosity drops rapidly to a minimum. Further mixing results in an increase in viscosity possibly due to over-solvation of the particles by the dispersion medium.

The dispersion medium for a polyvinyl chloride resin organsols consists of a weak solvent and a strong solvent termed respectively a diluent and dispersant. Too much diluent causes an increase in viscosity due to flocculation of the particles. This is also evidenced by a grainy, coarse structure of the organsol. On the other hand, too much diluent results in over solvation of the particles and if carried to extremes, may increase the viscosity to the point of gelation. The minimum viscosity point is the ideal balance of diluent and dispersant. It is sometimes desirable to use the organsol slightly on the dispersant-rich side. If the resin is a little over-solvated, a smooth shear thinning dispersion results. This avoids the danger, during evaporation of the solvent, of a shift to the diluent-rich side with resultant flocculation; the dispersant promotes fusion of the particles.

The organsol may now be applied by various coating methods to form a film on a substrate and then is usually heated rapidly to start fusion before all the dispersion medium is gone. This aids in the fusion. However, the film must not be heated too rapidly or blistering will occur. There are several advantages of organsol coating techniques over solvent coating. For a given viscosity, the solids concentration of an organsol may be much higher than a solution. Second, a much higher molecular weight resin may be used. The use of less expensive solvents is possible, and the rate of evaporation from an organsol is much faster than from a solvent because there is less affinity of a solvent for the polymer in an organsol.

The field of decorative and protective coatings constitutes one of the important outlets for polyvinyl chlorided homopolymers and copolymers. To utilize these resins in solution coatings, a compromise in drawn between the excellent chemical resistance of the homopolymer of vinyl chloride and the good solubility imparted by the copolymer. Reference to vinyl solution coatings, therefore, usually implies the use of a vinyl chloride-vinyl acetate copolymer. In organsols, however, initial solubility consideratinos are avoided since these systems are not solutions, but are dispersions of polymer particles in an organic medium. Therefore, organsol coatings can take advantage of the toughness, formability, chemical inertness, abrasion resistance and weatherability that high molecular weight and 100% polyvinyl chloride resins confer.

Organsols in a way are solvent thinned versions of plastisols. In use, most dispersion coatings contain some solvent for ease of application and hence fall into the organsol class by this definition. It is widely accepted in the field today that a plastisol can contain up to 10 per cent volatile thinner, but any PVC dispersion system with more than 10 per cent volatile thinner is regarded as an organsol. One worker regards organsol as those systems which do not contain enough plasticizer to form a wet paste in the absence of the volatile thinners. While the amount of plasticizer required to form a paste is largely dependent on the properties of the particular resin being used, this viewpoint does not serve to point out why organsols were a natural outgrowth of plastisols. If fluidity did not result in the resin plasticizer mixture at the level of plasticizer dictated by the end use requirements, then it became a simple matter to obtain the required fluidity by the addition of volatile thinner, while maintaining the resin-plasticizer which was required. Thus, for resin plasticizer mixtures of 50 phr plasticizer or greater, it is possible to have plastisols.

Today, vinyl dispersion resins in the market:(1) resins characterized by high molecular weight and low emulsifier content, designed primarily for organsols, (2) resins that have higher soap content and faster gelling properties that are intended mainly for plastisols, and (3) special resins for adjusting plastisol and organsol rheological properties and resins which fuse at temperatures as low as 275° F. Dispersion resins in this category are copolymers of vinyl chloride and other monomers.

When PVC dispersion resins are mixed with plasticizers, the mixture will remain dry until an amount of plasticizer has been added which is equal to the amount that can be absorbed or imbided by the resin particles. This amount was termed the "bound" plasticizer by Hay. The system at this resin-plasticizer ratio is a heavy paste. To obtain fluidity it is necessary to occupy with plasticizer the voids that enist between the resin particles that are now swollen by the "bound" plasticizer. The additional amount of plasticizer required for flow exists outside the resin phase and is called "free" plasticizer.

The quantity of "bound" plasticizer is normally about 50 parts plasticizer per 100 parts resin. The amount of "bound" plasticizer depends on many factors. Some of these are : average particle size of the resin, particle size distribution, surface area of the resin, resin porosity, and solvent power of the plasticizer for the resin. As additional or "free" plasticizer is added to obtain flow, the viscosity level attained will be directly related to the viscosity of the plasticizer itself. This is readily predicted by the Hay concept and has been observed by numerous workers in the field.

Organsols present a somewhat different situation in that the amount of plasticizer used is almost always considerably less than the "bound" amount. Indeed, organsols for coatings applications seldom exceed 25 phr plasticiser. The formulation technique, then, becomes one of adding the proper amouont of a suitable liquid to impart fluidity without causing flocculation (or depeptization) or oversolution of the resin particles. This is accomplised by the use of a thinner which is a combination of a dispersant and a diluent.

Dispersants are polar compounds which form strong attachments to the resin particles and aid in the wetting and dispersing of these particles. Ketones, esters and glycol ethers are common dispersants. Their ability to function in this role is directly related to their ability to serve as solvents for vinyl resins. Diluents are usually aromatic or aliphatic hydrocarbons or blends thereof. Diluents are used to balance and modify the wetting and swelling characteristics of the dispersants and to lower the cost and viscosity of the liquid medium. The proper balance of dispersant and diluent, to give the lowest viscosity, is determined by a study of the viscosity as a function of composition. This is accomplished by making several organsols in which the dispersant diluent ratio systematically varies and the viscosity of each is measured. An idealized organsol viscosity composition diagram is shown in Fig 12.3 below.

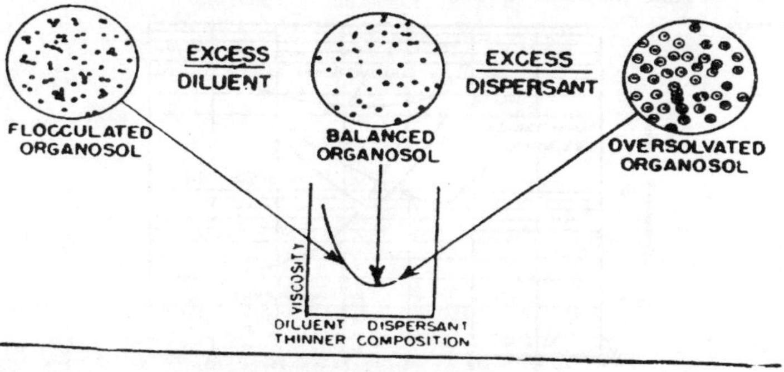

Fig. 12.3 — Effect of thinner balance on organsols

The curve shows of the effect of thinner composition or "balance" on organsol viscosity. On the lean side where there is an excess of diluent, the system tends to agglomerate and flocculate. On the rich side where there is an excess of dispersant, the resin particles are swollen excessively (oversolvated), and the organlsol shows high viscosity and poor viscosity stability. At the minimum point, the dispersant-diluent ratio is balanced to result in lowest viscosity and the best storage stability. It is this balance point, or perhaps slightly on the dispersion-rich thereof, that the formulator strives to be.

Glycol ethers, as a class, are valuable dispersants for use in organsols. While they do not yield dispersions that are as fluid as those formulated with ketones and esters, they offer more latitude in formulating. With the exception of methyl "cellosolve" solvent and "carbitol" solvent, a large excess of glycol ether can be used without causing an excessive increase in viscosity. For this reson, the glycol ethers are widely used as dispersants and thinners. For this reason, the glycol ethers are widely used as dispersants and thinners. They are particularly useful for overcoming the false body obtained in organsols contaminated by traces of water. In addition to providing wide formulating latitude, the glycol ethers can be used to good advantage as carriers for modifying resins that are added to organsols for specific end use requirements.

Because of their good compatibility and mild solvating action at normal temperatures,. plasticizers make excellent dispersants. The effect of plasticizer on the balance point of an organsol is illustrated in Figure 12.4.

Here two organsols are compared: one plasticized, the other unplasticized. The formulating ingredients in each case were otherwise the same.

Here two organsols are compared : one plasticized, the other unplasticized. The formulating ingredients in each case were otherwise the same.

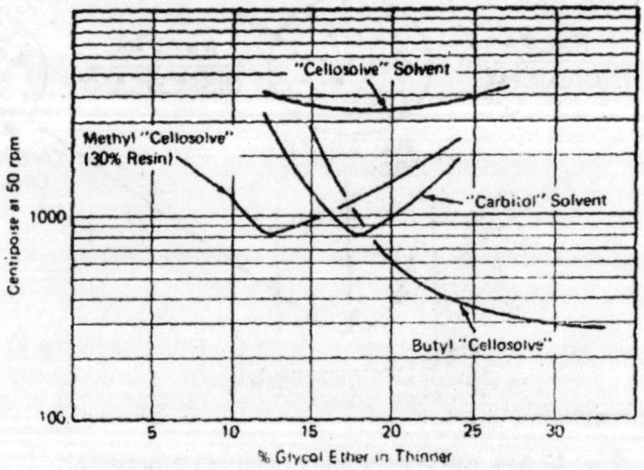

Fig. 12.4 Ogansol composition — viscosity diagram

The unplasticized system was composed of 33 per cent resin and 67 per cent thinner. However, the DOP is properly considered as a portion of the thinner, because of its dispersant ability, the plasticized organsol is seen to contain 67 per cent thinner also.

Without plasticizer, the balance point (A) is achieved with 25.5 per cent MIBK in the thinner, and the composition at this point is:

Resin	33.0
MIBK255 X 67	17.0
Xylene 60 x 50	30.0
Naphtheonic acid 40 X 50	20.0
	100.0

With plasticizer present at the 50 phr level, the balance point (B) is achieved with only 2 per cent MIBK in the thinner, and the composition at this point is:

Resin	33.0
DOP	16.5
MIBK 0.2 x 50.5	1.0
Xylene 60 x 49.5	29.7
Naphtheonic acid 40 x 49.5	19.8
	100.0

Thus, plasticized organsols require far less volatile dispersant to achieve balanced formulations and provide considerably lower viscosity at the balance point than do unplasticized formulations. For these reasons, the role of the plasticizer as a dispersant cannot be ignored when formulating organsols.

Diluents used in formulations can be aromatic or aliphatic hydrocarbons. Aromatic hydrocarbons such as xylene, have a strong swelling action on the resin and require only small proportions of dispersant to convert them to balanced organsol thinners. Aliphatic hydrocarbons, on the other hand, little swelling or wetting action on the resin. Hence, they require a higher percentage of dispersant, but yield organsols of lower viscosity. These effects are illustrated in Fig. 12.5.

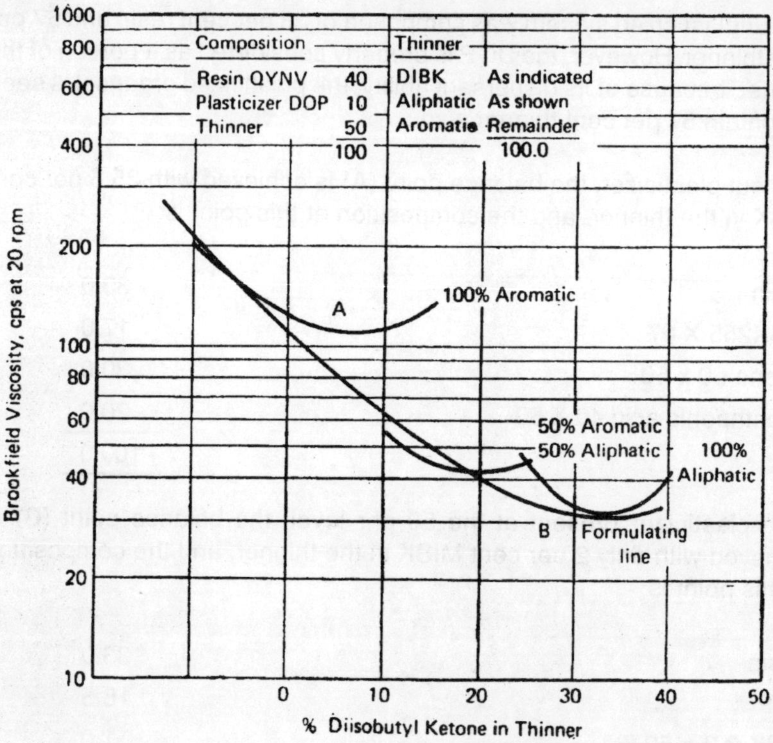

Fig. 12.5 Organsols viscosity with viscosity of aliphatic to arometic diluent

The organsol contained 25% DOP plasticizer based on resin weight. With a diluent composed of 100% aromatic hydrocarbon, a balance organsol was achieved with only 15% DIBK in the thinner (point A). The organsol formulation at this point was:

Resin Q Y N V	40
"Flexol" DOP	10
DIBK	7.5
Aromatic hydrocarbon	42.5
	100.0

With a diluent composed of 100% aliphatic hydrocarbons, a balanced organsol was achieved with about 43% DIBK in the thinner (point B). The organsol formulation at this point was.

Resin Q Y N V	40
"Flexol" DOP	10
DIBK	21.5
Aliphatic Hydrocarbons	28.5

Note that considerably lower viscosity was obtained with the non-swelling aliphatic hydrocarbon diluent.

Because the swelling action of aromatic diluents aids the fusion of the organsol film (particularly at low plasticizer levels) and because organosols are often modified with other polymeric materials that tolerate only limited amounts of aliphatic hydrocarbons, most organosol thinners contain a mixture of aromatic and aliphatic hydrocarbons as diluents.

PREPARATION OF DISPERSION COATINGS

The preparation of dispersion coatings involves the breaking of resin agglomerates. The individual dry resin particles are tightly held together in large clusters that require considerable work or higher sharing forces for reduction to the ultimate particle size of polymer.

Organosols are generally used as films of about 1 mil thickness, so they must by dispersed to a fineness of grind of at least 6 on the Hegman scale. Consequently, considerably more shear is required with plastisols.

Early technical brochures describing organosols dwelt heavily on the use of pebble mill or roller mills as production equipment. While such equipment is still being used in some instances, high speed dispersers are rapidly becoming the preferred type of equipment for organosol manufacture. Dispersion cost studies reveal the reason for this: high speed dispersers can disperse agglomerates for about one-tenth of the cost involved with a three roll mill and about one half to one-fifth of the cost of pebble milling. Resin suppliers responded to these economies by making available resins that are especially tailored to be readily dispersable in organosol formulations by means of high speed dispersers.

It is convenient to classify new organosols as consisting of dispersion resin and plasticizer as the primary film former, pigment for colour and protection, solution vinyl resin as modifier and film-forming aid, and thinner. From this view, two dispersion steps are readily seen, one for the pigment and the other for the dispersion resin. In organosol manufacture by high speed moving equipment it is common and sound practice to prepare first the solution vinyl resin portion of the formula and use this solution as the pigment dispersing medium. This ensures minimum pigment wetting by a portion of the film former. The strongest solvents in the formulation would be incorporated into this point of the mix.

The dispersion resin would be dispersed in a relatively non-solvating dispersant, diluent thinner, wherein the plasticizer required in the formula serves as part of the dispersant. This serves to improve the viscosity and viscosity stability of the finished coating. Any heat and light stabilizers or other modifiers would generally be added to this portion of the formula. The organosol would be completed by mixing the dispersion resin portion into the solution portion. Care should be taken to avoid excessive solvation of the dispersion resin, since this would result in high viscosity and loss of viscosity stability. For this reason, the upper temperature of the dispersion resin portion during manufacture should be 100° F or below.

Recommended procedures for dispersing agglomerated particles by means of high speed impellers have been developed by the Toronto society for Paint Technology. Salient points to observe are: (1) The peripheral speed oof the blade should be 4500-5000 ft./min. (2) The mixing tank diameter should be 2.8-3.0 times the blade diameter. Observation of these points will ensure that sufficient impact energy is available to disperse the agglomerates and that a working vortex is present through the mixing cycle.

The use of sand mills is described in U.S. 2,581, 414 and U.S. 2,855,156. The manufacturing procedure suggested for preparing an organosol on a sand mill is as follows.

Prepare a premix of dispersion resin, dispersant, diluent combinations (including plasticizers), stabilizers, pigments, and grinding aid. When homogenous, this mill base should have a viscosity of 60-65 krebs units. Pass this base through a sand mill at a rate of acid and sand level which will give 7.5 reading on a Hegman gauge. Add this dispersion to the solution resin portion of the formulation with strong agitation. Again, temperatures above 100° F should be avoided to obtain the best rheological properties of the formula.

As a starting point for pebble or ball mill grinding,it is suggesed that the mill be slightly over half full of pebbles to ensure proper cascading, and that the pebble plus organosol volume not be over three-fourth to four-fifths of the mill volume. Mill speed should be used that the pebbles tumble freely, and this varies with mill diameter and the viscosity of the charge being ground. Grinding time will vary with the effectiveness of the mill being used, with the viscosity of the organosol, and with the degree of dispersion required. Overnight grinding is often satisfactory. Long grinding times have been found to increase viscosity and gloss. By deliberately formulating the organosol slightly to the "richer" side of the balance point, the rate of grinding can be increased and the viscosity stability of the finished organosol can be improved.

FORMULATION OF ORGANOSOL COATINGS

Organosol coatings can be used on automobile dash boards, station wagon dacks, office furniture and partitions, lawn furniture and industrial and residential siding to name only a few of their many applications. In most of these applications, the thickness of the coating averages only about one mil. In coil coating applications, the coatings are exposed to temperatures high enough to effect proper fusion within sixty seconds. Obviously the demands of the coating with regard to thermal stability, flexibility, abrasion resistance, and resistance to weathering are severe in these end uses, and it is here that the advantages of high molecular weight polyvinyl chloride resins place the dispersion coatings high on the list of preferred coating materials.

Proper formulation of organosols for these demanding end uses requires a careful consideration of pigmentation. It has been found that a pigment content that is high enough to impart opacity toultraviolet light to the film is best means of stabilizing the polyvinyl chloride resin to UV degradation. It has been found that a resin/pigment ratio (using rutile Tio_2 pigment) of at least 100/75 is required to prevent discoloration upon long term outdoor exposure. Proper choice of pigment has been shown to have a significant influence onthe exterior durability of vinyl solution coatings. When formulating colours others other than white, the recommended practice is to replace Tio_2 with the same volume of the coloured pigment used. Exceptions are the very finely divided pigments such as carbon blacks and phthalicyamides, which are used at lower levels.

The ability to modify organosols with vinyl copolymer resins has previously been mentioned as a means of improving film formation. Another reason for the use of such resins is to impart adhesion of the organosol to a wide variety of substrates. The dispersion vinyl resins are non-adherent by nature and must be modified, or used over a suitable primer to gain adhesion. A typical formulation and performance date for a one-coat organosol are shown in Table 12.0.

TABLE 12.0

PERFORMANCE OF ONE-COAT ORGANOSOLS

Ingredients		*Per cent by weight*
Dispersion Resin Portion		
"Bakelite" vinyl resin QyNV-1		14.53
Rutile Tio_2		24.21
"Flexol" 10-10		4.84
Licithin grinding aid		0.24
"Bakelite" resin ERL-4221		1.21
Tin stabilizer		0.24
Di-isobutyl ketone		2.18
"Solvesso" 150		19.61
Solution Resin Portion		
"Bakelite" vinyl resin VMCC		9.69
Diisobutyl ketone		5.34
Isophorone		3.87
"Solvesso" 100		14.04
		100.00%
	Pass IT-2T bend	mt/gal 10.2 lbs.
Gloss	55-60	
Pencil hardness	H-2H	% N.V.by wt. 54-96

In those applications where the flexibility and long-term exposure requirements indicate the use of an organosol containing a higher proportion of dispersion resin than that possible with one-coat formulas, a two-coat system would be used.

Primers for two-coat organosol systems are of two types. When the topcoat contains 25 parts plasticizer or less per 100 parts resin, a primer based on an adhering vinyl resin has given excellent results. When the topcoat is more highly plasticized, the primer must be cross-linked to some extent in order to resist softening and loss of adhesion brought about by migration of plasticizer from the topcoat into the primer.

Some primer formulations are given below.

PRIMER FOR LIGHTLY PLASTICIZED ORGANOSOLS

Ingredients	*Per cent by wt.*
"Bakelite" resin VMCH	20
"Bakelite" resin ERL-2774	1.5
TiO_2	20
Methyl isobutyl ketone	58.5
	100.0 %

CROSSLINKED PRIMER FOR ORGANOSOLS

Ingredients	*Per cent by wt.*
"Bakelite" resin VMCH	14.3
"Bakelite" resin BKR-2620	14.3
Methyl isobutyl ketone	71.4
	100.0%

CROSSLINKED PRIMER FOR ORGANOSOLS

"Bakelite" resin VMCH	5.4
"Bakelite" resin VyNS	9.2
"Bakelite" resin BUR-2620	5.4
Methyl ethyl ketone	33.2
Methyl isobutyl ketone	23.4
Toluene	23.4
	100.0%

Topcoat formulations that have been used with these primers to complete the two coat system can be similar to that shown in the following formulation.

HIGHLY CROSS-LINKED PRIMER FOR PLASTISOLS

Ingredients	*Percent wt.*
"Bakelite" phenolic resin solution BKSA-2750	41.9
Dicyandiamide	1.31
Cyclohexane	21.90
Dimethyl formamide	7.45
Methyl isobutyl ketone	15.48
"Carbitol" solvent	10.96
	100.0%

TWO-COAT ORGANOSOL TOPCOAT

Ingredients	*Per cent by wt.*
Solution Base Grind	
"Bakelite" vinyl resin VyHD	7.29
Diisobutyl ketone (DIBK)	7.65
Isophorone	5.46
"Solvesso" 100	5.46
Titanium dioxide	18.23
"Solvesso" 150	7.65
Rutile, non chalking lecithin grinding aid	0.18
Organosol Base Grind	
"Bakelite" vinyl resin RyOH-1	24.28
"Flexol" 10-10	7.29
Di-isobutyl ketone (DIBK)	2.33
"Solvesso" 150	13.21
Tin stabilizer	0.24
"Bakelite" epoxy resin ERL-2774	0.73
	100.0%

STRIATED ORGANOSOL

"Bakelite" resin QyKV	30.7
"Bakelite" resin ERL-4221	4.0
"Flexol" 10-10	12.2
TiO_2 rutile	9.2
Barytes ≠1	30.7
Di-isobutyl ketone	1.4
"Solvesso"150	11.8
	100.0%

SPATTER FINISH ORGANOSOL

"Bakelite" resin QyKy	6.1
"Bakelife" resin VMCC	14.9
Calcium carbonate	10.9
TiO_2 rutile	6.9
Orgnesium silicate	1.9
"Cymel"301	2.7
"Flexol" 10-10	2.1
Diacetone alcohol	5.3
"Solvesso" 100	16.0
Xylol	10.6
"Cellosolves" acetate	5.3
Methyl isoamyl ketone	5.3
Di-isobutyl ketone	10.0
Lecithin grinding aid	0.1
Tin stabilizer	0.2
	100.0%

Special effects or performance properties can be formulated into organosols by means of additives. Modifying agents must be compatible with the polyvinyl chloride resin so as to avoid decreasing the weatherability of the final coating.

Organosol formulations for developing surface effects described as striations, or pebble texture are given below. Here the effects are derived from a combination of formulation ingredients and spray techniques. A modification to reduce blushing upon immersion in hot water would be the cross-linked organosol. Finally, the addition of small amounts of wax or low molecular weight polyethylene has been used to good advantage to reduce the tendency of low gloss formulations to metal work or burnish.

PEBBLE TEXTURED ORGANOSOL

Bakelite vinyl resin VyHH	12.2
Toluene	24.5
DIBK	27.5
"Flexol" plasticizer 10-10	7.3
"Bakelite" epoxy resin ERL-2774	1.0
17 per cent black in DOP	0.5
60 per cent Tio_2 in DOP	8.6
"Bakelite" vinyl resin QyPM	15.2
Tin stabilizer	0.2
	100.0%

THERMOSET ORGANOSOL

Bakelite resin QyOH-1	35.9
"Cymel" 301	2.9
"Bakelite" resin ERL-2274	3.6
"Varsol" No.1	14.4
Di-isobutyl ketone	5.4
"Santicizer" 141	28.8
"Bakelite" resin yMCC	7.2
"Bakelite" resin BKR-2620	1.8
Flexibility: Pass OT bend	100.0%

Boiling water resistance, adhesion-Excellent
10 recovery Blush-None.

In conclusion, dispersion coatings are highly versatile vehicles offering outstanding weatherability, formidability, abrasion resistance, and chemical resistance. Then offer the economic advantages of high solids content and high film thickness in one pass. The broad formulating latitude possible with dispersion coatings permits the formulation of a wide range of effects and properties that find use in ever expanding range of applications. Combined with improvements in raw materials, formulating technology and application technology, these reasons are truly bringing to fruition the fondest dreams of those early workers who in late 1940's, laboured so well in bringing to today's coatings formulator the technology of dispersion coatings.

• *Chapter 11* •

SILICONES

INTRODUCTION

Silicones are compounds containing silicon, oxygen, and one or more organic groups with the organic radicals attached to the silicone atoms. Their history dates back to the ninteenth century, when Dumas predicted the possibility of the existence of organo-silicone compounds.

The first systematic work was carried out by Professor F.S. Kipling during the first half of the twentieth century. However, just prior to the outbreak of the second world war certain industrial organisations began to show interest in silicone polymers.

Because of their good thermal stability, high electrical insulation, consistency of properties over a wide temperature range, water repellency etc. they find use in a wide variety of applications. The silicone polymers are available in the form of fluids, greases, rubbers and resins. They find applications in cosmetics, aircrafts, or antifoams agents in food and chemical industry, treatment of leather and textiles to give them special effects, masonry water repellents, glass and textile sizing agents and foam stabilizers.

NOMENCLATURE

Kipling first used the word 'silicone' to denote the organo-silicone analogus of ketones. He quickly realized that such materials were polymeric having the structure.

$$\begin{array}{c} R' \\ | \\ Si = O \\ | \\ R \end{array} \qquad n$$

The simplest member of the series is silane

```
      H
      I
H - Si - H
      I
      H
```

The hydrogen atoms of this material may be replaced by halogen, alkyl or aryl groups giving compounds such as.

```
      H
      I
H - Si - H        or
      I
      Cl
```

Monochlorosilane Diphenyldichlorosilane

The basic structure of the building blocks from which silicone polymers are produced is:

- Si - O - Si -

This grouping is designated as the siloxane linkage and is the characteristic structure to be found in all silicone polymers. A compound consisting of a large number of such groupings is referred to as a polysiloxane.

PROCESSING TECHNIQUES FOR SILICONE ELASTOMERS

A silicone elastomer stock is compounded and processed on the same type of equipment as used for organic rubbers. It can be mixed on a two roll mill, in a Banbury or in a dough mixer. The curing agent should always be added on a mill to avoid premature set-up. Unvulcanized silicone elastomer is softer and weaker than organic rubber, and a scrapper blade attachment on the mill is recommended for removing the silicone compound. After compounding the next step is to cure rubber. The first stage of curing is carried out in a press, hot air chamber or steam vulcanizer, the process being referred to as set-cure. The second stage is carried out in an air-circulating oven and is especially necessary in order to develop the optimum physical properties required for many applications and for maximum resistance to compression set.

Fully compounded silicone stocks may be moulded, extruded, laminated, calendered or applied from solvent dispersion. Conventional rubber processing machinery is used and should include a two-roll mill equipped with scrapper blades, a steam or electrically heated moulding process operating at temperatures between 100-150^{0} C with provision for water cooling. A steam vulcanizer capable of operating at pressures up to 100 1b/in^{2} should also be available. In addition, a forced air-draught circulating oven is essential to obtain an adequate final cure for optimum physical properties.

MANUFACTURE OF SILICONE FLUIDS

Manufacture of silicone fluids involves following three important steps.

(1) Hydrolysis (2) Catalystic equalibration (3) Devolatization.

These fluids are preferably made in a batch process. In a batch process, a weighed excess of water is placed in a glass lined jacketed reactor. Dimethylchlorosilane is run through a dispersion nozzle and the contents are agitated well. The reaction is carried out under reflux. Although the reaction is endothermic, the absorption of hydrochloride gas evolved in the reaction generates enough heat to make the reaction exothermic and therefore it becomes necessary to cool of reactants. When the reaction is completed, the oily polymer layer is allowed to separate from the dilute acid phase which is then drawn off. The oil is then neutralized in a separate operation by washing with sodium carbonate solution. The neutral solution at this stage consists of cyclic and linear polymers. Cyclic polymers constitute 20-80% of the total products. In order to achieve a more linear polymer but with a random molecular weight distribution and also to stabilize the viscosity it is a common practice to equilibrate the fluid by heating with a catalyst such as dilute sulphuric acid. To check the degree of polymerization, chain stoppers such as mono-functional trimethyl-chlorosilane is added. In practice for fluids of viscosities less than 1,000 centistokes, the equilibration reaction takes a number of hours at 100-150^{0} C. The volatile low molecular weight products are finally removed from the batch using a vacuum still.

COMPOUNDING

(a) FLUIDS

Silicone fluids are normally used without fillers or additives, therefore, very little compounding is necessary. However, in fluids for the production of greases inert fillers are added such as silica and carbon black as well as metallic soaps, e.g. lithium octoate.

(b) RESINS

Relatively little compounding is required with silicone resins and they are generally supplied either solventless or in solutions of xylene and toluene.

(c) ELASTOMERS

Unfilled silicone gums have negligible mechanical strength and must therefore be reinforced by the addition of a filler. The fillers are classified as reinforcing or semi-reinforcing and non-reinforcing. The reinforcing fillers commonly used are precipitated and fume silicas. There are several fillers of which the following are frequently used and include diatomaceous earth, quartz, calcium carbonate and precipitated calcium silicate.

Special additives are frequently used in conjunction with silicone elastomers to provide certain enhanced properties including improved heat stability and reduction in compression set. Heat stability is normally improved by the addition of ferric oxide, ferric octoate or barium zirconate. Silicone elastomers may be readily pigmented by the addition of heat-stable inorganic oxides such as those of iron, nickel, chromium, titanium or cadmium.

APPLICATIONS

(a) FLUIDS

The silicone fluids have certain advantages over hydrocarbon oils such as small viscosity change with temperature and non-sticking properties, they are now being used more and more in aircraft hydraulic systems. Antisticking characteristics have led to at least two large uses namely in polishes and as mould release agents in plastics and rubber moulding.

Silicone oils may be used in form of an aqueous emulsion or solvent solution for mould release applications. They offer a unique combination of properties viz. inertness, heat resistance, low surface tension combined with good lubricating power. These materials have now replaced many of the more conventional mould release materials such as soap and preparation of the mould release agent would be as follows.

Dimethyl silicone fluid	35 parts
Emulsifier	2 parts
Water	63 parts

The above ingredients are mixed together and then diluted to a concentration of around 1 per cent.

The use of silicone fluids in car and furniture polishes has grown in popularity over the past few years. Normally about 2-4 per cent is added to either wax or waxless formulation and in the case of the wax polish the silicone fluids serve to lubricate the micro crystalline wax.

Silicone fluids are now widely used in the paint industry as antiflotation and anti-sticking agents. The addition of a small amount of a low viscosity dimethyl silicone fluid (1-50000 ppm) will assist in the grinding and dispersion of the pigment as well as inhibiting flotation and flow lines. They are also used in the production of polyurethane foams to control certain characteristics such as cell size. Silicone anti-foams are now widely used in food manufacture and sewage disposal.

One of the earliest uses of silicone fluids was as a water-repellent treatment for a wide variety of surfaces. They are now being used extensively for treating textiles, paper and leather. In the textile treatment the silicones not only confer excellent resistance to water but also to staining.

(b) RESINS

The film-forming properties of silicones resins are not as good as those of the more conventional organic polymers, but they do possess greater heat stability. Paints based on silicone resins and aluminium pigments can effectively withstand direct heating to around 700° C. Their overall cost can be reduced by blending them with organic coating materials such as glyptals, urea and phenol formaldehyde as well as the epoxy resins. The aluminium-based silicone paints are used for coating certain parts of jet engines which are subjected to high temperatures.

The silicone resins have found extensive use in high temperature insulation for electrical equipment. Other interesting applications for silicone resins include the water proofing of masonry and utilization as a release agent. Silicone containing solvent may be sprayed on brick work and on the subsequent evaporation of the solvent the bricks are left with a coating of silicone resin and are thus water repellent. As a mould release agent they offer an advantage over the fluids in that their effect is semi-permanent. The baking industry has used silicone resins for coating bread tins and they have found that they are able to obtain many hundreds of satisfactory releases before the treatment wears off.

Silicone resins have also been used in preparing moulding powders suitable for the compression and transfer moulding techniques. These resins are expensive and although the overall price may be reduced by addition of fillers such as asbestos powder or chopped glass wool.

Another use for these resins is in the preparation of laminates with glass fibre, asbestos and mica as the reinforcing material. Such laminates may be manufactured by press moulding at both high and low pressures, by vacuum bag moulding, or by filament winding. The resin is normally applied from a solvent solution usually of the high-boiling aromatic type such as xylene or toluene and is pre-cured on the reinforcing material. The main field of application is in the aircarft industry, where heat resistance is required, or in the electrical industry where the insulating properties are of prime importance.

(c) ELASTOMERS

Undoubtedly the growth and popularity of the use of silicone elastomers can do a large extent be attributed to the requirements of the aircraft and electrical industries. The main uses of silicone elastomers in the aircraft industry are for door seals, hot air ducts, flexible sleeving, gaskets and vibration dampers. The fluorinated silicone elastomers are now widely used for such applications where their outstanding resistance to chemicals and fuels may be used effectively.

A relatively big market for these elastomers is for the insulation sleeving used on power and control cables in ships. There are many advantages in using silicone rubber as an insulator, namely resistance to oxidation, ozone and a variety of chemicals. One particular advantage that is gained for use with cables in ships is that in the event of a fire on board, the silicone would burn, leaving a silica ash which would have sufficient insulating value, possibly to allow the ship to return to the base.

They are used in domestic and industrial appliances. Typical applications include use as oven-door seals, cable insulation, belting gaskets and canking pastes for sealing joints. More and more uses are being found for silicone elastomers in the medical field, e.g. tubing, vial stoppers, gaskets, teats and heart valves. An important use is for tubing on blood transfusion equipment and it has been found in service that such tubing is unaffected by 30 heat sterilizations involving exposure to steam at 20 lb/in^2 pressure for 30 minutes each time.

The cold-curing silicone elastomers are also used extensively in a variety of applications including sealing, canking, potting, encapsulating and impregnating. They are encapsulating delicate and electronic components especially where severe humidity conditions are to be met. Electrical equipment such as resistors, capacitors and transformers may also be encapsulated quite easily.

Table 8.0 PHYSICAL PROPERTIES OF SOME SILICONE FLUIDS

Fluid	Viscosity at 25°C cS	Permittivity at 25°C (100 c/s)	Freezing point (°C)	Boiling point (°C)	Flash point min. (°F)	Thermal conductivity cal cm. sec cm² °C at 50°C	Specific gravity at 25°C/25°C	Refractive index at 25°C
MS 200/3	3	2·52	−65	70–100	215	0·00027	0·90	0·39
			Pour point					
MS 200/10	10	2·65	−65	>200	325	0·00032	0·94	1·40
MS 200/20	20	2·68	−60	>200	520	0·00034	0·96	1·40
				Volatility after 48 hr at °C / per cent				
MS 200/500	500	2·75	−50	200 / <2	600	0·00038	0·97	1·403
MS 200/12 500	12 500	2·82	*Solidification temp.* −46	200 / <2	600	0·00038	0·97	1·403
			Freezing point					
MS 510/50	50	2·7	−70	250 / 10	525	—	0·99	1·42
MS 510/550	550	2·8	−70	250 / 6	525	—	0·99	1·43
MS 550	100–150	2·9	−50	250 / 15	575	0·00035	1·06–1·08	1·49–1·50

Polymer Technology

Table 8.1 TYPICAL PROPERTIES OF SOME SILICONE RESINS

Property of cured resin	Coating resins MS 935	Coating resins MS 994	Impregnating varnish MS 997	Impregnating varnish MS 1360	Bonding resins MS 840	Bonding resins MS 2103
Electric strength, film thickness 10 mil (V/mil)	>1000	>1500	>1000	>1500	>1000	>1000
Power factor at 10^2 c/s	0·003	0·001	0·006	0·005	0·003	0·002
Power factor at 10^6 c/s	0·004	0·001	0·007	0·013	—	0·002
Permittivity at 10^2 c/s	2·9	2·8	3·1	3·6	2·9	2·9
Permittivity at 10^6 c/s	2·7	2·8	3·0	3·5	—	2·9
Craze life (min, hr at 250°C)	800	3000	1000	—	—	—
Flex life (min, hr at 250°C)	100	1000	250	—	—	—
Property of resin solution						
Solids content (per cent)	50	50	50	50	80	60
Solvent	Xylene	Xylene	Xylene	Cresylic Acid	Acetone	Toluene
Viscosity at 25°C cS	80–150	80–125	100–200	4300–8600	350–1750	60–125
Processing	Require curing at 200–250°C			Cures at 50°C above vinyl formal wire enamels	Will rapidly air dry tack-free to form a soft film. Require curing at 250°C to form hard non-thermoplastic bond.	

PROPERTIES

Certain properties are common to all silicones, of which the most important are their exceptional stability to heat, cold and oxidation.

(a) FLUIDS

The influence of temperature on the viscosity of methyl silicone fluids is relatively small. They also exhibit unusually high resistance to mechanical shearing, particularly in hydraulic systems. They are also highly water repellent and water will condense discreet droplets on surfaces previously treated by the fluids. Dimethyl silicone fluids are colourless, odourless, nontoxic and physiologically inert. They are resistant to oxidation, have excellent resistance to a wide variety of chemicals, and are available in a wide range of viscosities. Some physical properties are given in Table 8.0.

(a) RESINS

The physical properties of silicone resins are dependent to a large extent on the Me:Si ratio; and it has been found that a ratio between 1:3 and 1:5 gives the most useful products. Resins prepared with such ratios exhibit excellent stability at high temperatures and are also resistant to moisture. The excellent thermal electrical equipment that has been impregnated with these resins. These resins possess good chemical resistance specially to dilute mineral acids and alkalies. Their resistance to many organic solvents such as toluene and xylene is not good. The properties of some silicone resins are given in Table 8.1.

(c) ELASTOMERS

Silicone elastomers may now be produced with tensile strengths in the region of 1500 lb/in^2. They remain serviceable and stable over a wide temperature range from as low as 70° C to as high as 250° C. They also possess excellent electrical resistance and insulating properties. Typical properties of silicone elastomers are listed in Table 8.2.

Silicone elastomers are generally resistant to a wide variety of chemicals and in general will resist the attack of oxidizing agents, weak acids, weak bease, salts and vegetable acids. They will swell in the presence of strong acids and bases, chlorinated solvents, and reducing agents but they are not attacked chemically and will normally return to the original shape on removal from the source of the chemical. These elastomers do not harden up and become brittle over a wide range of temperature as do the conventional natural and synthetic organic elastomers.

Table 8.2 TYPICAL PROPERTIES OF SILICONE RUBBER

Temperature stability (°C)	−100 to + 250
Specific gravity at 25°C	1·0–2·0
Hardness (B.S. deg.)	40–85
Tensile strength (lb/in²)	700–1500
Ultimate elongation (%)	100–400
Compression set (% at 150°C)	10–70
Brittle point (°C)	−110 to −60
Tear strength (lb)	4–5
Electric strength (V/mil)	250–600
Permittivity at Mc/s	3·0–4·0
Power factor (1 Mc/s)	0·001–0·007
Coefficient of cubic expansion/°C	approx. 0·0007
Thermal conductivity (cal cm/cm sec)	approx. 5×10^{-4}
Specific heat (cal/°C/g)	0·275 to 0·325

• *Chapter 12* •

UREA FORMALDEHYDE RESIN

INTRODUCTION

The reaction between urea and formaldehyde has been known since Halzer first isolated methylene urea in 1881. Synthetic production of urea was achieved some fifty years earlier in 1828. Commercial interest was not aroused in the reactions between urea and formaldehyde until a patent was granted in 1918. The next few years saw consolidation of the early development work on the amino plasts and large scale production of urea formaldehyde moulding powders began in 1938; extension of used glues followed soon after. The use of such resins has now become so firmly established for such applications as moulding powders, adhesives, textile treatments and surface coatings.

The advantages offered by the amine resins emerge from their initial water solubility, nonflammability, hardness, are resistance and absence of colour in cured polymers. The absence of colour of these resins has made them most suitable for production of beautiful, translucent shades of any desired colour from slightest white cream or any pastel or opaque shade. Choice of colour makes them more suitable in decorative field.

The base urea resins are clear water-white syrups or white powders. Correctly cured mouldings are colourless and tasteless which makes them eminently suitable for domestic articles.

RAW MATERIALS

UREA

It is a white crystalline organic compound melting at 132° C. It is soluble in water and slightly soluble in alcohol. It gives ammonia at 30° C. Resin grade urea is more pure than fertilizer grade.

Urea can be produced by various methods, of which probably the most important is the reaction under pressure if carbon dioxide with ammonia in siliver lined autoclaves. Urea may also be synthesized by the acid hydrolysis of cyanamide.

THIOUREA

It is another important raw material used in the manufacture of urea formaldehyde resins.

Thiourea has white, lustrous crystals melting at 180-182° C, soluble in cold water and alcohol. This material is sold in bags. It is made on an industrial scale from ammonium thiocyanate, which is a by-product of coke oven operations, and also from cyanamide and hydrogen sulfide.

CHEMISTRY OF RESINIFICATION

The basis of the chemistry of the interaction of urea and formaldehyde is the formation of monomethylol and dimethylol urea. Monomethylol urea is obtained after mixing equimolour proportions of urea and formaldehyde urea is prepared in a similar manner using 2 moles of formaldehyde per mole of urea. On a commercial scale the formalin (35-40%) w/v in water is adjusted to a pH of 7.5 using sodium potassium hydroxide. The following reaction take place.

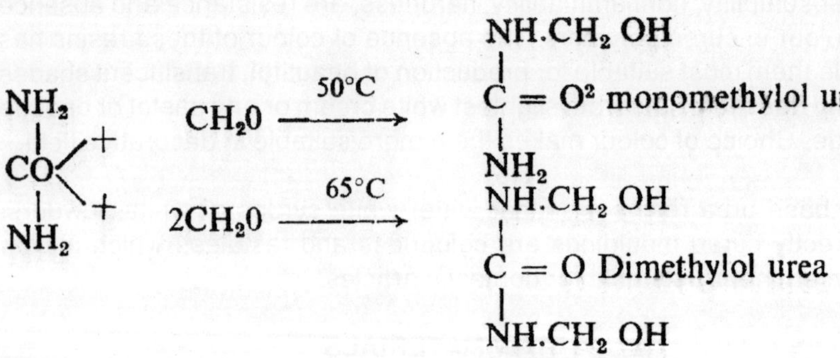

The methylol compounds so formed are relatively unstable and will condense in the presence of a catalyst on heating to produce methylene derivatives which ultimately become cross-linked and infusible products.

The functionality of monomethylol urea can be considered as 2 and that of fomaldehyde as 2, therefore, this system will not cross link. Dimethylol urea, formed from two moles of formaldehyde has a functionality of 4 and will cross link to give the thermosetting resin.

When the crystalline monomers (monomethylol and dimethylol urea) are heated at their fusion points (110-165° C), they become reactive melts. Some formaldehyde is lost under these conditions and resolidification in resinous form takes place due to thermally induced polymerization. Polymerization is usually initiated and promoted in solution under the catalytic influence of hydrogen.

EQUIPMENT FOR UREA FORMALDEHYDE RESIN MANUFACTURE

The major equipment required for urea formaldehyde resin manufacture consists of a (1) Reaction kettle (2) Condenser (3) Receiver etc.

REACTION KETTLE

The reaction kettle is the main item of equipment required for resin manufacture.

A view of the kettle used in the manufacture of this resin is given below.

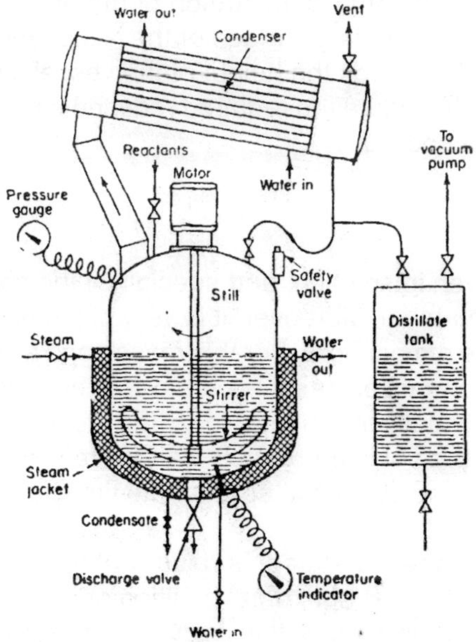

Fig 3.0 Reaction Vessel for urea formaldehyde resin manufacture.

The kettle is a cylindrical vessel with dish bottom and dome top, usually containing a jacket over most of the lower part for heating the contents. The agitator is of the anchor type or gate type and usually runs at a speed of 35-60 rpm. It is closely fitted to the sides of the tank for a scraping action and mixing of the viscous mixtures thoroughly. It is constructed most commonly of stainless steel, although ordinary steel, nonferrous alloys and even glass-lined tanks are used. They very in sizes from 300 to 2000 gallons capacity. A vapour line is attached to the reactor, the other end of the line is connested to an overhead condenser, which can be used for refluxing the reaction mixture in the early stages,or stripping off the water of condensation, during the later stages of the reaction. Feed inlet for the reactants, a recording thermometers, and slight glasses are attached to the top of the reactor through suitable flanged openings. A large bottom outlet contains a gate type valve or flash bottom valve for easy discharge of viscous resinous product, either into shallow pans for hardening, or directly on the cement flour which should contain the cooling pipes embedded below the surface for a fast setting of the resin.

During the part of the reaction where-heat is required, the vessel will not be more than two-thirds full. After dehydration of the product it may be less than one third full. After dehydration of the product it may be less than one third full. The heating surface or the jacket, therefore, need not extend more than two-thirds the height of the vessel, and such a jacket will obviously accommodate the required reduced volume of the product when employed for cooling.

CONDENSER

Formaldehyde, even in solution, and specially if the solution is heated, is a very volatile material. Moreover, it is very unpleasant if it is allowed to vaporise into the atmosphere. For this reason and also for condensing water vapours, the reaction vessel is fitted with an efficient condenser. The condenser is usually of a tubular form and the condensing system is so arranged that the volatile products can be refluxed, and unwanted water drained from the system at appropriate time.

The condenser, as already stated, is usually of the shell and tube type and is placed in an almost horizontal position or at a slight angle to the horizontal. With a wide vapour line from the vessel to the top of the condenser. The material of construction of the condenser shell, tubes and other accessories is generally the same as that of the vessel. For refluxing a pipe from the lower end leads back to the top of the still through a U-bend trap. However, by altering the setting of the two valves, the distillate can be led into distillate-receiver tank. In the first position, the condenser system is used as reflux condenser and in the end it can be used for distillation.

Rapid water removal is often of vital importance, and for this reason the capacity of the condenser must be adequate enough to facilitate this process. Some idea of the size of condenser used can be obtained from the following date. For a 1,000 gallon capacity reaction vessel a condenser containing 320, 3/4 in O.D. stainless tubes, 8 ft. long was employed. A 500 gallon capacity urea-formaldehyde plant may have a condenser with 120 nickel tubes, 7 ft, 7 5/8 in. long. Both forms of condenser, i.e. with vapour inside and outside the tubes have been used, but the former arrangement is more popular.

RECEIVER

The distillated receiver is to receive the water and any formaldehyde condensed in the condenser. It is sometimes necessary to operate the system under reduced pressure to have low temperature in the reaction kettle. So the distillate receiver is connected to the vacuum pump.

Two distillate receivers are generally provided both of mild steel, and together provide accommodation for distillate equivalent to 80 per cent of the total volume handled in the main reaction vessel. These receivers are arranged to be used in series or parallel.

When resin formation is complete in the kettle, it is necessary to dehydrate the product, and this is done by subjecting it to a vacuum, after some cooling to arrest polymerization.

In is often considered useful to include a sight glass in the condensate line leading to the receiver, for it provides a ready means of ascertaining precisely when distillation has ceased.

HEATING MEDIUM

For urea formaldehyde resin manufacture, steam heating is used. But when higher temperatures are required, it is usual to employ some after media like dowtherm. A suitable steam boiler for steam heating and a thermopack boiler for oil heating can be used.

MANUFACTURING PROCESS

LABORATORY PREPARATION

The apparatus required for the preparation of urea formaldehyde resin consists of (1) 1 litre bolthead flask with reflux condenser, (2) Buchner vacuum filteration apparatus (3) vacuum distillation apparatus with air bubbling tube and screw clip (4) Thermometer (110° C) (5) Hot water bath etc.

PROCEDURE

(a) 120 g. urea are dissolved in 315 cc. 40 per cent formalin without warming and the pH adjusted to 8.5, using N/1 sodium hydroxide solution and B.D.H. universal indicator. 1 cc. 0.880 ammonia are added, and, if transluent mouldings are required, the solution is filtered by means of a Buchner vacuum apparatus. The solution is boiled under a reflux condenser for 30 minutes, adjusted to pH 5.5 with N/1 lactic acid and B.D.H. universal indicator, boiled under reflux for 15 minutes and the pH adjusted to 8 with approximately N/1 sodium hydroxide and B.D.H. universal.

The liquor is vacuum distilled from a water bath maintained at 65-70° C at a pressure of about 25 mm mercury, i.e. 1 in. to give a syrup.

The resin is used for making a moulding material. The U.F ratio used in this experiment is 1:2.1, not the preferred ratio for moulding materials of about 1:1.5. The reason for this is that a higher proportion of formaldehyde gives a more stable resin liquor, better suited to experimental work, which may have to be carried out during broken periods of time. Moulding materials made from high formaldehyde ratio resins will give passing trouble during moulding; extra urea is therefore added when making a moulding material from this urea formaldehyde resin.

(b) 300 cc. 40 per cnet formaline are warmed gently to about 35° C and 0.33 magnesium carbonate is then added. The formalin is stirred until it is neutral to B.D.H. universal indicator and allowed to stand until it cools to 15-20° C. 8.5 cc. of 0.880 ammonia and 165 g. urea are added and the solution stirred. The temperature is allowed to rise to 35-40° C and the liquor allowed to stand for two hours. A syrup is formed which is used to prepare a moulding material. The resin syrup made by this method has U.F. ratio 1:1.45.

COMMERCIAL PREPARATION

The raw materials required to produce 500 kg. Urea formaldehyde resin are :

Formalin (37%)	:	400 kg
Urea	:	200 kg
Ammonia	:	9 kg

Formaldehyde (37%) is charged to the reaction kettle. Required amount of urea is then added. The reactants are mixed well. Mole ratio of urea and formaldehyde is adjusted to 1:1.5 to 2.1. The alkaline catalyst, i.e. N/l sodium hydroxide solution. The pH in the kettle should be adjusted to 8.5 and tested by a B.D.H indicator.

Urea dissolves in fomalin in the reactor. The reactants are heated. On boiling the reactants, a viscous syrupy mass is obtained. The reaction takes 2 hours. However, before a syrup mass is formed, the reaction can be carried out and controlled at different stages to give resin suitable for different applications. At stage A, the resin is in a liquid state and contains mono and dimethyl ureas. It may be used at this stage for sizing of fabrics, crease proofing, coating of papers for water proofing and formation of plastic laminates. But B stage resins are suitable for moulding compounds. The mixture is acidified with phosphoric acid or lactic acid to a pH of 5.0 and heated to 60° C under vacuum for further condensation and removal of water by distillation. As cellulose is frequently used as the filler in urea plastics, alpha stock is added to the mixture for thorough penetration.

APPLICATIONS

The major applications of urea formaldehyde resins are in the following industries.

1. Adhesives
2. Chip board making
3. Paper industry
4. Surface coatings
5. Moulding powders
6. Laminated plastics
7. Miscellaneous

1. ADHESIVES

The principle of bending wood with urea formaldehyde resin makes use of the fact that the latter may be hardened at temperature even below 100° C in the presence of accelerators. If, therefore, the resin solution containing an accelerator is employed for the bonding of wood, hardening takes place even on long standing in cold or after a few minutes at 80-100° C depending on the nature and quantity of accelerator used. The hardened resin layer bends the piece of wood or wood in manner similar to that of common glues, but bending is resistant to cold water. It also resists the attack on the moulds and typical climate.

LABORATORY PREPARATION

The apparatus required for the preparation of cold setting gap filling urea formaldehyde adhesive include (1) 1 litre bolthead flask with reflux condenser (2) vacuum distillation apparatus with air bubbling tube and screen clip (3) hot water bath (4) pieces of wood about 6 in x 2 in x 1/2 in (5) clamps.

PROCEDURE

100g urea, 270 cc 40 per cent formalin and 5cc N/l sodium hydroxide solution are mixed in the flask to give a solution of pH of about 8, as indicated by B.D.H. indicator. The solution is boiled under reflux for 5 minutes, and then adjusted to pH 4.5-5.0, with N/l lactic acid, using B.D.H. universal indicator. Boiling is continued for a further 30 minutes under reflux. The liquor is adjusted to pH of 7.5 with N/1 sodium hydroxide solution and vacuum distilled from a water bath at about 70° C at a pressure of about 25 mm, i.e. 1 in, to give a thickish syrup.

The gap filler is made by mixing 10g wood flour (80-120 mesh) with 20 cc benzyl alcohol or furfural.

APPLICATION

100g of resin, all of the gap-filler type and 1g of ammonium chloride are thoroughly mixed. Then, within the course of an hour or so the adhesive is applied to about 1 in. of one surface of each of the pieces of wood. The pieces are placed together in pairs with end to end overlapping contact, clamped in position and allowed to stand overnight. The adhesion is empirically tested by putting one end of the assembly in a Vice and breaking the joint open with a hammer blow. A good joint should show wood failure when breaking, that is, there should be splinters of wood torn away with the adhesives.

COMMERCIAL PREPARATION

The urea formaldehyde resin for adhesive use is made by condensing 2 moles of formaldehyde with one of urea. The initial pH of the reaction medium is usually neutral or slightly alkaline to allow the formation of the methylol ureas, and then raised to a mildly acid medium (pH = 5) to ensure a steady rate of condensation. The reaction can be followed by viscosity measurements and the tendency of the resin to be hydrophobic. At a predetermined stage the process is stopped by neutralization and the resin is then either dehydrated under vacuum to give a viscous product of 1-10 poises and 60-70 per cent solids content or spray dried to give a resin powder. The resin syrup can then be stabilized by the addition of weak bases or by protective colloids such as starch. The liquid product has a shelf life of between 3-9 months whereas the spray dried powder is usable for periods up to two years.

There are two types of glueing with these adhesives:

1. Glueing in the cold
2. Glueing in the hot

Cold Glueing

In the cold glueing more amount of accelerator is used. The glue and accelerator mixture then remains unusable for some hours until it becomes ineffective through hardening. The mixture is then employed for glueing of the wooden objects during this preliminary period, and the bonding is completed while the pieces are in the press. The final curing is accomplished by standing the bended piece at room temperature for some days.

Cold pressing methods are used for the preparation of inferior grade plywood, furniture, interior doors, general assembly glueing and bending of decorative laminates to substructures such as hard boards and plywood. Both solid and liquid urea resins are available for cold press glueing. They require and added catalyst and may be used unextended or with varying amounts of cereal flour as extender. Shell floors, walnut or peanut are usually incorporated to control flow and limit penetration of the glue line.

Pressure required for cold pressing will vary from mere contact to a maximum of about 200 psi depending on the type of adhesive and the nature of the product. Plywood presses for cold set adhesives operate from 150-200 psi. For low density woods such as popular, mahogany, or gum, pressure of 150-175 psi is desirable. For the denser woods such as maple, coak or birch, pressures from 175 to 200 psi are recommended.

A formulation of cold setting adhesive is given below.

FORMULATION

Ingredients	*Qty. in lbs.*
Urea formaldehyde resin	100
Shell flour	15
Wheat flour	25
Water	100-110
Hardener	5
Working life, hr. at 70° F	4
at 80° F	2
at 90° F	1

Highest proportion of formaldehyde enhances the stability of the product in solution form, increases water tolerance and a highest sensitivity to atmospheric moisture.

Hot Glueing

For production of plywood or flat veneer work hydraulic presses with multiple openings are usually used, operating at a pressure of 30-300 psi according to the type of wood, so that porous structure is not destroyed. Temperature used is usually 90-100° C and time required varies from 5-10 minutes after reaching this temperature. Temperatures over 100° C are risky as the moisture of the wood and glue may give steam blisters. Lower temp, say of 80-90° C, though take more time to cure but offer an advantage that cured plywood display less tendency to warp on drying and they stay flat better.

The accelerators or hardeners employed usually consist of ammonium chloride.

The use of fillers is an important feature of the application of these glues, partly because of the economic consequences and are necessary from technical point of view because correct use of fillers prevents the glue being squeezed out of joint under pressure or absorbed into the wood itself so that formation of "starved joints" is prevented. As a rule, 20-50 per cent filler is used and for plywood it is up to 100 per cent.

2. CHIPBOARD INDUSTRY

Another important application of urea formaldehyde glues at present is in the manufacture of chipboard. The wood chips are mixed with about 10 per cent of the resin hardener solution and the mixture is pressed in a multi-die light press for about 8 minutes at 150° C. Since the odour of formaldehyde is disagreeable, it is important that a little of the pungent chemical is released up to the press shop during the opening of the press. For this reason the resin should have low formaldehyde content. Since a low degree of polymerization is necessary to ensure good dispersion a rather low formaldehyde/urea is necessary to achieve a low rate of formaldehyde content.

Typical formulation of adhesive for chipboard industry is given below.

Ingredients	*parts by wt.*
Urea	155.5
Formaldehyde (37 per cent)	382
Catalyst	as required.

Reactants are charged to the reactor and the pH adjusted to 7.5-8 by means of aqueous solution of caustic soda. They are heated and allowed to reflux. Cloud test is done and formic acid is added to make the pH at 5.5-5.6. Now the contents are again refluxed till desired viscosity is obtained. pH is again brought to 7.5 by NaOH solution and after that water is evaporated till 65 per cent solid contents are obtained.

3. PAPER INDUSTRY

The binding force between cellulose fibres which converts them into a paper web is largely that of hydrogen bending between polymer chains. This same force exists within the polymer structure of urea resins and is responsible in part for properties of strength.

In the treatment of paper, urea resins were first used on a limited scale by so-called tub application to impart wet strength to the fibre and as an adhesive in corrugated-box board making. However melamine formaldehyde resin is more in use in the paper industry.

The urea resin for use in paper industry is prepared by modifying with about 10 per cent (calculated on the urea) of an organic base, such as tetraethylene pentamine, of vanidine or triethanolamine and hydrochloric acid. An acid resin is produced which is neutralized to give a good shelf life, but which is made slightly acid again before being used to treat the paper.

Limited use has been made of anionic resins made by condensing urea and formaldehdye in the presence of 10 per cent (calculated on the urea)of sodium metabisulphite, alum must be added to the paper, suspension to precipitate the resin on the fibre. The method is very cheap and gives fair results on kraft paper but not with types of pulp.

Urea resins improve the wet strength of paper, mainly for packing, to improve adhesion to the pulp and present losses along with with effluent water. Resin with positively charged particles is used which adheres to the negatively charged particles of pulp. The resin is cured as the paper passes over hot rollers during the drying process.

4. SURFACE COATINGS

The resins that have been modified by the introduction of an alkyl group are used for the production of coatings by mixing them with alkyds processed oils and plasticizers. Such resins are usually supplied in 50 per cent solutions in mixtures of naphthas and alcohols.

Coatings are usually baked at temperatures ranging from 225 to 325° F, although special catalyzed resins may be made to conform with low temperature force dry schedules. The urea resin content of such coatings hardens by polymerization as contrasted to evaporation and or oxidation of usual alkyd, oil or lacquer film.

Urea formaldehyde coatings are resistant to breakdown and discoloration when subjected to sunlight and exterior exposure. When formulated with coconut and castor oil alkyds, their clarity and colour retention properties produce hgih quality coating for refrigerators, kitchenware, bathroom and hospital etc. In combination with alkyds they have shown outstanding interior and exterior durability.

At the present time urea resins are used with alkyds in proportions varying from 1:2 to 1:20. Both oxidizing and non-oxidizing alkyds, from phthalic anhydride or from isophthalic aicd, are used. Nonoxidizing alkyds provide better resistance and colour retention. Baking conditions for film cure may vary from 40 min. at 90° C to 1 min at 260° C depending on whether or not a catalyst is used.

5. MOULDING POWDERS

The base resin for use in moulding powders is produced in fairly low state of condensation. Urea-formaldehyde molar ratios of about 1:1.5 are preferred. The condensation is carried out under faintly alkalin conditions. The process of manufacture has already been described.

There are two general methods used for converting the resin into a moulding powder. One, which is termed the wet process consists of kneading the filler (wood flour or bleached wood pulp) with the aqueous resin until the filler becomes thoroughly impregnated. The resultant mix is then broken up into fine crumbs and dried to the required plasticity. At this stage the material is in a form similar to coarse dessicated coconut and is placed in a ball mill together with catalyst (hexamine), lubricants (stearates) and pigments. It is then ground to a fine powder and finally sieved to remove any coarse particles. The resultant moulding powder may be too bulky for certain applications and can be densified by granulating either on heated mixing rolls or in a Banbury mixer.

The other method, termed as the dry process, merely consists of mixing the condensed resin with fillers, catalyst, lubricants, and pigments on heated mixing rolls. At the correct temperature the mix resinifies and can then be shuted off and finally granulated.

The manufacture for moulding powders and the type of fillers and other ingredients used are described in detail in the following pages.

The ingredients used in the moulding powders include :

(1) Pigments
(2) Hardener
(3) Stabilizer
(4) Filier
(5) Mould and release agent
(6) Plasticizer

Pigments

A wide variety of pigments is now used in the manufacture of moulding powders. Their principal requirement is that they should not affect the stability or moulding characteristics of the powder, that they should be stable to processing conditions; the unaffected by the conditions of service including the insolubility in any solvents with which the mouldings might come into contact and should not interfere with electrical properties. For cream/whiteners, zinc, oxide and titanium dioxide could be used. For blue shades ultramarines may be used. Organic pigments such as azo pigments, Hansa yellows and phthalocyanin blues are used.

Hardener

In order to obtain sufficient rate of cure at moulding temperatures, it is usual to add about 0.2-2 per cent of the hardener. This functions by decomposing or hydrolysis at moulding temperatures to give an acidic body that shall accelerate the cure rate. A very large number of such latent acid catalysts have been described in the literature of which some of the most prominent are ammonium sulphonate, ammonium phenoxymate and trimethyl phosphate. Hardener should be non-corrosive and non-staining to moulds and non-reactive towards pigments.

Stabilizer

Especially urea formaldehyde has a limited shell life but some improvement is made by incorporating a stabilizer such as hexamine into the system. In some formulations the cure rate and the related time for flow are controlled by keeping the latent acid catalyst fixed and adjusting the stabilizer. Stabilizer is also necessary to absorb free acid developed.

Fillers

Where colour of the mouldings is not complete, wood flour is used as the filler. For all decorative mouldings, a pure cellulose filler which gives a somewhat thick coloured base is the filler most extensively used. Bleached sulfite cellulose is well suited for urea formaldehyde compounds but a trace of yellowish tint is inevitable in most cases. For higher demands on colour a still more purified cellulose containing a high proportion of cellulose and usually sold by this name, is satisfactory. Another criterian for cellulosic filler is that it should be free from dirt.

α - Cellulose Paper

Pure cellulose filler has advantage of light colour over wood flour but because of its fibrous nature it imparts mechanical strength to mouldings. Another remarkable difference is that cellulose filled amino mouldings have a surprising translucency which is desired from decorative mouldings. Also these fillers absorb the reaction water that is formed during last curing and thus render water hardened by its absorption.

α - cellulose is a colourless paper. It is produced by a special alkaline treatment of wood pulp. It also, increases the hardness of many filled plastics without increasing the density. Usually 30-40 per cent cellulose is used in moulding compositions based on the weight of the syrup.

Wood Flour

It is the cheapest filler and is also widely used but gives opaque mouldings, because it is inherently of brown colour, leads to limitation in colour range. Also it is used where strength is desired.

For urea formaldehyde, fabric fillers and mineral fillers are not commonly used. Usually 30-40 per cent of cellulose is used in the moulding compositions.

Other Fillers

However in order to get properties not obtainably by cellulosic fillers, inorganic fillers are used. They include asbestos and glass fibre.

Hardening of fillers, in particular of fibrous cellulosic fillers merit some consideration. Wood flour may be incorporated in the resin, namely by mixing wood flour and other ingredients on hot friction rolls. After a few minutes a homogeneous plastic sheet is formed which after cooling it can be ground into powder. However, in decorative, translucent, or opaque mouldings, cleanliness requires prime consideration, i.e. it is essential to keep away the mechanical dirt.

Mould Release Agents

One requirement of the moulder is that moulded article be easily removable from the mould without the necessary of lubricating the mould every now and then. To achieve this, a small amount of a mould lubricant is added to the compound. This must be distributed well by careful mixing. Stearate of zinc, magnesium or stearic acid, waxes etc. are employed for this purpose. The percentage is usually of the order of 0.2-0.5 per cent. Stearates of the alkali and alkaline metals are unsuitable. Other lubricants are oxidized paraffin wax, sulfonated castor oil etc.

Plasticizer

Their main virtue is that they enable more highly condensed resins to be used and thus reduce shrinkage whilst maintaining good flow temperatures. Glycerol-tolyl ether, for example, mono cresyl glicidyl ether is used for this purpose. Plasticizers are also included in common grades to improve the flow.

MANUFACTURE OF UREA MOULDING POWDER

First of all urea is condensed with aqueous formaldehyde in basic, neutral or very weakly acidic medium to a solution of methylol compounds. The most preferred preparations are 1-2 moles formaldehyde per mole of urea and 2-5 moles of formaldehyde. These resin syrups are used to impregnate cellulose fibre and then by mixing, drying, comminuting and densifying operations to produce saleable moulding powder. The following processes, with certain alterations are most widely used commercially. These variations often concern only the mechanical steps as there have been many changes in last ten to twenty years.

MIXING PROCESS

A Banbury mixer is charged with the amino resin solution which is usually still in a well flowing, medium viscous state. After the resin is warmed to decrease the viscosity (e.g. to 50-60° C), the desired amount of the cellulose sheet or shredded cellulose sheet is slowly added during mixing. Linters may also be used in sheet form, and even moist cellulose sheet containing substantial quantities of water. In all these cases the moisture content of the cellulose has to the determined by analysis and to be considered in the calculation of proportions. Usually a part of lubricating agent is added here in order to avoid sticking in the subsequent test mouldings. By kneading cellulose sheets are disintagrated into individual fibres and at the same time homogeneously impregnated. It is essential to arrive finally at a uniform, crumbly still moist mass that falls apart easily. Carefull control of the condensation stage of the resin and the correct water content of the mixtures are necessary. Too concentrated or too viscous may produce a heavy mass not suitable for efficient drying. A thin resin solution or too much water produces a mix in which the individual fibres do not stick together and, therefore, after drying and grinding undesirable, loose, fluffy product of low density is obtained. Final mixing may take place at a temperature around 75° C.

For drying the impregnated mass is transferred to the dryer or conveying

Bireen dryer. The moist mass is brought to the desired state of dryness by circulating hot air and at the same time condensation of the resin is further advanced. On the drum dryer temperatures used are 70-120° C. By continuously taking samples and immediately moulding a test sample, the drying conditions are corrected, based on the flow and other moulding characteristics of the test piece. On leaving the hot drum the dried material should be in the form of irregular granules of 1/8-3"/8 diameter and should be capable of being somewhat compressed in handling while hot, quite hard when cold. (Flow at this stage must be high, as some is lost in further processing steps. Flow must be a reflection of the stage of condensation, not of moisture content; this latter may cause clouds, white stains, excessive flow or even blisters.

Water content, periodically measured, should not run over 3-4 per cent and it is therefore an advantage to have the dried mass cool in closed containers in order to avoid excessive moisture pick up from air during wet weather.

Next the dried mass is ground, grinding of the raw moulding compositions obtained is mostly done in a hammer mill or any impact pulverizer. This gives a somewhat coarse powder with few fuzzy, tougher fibres. The powder is then ball milled to obtain a satisfactory density. This is done in one step simultaneously with finishing.

The finishing step from the raw product to the saleable moulding powders involves colouring to the desired shades by adding dyes or pigments in the proper amount, adding a mould release agent and after curing agents also to correct the cure speeds.

Manufacturer does not need large inventory of all standard colours of a moulding compound. From this the standard or extra colours can be made for the customer within a few days. Another valuable asset is that this method does not require colour correctly. The first time it may be corrected while still in ball mill.

MIXING PROCESS INCLUDING FINISHING STEPS

This process is a simple method of amino resin moulding compositions. The amino resin and the cellulosic filter as well as all additives for the final formulation of the end product including colourant, lubricating agents are mixed in a large closed Werner Pleiderer type mixer and subsequently dried and granulated in the same manner. First the resin syrup and cellulose are thoroughly mixed and disintegrated and the cellulose impregnated. Additional substances may be added a any desired stage. Dehydration of the mix is effected by applying vacuum or circulating hot air. Usually both means are embined. Finishing is rather a delicate operation particularly when new shades have to be matched, and only long experience enables one to end up with a powder that possesses all the properties. All the ingredients are mixed in the large mills that are at the same time used to densify the raw product.

However, for finishing operations many details are necessary. For example because of its lubricating action not all of the mould release agents may be added in the start, because it makes ball milling take more time. Many pigments develop the proper shade for the finished product only when milled for a predetermined time, and this time is variable with various size ball mills. Ball mills require a lining and filling with grinding ball that do not produce off-colour in the product because of contamination. A tough ceramic lining and ceramic or flint balls are often used and found satisfactory.

The major advantage of using separate finishing steps is that the mixer is kept running and drying proceeds while fresh surfaces of the wet material are exposed to the hot air.

After several hours of drying the material turns into soft, then hard granules but some larger lumps remins. These large lumps are not sufficiently dry inside and so are screened off and used in next batch. The dry granulated main part of the batchis passed through an impact mill after cooling to produce a dense sandy moulding powder ready for use.

The surfaces of the moulded articles made from this method are not of the same high density as from products of the previous method. Also this method does not allow correction of shade. But it is easy to adopt, space saving and economical.

MOULDING OF UREA MOULDING POWDERS

The moulding of the urea moulding powder is basically same as for phenolic moulding powder earlier described. But ureas demand care in avoiding dirt and also they are more sensitive to oven cure. This can be explained by the difference in the temperature ranges at which these resins can be successfully moulded.

1. Phenolic resins = 150-200° C
2. Urea formaldehyde = 140-160° C

Over sensitivity of the urea formaldehyde resins is due to the fact that oven curing rapidly decomposes the resin and oven cured articles have blisters.

MOULDS

The moulds used for urea resins are the same as used for phenolics, i.e. hand operated, semi or fully automatic presses.

The moulds are heated by electricity. Chromium plated moulds are generally satisfactory.

PROCESS

The moulding steps in the manufacture are of the following type:

The mould is heated to the optimum temperature. A weighed or measured amount of the moulding compound is filled into the the cavity and the plunger begins to close. As soon as the plunger touches the composition, pressure builds up and the compound is compressed and heated simultaneously. The material is now softened by heat, the pressure of the line drops and mould closes. The soft material by its capacity to flow under pressure, fills all the empty places of the mould, thus forming the article in its details. With urea formaldehyde the breating cycle has to be extended at this time. Moisture, water of reaction, trapped air and some excess formaldehyde escape in a few seconds so that they cannot cause moulding faults such as blister and clouds. The mould is closed again and proper curing pressure and mouding temperature are applied for the correct time. The fully cured article can then be easily taken out of the mould while still hot and when cooled can be finished by removing flash etc.

Especially with urea formaldehyde compounds, the hot moulded article is still somewhat soft and the larger articles may even deform on cooling. Deformation can be controlled by letting the article shrink while cooling on simple frames, usually wood, so that it cools while keeping its desired shape.

Since the flow characteristics of melamine formaldehyde moulding compositions are better, they are very often transfer moulded. But urea formaldehyde moulding compositions are rarely moulded in transfer moulding presses because of their lesser flow and tendency to cure fast in the moulds.

Urea formaldehyde moulding powders are used extensively for the production of electrical accessories due to the fact that in addition to having the required mechanical strength and rigidity they can also be moulded round metallic inserts. The formaldehyde moulding powders are, therefore, generally favoured for nearly all electrical accessories except for lampholders for which melamine formaldehyde is used because of its greater resistance to embrittlement on prolonged exposure to high temperature.

6. LAMINATED PLASTICS

A laminate is essentially a multilayered combination of thermoset resin and fibrous filler in sheet form. Laminates generally have flat or panel-like form. However, they can be postformed into simple or compound curvatures so that its dinstinction from moulded resins arises mainly from the manner in which the two are fabricated.

For the manufacture of a laminated resin, a fairly advanced state of condensation is desired. Urea formaldehyde resin requires an acid catalyst to effect hardening.

The urea-thiourea-formaldehyde system was the first amine resin to be applied commercially for this purpose. Cellulose filled laminates were used for table tops, light diffusers, and refrigerator door liners.

7. MISCELLANEOUS APPLICATIONS

Quite distinct from the use as a resin or plastic is the current application of polymethyl thylene ureas (F/U:1) in fertilizers for lawn and garden use. The particular advantage offered is the gradual release of nitrogen to the soil through slow hydrolysis and decomposition rates.

IMPORTANT VARIABLES AND THEIR CONTROL IN THE MANUFACTURE OF MOULDING POWDERS

There are certain variables that should be controlled for production of quality grade amino moulding powders. For this various factors that influence the product should be carefully considered. Following are importants variables:

PURITY OF THE REAGENTS

Every commercial grade of formalin has some methanol from its manufacturer to stabilize the formalin solutions. Urea moulding powders made from the methanol containing formalin solution have higher rate of water absorption than with methanol free formaldehyde. To avoid this, it is preferably to use unstabilized formalin for urea moulding powders.

AMOUNT OF REACTANTS

The molar ratio of formaldehyde to urea taken is generally 1.6:1 with the formaldehyde in the form of aqueous solution. This solution always contains some formic acid and is therefore neutralized with alkali or ammonia before addition of urea. After urea is dissolved, methylol formation is achieved resulting the components at a moderate temperature (say 50° C) for a few hours. A turbid solution or a slurry of methylol compounds develops, which can be used after further reaction to impregnate the filler.

pH CONTROL

The control of pH during the reactions of urea with formaldehyde is of paramount importance for production of resin solutions. Formalin solutions always contain some formic acid often from 0.05-1%, which is altogether too much to be usable in these reactions. If the acid is not removed before reaction with urea this small amount can act as a catalyst and the reactor shall be uncontrollable. In this case, the reactants will heat up and form a soft, white gel, which soon is transformed into a block of white, gelled, hard resin that is worthless for further production.

Another suitable way to condense urea and formaldehyde is to start the reaction with one mole urea and some excess formaldehyde. For example 2-2.3 moles of formaldehyde will hold the pH strictly between 7.5 and 8.5 while heating to near the boiling point of the solution. After the formation of the methylols, the rest of urea is added at lower temperature, as described above, to deal with the rest of formaldehyde. The urea-formaldehyde so obtained is clear any may be further condensed to the desired viscosity.

CONTROL OF REACTION

Careful pH control during the reaction of urea or melamine with formaldehyde in combination with repeated tests for solubility and viscosity are the methods used to contral the molecular weight of the mass.

Also repeated or even continuous determinations of pH during reaction are highly recommended because in warm formaldehyde solutions exposed to air, formaldehyde itself is oxidised to formic acid.

The increase in molecular size can easily be seen in the U.F. reaction by measuring viscosity and the m-f resins by determining solubility of the respective solutions during condensation. A m-f resins can be evaluated very well diluting a sample of 5 ml at 20° C with H_2O Nos. of mls. of H_2O added to reach permanent turbidity is a satisfactory means of estimating the condensation stage of the given resin solution.

FORMULATION OF MOULDING POWDERS

Formulation of moulding powders depends upon two factors:

1. Properties desired
2. Cost

Resin is prepared in syrup form and its proportion is determined by the properties aimed at, but should be enough to impregnate the filler particles. The filler, apart from the resin syrup, is the most important ingredient. It is generally 30-40 per cent by weight of resin syrup. Hardener is generally 0.2-2 per cent on the total powder weight. The precise quantity of hardeners depends upon the strength of acid liberated, the moulding powder composition, the processing conditions, and the rate of cure desired. Plasticisers are generally added to the extent of 2-7 per cent of the wt. of resin syrup. The pigment is generally 1-2 per cent of the syrup weight. The selection of proportion of colouring matter require some experience in the line. Proportion of inorganic fillers is usually high, up to 50 per cent of syrup.

Typical formulations for urea formaldehyde powders are given below.

UREA FORMALDEHYDE MOULDING POWDER

First of all resin syrup is made by taking molar ratio of formaldehyde/ urea to 1.4-1.5. This resin syrup is the basis of formulation. Typical formulation is given below.

Ingredients	*Parts by weight*
1. Resin syrup	200
2. Cellulose paper or disintegrated sulfite wood pulp	65
3. Zinc stearate	2
4. Monocresyl glycoryl ether	24
5. Chloroacetamide	4
6. Colorant	1-3 parts

For wood flour filled powders filler is fine wood flour and its weight on above formulation is about 80 parts.

Urea formaldehyde forms of both open cell and closed cell types are available. The open cell type, prepared by air foaming and setting a phosphoric acid catalyzed syrup, is used for thermal insulation and for the support of floral displays. In another application microscopically small hollow spheres of resin, 2-60 microns in diameter, made by special spray drying sector techniques, are used with binders for low density aggregate in light weight structural members and insulation.

These resins have been used to saturate wood for stabilization purposes and prepare densified wood, with gypsum of develop high strength rapidly, and to make surgical bandage for casts of high strength and low weight.

PROPERTIES OF MOULDING POWDERS

A specification for 'Aminoplastic Moulding Materials' is covered by B.S. 1322:1956. Some important properties of these powders are given below.

Property	*U.F.Resin*
Specific gravity @ 15° C	1.48-1.52
Tensile strength lb/in^2	5000-7000
Impact strength ft/lb. in notch	0.26
Compressive strength lb/in^2	25-35000
Dielectric strength V/nil	300-400
Thermal conductivity cal/sec/cm^2/C/10-4	7-10

• *Chapter 13* •

PROJECT PROFILES

PLANT ECONOMICS OF PHENOL FORMALDEHYDE RESIN

Rated Plant Capacity = 1.00 Mt./Day

LAND & BUILDING = Rs. 3,60,000.00
(Land required 500 sq. mt.)

PLANT & MACHINERY

1. Reactor
2. Melting tank
3. Storage tanks
4. Melting tank
5. Vacuum Pump.
6. Pipe lines, valves and fittings
7. Resins coolers, S.S. pan rectangular
8. Boiler
9. Water tank
10. 5 H.P. motor for vacuum pump
11. 3 H.P. motor for reactor
12. Process pump for pumping formaldehyde to the material tanks
13. Thermostats
14. Thermometers, viscometers, flow meters and pH meters
15. Other miscellaneous instruments

FIXED CAPITAL

1. Land & Building	Rs.	3,60,000.00
2. Plant & Machinery	Rs.	5,03,000.00
3. Other Fixed Assets	Rs.	87,000.00
TOTAL	Rs.	9,50,000.00

TOTAL WORKING CAPITAL/MONTH

1. Raw Material	Rs.	6,37,450.00
2. Salary & Wages	Rs.	26,250.00
3. Utilities & Overheads	Rs.	42,100.00
TOTAL	Rs.	7,05,800.00

TOTAL CAPITAL INVESTMENT

Total Fixed Capital	Rs.	9,50,000.00
Total Working Capital for 2 months	Rs.	14,11,600.00
TOTAL	Rs.	23,61,600.00

TURN OVER/ANNUM

300 tonnes Phenol Formaldehyde Resin	Rs.	1,05,00,000.00

PROFIT SALES RATIO = 14.17 %

RATE OF RETURN = 63.01 %

BREAK EVEN POINT (B.E.P) = 36.90 %

PLANT ECONOMICS ON POLY AMIDE RESIN

Rated Plant Capacity	=	1.00 Ton/Day
LAND & BUILDING	=	Rs. 16,27,500.00

(Land required 800 sq. mts.)

PLANT & MACHINERY

1. Reaction vessel
2. Condenser
3. Vacuum pump
4. Storage tank
5. Drum filling machine
6. Laboratory testing equipments
7. Misc. pipe & pipe fittings, valves etc.

FIXED CAPITAL

1. Land & Building	Rs.	16,27,500.00
2. Plant & Machinery	Rs.	6,60,000.00
3. Other Fixed Assets	Rs.	1,75,000.00
TOTAL	Rs.	24,62,500.00

TOTAL WORKING CAPITAL/MONTH

1. Raw Material	Rs.	14,15,000.00
2. Salary & Wages	Rs.	60,750.00
3. Utilities & Overheads	Rs.	82,200.00
TOTAL	Rs.	15,57,950.00

TOTAL CAPITAL INVESTMENT

Total Fixed Capital	Rs.	24,62,500.01
Total Working Capital for 3 months	Rs.	46,73,850.00
TOTAL	Rs.	71,36,350.01

TURN OVER/ANNUM

Sale of 300 mt of Poly Amide Resin	Rs.	2,40,00,000.00

PROFIT SALES RATIO = 15.40 %
RATE OF RETURN = 51.79 %
BREAK EVEN POINT (B.E.P) = 38.31 %

PLANT ECONOMICS ON POLYESTER RESINS

Rated Plant Capacity = 2.00 Ton/Day

LAND & BUILDING = Rs. 24,40,000.00
(Total land area 1000 Sq.mts.)

PLANT & MACHINERY

1. Jacketed Reaction Vessel
2. Premelter
3. Condenser with accessories
4. Dowthern vapourizer with burner and accessories.
5. Dowtherm storage tank (S.S.tank)
6. Liquid dowtherm condenser.
7. Dowtherm condensate receiver
8. Liquid dowtherm cooler
9. Vapour scrubber with sludge tank
10. Resin receiving tank
11. Water Chiller
12. Pumps, valves, motors, structures, fitting pipes etc.
13. PVC sintex tank

FIXED CAPITAL

1. Land & Building	Rs.	24,40,000.00
2. Plant & Machinery	Rs.	36,45,000.01
3. Other Fixed Assets	Rs.	5,45,000.00
TOTAL	Rs.	66,30,000.01

TOTAL WORKING CAPITAL/MONTH

1. Raw Material	Rs.	24,39,194.00
2. Salary & Wages	Rs.	82,194.00
3. Utilities & Overheads	Rs.	1,92,000.00
TOTAL	Rs.	27,13,388.00

TOTAL CAPITAL INVESTMENT

Total Fixed Capital	Rs.	66,30,000.01
Total Working Capital for 3 months	Rs.	81,40,164.00
TOTAL	Rs.	1,47,70,164.01

TURN OVER/ANNUM

Polyester Resin 600 MT	Rs.	3,90,00,000.00

PROFIT SALES RATIO = 7.59 %
RATE OF RETURN = 20.05 %
BREAK EVEN POINT (B.E.P) = 61.82 %

PLANT ECONOMICS (ALL FIG. IN LACS) ON POLYCARBONATE RESIN

Rated Plant Capacity = 36.00 Mt./Day

LAND & BUILDING = Rs. 663.50
(Land area 25 Acres)

PLANT & MACHINERY

1. Stainless Steel Storage bin
3. FRP lined S. S. Storage bin
4. Reaction vessel (S.S.)
5. S. S. Vacuum Systems
6. Vacuum Pump with motor and accessories
7. Phenol Condensor
8. Phenol Storage Tank
9. Cooling Tower (FRP lined) with pump & accessories
10. PVC (Sintex) water storage tank
11. Boiler
12. Micro processor based computer control system
13. Process Control equipments and instrumentation
14. Laboratory Equipments & instruments
15. Palletiser
16. Automatic Weighing,filling and bag sealing machines
17. Conveyor belt and bucket elevators
18. Platform, Structures, and other fittings

FIXED CAPITAL

1. Land & Building	Rs.	663.50
2. Plant & Machinery	Rs.	10,650.24
3. Other Fixed Assets	Rs.	5,078.00
TOTAL	Rs.	16,391.74

TOTAL WORKING CAPITAL/MONTH

1. Raw Material		Rs.	692.40
2. Salary & Wages		Rs.	21.95
3. Utilities & Overheads		Rs.	28.80
	TOTAL	Rs.	743.15

TOTAL CAPITAL INVESTMENT

Total Fixed Capital		Rs.	16,391.74
Total Working Capital for 3 months		Rs.	2,229.44
	TOTAL	Rs.	18,621.18

TURN OVER/ANNUM

By Sale of Polycarbonate Resin Pallets 10800 MT	Rs.	15,120.00

PROFIT SALES RATIO = 14.58 %

RATE OF RETURN = 11.84 %

BREAK EVEN POINT (B.E.P) = 65.80 %

PLANT ECONOMICS ON UREA FORMALDEHYDE RESIN

Rated Plant Capacity = 1.00 Ton/Day

LAND & BUILDING = Rs. 4,35,000.00
(Land required 500 sq.mt.)

PLANT & MACHINERY

1. Formaldehyde storage tank
2. Reactor
3. Condenser
4. Condensate receiving tank
5. Ammonia storage
6. Urea storage tank
7. Baby boiler
8. Storage for sod hyd.
9. Storage for Resin
10. Misc. equipment like pump etc.

FIXED CAPITAL

1. Land & Building	Rs.	4,35,000.00
2. Plant & Machinery	Rs.	6,81,500.00
3. Other Fixed Assets	Rs.	1,60,000.00
TOTAL	Rs.	12,76,500.00

TOTAL WORKING CAPITAL/MONTH

1. Raw Material	Rs.	2,21,875.00
2. Salary & Wages	Rs.	60,720.00
3. Utilities & Overheads	Rs.	1,20,800.00
TOTAL	Rs.	4,03,395.00

TOTAL CAPITAL INVESTMENT

Total Fixed Capital	Rs.	12,76,500.00
Total Working Capital for 3 months	Rs.	12,10,185.00
TOTAL	Rs.	24,86,685.00

TURN OVER/ANNUM

300 tonnes of U.F. Resin	Rs.	66,00,000.00

PROFIT SALES RATIO = 17.42 %
RATE OF RETURN = 46.24 %
BREAK EVEN POINT (B.E.P) = 56.29 %

PLANT ECONOMICS ON ACRYLIC COPOLYMER EMULSION

Rated Plant Capacity = 500.00 Kgs/Day

LAND & BUILDING = Rs. 25,75,000.00
(Land required 1500 Sq.Mt.)

PLANT & MACHINERY

1. Vessel (A) stainless steel
2. Vessel (B) stainless steel 5 cubic meter Capacity with stirrer & other necessary arrangement.
3. Vessel (C) stainless steel 6.25 cubic meter capacity with stirrer & other necessary arrangements.
4. Centrifuge
6. Monomer storage tanks.
7. Boiler
8. Deionization plant.
9. Vacuum pump.
10. Cooling tower.
11. Beam scales and weighing bridge & liquid filling machine.
12. Instrumentation & process control equipment.

FIXED CAPITAL

1. Land & Building	Rs.	25,75,000.00
2. Plant & Machinery	Rs.	26,05,000.00
3. Other Fixed Assets	Rs.	7,20,000.00
TOTAL	Rs.	59,00,000.00

TOTAL WORKING CAPITAL/MONTH

1. Raw Material	Rs.	4,32,000.00
2. Salary & Wages	Rs.	88,875.00
3. Utilities & Overheads	Rs.	1,34,300.00
TOTAL	Rs.	6,55,175.00

TOTAL CAPITAL INVESTMENT

Total Fixed Capital	Rs.	59,00,000.00
Total Working Capital for 3 months	Rs.	19,65,525.00
TOTAL	Rs.	78,65,525.00

TURN OVER/ANNUM

Sale of 1,50,000 Kgs. of Acrylic Co-polymer emulsion.	Rs.	1,35,00,000.00

PROFIT SALES RATIO = 25.35 %

RATE OF RETURN = 43.51 %

BREAK EVEN POINT (B.E.P) = 48.99 %

• Chapter 14 •

PRESENT MANUFACTURERS/DEALERS/ SUPPLIERS OF SYNTHETIC RESINS

Resins - Synthetic

Anuvi Chemicals P.Ltd
25E/4, Model Town,
Bal Rajeshwar Road,
Mulund (W),
Mumbai-400080.
Phone : (022)-5653818
Fax : (022)-5645455.
E-Mail: anuvi@bom2.vsnl.net.in

Asian Paints (India) Ltd.
Nirmal 5th Floor,
Nariman Point,
P.B.No. 11701,
Mumbai -400021
Phone : (022)-2024544,
Fax : (022)-2028993

Auchtel Products Ltd.
142/C, Victor House,
N.M. Joshi Marg,
Lower Parel (W),
Mumbai - 400013.
Phone : (022)-4974211,4933975,
Fax : (022)-4939755,4974211
E-Mail : auchtel@vsnl.com

Berger Paints India Ltd.
Berger House, 129,
Park Street,
Kolkata-700017.
Phone : (033)-299724-8,
Fax : (033)-2499729,2499009.
E-Mail :
berger@giasc101.vsnl.net.in

Bombay Paints Ltd
B.D. Patil Marg,
Gavanpada,
Chembur,
Mumbai -400074.

Coates of India Ltd.
Transport Depot Road,
Kolkata - 700088 (W.B)
Phone : (033)-4792584,4793311,
Fax : (033)47952167

Goodlass Nerolac Paints Ltd.
Nerolac House,
Ganparao Kadam Marg,
Lower Parel, Post Box 16322,
Mumbai - 400013 (Maharashtra)
Phone - (022)-4934001,4934003,
Fax : (022)-4936296,4973704

Harshadrai Navnitrai & Bros
Ladi Road,
Jetpur - 360370,
Gujarat
Phone : (02823)-20474,21579

Epoxy Resins

Ciba Speciality Chemicals (I) Ltd.
Off. Aarey Road,
Goregaon (East),
Mumbai-400063.
Phone : (022)-8403221,8403222,
Fax : (022)-8421532,

Dhaval Dyes,
C1/5, G.I.D.C. Estate,
Vithal,
Udyognagar - 388121,
Gujarat
Phone : (02692)-46143,47890
Fax : (02692)-02692-47890

Forrum Corp
313/16/6 G.I.D.C. Estate,
Ankleshwar - 393002,
Gujarat,
Phone (02646)-24018,23923

International Technology Corp
Plot B-31, Near Monginis,
New Link Road,
Andheri West,
Mumbai-400053.
Phone :(022)-6324471,6401332
Fax : (022)-6324471

Narkhede Chemicals
3, Vrindavan Building,
Krishnadham Society,
S.D.Marg,
Panchpakhade,
Thane 400602,
Maharashtra.
Phone : (022)-5680520,
Fax : (022)-5441996.
E-Mail :
narkhedechemicals@vsnl.com

Parikh Resins & Polymers Ltd
54/38, Nayaganj,
Kanpur- 208001
Uttar Pradesh,
Phone : (0512)-313019,363032
Fax : (0512)-310630
E-Mail: parikh@1w1.vsnl.net.in

Ruia Chemicals P.Ltd
AB/243, Sector-1,
Salt Lake City,
Kolkata - 700064
Phone : (033)-3597726,3597727
Fax : (033)-3597727

SIP Industries Ltd.
116, Radhakrishnan Salai,
Mylapore,
Chennai-600004
Phone : (044)-8530512,8591038.
Fax : (044)-8530289.
E-Mail : sipil@siptech.co.in

Melamine Formaldehyde Resins

Anu Synth Chem Industries
Plot No. 79,
Kundaim Industrial Estate,
Kundaim-403115,
Goa
Ph:.0834-395287
Fax: 395287

Atul Ltd.
At P.O. Atul,
Distt. Valsad
Atul - 396020
Gujarat
Ph:.02632-33621,33622
Fax: 33631, 33639

Pay Rs.1500/- for
Classified Advertisement only.

Phenol Formaldehyde Resins

ABR Organics Ltd.
A-3, Madhava Apartments,
2-2-23/41/4&5,
Bank Colony, Bagh Amberpet,
Hyderabad - 500013 (A.P)
Phone : (040)-7619059.
Fax : (040)-7640873.
E-Mail: abrorg@hd2.vsnl.net.in
Website : http://
www.abrorganics.com.

Amberlite Polymers P.Ltd.
3-6-69/2/1, Basheerbagh,
Near Skyline,
Hyderabad - 500029
Phone : (040)-3221885,3236573.
Fax : (040)-3221885.
E-Mail
:amberlitepolymers@yahoo.com.

Bakelite Hylam Ltd.
7-2-1669, Sannat Nagar,
P.O.Box No. 1908,
Hyderabad - 500018 (A.P)
Phone : (040)-3702641,3702642
Fax : (040)-3702672,

Chem Aux Products
1 Jawaharlal Nehru Road,
Anakaputhur,
Chennai -600070 (T.N)
Phone : (044)-2480443
Fax : (044)-2367616
E-Mail : gsamr@md3.vsnl.net.in

Esterkote Pvt. Ltd.
18, 2nd Floor, Balaram Road,
Adyar, Chennai - 600020 (T.N)
Phone : (044)-4416558.
Fax : (044)-4420388
E-Mail : esterkot@md3.vsnl.net.in

Filtec Research & Manufacturing Co.
18-26 Dev Prayag,
Ravi Industrial Compound,
Hajuri Lane,
Naupada,
Thane -400602,
Maharashtra.
Phone : (022)-5334073,5364173.
Fax : (022)-5335614m5424760
E-Mail : filtec@bom@.vsnl.net.in

Forace Polymers P.Ltd
10th KM stone, Delhi-Hardwar
Road,
Dist. Hardwar,
Bahadrabad - 249402,
Uttar Pradesh.
Phone : (0133)-451824,451823,
Fax : (0133)-451823.

Furnova Polymers Ltd.
12-B, Welfare Chambers,
Ground Floor,
Plot No. 73, Sector 17, Vashi,
Navi Mumbai-400703, Maharashtra.
Phone : (022)-7891141,7894303,
Fax : (022)-7893935.
E-Mail : furnova@vsnl.com.

Urea Formaldehyde Resins

Chemox Industrial Corp.
33 A, Vatsa House,
Janma-Bhoomi Marg,
Fort, Mumbai-400001.
Phone : (022)-2870133,2874119
Fax : (022)-8574487

Gayatri Chemical Industries
4, Masalawala Complex,
2nd Floor,
Above Central Bank of India,

Opp. Railway Station,
Ankleshwar - 393002
Gujarat
Phone : (02646)-50276
Fax : (02646)-50614

Harish Acro Polymer P.Ltd.
205, Barodiya Tower,
D-12, Cenral Market,
Prashant Vihar, New Delhi-110085
Phone :(011)-7268125,7864385,
Fax : (011)-7864385,

Hemco Plastic Industries
2, Sonawala Chawl,
sonawala X Road No.2.
Goregaon (East),
Mumbai-400063
Phone : (022)-8734551
Fax : (022)-8733274,

Hindustan Adhesive and Chemicals
48, Dum Dum Road,
Kolkata-700074
Ph. (033)-5514755,5513285
Fax : (033)-5514755

Indian Recaply Enterprises P.Ltd.
P-198, C.I.T. Scheme VII-M,
Kolkata -700067
Phone : (033)-3346433,3346448,
Fax : (033)-3343942.

Macro Polymers P.Ltd
165, G.V.M.M. Odhav.
Ahmedabad - 382445
Gujarat
Phone : (079)-2871966,2894305
Fax. (079)-7540767,
Email. mayank@ad1.vsnl.net.in

Punjab Dyes & Chemicals
31, Near City Telephones Exchange,
Amritsar - 143006, Punjab
Phone : (0183)-552039,292985
Fax : (0183)-554983

Polyester Resins

Eastern Chemofarb Ltd.
S Park Mansions,
57 Park Street,
Kolkata - 700016.
Phone : (033)-2291793,2291539
Fax : (033)-4753368
Email : renshel@vsnl.com

Hardik Chemicals
220, Anand Mangal,
Behind Omkar House,
C.G. Road,
Ahmedabad-380009
Gujarat
Phone : (079)-468286

H.K.Enterprise
Aniket C.G.Road,
Navrangpura,
Ahmedabad-380009,
Gujarat
Phone : (079)-6565429,468752
Fax : (079)-6561910.
Email.hkal.ahd@sprintrpg.ems.vsnl.net.in

Jalaram Trading Co
4201/AG.I.D.C. Estate,
Near Crystal Chakdi,
Ankleshwar - 393002,
Gujarat
Phone - (02646)-22039,

Mittal Industries
Plot No. 1502, Phase I,

G.I.D.C.Estate,
Naroda, Ahmedabad-382330
Gujarat,
Phone : (079)-2821716,2819083.
Fax : (079)-2820511.

Narchem Industries
07, Monica Apartment,
Opposite Gurukul Society,
Panchpakhadi,
Thane-400602,
Maharashtra.
Phone : (022)-5265742
Fax : (022)-5365214

Nirav Chemical Industries,
18, Laxmi Estate,
Behind Dena Bank,
Gujarat Bottling Road,
Rakhial, Ahmedabad-380023,
Gujarat
Phone : (079)-2740654,2744082.
Fax : (079)-468201.

Alkyd Resins

Era Paints & Adhesives P Ltd.
17, Chandi Ghosh Road,
Kolkata-700040
Phone : (033)-4716702, 471568.

Krishi Oils Ltd.
Plot Nos. 91-94,
Sector-II, Dist.
Dhar, Pithampur -454775,
Madhya Pradesn.
Phone : (07292)-513015, 53388.
Fax : (07292)-513015

Macro Polymers P.Ltd
165, G.V.M.M.,
Odhav.
Ahmedabad - 382445,
Gujarat
Phone : (079)-2871966,2894305
Fax. (079)-7540767,
Email. mayank@ad1.vsnl.net.in

M.P. Dyechem Industries
59 & 63, Sector A,
Sanwer Road,
Industrial Area,
Indore-452003,
Madhya Pradesh,
Phone : (0731)-420325,420775
Fax : (0731)-420136

Neeraj Paints & Chemicals
P-5, Industrial Area, Site I,
B.S.R. Road, Distt. Ghaziabad,
Uttar Pradesh.
Phone : (0575)-718726,718727
Fax : (0575)-701611.
Email : neeraj@focusindia.com.

Niharika Paints & Chemicals P.Ltd.
41, Princep Street,
5th Floor,
Kolkata-700072.
Phone : (033)-266384,260718
Fax : (033)-268636.

Rang Krupa Enterprise
3454 G.I.D.C. Estate.
Ankleshwar-393002,
Gujarat
Phone : (02646)-24991

Raysinet Kemikal Co.
31 To 35, 74 & 75 Industrial Estate,
Dist. Durg, Bhilai - 490026,
Madhya Pradesh.
Phone : (0788)-356132,356173

• Chapter 15 •

RAW MATERIAL SUPPLIERS

Shankar Dyes & Chemicals
1209, Shankar Building, Gali No.11,
Sadar Bazar, Delhi-110006
Ph.: 3673462, 3558239, 3616830
Fax : 3558239
Branch : 119, Tilak Bazar, Delhi-1100006
Ph.: 3970589, 3959574, 3912061
Email : djeswani@sattiya.net.in
Website :www.shankardyesandchemicals.com
Specialist in all types of Chemicals & Dyes Products
(See advertisement in starting of this book)

Acrylic Acid

Abhilash Chemicals P.Ltd.
26-D, Ganesapuram, K. Pudur,
Madurai - 625007, Tamil Nadu.
Phone : (0452)-539566.
Fax : (0452)-539286.
Br. Office : C/29,
Vijay Smruti, 19th Road,
Chembur,
Mumbai North Taluk,
Madurai - 625305,
Tamil Nadu.
Phone : (0452)-870260
Estd. 1990. (Private Limited Company).

Aishwarya Chemicals
101/12, Om Apartments,
Medavakkam Tank Road,
Kilpauk,
Chennai - 600010 (T.N)

Arpan Industries,
10, Umang Society,
Near Jawahar Chowk,
Maninagar, Ahmedabad 380008,
Gujarat. Phone : (079)-2114283.
Fact : 7, Sarvoday Estate,
Isanpur,
Ahmedabad - 382443
Gujarat.
Phone : (079)-5328364

BASF India Ltd.
Rhone-Poulene House,
S.K. Ahire Marg,
Worli, Mumbai-400025.
Phone : (022)-4930730.
Fax : (022)-4950512. Br. Office:
(1) Karaka Building 1,
Ashram Road,
Navrangpura,
Ahmedabad - 380009,
Gujarat. Phone : (079)-6583074.
Fax : (079)-6581477. (2)
7, Basant Lok,
Vasant Vihar, New Delhi- 110057.
Phone : (011)-6147593.
Fax : (011)-6142862.

Dai-Ichi Karkaria Ltd,
Liberty Building,
Sir Vithaldas Thackersey Marg,
Mumbai-400020.
Phone : (022)-2015985,2017130,2015973.
Fax : (022)-2096976.
Telex : 011-83222
Email : daiichi@diklpun.aworld.net.

Jay Nakoda Industries,
5, Fulwadi Co-Operative Society,
Near Amarapali Theatre,
Gomtipur, Ahmedabad-380021,
Gujarat,
Phone : (079)-2114031,334661,332105.
Fax : (079)-2111544.
Email : meca@ad1.vsnl.net.in

Calcium Carbonate

Paras Mimneralas & Alloys
N1A/27, Kirti Nagar,
New Delhi-110015
Tel :5434766,5414322,5122484
Fax : 5121874

Calchem Industries India Ltd.
Factory Unit No. 1,
62, MIDC Industrial Area,
Village-Dhatav,
Roha-402116 Dist. Raiged (M.S)
Tel : (02194)-63734/63832
Unit No. 2 .
30, Industrial Area,
Poanta Sahib - 173025 (HP)
Tel : (01704)-23609/23598
E-mail : calchem@pn3.vsnl.net.in

Bajaj Rubber Co.
15, Khurshid Market,
Sadar Bazar,
Delhi-110006
Phone : 3626038, 3535592, 35347701
Fax: 011-3612498
E-Mail : anilchemical@yahoo.com

Jaimurty Minerals & Chemicals Pvt.Ltd.
Factory. 82,Industrial Area,
Poanta Sahib-173025
(Himachal Pradesh)
Tel : (01704)-23166/23527
E-Mail : calchem@bom5.vsnl.net.in
New Delhi : 102, South Ext.
Plaze-I,
M.Moth, NDSE Part-II,
New Delhi - 110049
Tel : (011)-6255122,6255272,6255742
E-Mail : calchem@nda.vsnl.net.in

Akay Chemicals
5-J.V.Chotai Complex,
Vazari Chowk,
M.G.Road, Junagarh - 362001,
Gujarat Phone : (0285)-625922, 651921,651990,625925,650930,6223340.
Fax : (0285)-650930.

Gujarat Clay Mills P.Ltd.
Microfine House,
Qureshi Nagar,
Kurla (East),
Mumbai - 400070.
Phone : (022)-5228688,5228689
Fax : (022)-5230932

Gumpro Chem
56, C.P.Tank Road,
Mumbai - 400004.
Phone : (022)-3827671,3827672.
Fax : (022)-3804564.
Email : gumpro@vsnl.com.

K.Mohan & Co.
12/14, Moores Road,
Moores Garden,
Chennai - 600006 (T.N)
Phone : (044)-8271320,8277704
Fax : (044)-8572388.
Email : kaymohan@vsnl.com.
Web:http//www.metroindia.com/kaymohan.

Lime Chemicals Ltd.
Prem Estate, 2nd Floor,
Near Sant Savater,
Cross Road No. 1,
Mustafa Bazar,
Mazgaon, Mumbai - 400010.
Phone : (022)-3714083,3714151,
Fax : (022)3775647.
Email : info@limechem.com.
Web: http://www.limechem.com.

Margee Minerals (P) Ltd.
711, Saffron Complex, Fatehgunj,
Vadodara -390002,
Gujarat.
Phone : (0265)-786770.
Fax : (0265)-445103.

Butanol

Rita Corp.
Rita Chem Industries,
B Block, 37 Sujal Mansion,
Bhangawadi,
Kalbadevi Road,
Mumbai-400002.
Phone : (022)-2002645.
Fax : (022)-2078262.

Adinath Petrochems,
B-56, Siddhi Apartment,
Ashok Nagar, Kandivli (E),
Mumbai- 400001.
Phone : (022)- 8877557.
Fax : (022)-8873934.
Email : adipetro@vsnl.com.
Web : http://www.adinath.com.

Aroma Organics P.Ltd.
106-110, Krishna Bhawan,
22/B, Shivji Devshi Marg,
Deonar, Mumbai-400088.
Phone : (022)-5575010,5575012,-13
Fax : (022)-5564200.
Email :
suneel.jain@gems.vsnl.net.in.

B.R.International,
90/92, Kazi Sayed Street,
29, Hemprakash, Mumbai-400003.
Phone : (022)-3433605, 3438037.
Fax : (022)-3440235.

Chandranil Dye-Chem Corp.
2/26, Mansoor Building,
96, Princess Street,
Mumbai-400002.
Phone : (022)-2011038,2074299,
Fax : (022)-2011038.
Email : cdc@ bom5..vsnal.net

Chemico,
10/18,Old Hanuman Lane,
Princess Street,
Mumbai-400002.
Phone : (022)-2006427,2062483.
Fax : (022)-2017623.
Email : dwijesh@bom5.vsnl.net.in.

Drier

Arihant Dye-Stuffs (India)
6, Tripathi Sadan, 110,
S.V. Road, Jogeshwari (w),
Mumbai-400102.
Phone : (022)-6790450,
Fax : (022)-6797299.
Email : ramesh@bom4.vsnl.net.in

Nixon Chemical P.Ltd.
Copper Roller's Premises,
2nd Floor, L.B.S. Marg,
Bhandup (West),
Mumbai-4000078.
Phone : (022)-5679134,5679135.
Fax : (022)-5676519.
Email : lumipon@bom4.net.in

Dhaval Industries,
16/18, Garibdas Street 8,
Madiar Mansion, Vadgadi,
Mumbai-400 003.

General Traders.
29 & 97, N.R.K. Rajarahinam Street,
Sivakasi -626123, Tamil Nadu
Phone : (04562)-74014,74310,
Fax : (04562)-72810.

OMG Asia Pacific Co. Ltd.
208, Anand Estate,
189/A. Sane Guruji Marg,
Mumbai-400011.
Phone : (022)-3010740.
Fax : (022)-3015106.
Email : vsamir@bom5.vsnl.net.in.
Web : http://www.omgi.com.

Castor Oil - Dehydrated

Jayan Oil Mills,
13, Sitafalwadi,P.O.Box No. 6209,
Dr. Mascarenhas Road, Mazgaon,
Mumbai - 400010
Phone : (022)-3738810,3738811,
Fax : (022)-3738107
Telex : 011-75677
Email :
udeshi@giashm01.vsnl.net.in
Web : http://www.jayantoil.com.

Ricinash Oil Mill Ltd.
301,Shah & Nahar Industrial Estate,
Dr.E.Moses Road, Worli,
Mumbai-400026
Phone : (022)4921168
Fax : (022)-2028993.

Dhaval Industries,
16/18, Garibdas Street 8,
Madiar Mansion, Vadgadi,
Mumbai-400 003.

Mahendra & Co.
116,Keshavji Naik Road,
Chinchbunder,
Mumbai-400009.
Phone : (022)-3738240,3751750.
Fax : (022)-3730388

Nucleus Chemicals & Marketting
8, Dheeraj Apartment,
Jata Shankar Desai Road,
Opp. Bus Stop,
Near Railway Station,
Mulund (W),
Mumbai - 400080
Phone : (022)-5601380.
Fax : (022)-5611331.

Dispesion Resins

Malli Polymers P.Ltd.
5, Fulwadi Co-operative Society,
Near Amarpali Theatre,
Gomipur,
Ahmedabad-380021,
Gujarat
Phone : (079)-2114031,332105,
Fax : (079)-211544.
Email : meca@ad1.vsnl.net.in

Polymerphic Systems (P) Ltd.
18/1072, Jeevan Bhima Nagar,
Anna Nagar (W) Extn.
Chennai - 600101
Phone : (044)-6255117
Fax : (044)-627162

Shri Ganesh Petrochem
Outside Saloonagate,
Near Chaklashi Bhagole,
Nadiad 387001,
Gujarat
Phone :(0268)-62308,(R)62985

Chemex Corp
4, Nutan Para Road,
Lilush, Howrah,
West Bengal
Phone : (033)-6652835.

Rattan Singh Jaswant Singh
B-VII, 500 Saban Nagar,
Ludhiana -141008 Punjab
Phone : (0161)-722879,725674,710104
Fax : (0161)-725674

Ethylene Glycol

Evans India,
16, Saraswati Sadan,
115, Keshavji Naik Road,
Mumbai-400009.
Phone : (022)-3752129,3773060,

India Glycols Ltd.
C-124, Okhla Industrial Area,
Phase I,
New Delhi-110020.
Phone : (011)-6815772,6815185,
Fax :(011)-6810390,68194190.
Telex : 031-753431,75186IGLIN.
Email : igldelho@del2.vsnl.in.

Rita Corp.
Rita Chem Industries,
B Block, 37 Sujal Mansion,
Bhangawadi,
Kalbadevi Road,
Mumbai-400002.
Phone : (022)-2002645.
Fax : (022)-2078262.

Reliance Industries Ltd.
Maker Chambers IV, 3rd Floor,
222, Nariman Point, P.B.No. 11717,
Mumbai - 400021.
Phone : (022)-2842384,2842331,
Fax : (022)-2042268,2880391
Telex : 86542,82950
Web:http://www.ril.com.

National Organic Chemical Industries Ltd.
Mafatlal Chambers, B-Wing,
2nd Floor,
N.M.Joshi Marg, Lower Parel (E),
Mumbai-400013.
Phone : (022)-3016566,
Fax : (022)-3016570,3091855.

Fumaric Acid

Ganesh Anhydride Ltd
Ganesh House, Makwana Lane,
Marol Naka, Andheri (East),
Mumbai-400059.
Phone : (022)-8502096.
Fax : (022)-8505529

Herdillia Chemicals Ltd.
Air India Building,
13th Floor, Nariman Point,
Mumbai-400021.
Phone : (022)-2024224
Fax : (022)-2880942,204379
Email : herdho@bom3.vsnl.net.in
Web:http://www.herdillia.com.

ICS Industries
16, India Exchange Place,
3rd Floor, Room No. 9,
Kolkata-700001.
Phone : (033)-2203876,2203558.
Fax : (033)-2203558
Email : icsco@cal.vsnl.net.in.

Pure Chem P.Ltd.
8/10, Bora Bazar Street,
2nd Floor, Fort, Mumbai-400001.
Phone : (022)-2618787.
Fax :(022)-2610670

Godrej Soaps Ltd.
Phirojsha Nagar,
Eastern Express Highway,
Vikhroli (East),
Mumbai-400079.
Phone : (022)-
5171556,5172384,5170861
Fax : (022)-5171525,5171717,
Telex : 011-71480
Web: http://www.godrejindia.com.

Jocil Ltd.
Arundelpet, P.O.Box 216,
Guntur -522002.
Andhra Pradesh.
Phone :(0863)-290190 to 290192.
Fax : (0863)-290090.
Email :
jocil@jocil.xeevga.ems.vsnl.net.in.

Kamani Oil Industries
Pooran Asha,
317, Narsi Natha Street,
Mumbai-400009.
Phone : (022)-3451812,3420241,
Fax : (022)-3435964.

Kashu-Chem P. Ltd.
C-44, Radhika,
Happy Home Dwarkesh Co-op.Sec.
Poisar, Kandivali (W),
Mumbai-400067.
Phone :(022)-802006

Glycerine

Alloied Chemical Corp
658, G.I.D.C. Estate,
Road No. 54,
Makarpura,
Vadodara -390010.
Gujarat.
Phone : (0265)-642945.
Fax : (0265)-332953.

Apex Chemicals
28, Vithaldas Road,
Mumbai-400002.
Phone. (022)-2053560,2054833,

Colgate-Palmolive (India) Ltd.
Colgate Research Centre,
Main Street,
Hiranandani Gardens,
Powai,
Mumbai-400076.
Phone : (022)-5705060,
Fax : (022)-5705088.

Deepak Chemicals
2207, PhaseIV, G.I.D.C. Estate,
Vatva, Ahmedabad-382445,
Gujarat
Phone : (079)-5831878.
Fax : (079)-5834062,7419595.
Email : deepak@ad1.vsnl.net.in
Web: http://
www.deepdakchemicals.com.

Iron Oxide (Red)

Anirox Pigments Ltd
Lords, 3rd Floor,
7/1, Lord Sinha Road,
Kolkata -700071.
Phone : (033)-2822378,2826633.
Fax : (033)-2823086,4758433.
Email : anirox@vsnl.com.
Web: http://www.anirox.com

Pay Rs.1500/- for
Classified Advertisement only.

Anuj Industry
Plot No.16B, Ist Phase,
K.I.A.D.B. Industrial Area,
Bangalore Road,
Bellary (Hubli)-583102,
Karnataka.
Phone : (08392)-50061,50220
Fax : (08392)-50220.

Bharti Chemicals
177-178, Vithal Udyognagar,
V.V.Nagar,
Vithal Udyognagar-388121.
Gujarat.
Phone : (02692)-36034.
Fax : (02692)-36618.
Email: silverline@pcbbs.net.

Bajaj Rubber Co.
15, Khurshid Market,
Sadar Bazar,
Delhi-110006
Phone : 3626038, 3535592,
35347701
Fax: 011-3612498
E-Mail : anilchemical@yahoo.com

Chanakya Chemicals & Pigments P.Ltd.
1st Floor, Ambica Complex,
Thiruvalluvar Salai,
Dist. Namakkal, Velur,
Tamil Nadu
Phone : (04268)-21131

Linseed Oil

M.P.Dyechem Industries
59 & 63, Sector A,
Sanwer Road Industrial Area,
Indore -452003,
Madhya Pradesh
Phone : (0731)-420325,420775
Fax : (0731)-420136

Viscus Oils P.Ltd.
55/1/2C, New Palasia,
Indore-452001,
Madhya Pradesh,
Phone : (0731)-533710,432205
Fax : (0731)-431168, 538226
Telex : 0735-6313

Methanol

Aarti Drugs Ltd.
Plot No. 109-D,
Mahendra Indl. Estate,
Road No. 29.
Sion (E),Mumbai-400022
Phone : (022)-4072249.
Fax : (022)-4073462.4070144
Email : aarti@giasbm01.vsnl.net.in.
Web : http://www.aartigroup.com.

Acharya Chemicals
B-2/11, Jawahar Darshan,
Shri Khandewadi,
Off.Manpada Road,
Dombivli -421201
Maharashtra.
Phone : (0251)-448256,470604,
Email : acharyachem@vsnl.com.

Advanced Laboratories (P) Ltd
A-86, PIPDIC Industrial Estate,
Mettupalayam,
Pondicherrry-605009,
Pondicherry.
Phone : (0413)-371176.

Advance Petrochemicals Ltd.
93, New Cloth Market,
Ahmedabad-380002,
Gujarat
Phone : (079)-2124097,2164795.
Fax : (079)-2165386,5322219.
Telex : 0121-6807 APL IN
Email : goenka@wilnetonline.net.

Methyl Ethyl Ketone

Cetex Petrochemicals,
Manali, Chennai -600068.
Phone : (044)-5941358,5941359
Fax : (044)-5941835.
Email :
cetex.fac@cetex.sprintrpg.cms.vsnl.net.in
Web : http://www.cetexpetro.com.

Chemilite Industries
42/14, Babu Genu Road,
Mumbai-400002.
Phone : (022)-2050805,
Fax : (022)-2061582.

Gujarat Carbon & Industries Ltd.
Offtel Towers. 6th Floor,
R.C.Dutt Road,
Vadodara -390007.
Gujarat

Rita Corp
21, Chewool Wadi.
1st Floor.P.O.Box.No.2722,
Dr. M.B. Velkar's Street,
Kalbadevi Road,
Mumbai-400002.
Phone : (022)-2056895 (R) 8894226.
Fax : (022)-8899598

Phthalic Anhydride

Peroxides Ltd.
Leelavai Building,69,
Armenian Street,
Chennai - 600001.
Phone : (044)-5222101.
Fax : (044)-5229600.
Email : cps@giasmd01.vsnl.net.in

Herdillia Chemicals Ltd.
Air India Building, 13th Floor,
Nariman Point, Mumbai-400021
Phone : (022)-2880942,2042379.
Email : herdho@bom3.vsnl.net.in
Web: http://www.herdillia.com.

IG Petrochemicals Ltd.
401/404, Raheja Centra,
Free Press Journal Marg.
214, Nariman Point,
Mumbai-400021
Phone :(022)-2840714,2160534.
Fax : (022)-2836392,2040747.
Email : igpetro@vsnl.com.
Web : http://www.igpetro.com

Mysore Petrochemicals Ltd.
401/404, Raheja Centre,
Free Press Journal Marg,
214 Nariman Point,
Mumbai-400021.
Phone : (022)-2840714,2928435.
Fax : (022)-2040747,2836392.
Telex : 011-83928

Thirumalai Chemicals Ltd.
Thirumalai House, Plot No.101/102,
Road No. 29.
Sion-Matunga Estate Scheme N0.6,
Sion East, Mumbai-400022.
Phone : (022)-4017834,4017841.
Fax : (022)-4011699,4017869
Email : thirumalai@gnbom-tcl.global.net.in.

Pigment Binders

Arpan Industrial
10,Umang Society,
Near Jawahar Chowk,
Maninagar,
Ahmedabad-380008.
Gujarat.
Phone : (079)-2114283.

Chemox Industrial Corp
33A, Vatsa House,
Janmabhoomi Marg.
Fort, Mumbai-400001.
Phone : (022)-2870133,2874119
Fax :(022)-8574487.

Engineer's Poly-Chem
25/2, Pillayar Koil Street,
Bhavani Road, Post Box No.23.
Perundurai -638052.
Tamil Nadu.
Phone : (04294)-20730.
Fax : (04294)-21482.

Indian Chemical Industries,
Bhavani Chambers,
Near Times of India.
Ashram Road, Ahmedabad-380009
Phone : (079)-6587210,6582858,
Fax : (079)-6581889.
Telex : 121-6987-ICI IN.
Email :icidyes@ad1.vsnl.net.in.

Polyols

Jayan Oil Mills
13,Sitafalwadi,P.O.Box No. 6209,
Dr. Mascaraenhes Road,
Mazgaon,
Mumbai-400010.
Phone : (022)-3738810,
3738811-12-13
Fax : (022)-3738107,3730831.
Telex : 011-757677
Email :
udeshi@giasbm01.vsnl.net.in.

Polymermann (Asia) P.Ltd.
C-17, Kilfire House,
Dalia Industrial Estate,
Opp. Laxmi Industrial Estate,
Andheri (West),
Mumbai-400053.
Phone -(022)-6366252,(5 lines).
Fax : (022)-6367010.
Email :
polymer.replexp@gems.vsnl.net.in.

Southern Chemicals
504, Meridian Apartments,
Basheerbagh,
Hyderabad-500063
Phone : (040)-
3225550,3224223,3227429
Fax : (040)-3223177
Email : schem@hd1.vsnl.net.in.

Mica Agencies,
2, Ratnadeep,
Mahant Road Extension,
Vile Parle (East).
Mumbai-400057.
Phone : (022)-6111653, 6161316
Fax : (022)-6124315.
Email : tamhini@bom5.vsnl.net.in

Bhashaaver Mining Corp
23, Govardhan Niwas,
2nd Floor, 2nd Khatar Gallai,
Thakurdhwar,
Mumbai-400002.
Phone -(022)-4220422,4377651.
Fax : (022)-4379784.

G.K.Metal Powder Mfg.Co.
5,Vraj Bhavan, Khetwadi,
4th Lane, Sardar V.P.Road,
Post Box No. 3630,
Mumbai-400004.
Phone -(022)-3882450.
Fax :(022)-3895400.

Gujarat Clay Mills P.Ltd.
Microfine House, Qureshi Nagar,
Kurla (East),.
Mumbai-400070.
Phone : (022)-5228688,5228689.
Fax : (022)-5230932,

Polyvinyl Acetate Emulsions

Almex Laboratories P. Ltd.
G-1, Plot No. 251,
Road No. 15,
Jawahar Nagar,
Goregaon (West)
Mumbai-400062.
Phone : (022)-8748635.
Fax : (022)-8748924.

A.Sabar Chem
4, Mahavir Industrial Estate,
Navghar, Vasai Road (East),
Dist. Thane, Vasai - 401210,
Maharashtra.
Phone : (0250)-334184.

Organics (India)
1102 -A, Phase -III,
G.I.D.C. Estate,
Ahmedabad-380007,
Gujarat.
Phone : (079)-5833697

Auxi Chem Industries
30, Ahmedabad Building Material
Co.Op.Society,
Opp. Central Ware House,
N.I.D.C. Lambha,
Ahmedabad, Gujarat
Phone : (079)-5890076, (R) 5331347

Polyvinyl Alcohol

Ashok Chemicals
43, Princess Street,
3, Devkaran Mansion,
Mumbai-400002
Phone : (022)-2064853,2084293.
Fax : (022)-2091459,
Email : apshah@bom5.vsnl.net.in.

Pay Rs.1500/- for
Classified Advertisement only.

Chemox Industrial Corp
33A, Vatsa House,
Janmabhoomi Marg.
Fort Mumbai-400001.
Phone : (022)-2870133,2874119.
Fax : (022)-8574487

Mittal Industries
Plot No. 1502, Phase I,
G.I.D.C. Estate,
Naroda Ahmedabad-382330,
Gujarat.
Phone : (079)-2820511.

Orinco Chemical Industries,
76/78, Issaji Street, Guru Sadan,
5th Floor, Vadgadi, Mumbai.400003.
Phone : (022)-3430791.

Poly-Resins
L-11, SIDCO Industrial Estate,
Kodungaiyur.Chennai-600118.
Phone : (044)-5375755.
Fax : (044)-5375755.

Shree Vinayak Industries,
2, Violete Villa, West Avenue Road,
Santacruz (West),
Mumbai-400054.
Phone : (022)-
6461069,6495100,6040460.
Fax : (022)-6042275.
Email : fineotex@hotmail.com.

Phenol

Coalchem
101, Light Industrial Area,
Bhilai - 490026
Madhya Pradesh.
Phone : (0788)-382670,381171,
Fax : (0788)-381365
Email :
coalchem@bom6.vsnl.net.in

Deeaar Laboratories
602/A, President Plaza,
Near RTO, Ring Road,
Surat - 395003,
Gujarat
Phone : (0261)-472670.
Fax : (026)-472670

De-Fine Labs
13/8, Dattatray Apartments,
Shiv Mandir Road,
Shiv-Ganganagar,
Ambernath -421501,
Maharashtra.
Fax : (0251)-682944.

Eastern Chemicals
48-12-7,Prakasam Road,
Srinagar, Akkayaapalem,
Visakhapatnam - 530016
Andhra Pradesh.
Phone : (0891)-551653
Fax : (0891)-540589

G.Chemie
5, Vruj Bhavan, 2nd Floor,
Khetwadi, 4th Lane,
Sardar V.P.Road,
Post Box 3630,
Mumbai-400004.
Phone : (022)-3882450
Fax : (022)-3895400

Starch

Amishi Drugs & Chemicals
Plot No. 622, Phase IV,
G.I.D.C. Estate, Naroda,
Ahmedabad-382330,
Gujarat.
Phone : (079)-2821857
Fax : (079)-2821176,6745407

Anil Starch Products Ltd.
Anil Road, Post Box No. 10009.
Ahmedabad-389025,
Gujarat
Phone : (079)-2123222.
Fax : (079)-2110731,
Telex : (079)-121-6544 NILA IN
Email : mktg@gnahd-anil.globalnet.ems.vsnl.net.in
Web : http://www.angelfire.com/co/anlist.

Gujarat Ambuja Exports Ltd.
Ambuja Tower Navrangpura,
Opposite Memnagar Fire Station,
P.O.Navjivan, Ahmedabad-380014,
Gujarat.

Kalpana Chemicals Ltd.
Road, No.5,
Nacharam Industrial
Development Area,
Hyderabad - 500076
Phone : (040)-7173241,7174445,7171178.
Fax : (040)-7171946.
Telex : 0425-7017 KCPL IN

Soyabean oil

Durga Agro Industries
3rd, Floor, Arya Samaj Mandir,
Kishan Gunj,
Hyderabad
Phone : (040)-4015662.

Foods Fats & Feriliser's Ltd.
Green House, 2nd Floor,
Green Street,
G.P.O. Box No. 10066,
Fort, Mumbai-400023
Phone : (022)-2662136,2661846,
Fax : (022)-2664115.
Telex : 011-82503 FFFB IN.

Email : fffb@vsnl.com.

M.P.Dyechem Industries
59 & 63, Sector A,
Sanwer Road Industrial Area,
Indore -452003, Madhya Pradesh.
Phone : (0713)-420325,420775.
Fax : (0731)-420136

Styrene

L.G.Polymers (India) P.Ltd.
R.R.Venkatapuram,
Vishakhapatnam - 530029.
Andhra Pradesh
Phone : (0891)-520455,520458
Fax : 520338,520528
Email : inso@lgpi.co.in

Sig-Chem Products
21, Chewool Wadi,
Dr. M.B.Velkar's Street,
Kolbhat Lane, Ist Floor,
Kalbadevi Road, Mumbai-400002.
Phone : (022)-2056895,R-8894226.

Titanium Dioxide

Associated Cement Companies Ltd.
CRS Complex, LBS Marg,
Thane-400604.
Phone : (022)-5323631,5320962
Fax : (022)-5320962
E-Mail : rcd@giasbm01.vsnl.net.in

Bajaj Rubber Co.
15, Khurshid Market,
Sadar Bazar,
Delhi-110006
Phone : 3626038, 3535592, 35347701
Fax: 011-3612498
E-Mail : anilchemical@yahoo.com

Cochin Minerals And Rutile Ltd
P.B.No. 73, XVIII/219,
Market Road,
Alwaye-683101
Kerala
Ph:.0484-626789,
Fax: 0484-625674
E-Mail : sachexim@vsnl.com

Toluene

Allied Chemicals Corp.
658,G.I.D.C.Estate, Road No. 54.
Makarpura, Vadodara -390010,
Gujarat.
Phone : (0265)-642945
Fax : (0265)-332953

Ases Chemicals Works
Brahm Bagh, Jalori Gate,
Jodhpur -342001, Rajasthan
Phone (0291)-30437,37882
Fax : (0291)-38266

Vinyl Acetate

Pidilite Industries Ltd
RamKrishna Mandir Road.
Off. M.Vasanji Road,
Andheri (E), Mumbai-400059
Ph. 022-8387240,8387241
Fax : 8384989,8367459
E-Mail :pil@pidilite.com
Website : www.pidilite.com

Urea Melamine Formaldehyde Resins

Anu Synth Chem Industries
Plot No. 79,
Kundaim Industrial Estate,
Kundaim-403115, Goa
Ph:.0834-395287

Fax: 395287

Atul Ltd.
At P.O. Atul, Distt. Valsad
Atul - 396020
Gujarat
Ph:.02632-33621,33622
Fax: 33631, 33639

Xylene Mixed

Ases Chemicals Works
Brahm Bagh, Jalori Gate,
Jodhpur -342001, Rajasthan
Phone (0291)-30437,37882
Fax : (0291)-38266

Reliance Industries Ltd.
Maker Chambers IV, 3rd Floor,
222, Nariman Point, P.B.No. 11717,
Mumbai 400021.
Phone : (022)-2842384,2842331,
Fax : (022)-2042268,288
Telex : 86542,82950
Web:http://www.ril.com.

Zinc Oxide

A. Kumar & Co
30/2, Ellisbridge Shopping Centre,
Opp Town Hall Ashram Road,
Ahmedabad-380006 Gujarat
Phone : (079)-6578457, (R)6440733
Fax : (079)-6577585

Amvee Chemicals
Saket, Baptista Road.
Vile-Parale(West)
Mumbai-400056.
Phone -(022)-6161504,6141485
Fax: (022)-6117049,

Bajaj Rubber Co.
15, Khurshid Market,
Sadar Bazar,
Delhi-110006
Phone : 3626038, 3535592,
35347701
Fax: 011-3612498
E-Mail : anilchemical@yahoo.com

Zinc Stearate

Chopra & Co.
B-8, Sardar Nagar,
Near C.C.Colony,
Delhi-110009
City Off. 7-U.A.
Jawahar Nagar, Delhi-110007
Tel : 7137247,7134803,
7464804,3918234
Fax: 7134803
E-Mail : chopra@delhi.guide.com

Aggrawala Organic Industrial
E-79(A), Indrapprastha Industrial
Area, Road No.4.,Kota 324000
Rajasthan
Phone : (0744)-421987, 429522.
Fax : (0744)-429522.

Arti Chemical Industries
L-141, G.I.D.C. Estate Odhav,
Ahmedabad-322 415
Ph:. 079-2874273

Bajaj Rubber Co.
15, Khurshid Market,
Sadar Bazar,
Delhi-110006
Phone : 3626038, 3535592,
35347701
Fax: 011-3612498
E-Mail : anilchemical@yahoo.com

Pay Rs.1500/- for
Classified Advertisement only.

• Chapter 16 •

SUPPLIERS OF PLANT AND MACHINERY

Complete Plant Suppliers for Resins

Aristo Engineers
J-3 Vikas Udyog Nagar,
Bhayandar (E) - 401105
Phone : 8195268,8192568
Email : aristoeg@vsnl.com

Tanks (Storage and others)

India Tube Mills & Metal Industrial Ltd.
L.B.Shastri Marg, Vikhroli,
Mumbai-400083.
Phone (022)-5781541,
Fax : (022)-5784443.

Indian Sugar & General Engineering Corp
Yamuna Nagar,
Yamunanagar-135001, Haryana.
Phone : (01732)-51700
Fax : (01732)-50250.
Email : isgec@nde.vsnl.net.in

Dolphin Engineering Enterprise,
45/A, Parishram, Narayam Estate,
Bharuch - 392001, Gujarat
Phone : (02642)-40659

Multi Engineering Services
201, Gulistan E. Hind,
N.S.Road No.10,
Mumbai- 49
Phone : 6202232
Fax : 6237609
Email : multiengg@yahoo.com

Cosywo Engineering Company
15 Laxmi Co Op Industrial Estate
Amraiwadi Road,
Ahmedabad-380026
Telefax : 079-2748168,2748001
Email : cosywo@usa.net
Website : www.indianic.com/cosywo

Dipesh Engineering Works
3, Sheroo Villa, 87,J.P.Road,
Near Andheri Sports Complex,
Andheri (W),
Mumbai-400053.
Phone : (022)-6336729,6315507,
Fax : (022)-6315507
Email : dew@vsnl.com.

Chemac Eqpts. Private Limited
M.J.D'Souza Comp.,
Safedpool,
Sakinaka,
Mumbai - 400 072
Tel : 851 0777/6986, 859 2352

Telefax : 851 6986
E-mail - chemac @ bom4.vsnl.net.in

Internationl Engineers
PP. 4, Gali No. 10,
Anand Parbat Industrial Area,
New Delhi - 110 005
Tel : 5812557, 5751194/011-6422422

Laxmi Engineering Works
C-7, DSIDC Industrial Complex,
Rohtak Road, Nangloi,
Delhi - 110 041
Tel : 5472482, 5473255/011-5587597

Navyug Industries
C-11/1, Mansrover Garden,
New Delhi - 110 015
Tel : 5432689

Premier Engineering Works
B-136, Phase - I,
Okhla Industrial Area,
New Delhi - 110 020
Tel : 6818 8210

Condensor

Aristo Engineers
J-3 Vikas Udyog Nagar,
Bhayandar (E) - 401105
Phone : 8195268,8192568
Email : aristoeg@vsnl.com

Reactors

Aristo Engineers
J-3 Vikas Udyog Nagar,
Bhayandar (E) - 401105
Phone : 8195268,8192568
Email : aristoeg@vsnl.com

New Multifab Engineers Pvt. Ltd.,
225, Gala Complex, 2nd Flr.,
D-Upadhyaya Marg,
Mulund (West),
Mumbai - 400080
Ph : 022-5613136, 5611291
Fax: 022-5646325

Dipesh Engineering Works
3, Sheroo Villa, 87,J.P.Road,
Near Andheri Sports Complex,
Andheri (W),
Mumbai-400053.
Phone : (022)-6336729,6315507,
Fax : (022)-6315507
Email : dew@vsnl.com.

India Tube Mills & Metal Industrial Ltd.
L.B.Shastri Marg, Vikhroli,
Mumbai-400083.
Phone (022)-5781541,
Fax : (022)-5784443.

Indian Sugar & General Engineering Corp
Yamuna Nagar, Yamunanagar-135001, Haryana.
Phone : (01732)-51700
Fax : (01732)-50250.
Email : isgec@nde.vsnl.net.in

Mitachem Pulveriser Industries
3, Max Industrial Estate,
Rakhial, Ahmedabad - 380 023
(Gujarat)
Ph : 079- 2746646, 2743109

Ball Mill

New Multifab Engineers Pvt. Ltd.,
225, Gala Complex, 2nd Flr.,
D-Upadhyaya Marg,
Mulund (West),
Mumbai - 400080

Ph : 022-5613136, 5611291
Fax: 022-5646325

Mitachem Pulveriser Industries
3, Max Industrial Estate,
Rakhial, Ahmedabad - 380 023
(Gujarat)
Ph : 079- 2746646, 2743109

Cosywo Engineering Company
15 Laxmi Co Op Industrial Estate
Amraiwadi Road,
Ahmedabad-380026
Telefax : 079-2748168,2748001
Email : cosywo@usa.net
Website : www.indianic.com/cosywo

Mohr Corporation
25255, Southfield Road
Southfield, MI 48075
USA

New Lahore Welding & Engg. Works
B-74, Mayapuri Indl. Area
Phase I, New Delhi- 110 064
Ph: 5134409, 5132209
Fax: 011-5490053

Suryatronics Private Limited
Plot No. 3a/1 & 2 IDA
Cherapally, Hyderabad- 500 051

Ferro Tech Engineers
P.O. Box no. 7078,
Pratap Bhawan Ground Floor 5
Bahadur Shah Zafar Marg
New Delhi- 110 002
Ph: 3313670, 3351830, 3351848
Fax: 3739855, 3324082

Neu-Tech
18/32, Street No. 5,
Railway side,
Anand Parbat Industrial Area,
New Delhi - 110 005
Tel : 5722678

Cooling Tower

Ion Exchange (India) Ltd.
Tiecicon House, Dr. E.Moses Road,
Mahalaxmi, Mumbai-400001.
Phone : (022)-4939520,4939523,
Fax : (022)-4938737

Nilesh Cooling Components Pvt. Ltd.,
G/4, Nimesh Park, Ellisbridge,
Ahmedabad - 380006 (Guj.)
Ph : 079-462025
Fax: 079-462025

HDPE Storage Vessels

Jet Fibre Pumps & Equipments P.Ltd.
17-B, Swaga Complex, Selat
Bhuwan, Maninagar,
Ahmedabad-380008, Gujarat
Phone : (079)-5325385.
Fax : (079)-5322513.

Plastofab Engg.
874, Old GIDC, Katargam,
P.O. Box. No. 509,
Surat - 395008
Gujarat
Ph : 0261-480220
Fax : 0261-480220

Pumps

Jet Fibre Pumps & Equipments P.Ltd.
17-B, Swaga Complex, Selat
Bhuwan, Maninagar,

Ahmedabad-380008, Gujarat
Phone : (079)-5325385.
Fax : (079)-5322513.

Plastofab Engg.
874, Old GIDC, Katargam,
P.O. Box. No. 509,
Surat - 395008
Gujarat
Ph : 0261-480220
Fax : 0261-480220

Boilers

Chem Engineering Co.
Plot 517, Sector 25, Nigdi,
Pune 411044.
Phone :(020)-784792,782605
Fax : (020)-782605,789822

Chemtex Engineering Enterprises,
Plot No. 277-278.,
Opp. Shed No- L-1, G.I.D.C.
Industrial Estate,
Odhav, Ahmedabad-382415,
Gujarat.
Phone : (079)-2871180,2871280,
Email : chemtex@vsnl.net.in

Fluidtech Boilers P.Ltd.
2703, Phase-IV, G.I.D.C. Vatva,
Ahmedabad-382445 Gujarat
Phone - (079)-5830105, 5830106
Fax : (079)-5830041.
Email : fluidltd@vsnl.com
Website : http://
www.infoquestindia.com/fluidtech.

Double Ace Engineers
1/3, Siddharth Nagar-3,
Next to Siddhi Vinayak Temple,
S.V.Road, Goregaon (West),
Mumbai-104.
Tel : 91-22-8728436,8771948
Fac : 91-22-8740466
Wesite : www.doubleaceboiler.com
Email : dblace@bom5.vsnl.net.in

Maxima Boilers Pvt. Ltd.
G-14, Meghal Service Industrial
Estate
Devidayal Road Mulund (W),
Mumbai - 400080
Tel : 5646815,5612759
Fax : 5670030
Email : maxima@bom8.vsnl.net.in

Indcon Boilers Ltd.
D-170, Okhla Indl.Area, Phase-1,
New Delhi - 110020
Ph. 6811440,6811441,6811442
Fax : 011-6812425
Email : pnmpsa@del2.vsnl.net.in

Lal Sons Boilers
A-45, Maya Puri Indl. Area,
Phase-1
New Delhi-110064
Phone : 5138121-5143223
Fax : 5147483

READ
HI-TECH PROJECTS
(MONTHLY INDUSTRIAL MAGAZINE)

Avail your free copy from :
Engineers India Research Institute
4449, Nai Sarak, Main Road,
Delhi - 110006
Ph.: 3918117, 3916431,
3920361, 3960797
E-mail : eirisidi@bol.net.in

Market Survey Cum

Detailed Techno Economic Feasibility Reports

EIRI Consultants & Engineers have recently prepared the following **"Market Survey Cum Detailed Techno Economic Feasibility Reports"** which are having great future prospect. The **Detailed Project Reports** will also help you

- ***To get Loan/Finance from Banks/Financial Institutions.***
- ***To set up your own Industry/Unit (For SSI/Medium/Large Scale Unit).***
- ***To have Detailed and Exhaustive Data on any required Items/Projects.***

Each Report Rs. 3675/-

'ENGINEERS INDIA RESEARCH INSTITUTE' (EIRI) The Premier and Trusted Industrial Consultancy Organization from last 24 Years, offer Complete Consultancy, Liaisoning Jobs, Foreign Collaborations, Buy Back Arrangements etc. alongwith **"Market Survey Cum Detailed Techno Economic Feasibility Reports"** to the entrepreneurs as well as established Industrialists.

WHY EIRI ONLY ? Because **'EIRI'** is having (1) Well equipped data bank cum library. (2) Fully expertise team of consultants, technocrats & engineers for prepairing **"Market Survey Cum Detailed Techno Economic Feasibility Reports"** on any items in Small/ Medium/ Large Scale. (3) Record quantity of over ***32,000*** **"Market Survey Cum Detailed Techno Economic Feasibility Reports"** readily available. (4) More than thousands satisfied clients. (5) Vast experience of more than 24 years. (6) **'EIRI'** is being undertaken plants on turnkey basis and (7) Latest and detailed authentic informations Covered in each **"Market Survey Cum Detailed Techno Economic Feasibility Reports"** and many more plus points which stands **'EIRI'** on top.

BRIEF CONTENTS

BEGINING : Project Introduction, Brief History of the Product, Properties, BIS (Bureau of Indian Standard) Specifications & Requirements, Uses & Applications.

MARKET SURVEY : Present Market Position, Expected Future Demand, Installed Capacity, Actual Production & Demand, Statistics of Imports & Exports, Export Prospect, Names & Addresses of Existing Units (Present Manufacturers), List of Buyers.

MANUFACTURING PROCESS : Detailed Process of Manufacture, Selection of Process, Flow Sheet Diagram, Production Schedule.

RAW MATERIALS : List of Raw Materials, Properties, Availability of Raw Materials, Required Quantity of Raw Materials, Cost of Raw Materials, Suppliers of Raw Materials.

PLANT & MACHINERY : List of Plant & Machineries, Miscellaneous Items & Accessories, Instruments, Laboratory Equipments & Accessories, Plant Location, Electrification, Electric Load & Water Maintenance, Suppliers/Manufacturers of Plant & Machineries, Specifications of Machineries & Equipments.

PERSONNEL REQUIREMENTS : Requirement of Staff & Labour, Personnel Management, Skilled & Unskilled Labour, Manageriol Staff/Expert, Accountant etc.

LAND & BUILDING : Requirement of Land Area, Rates of the Land, Built up Area, Construction Schedule, Plant Layout, Cost of Boundry Wall etc.

FINANCIAL ASPECTS : Cost of Raw Materials, Cost of Land & Building, Cost of Plant & Machineries, Fixed Capital Investment, Working Capital, Project Cost, Capital Formation, Cost of Production, Profitability Analysis, Break Even Point (BEP), Cash Flow Statement for 5 to 10 Years, Depreciation Chart, Foreign Collaboration (if possible), Conclusion, Projected Balance sheet, Land Man Ratio.

ADDRESSES : Present Manufacturers, List of the Buyers, Plant & Equipment Suppliers/ Manufacturers, Raw Material Suppliers/Manufacturers etc.

LIST OF THE READY AVAILABLE DETAILED PROJECT REPORTS @ Rs. 3675/- EACH

AUTOMOBILES, MECHANICAL & METALLURGICAL

1. AGRICULTRAL EQUIPMENTS
2. AGRICULTRAL EQUIPMENTS INCLUDING THRESHERS
3. AIR BRAKE HELICAL COIL
4. AIR COOLER
5. AIR FILTERS(FOR SCOOTER CAR & EXCAVATORS ETC.)
6. ALUMINIUM & ALUMINIUM ALLOYS FROM ALUMINIUM SCRAP TO MAKE UTENSILS (INDUCTION FURNACE MELTED)
7. ALUMINIUM ALLOY WHEELS
8. ALUMINIUM ALLOYS FROM ALUMINIUM SCRAP TO MAKE UTENSILS (INDUCTION FURNACE)
9. ALUMINIUM HOT & COLD ROLLING MILL
10. ALUMINIUM BOTTLE MANUFACTURING (COLD EXTRUSION OF ALUMINIUM)
11. ALUMINIUM/COPPER CABLE LUGS
12. ALUMINIUM CANS FOR BEER PACKAGING
13. ALUMINIUM CANS FOR CAPACITORS
14. ALUMINIUM CAPS FOR INJECTION VIALS
15. ALUMINIUM EXTRUSION
16. ALUMINIUM FURNITURE & HARDWARE
17. ALUMINIUM SHEET ROLLING MILL
18. ALUMINIUM UTENSILS
19. ALUMINIUM UTENSILS & SCHOOL BOXES
20. ALUMINIUM WIRE DRAWING AND SUPER ENAMELLING FOR WINDING
21. ANODISED ALUMINIUM UTENSILS
22. ANODIZING OF ALUMINIUM
23. ANTIMONY OXIDE FROM LEAD SCRAP
24. ARC WELDING FILTER GLASS
25. ALUMINIUM FOIL CUTTING & ROLL MAKING
26. AUTO FLAPS FOR TRUCKS & BUSES
27. AUTOMOBILE WORKSHOP (GARAGE & SERVICE CENTRE)
28. AUTO GEARS
29. AUTO HORNS
30. AUTO LEAF SPRING
31. AUTO TUBES
32. AUTO PISTON RING
33. AUTO PISTON
34. BAKERY AND BISCUITS EQUIPMENTS FABRICATION
35. BALL POINT PEN REFILLS
36. BALL ROLLER & TAPER BEARING
37. BAND SAW BLADES
38. BARBED WIRE
39. BICYCLE SPOKES
40. BRAKE LINING ASBESTOES/ RESIN BASED & ASBESTOES FREE
41. BRASS ARTWARE/HOLLOW WARE CASTING (WITH THE HELP OF PHENOLIC RESIN)
42. BRASS CASTING
43. BRASS PIPES FROM BRASS SHEET WITH LONGITUDINALLY WELDING
44. BRASS WARE BY CASTING METHOD (BRASS ARTICLES VIZ. BRASS POOJA LAMPS AND OTHER CASTED)
45. BRIGHT BARS
46. BUFFING AND POLISHING INDUSTRY (JOB WORK)
47. BUTT HINGE (BRASS SHEET)
48. CARBON BRUSH HOLDER & SLIP RING
49. CO_2 WELDING WIRE ELECTRODES (COPPER/ COPPER ALLOY COATED M.S.WIRE)
50. CARBON FILM RESISTORS
51. CARBURETTORS
52. CAST STEEL PANES FOR MELTING FURNACE
53. CHEMICAL ETCHING OF STAINLESS STEEL
54. CHEMICAL RESISTANT IRON & STEEL
55. COLD FORM SECTION MILL
56. COLD ROLLED FORMING OF SECTION AND OTHER SECTIONS
57. COLD ROLLING OF MS STRIP
58. COLD TWISTED DE-FORMED RIBBED STEEL
59. COMPRESSOR (HERMETIC) FOR AIR CONDITIONERS
60. COMPRESSED NATURAL GAS (CNG KIT) FOR AUTOVEHICLE
61. CONTINUOUSLY CAST STEEL WIRE RODS (5 mm)
62. CONTINUOUS CASTING COPPER WIRE RODS
63. CONVEYOR BELTINGS
64. CONVEYOR BELT, TRANSM -ISSION BELT & V BELTS
65. COOKING RANGES
66. COPPER/BRASS SHEETS, CIRCLE & UTENSILS
67. COPPER FOIL
68. COPPER INGOTS, RODS MAKING & WIRE DRAWING
69. COPPER PRODUCTS FROM COPPER SCRAP
70. COPPER SMELTING PLANT
71. COPPER WIRE RODS FROM COPPER SCRAP
72. CORRUGATED BOX MAKING MACHINERY AND OTHER THEIR PARTS
73. CYLINDER LINER FOR AUTOMOBILES
74. DOOR LOCKS/PAD LOCKS
75. DRILL BITS & TOOL BITS
76. DRUM CLOSURES
77. ERW STEEL CONDUIT PIPE
78. EARTH MOVING EQPT.
79. ENGINE VALVES FOR AUTOMOBILES
80. FABRICATION OF HEAT EXCHANGER
81. FABRICATION OF STORAGE TANKS AND M.S. DRUM
82. FERROUS ALLOY NI-HARDY I.V CASTING
83. FERROUS Mn ALLOY CASTING BY ALUMINA THERMIC PROCESS
84. FERRO ALLOYS
85. FERRO SILICON & FERRO MANGANESE FROM DOLOMITE (SMS GRADE)
86. FIRE EXTINGUISHERS
87. FLIP-TONE CANS
88. FORGED CONECTING ROD
89. FORGING UNIT
90. FOUNTAIN PEN NIBS
91. FOUNDRY SAND
92. FUEL INJECTION SYSTEM
93. GALVANIZED M.S.STRIPS
94. GALVANIZING PLANT
95. GALVANIZED IRON WIRE
96. GAS WELDING TORCHES AND NOZZLES
97. GASKET SHEET
98. GATE GRILLS & WINDOW FRAMES
99. GENERATING SET (DIESEL)
100. HARD ANODISED ALUMINIUM
101. HOSPITAL WARES
102. HOSPITAL FURNITURES
103. HOT DIP GALVANIZING
104. HOT FORGED FASTENERS
105. HOT MIX PLANT
106. INJECTION MOULDED PLASTIC COMPOUNDS WITH TOOL ROOM
107. INJECTION MOULDED PLASTIC COMPONENTS AND METAL PIPE SPINNING UNIT
108. INVESTMENT CASTING
109. IRON/STEEL WIRE GAUGE
110. IRON TAWA
111. KNIVES (S.S.KNIVES)
112. KITCHEN SINK (S.S.)
113. L.P.G REGULATORS
114. MACHINE SCREWS & SELF TAPPING SCREWS
115. MARUTI WORKSHOP CUM SERVICE STATION
116. MAGNESIUM INGOTS & BULLETS CASTING

Price Rs. 3675/- for each "Detailed Project Report" Payable in advance through Draft/Cash/ M.O. in favour of "*ENGINEERS INDIA RESEARCH INSTITUTE*". 4449, Nai Sarak (D), Main Road Delhi - 110 006 *OR Ask by V.P.P.* • Ph : 3918117, 391 6431, 392 0361, 396 0797 •Fax : 91-11- 391 6431 •E-Mail : eirisidi@bol.net.in • WebSite : www.startindustry.com

117. MANUFACTURE OF TIN CONTAINERS
118. MANUFACTURE OF STORAGE TANKS, PRESSURE VESSELS, HEAT EXCHANGERS
119. MARK II HAND PUMPS
120. MARUTI WORKSHOP CUM - SERVICE STATION
121. MECHANICAL JACKS
122. METAL CUTTING DIE DESIGN
123. METAL CUTTING OF AND GRINDING WHEELS (ABBRASIVE CUTTING WHEELS)
124. METAL HOOKS & CLIPS
125. METAL SEPARATION (COPPER, TIN, LEAD) FROM SPENT WASH ACID
126. METALLIC RING JOINTS
127. METALLIC GASKET (SPIRAL WOUND)
128. MICROVEE & ABSOLUTE FILTER
129. MICROWAVE OVEN
130. MILD STEEL INGOTS
131. MINI STEEL PLANT
132. MODERN VEHICLE WORKSHOP
133. MOPED
134. M.S.HINGES
135. M.S.INGOT AND HR. STEEL STRUCTURALS
136. M.S.INGOT BY INDUCTION FURNACES
137. M.S.PIPES
138. M.S. WELDING ELECTRODE
139. MUFFLERS & SILENCERS FOR THREE WHEELERS
140. NAIL CUTTER WITH FILER & MANICURE
141. NICHROME WIRE
142. NICKEL LINED SCREENS
143. NON-FERROUS ALLOY ROLLING
144. NON-FERROUS FORGING
145. NON-FERROUS FOUNDRY
146. NON PRESSURE
147. INCANDESCENT LAMP
148. NUMBER COMBINATION LOCKS FOR LUGGAGES
149. NUTS & BOLTS
150. PAPER COATED ALUMINIUM AND COPPER WIRE
151. PETROMAX CONTAINER
152. PHOTO ETCHING OF STAINLESS STEEL PLATES
153. PIPE GALVANIZING PLANT
154. PISTON RING-AUTOMOBILE
155. PLANT PROTECTION EQUIPMENTS
156. PLATINUM LABORATORY APPARATUS
157. PRESSURE COOKER & ALUMINIUM UTENSILS
158. PRESSURE COOKER (ALUMINIUM)
159. PRESSURE DIE CASTING
160. PRINTED ALUMINIUM COLLAPSIBLE TUBES
161. PRINTED TIN CONTAINERS
162. PRINTING PRESS (CYLINDER MACHINE)
163. PUMPS FOR CHEMICAL INDUSTRY (SPECIAL)
164. RAILWAY SLEEPERS (M.S.)
165. RAZOR TWIN BLADE
166. R.C.C SPUN PIPES
167. RECONDITIONING OF M.S. DRUMS/BARRELS
168. RE-ROLLING COPPER AND BRASS SHEET AND RODS
169. RE-ROLLING MILLS
170. RESIN COATED SAND
171. RESIN CORED SOFT SOLDER WIRES
172. ROLLING MILL (BY INDUCTION FURNACE) & MANUFACTURE OF BARS, ANGLES, SQUARES, TUBES AND OTHERS
173. ROLLER BEARING & FORGING
174. ROLLING OF STAINLESS STEEL PATTA
175. RUBBER INSULATED PLIERS (HAND TOOLS)
176. RUBBING COMPOUND FOR AUTOMOBILES
177. SCIENTIFIC LABORATORY EQUIPMENTS
178. SCOOTER ASSEMBLING
179. SECONDARY LEAD EXTRAC-TION BY SCRAP BATTERY PLATES,PIPES & SHEET
180. SEAMLESS M.S. TUBES & PIPES
181. SELF TAPPING STEEL SCREW
182. SEWING NEEDLES
183. S.G. IRON & ALLOY STEEL
184. SHEET METAL PRODUCTS, (FERROUS/NON-FERROUS)
185. SHIP/MARINE CONTAINER
186. SHOCK ABSORBERS
187. SHOE EYELETS
188. SHOT AND GRITS BY AUTOMIZATION PROCESS
189. SHOVELS
190. SILICO MANGANESE ALLOYS
191. SILENCERS (MUFFLERS) EXHAUST & TAIL PIPE FOR ALL TYPES OF VEHICLES
192. SINTERED BEARING
193. SINTERED BUSHES
194. SINTERED METAL PRODUCTS
195. SOFT AND HARD FERRITES
196. SPANNERS
197. SPARK PLUGS
198. STEEL PLANT (ELECTRIC ARC FURNACE BASED- EAF)
199. SPHERIODAL GRAPHITE CAST IRON
200. SPRAY DRYER
201. STAINLESS STEEL HINGES
202. STAINLESS STEEL SHEET ROLLING TO PRODUCE STAINLESS STEEL UTENSILS
203. STAINLESS STEEL UTENSILS
204. STAPLE PINS,PAPER PIN, GEM CLIPS ETC.
205. STEEL CASTINGS
206. STEEL CHAIN
207. STEEL FOUNDRY
208. STEEL FURNITURES AND ELECTRICAL APPLIANCES
209. STEEL PLANT (MINI)
210. STEEL RODS AND COILS FROM SCRAPS
211. STEEL ROLLING MILL
212. STEEL STRIPS (COLD ROLLED) SILICON WITH GRAIN RIENTED FOR ELECTRIC USE
213. STEEL TRANSMISSION LINE TOWERS & ROLLING MILL TO PRODUCE STEEL SECTION
214. STEEL FURNITURES AND ELECTRICAL APPLIANCES
215. STEEL WIRE DRAWING AND GALVANIZING
216. STEEL WOOL
217. SUBMERGED ARC WELDED PIPES
218. SUBMERSIBLE PUMP MANUFACTURING
219. SUPER ENAMELLED COPPER WIRE
220. THREE WHEELERS
221. TIE-ROD ENDS
222. TIN CONTAINERS
223. TOOLROOM AND SHEET METAL PRODUCTS
224. TRACTOR TRAILERS
225. TRANSMISSION POWER FITTING
226. TUBULAR POLES
227. SUPER ENAMELLED COPPER WIRES
228 TUBULAR POLES FOR ELECTRICAL TRANSMISSION (BY FABRICATION PROCESS)
229. TUBULAR POLES OF M.S. & HIGH TENSILE STEEL
230. VACUUM CLEANERS
231. VACUUM FLASK (STAINLESS STEEL)
232. VALVES FOR REFRIGERATION AND AIR-CONDITION
233. VEHICLE WELDING & PAINTING
234. VENETION BLIND
235. WASHING MACHINES (AUTOMATIC & COMPUTERISED)
236. WATER CONTROLLER (AUTOMATIC)
237. WATCH STRAPS/CHAINS/ BRACELETS/BELT BRASS & STAINLESS STEEL
238. WATER COOLERS
239. WELDED WIRE MESH
240. WELDING ELECTRODES
241. WICK STOVES
242. WIND MILL WINDOW FRAME (FERROUS & NON-FERROUS)
243. WRIST WATCH

Price Rs. 3675/- for each "Detailed Project Report" Payable in advance through Draft/Cash/ M.O. in favour of *"ENGINEERS INDIA RESEARCH INSTITUTE"*. 4449, Nai Sarak (D), Main Road Delhi - 110 006 *OR Ask by V.P.P.* ● Ph : 3918117, 391 6431, 392 0361, 396 0797 ●Fax : 91-11- 391 6431 ●E-Mail : eirisidi@bol.net.in ● WebSite : www.startindustry.com

LIST OF FEW READILY AVAILABLE

'DETAILED PROJECT REPORTS' OUT OF 30,000 REPORTS

CHEMICALS (ORGANIC & INORGANIC)

244. ACETIC ANHYDRIDE
245. ACETIC ACID FROM ETHANOL
246. ACETYLENE BLACK
247. ACETYLENE GAS
248. ACETYLENE GAS & OXYGEN (INTEGERATED UNIT)
249. ACID SLURRY BY MANUAL PROCESS
250. ACTIVATED ALUMINA
251. ACTIVATED BLEACHING EARTH (ACTIVATED FULLERS EARTH)
252. ACTIVATED CARBON FROM CASHEWNUT SHELL
253. ACTIVATED CARBON FROM RICE HUSK
254. ACTIVATED CARBON FROM RICE HUSK, COCONUT SHELL & COCONUT POWDER
255. ACTIVATED CARBON FROM WOOD
256. ACTIVATED CARBON POWDER & GRANULES FROM COCONUT SHELL
257. ACTIVATED CARBON & SODIUM SILICATE FROM PADDY & RICE HUSK
258. ALUM FOR WATER TREATMENT
259. AEROSOL INSECTICIDES SPRAY (BAYGON, HIT, MORTEIN TYPE)
260. AGARBATTI SYNTHETIC PERFUMERY COMPOUNDS
261. ALCOHOL FROM POTATO
262. ALCOHOL FROM RICE GRAINS
263. ALCOHOL FROM RICE HUSK
264. ALCOHOL FROM MOLASSES
265. ALCOHOL, BEER, STARCH, LIQUID GLUCOSE, DEXTROSE, SORBITOL, VITAMIN-C, GERM OIL, CATTLE FEED ETC. FROM MAIZE
266. ALKYD RESIN
267. ALKYLATED PHENOL LIKE NONYL PHENOL, DODECYL PHENOL
268. ALUM (NON FERRIC)
269. ALUM (FERRIC)
260. ALUMINIUM INGOT BY BAUXITE
261. ALUMINIUM PHOSPHIDE
262. ALUMINIUM PHOSPHATE
263. AMINES & ALLIED PRODUCTS
264. AMMONIA GAS
265. AMMONIA GAS BOTTLING
266. AMMONIA LIQUOR
267. AMMONIUM CHLORIDE (PURE & TECHNICAL)
268. ANILINE
269. ARGON GAS
270. ARIEL TYPE DETERGENT POWDER
271. ANTHRAQUINONE
272. ANTIMONY TRIOXIDE
273. AZODICARBONAMIDE
274. BAKING SODA FROM ASH
275. BARIUM CARBONATE
276. BARIUM COMPOUNDS
277. BARIUM PEROXIDE
278. BARIUM-THIO-SULPHATE BANZENE
279. BARYTE POWDER
280. BEER PLANT
281. BELT PASTE (WITH BFS OIL)
282. BENZYL ACETATE, BENZYL BENZOATE, BENZYL ALCOHOL
283. BETA NAPHTHOL
284. BENTONITE POWDER
285. BENZIDINE
286. BIO GAS PLANT
287. BIO GAS FILLING IN CYLINDER
288. BI-CHROMATE OF SODIUM, POTASSIUM & AMMONIUM
289. BI-FUNCTIONAL BLACK MFGR. REACTIVE DYE (DYE FROM COTTON YARN DYEING)
290. BITUMINOUS ROAD EMULSION
291. BLACK PHENYL
292. BLACK SULPHUR
293. BLEACHING POWDER (STABLE)
294. BONE CRUSHING PLANT
295. BONE MEAL (CALCINED) ENRICHMENT WITH CALCIUM & PHOSPHORUS
296. BORIC ACID
297. B.O.N. ACID
298. BRANDY
299. BUTANOL
300. 1,4, BUTANEDIOL
301. BUTYL ACETATE
302. CAFFEIN FROM TEA WASTE
303. CALCINED LIME (DEAD BURNT DOLOMITE)
304. CALCINING OF MAGNESITE & DEAD BURNT MAGNESITE
305. CALCIUM ALUMINATE
306. CALCIUM CARBIDE
307. CALCIUM CARBONATE
308. CALCIUM CARBONATE (PRECIPITATED) FROM BY PRODUCT (LIME SLURRY & CARBON DIOXIDE)
309. CALCIUM CARBONATE (ACTIVATED & PRECIPITATED)
310. CALCIUM CHLORIDE
311. CALCIUM GLUCONATE
312. CALCIUM NITRATE
313. CALCIUM SILICATE BRICKS
314. CAMPHOR POWDER (SYNTHETIC)
315. CARBON DIOXIDE
316. CARBON BLACK FROM FERTILIZER WASTE
317. CARBOXY METHYL CELLULOSE (CMC)
318. CASEIN AND BY PRODUCTS
319. CASEIN FROM MILK
320. CATIONIC SOFTNER (STEARIC ACID BASED)
321. CAUSTIC SODA
322. CAUSTIC SODA FROM TRONA
323. CAUSTIC SODA, CHLORINE AND HYDROGEN GAS BY ELECTRO-LYSIS OF BRINE SOLUTION
324. CELLULOSE ACETATE MOULDING POWDER
325. CELLULOSE POWDER & MICRO CRYSTALLINE CELLULOSE POWDER
326. CEMENT COLOUR
327. CEMENT FROM FLY ASH & LIME
328. CEMENT TILES (GLAZED)
329. DOUBLE FIRING (HEATING)
330. CHELATED ZINC (ZN EDTA)
331. CHEMICALS FROM PRAWN HEAD
332. CHITIN & CHITOSAN FROM PRAWN SHELL WASTE
333. CHLORAL HYDRATE
334. CHLORAMPHENICOL
335. CHROMIC ACID (WITH POLLUTION CONTROL)
336. CHROMIC ACID (OXIDE) & BLUE OXIDE
337. CHLORINATED PARAFFIN WAX (CPW)
338. CHROMIC ACID
339. CEMENT PAINT & DISTEMPER
340. CITRIC ACID FROM LEMON
341. CITRIC ACID FROM MOLASSES
342. CLEANING OF COOLING SYSTEM AND BOILER
343. COAL TAR DISTILLATION
344. COBALT OCTOATE
345. COMPOST FOR MUSHROOM
346. COPPER OXYCHLORIDE
347. COPPER PHTHALOCYANINE BLUE & GREEN
348. CORRECTION FLUID
349. CYANURIC CHLORIDE
350. DEFOAMING AGENT FOR PAPER INDUSTRY
351. DE-NICKELING (ELECTROLYTIC PROCESS)
352. DETERGENT CAKE & POWDER
353. DETERGENT POWDER
354. DETERGENT CONCENTRATE (IDET 10)
355. DEXTROSE MONOHYDRATE & DEXTROSE ANHYDROUS POWDER FROM TAPIOCA STARCH
356. DI-BASIC LEAD STEARATE
357. DI CALCIUM PHOSPHATE
358. DICLOFENAL SODIUM SLOW RELEASE (SR) TABLES 100MG.

Price Rs. 3675/- for each "Detailed Project Report" Payable in advance through Draft/Cash/M.O. in favour of *"ENGINEERS INDIA RESEARCH INSTITUTE"*. 4449, Nai Sarak (D), Main Road Delhi - 110 006 *OR Ask by V.P.P.* ● Ph : 3918117, 391 6431, 392 0361, 396 0797 ●Fax : 91-11- 391 6431 ●E-Mail : eirisidi@bol.net.in ● WebSite : www.startindustry.com

359. DIETHYL OXALATE
360. DIMETHYL ORTHOPHTHALATE
361. DI-METHYL PHTHALATE
362. DICLOFENAC GEL
363. DIOCTYL PHTHALATE (DOP)
364. DI PHENYL GLYCERINE
365. DI PHENYL OXIDE
366. DINITRO-CHLORO BENZENE
367. DISTILLED WATER
368. DODECYL BENZENE SULPHONATE
369. DUSTLESS CHALK
370. EDTA & ITS SALTS
371. ELECTROLESS NICKEL PLATING ON PLASTICS
372. ENDOSULFAN
373. EPOXY RESIN BASED COMPOUND
374. ETHYL ACETATE
375. EHTYL ETHER
376. ETHYL ALCOHOL (POTABLE LIQUOR)
377. ETHYL HEXANOL
378. EXTRACTION OF ESSENTIAL OILS BY SUGAR CRITICAL FLUID (CARBON DIOXIDE) METHOD FROM FLOWERS, HERBAL & SPICES
379. FERRIC ALUM
380. FERRO CHROME LIGNO SULPHONATE
381. FERRO MANGANESE
382. FERRO SILICONE
383. FERRO VANADIUM FROM VANADIUM SLUDGE
384. FERROUS SILICATE
385. FERROUS SULPHATE
386. FERTILIZER FROM ANIMAL BLOOD & LEATHER WASTE
387. FLUORESCENT TUBE LIGHT POWDER
388. FOAMED PVC COMPOUNDING & ITS PRODUCTS
389. FORMALDEHYDE
390. FRACTIONAL DISTILLATION OF D.M.O (DEMENTHOLIZED OIL)
391. FRACTIONAL DISTILLATION OF ESSENTIAL OIL & MEDICINAL PLANT EXTRACT
392. FRICTION DUST (LIQUID & POWDER) FROM CNSL
393. FRUIT FLAVOURS
394. FURFURAL FROM RICE HUSK
395. GARLIC ACID
396. GASKET SHELLAC COMPOUND
397. GEAR OIL
398. GIBBERELLIC ACID
399. GLASS PUTTY
400. GLYCERINE
401. GOSSYPOL (POLY PHENOL) FROM COTTON SEED OIL
402. GUAR GUM POWDER
403. HAIR FIXER (HAIR GEL TYPE)
404. H - ACID
405. HENNA PASTE MAKING
406. HEPTAL DEHYDE
407. HIGH CARBON FERRO CHROME
408. HYDRATED CALCIUM SILICATE BRICK
409. HYDRATED LIME FROM SEA SHELL
410. HYDROCHLORIC ACID
411. HYDRO FLUORIC ACID
412. HYDROGEN PEROXIDE (BY AUTO-OXIDATION PROCESS)
413. ICE PACKS (SOLUTIONS TYPE, WHITE GEL TYPE, VIOLET SEMI SOLID POLYMER TYPE)
414. IMPROVING DROP POINT PARAFFIN WAX FROM 45-50°C TO 75-80°C
415. INDUSTRIAL ALCOHOL
416. INTEGERATED COMPLEX OF EASTER & ALLIED PRODUCTS (D.O.P, D.B.P, ETHYL ACETATE WIRE ENAMEL & CABLE JELLY)
417. IMFL (WHISKY) & COUNTRY LIQUOR
418. IRON OXIDE FOR MAKING FERITTE
419. IRON SULPHIDE
420. JUTE BATCHING OIL
421. KESH KALA TEL (HAIR DYE LOTION) (VASMOL 33, BLACK NITE TYPE)
422. L-LYSINE MONOHYDROCHLORIDE
423. LACTIC ACID FROM WHITE SUGAR BY FERMENTATION PROCESS
424. LDPE GRANULES FROM VIRGIN (LDPE RESIN)
425. LEAD EXTRACTION FROM BATTERY SCRAP
426. LEAD OXIDE (A) LEAD MONOXIDE
(B) LEAD TETRA OXIDE
(C) GREYLEAD OXIDE
427. LIQUID GLUCOSE & ITS BY PRODUCTS
428. LIQUID OXYGEN BOTTLING PLANT
429. LIQUID SHOE POLISH
430. LIQUID FLOOR POLISH
431. LUBE OIL VISCOSITY IMPROVED FOR P.P.G/P.E.G.
432. LUBRICANTS ASHLESS 100% COMBUSTION
433. MAGNESIUM CARBONATE AND MAGNESIUM BICARMONATE
434. MAGNESIUM HYDROXIDE POWDER
435. MAGNESIUM SILICATE
436. MAGNESIUM SULPHATE
437. MALACHITE GREEN
438. MALEIC ANHYDRIDE
439. MANGANESE SULPHATE
440. MANUFACTURING OF CARBON MONO-OXIDE WATER GAS
441. MENTHOL BOLD CRYSTALS FROM FLAKES
442. MENTHOL CRYSTAL & MENTHA OIL
443. MERCURIC OXIDE
444. METAL PRE-TREATMENT CHEMICALS
445. METHANE GAS BY SODIUM ACETATE & SODA LIME
446. METHYL ACETYL RICINOLATE
447. METOL
448. METOL FROM HYDROQUINONE & METHYLAMINE
449. MICANITE
450. MICRO NUTRIENT MIXTURE
451. MINERAL WATER
452. MINERAL WATER AND PET BOTTILNG PLANT
453. MINERAL WATER IN BOTTLES, GLASS AND POUCHES
454. MINI CEMENT PLANT (BY ROTARY KILN PROCESS)
455. MIXED FERTILIZER
456. MOSQUITO & FLIES REPELLENT AGARBATTI (INCENSE STICKS)
457. MONO CHLORO ACETIC ACID
458. MONOCROTOPHOS (TECHNICAL)
459. MOSQUITO COIL
460. MOSQUITO COIL & MAT
461. MOSQUITO MAT
462. MOTHER TINCTURE & BIO CHEMIC MEDICINES
463. NAPHTHALENE & PHENYL (INTEGRATED UNIT)
464. NATURAL MINERAL WATER BY REVERSE OSMOSIS PROCESS
465. NICKEL PLATING BRIGHTNER (PRIMARY OR CARRIER BRIGHTNER & SECONDARY BRIGHTNER)
466. NICKEL SULPHATE
467. NICOTINE FROM TOBACCO WASTE
468. NICOTINE SULPHATE FROM TOBACCO WASTE
469. NITRO BENZENE
470. NITRO CELLULOSE SANDING SEALER/LACQUER
471. NITRO MUSK
472. NITROGEN & OXYGEN GAS PLANT
473. NON-IONIC SURFACTANT (WETTING AGENT)
474. NO-CARB PASTE
475. OCTANOL
476. ORTHO NITRO PHENOL
477. OXALIC ACID FROM MOLASSES
478. OXALIC ACID FROMRICE HUSK
479. OXALIC ACID FROM TREE BARK
470. OXALIC ACID FROM WASTE VEGETABLES
471. OXYGEN GAS PLANT
472. OXYGEN GAS PLANT (AIR SEPERATION METHOD)
473. PARA-AMINO BENZOIC ACID
474. PARA-AMINO PHENOL
475. PARA TOLUENE SULPHONIC ACID
476. PECTIN FROM RAW PAPAYA
477. PERFUME (LEMON & OTHERS)

Price Rs. 3675/- for each "Detailed Project Report" Payable in advance through Draft/Cash/M.O. in favour of *"ENGINEERS INDIA RESEARCH INSTITUTE"*, 4449, Nai Sarak (D), Main Road Delhi - 110 006 *OR Ask by V.P.P.* ● Ph : 3918117, 391 6431, 392 0361, 396 0797 ●Fax : 91-11- 391 6431 ●E-Mail : eirisidi@bol.net.in ● WebSite : www.startindustry.com

Pay Rs. 8,000/- Only

for Tailor made Report We (EIRI) are fully capable to prepare any report as per your requirements

478. PESTICIDE PREPARATION USING NEEM FRUIT & SEEDS (MARGOSA)
479. PET BOTTLES FROM PRE-FORM
480. PET PREFORM FROM RESIN FOR PET BOTTLES
481. PETROLEUM JELLY
482. PHENOL
483. PHENYL
484. PHENYL (BLACK) IN LIQUID FORM
485. PHTHALIC ANHYDRIDE
486. PHOSPHORIC ACID FROM ROCK PHOSPHATE
487. PHOSPHORUS BY CHEMICAL PROCESS
488. PHOTO EMULSION FOR ROTARY SCREEN PRINTING
489. PHTHALOCYANINE BLUE
480. PIGMENT EMULSION FOR TEXTILE
481. PIGMENT GUM
482. PLANT GROWTH REAGEN BASED CHLOROTHYL TRIMETHYL AMMONIUM CHLORIDE
483. PLANT HARMONES BASED ON 2,4-DICHLORPHENOXY ACENTIC ACID & NAPHTHALENE
484. PLASTICINE (MODELLING CLAY)
485. PLASTIC WASTE REPROCESSING
486. PLASTER OF PARIS BANDAGES
487. POLYESTER RESIN (G.P. GRADE LAMINATE GRADE, ELECTRICAL GRADE)
488. POLY VINYL ACETATE
489. POLYVINYL ACETATE EMULSION
490. POLYURETHENE FOAM
491. POTASSIUM DICHROMATE/ BICHROMATE
492. POTASSIUM IODATE
493. POTASSIUM NITRATE
494. POTASSIUM PERMAGNATE
495. POTASSIUM PER SULPHATE
496. POTASSIUM SULPHATE (FERTILIZER GRADE)
497. POTASSIUM PER OXY DI-SULPHIDE
498. POTASSIUM SILICATE
499. POTASSIUM STEARATE
500. POWER ALCOHOL
501. PVC RESIN FROM ETHYL ALCOHOL
502. PYRIDINE & ITS DERIVATIVES
503. RAPID FAST DYES (ONLY PROCESS)
504. REACTOR (CHEMICAL)
505. RECLAMATION OF USED ENGINE OIL (BY CLAY & VACUUM DISTILLATION PROCESS)
506. RECLAMATION OF SPENT BLEACHING EARTH
507. RECLAMATION OF NICKEL SPENT CATALYST FROM VANASPATI INDUSTRY
508. RECTIFIED SPIRIT FROM MOLASSES & MAHUA FLOWERS
509. RECTIFIED SPIRIT FROM RICE STRAW
510. RED OXIDE PAINT/PRIMER (ANTI CORROSIVE) BASED ORGANIC RED PIGMENTS
511. REMOVAL OF ANTIMONY FROM LEAD SCRAP
512. RESORCINOL
513. ROSIN SIZING AGENT
514. RESORCINOL
515. SALINE AND INJECTION WATER
516. SALICYLIC ACID
517. SANTONIN
518. SENNOSIDES FROM SENNO LEAF
519. SHOE POLISH
520. SILICA GEL (BLUE SELF INDICATING PROCESS)
521. SILICONE EMULSION
522. SILICONE FROM RICE HUSK
523. SILICON FROM SILICA (SEMI CONDUCTOR GRADE)
524. SILICONE RESINS
525. SILICONE SPRAYSILVER BRAZING FOIL
526. SILVER EXTRACTION FROM WASTE HYPO SOLUTION
527. SILVER NITRATE
528. SILVER PARTS FOR CERAMIC CAPACITOR SINGLE SUPER PHOSPHATE & MIXED FERTILIZER (NPK)
529. SINGLE SUPER PHOSPHATE (S.S.P) & SULPHURIC ACID
530. SODA ASH
531. SODA ASH FROM NATRON
532. SODA WATER BOTTLING PLANT (CARBONATED BEVERAGE)
533. SODIUM ALUMINATE
534. SODIUM BI-CARBONATE (BAKING SODA) FROM SODA ASH
535. SODIUM CHLORITE
536. SODIUM CHROMATE SODIUM CYCLAMATE
537. SODIUM DI-CHROMATE
538. SODIUM DI-CHROMATE & SODIUM SULPHATE AS BYE PRODUCTS
539. SODIUM HEXA META PHOSPHATE
540. SODIUM HYDROSULFITE
541. SODIUM HYPO CHLORIDE (BLEACH LIQUOR)
542. SODIUM ISO-PROPYL XANTHATE
543. SODIUM LAURYL SULPHATE
544. SODIUM LAURYL SULPHATE & SODIUM LAURYL ETHER SULPHATE
545. SODIUM NITRATE
546. SODIUM PETROLEUM SULPHONATE (EMULSIFIER)
547. SODIUM SILICATE FROM SILICA & SODA ASH
548. SODIUM SILICATE FROM (1) PADDY SILK HUSK 2) & SILICA
549. SODIUM CARBONATE & SILICA
550. SODIUM SULPHATE
551. SODIUM SULPHIDE BY BARIUM SULPHATE PROCESS
552. SODIUM SULPHIDE FROM AMMONIA & SODIUM CHLORIDE
553. SODIUM SULPHITE
554. SODIUM TRI-POLY PHOSPHATE
555. SOFTENER (CATIONIC ANIONIC & NON-IONIC)
556. SPIRIT FROM PINE APPLE
557. STANNOUS CHLORIDE
558. STEARIC ACID
559. STEARATES MANUFACTURE (CALCIUM, ZINC, ALUMINIUM, MAGNESIUM STEARATES)
560. SULPHUR FROM PYRITES & SLAG
561. SULPHUR CRYSTALS/LUMPS
562. SULPHURIC ACID
563. SULPHURIC ACID FROM DCDA PROCESS
564. SUPER PHOSPHATE (S.S.P)
565. SYNTHETIC IRON OXIDE (YELLOW)
566. SYNTHETIC RED & WELLOW IRON OXIDE FROM IRON FILLING & PICKLE LIQUOR
567. TARTARIC ACID
568. TOILET CLEANER
569. TOLUENE AND SBP FROM

Price Rs. 3675/- for each "Detailed Project Report" Payable in advance through Draft/Cash/M.O. in favour of *"ENGINEERS INDIA RESEARCH INSTITUTE"*. 4449, Nai Sarak (D), Main Road Delhi - 110 006 *OR Ask by V.P.P.* ● Ph : 3918117, 391 6431, 392 0361, 396 0797 ●Fax : 91-11- 391 6431 ●E-Mail : eirisidi@bol.net.in ● WebSite : www.startindustry.com

CRUDE NAPHTHA
570. TRIMETHYL AMMONIUM CHLORIDE
571. TRIPHENYL PHOSPHITE (T.P.P)
572. ULTRAMARINE BLUE (LIQUID)
573. UREA FORMALDEHYDE & MELAMINE FORMALDEHYDE POWDER
574. UNDECYLINIC ACID
575. VINYL ACETATE MONOMER
576. VITAMIN C
577. VITAMIN E
578. WASTE WATER TREATMENT PLANT FOR INDUSTRIAL SECTOR IN INDIA (ONLY MARKER SURVEY)
579. WIRE DRAWING LUBRICANT
580. WIRE ENAMEL
581. XANTHATES
582. YELLOW DEXTRIN
583. ZINC CHLORIDE
584. ZINC OXIDE
585. ZINC PHOSPHATING BY COLD PROCESS
586. ZINC SILICATE
587. ZINC STEARATE
588. ZINC SULPHATE
589. ZINC SULPHATE MONOHYDRATE
590. ACID BLACK
591. AURAMINE'O'
592. AZO DYES STUFF
593. DYE & DYE INTERMEDIATE
594. DYE INTERMEDIATES
595. MALACHITE GREEN
596. METHYLENE BLUE
597. PHTHALOCYANINE BLUE
598. PHTHALOCYANINE BLUE & GREEN
599. REACTIVE DYES
600. SULPHUR BLACK DYE
601. VAT DYES
602. WATER CHILLING PLANT
603. WADDING OIL (100%) FOR WADDING OF COTTON HOSIERY CLOTH IN THE DYEING PROCESS
604. WHITE OIL
605. WAX FLOOR POLISH

ELECTRICAL, ELECTONICS, COMPUTERS AND INFOTECH/IT PROJECTS

606. AIR CONDITIONING
607. ALUMINIUM ALLOY CONDUCTOR
608. ALUMINIUM CABLE
609. ALUMINIUM ELECTROYTIC CAPACITORS
610. AUDIO CASSETTE ASSEMBLING & RECORDING
611. AUDIO CASSETTES DUPLICATING RECORDING
612. AUDIO CASSETTES & AUDIO STUDIO
613. AUDIO CASSETTES PLANE & RECORDED
614. AUDIO MAGNETIC HEADS
615. AUDIO MAGNETIC TAPE
616. AUDIO/VIDEO CASSETTES
617. AUTO BULB/LAMPS
618. AUTOMATIC VOLTAGE STABILIZER
619. BATTERY PLATES
620. BACK OFFICE (Rs. 5000/-)
621. B/W TV & COMPUTER MONITOR PICTURE TUBE
622. BREAD BOARDS
623. CALL CENTRE
624. CAMERA (35 MM)
625. CAPACITORS
626. CARBON ELECTRODE USED FOR BATTERY CELL
627. CARBON POTETIOMETERS
628. CEILING FAN
629. CERAMIC INSULATOR
630. CHILDREN INFOTECH TRAINING INSTITUTE (Rs. 5000/-)
631. CHOKE AND PATTI
632. CHOKE AND STARTER
633. CHOKE USED FOR FLUORESCENT LAMPS
634. COLOUR TELEVISION
635. COLOUR AND BLACK & WHITE TELEVISION
636. COMPACT DISC
637. COMPACT DISC PLAYER (AUDIO/VIDEO)
638. COMPUTER EDUCATION INSTITUTE
639. COMPUTER ASSEMBLY
640. COMPUTER HARDWARE
641. COMPUTER KEYBOARD
642. COMPUTER PERIPHERALS
643. COMPUTER PRINTERS
644. COMPUTER RIBBON
645. COMPUTER RIBBON REINKING OR REFILLING
646. COMPUTER STATIONERY
647. COMPUTER STATIONERY & IMPORTED HARDWARE PARTS

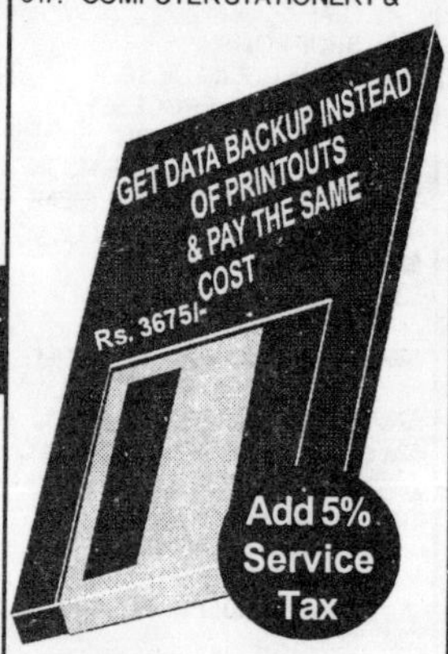

648. COMPUTER TERMINALS
649. COMPUTERISED WASHING MACHINE (AUTOMATIC)
650. COMPUTER SOFTWARE
651. CONDENSER FOR MOTOR USING MPP FILM
652. CONTENT DEVELOPMENT CENTRE (EOU) (Rs. 5000/-)
653. CONTROL PANEL BOARD
654. COOLING COIL FOR AIR CONDITIONERS
655. COPPER STRIP COIL FROM SCRAP
656. CORDLESS TELEPHONES
657. CYBER CAFE
658. CYBERKIOSK (Rs. 5000/-)
659. DATA PROCESSING CENTRE (Rs. 5000/-)
660. D.C. MICRO MOTORS
661. D.G.SETS
662. DISH ANTENNA AND CABLE T.V. NETWORK EQUIPMENT
663. DISTRIBUTION TRANSFORMERS & REPAIRS
664. DOMESTIC ELECTRICAL APPLIANCES- ROOM COOLER, WASHING MACHINE, WATER HEATER, ELECTRIC ROOM HEATER
665. E-SCHOOL
666. E-COMMERCE/BUSINESS
667. ELECTRIC ENERGY METER
668. ELECTRIC FANS
669. ELECTRIC HORN FOR AUTOMOBILE
670. ELECTRIC LAMP/GLS (INCANDESCENT LAMP)
671. ELECTRIC MIXER
672. ELECTRIC MOTORS UP TO 10 HP. REWINDING OF ALL TYPES OF MOTORS WATER PUMPS
673. ELECTRIC MOTOR WINDING (FOR FAN, MIXIES, ETC.)
674. ELECTRIC STEAM IRON
675. ELECTRICAL APPLIANCES
676. ELECTRICAL FIXTURES
677. ELECTRICAL STAMPING
678. ELECTROLYTIC CAPACITORS
679. ELECTROMAGNETIC RELAY
680. ELECTRONIC BALAST/CHOK
681. ELECTRICAL CHOKE
682. ELECTRONIC DIGITAL WATCHES
683. ELECTRONIC DIGITAL WEIGHING MACHINE
684. ELECTRONIC FIRE ALARM
685. ELECTRONIC GAS STOVE LIGHTERS
686. ELECTRONIC PRESSURE INDICATORS, ELECTRICALS, ELECTRONIC LIQUID LEVEL INDICATORS, ELECTRONIC TEMPERATURE INDICATOR, DIGITAL TACHOMETER
687. ELECTRONIC TELEPHONE INSTRUMENTS
688. ELECTRONIC TOYS
689. ELECTRONIC WATCHES & CLOCKS
690. FAX MACHINES
691. F.H.P MOTORS
692. FLOPPY DISKETTES
693. FLUORESCENT LAMP STARTER
694. FLUORESCENT TUBULAR

Price Rs. 3675/- for each "Detailed Project Report" Payable in advance through Draft/Cash/M.O. in favour of *"ENGINEERS INDIA RESEARCH INSTITUTE"*. 4449, Nai Sarak (D), Main Road Delhi - 110 006 *OR Ask by V.P.P.* ● Ph : 3918117, 391 6431, 392 0361, 396 0797 ●Fax : 91-11- 391 6431 ●E-Mail : eirisidi@bol.net.in ● WebSite : www.startindustry.com

LAMPS WITH INTRODUCTION TO MERCURY VAPOUR LAMP
695. FRANCHISEE COMPUTER EDUCATION CENTRE (Rs. 5000)
696. GAS DETECTOR (L.P.G)
697. GENERATOR SET & PUMP SETS
698. GENERATOR (BATTERY OPERATED)
699. GIS SERVICE CENTRE (GEOGRAPHICAL INFORMATION SYSTEMS)
700. HARDWARE FITTING FOR TRANSMISSION LINE (OVERHEAD LINE MATERIAL
701. HEADERS FOR TRANSISTOR ICS SEMI CONDUCTOR
702. H.T & L.T INSULATORS
703. H.T & M.V INDUSTRIAL CUBICAL SWITCH BOARD
704. INFORMATION MOVING DISPLAY (L.E.D TYPE)
705. INSURANCE CLAIM PROCESSING CENTRE (EOU) (Rs. 5000/-)
706. INTEGRATED CIRCUITS
707. INTERNET BASED STOCK TRADING (Rs. 5000/-)
708. INTERNET SERVICE PROVIDER (I.S.P.)
709. JELLY FILLED TELEPHONE CABLES
710. LAP TOP COMPUTERS
711. LEAD ACID BATTERIES
712. LEAD ACID BATTERY PLATES AND ASSEMBLING OF BATTERY
713. LEGAL TRANSCRIPTION & SECRETARIAL SERVICES CENTER (EOU)(Rs. 5000/-)
714. LIGHT EMITTING DIODES (L.E.D)
715. LINEAR ICS TRAINER KIT
716. LOUD SPEAKER
717. L.T TRANSFORMER REPAIRING
718. MEDICAL TRANSCRIPTION CENTRE
719. METAL FILM RESISTORS
720. METALLISED POLYPROPYLENE, POLYESTER FILM CAPACITOR
721. MICA BASE ELECTRONIC COMPONENTS
722. MICA PAPER WASTE PAPER FROM MICA WASTE
723. MICRO PROCESSORS TRAINER KITS BASED ON MICRO PROCESSORS
724. MINI COMPUTER (PERSONAL COMPUTER)
725. MINIATURE CIRCUIT BREAKER (M.C.B)
726. MINIATURE WATCH BATTERIES (BUTTON CELL)
727. MIXER/GRINDER (MIXI)
728. MONO CHROME COMPUTER MONITOR
729. MOTOR START ELECTROLYTIC CAPACITOR
730. MULTI LAYER P.C.B
731. MULTIPLE RELAY FOR LOW VOLTAGE
732. NEON INDICATOR
733. NEON SIGN MANUFACTURE
734. OPTICAL FIBRE CABLES
735. ON LINE SHOPPING MALL (Rs. 5000/-)
736. OPTO MECHANICAL & ELECTRICAL EQUIPMENTS
737. PHOTO COLOUR LAB
738. PICTURE TUBE (B/W)
739. PLAIN PAPER COPIER
740. PLASTIC FILM CAPACITORS
741. POLYESTER CAPACITORS
742. PORTABLE GENERATOR SET
743. PORTAL
744. PORTABLE TELEVISION(TV)
745. POWER CAPACITORS
746. POWER INVERTERS
747. POWER PLANT
748. POWER TRANSFORMERS UP TO 600 KVA
749. PRINTED CIRCUIT BOARD
750. PVC WIRES & CABLES
751. RE-CONDITIONING OF PICTURE TUBE
752. RESIN CAST CT & PT (1 KV)
753. SEMI CONDUCTOR DEVICE
754. SEMI CONDUCTORS FOR TRANSISTORS & DIODES
755. SETTING UP OF A VIDEO STUDIO
756. SMOKE DETECTORS
757. SOLAR CELLS
758. SOLAR MODULES
759. SOLAR PHOTO VOLTAIC SYSTEM
760. SOLDER FLUXES
761. SOLAR WATER HEATING PANELS
762. STEEL FURNITURE & ELECTRICAL APPLIANCES
763. STEREO AMPLIFIERS
764. STEREO CASSETTE RECORDERS/PLAYERS
765. STREET LIGHT FITTINGS SURGE SUPPRESSOR
766. TANTALUM CAPACITORS
767. TEFLON COATED ELECTRIC CABLE
768. TELEMEDICINE (DISTANCE HEALTH CARE) (Rs. 5000/-)
769. TELEPHONE CORD/CABLE
770. TELEPHONE (PUSH BUTTON TYPE)
771. TELEPHONE (PUSH BUTTON & CORDLESS)
772. TELEVISION (CTV & B/W)
773. TELEVISION (3-D)
774. TELEVISION DEFLECTION COMPONENTS
775. TELEVISION SIGNAL BOOSTERS
776. TELEVISION TUNERS
777. TRACTION BATTERIES
778. TRAINING INSTITUTE OF MEDICAL TRANSCRIPTION
779. TRANSFORMER FOR B/W TV
780. TRANSFORMER FOR VOLTAGE STABILIZER & E.H.T
781. TRANSMISSION POWER LINE FITTING
782. TRANSMISSION TOWER FITTING
783. TV AUDIO EQUIPMENT CABINETS & THEIR ASSEMBLING UNIT
784. UN-INTERRUPTED POWER SUPPLY (U.P.S)
785. VARIABLE FREQUENCY
786. VARIABLE VOLTAGE A.C. DRIVE
787. VIDEO CASSETTES (COMPLETE MANUFACTURING & ASSEMBLING)
788. VIDEO CASSETTES RECORDER (V.C.R)
789. VIDEO FILM STUDIO
790. VOLTAGE REGULATOR FOR AUTOMOBILES
791. VOLTAGE STABILIZERS
792. VOLTAGE STABLIZER & T.V. GAIN BOOSTER
793. WAX AND CHEMICAL COATED, BRAIDED TINSEL WIRE
794. WEBSITE DESIGN & E-MAIL REGISTERING
795. WELDING ELECTRODES
796. WIND ENERGY POWER PROJECT (10 MW) WIRE WOUND POTENTIOMETERS

FOOD, AGRO FOOD, PROCESSED FOOD, AGRO PLANTATION, CULTIVATION, FARMING, DAIRY/MILK, TOBACCO/PAN MASALA, BREWERY & DISTILLERY, EDIBLE OILS, EOU FOOD PRODUCTS AND ALLIED PRODUCTS

797. ALCOHOLIC BEVERAGES & VENEGAR FROM COCONUT WATER
798. ALCOHOL DRINKS FROM ETHYL ALCOHOL BY MIXING OF VARIOUS FLAVOURS
799. ANTI SCALE COMPOUND FOR ADDING INTO SUGAR JUICE BOILING
800. APPLE JUICE CONCENTRATED & DEHYDRATED FRUIT & VEGETABLES
801. ARTIFICIAL FISH MEAL FOR POULTRY FEED
802. AUTOMATIC BISCUIT PLANT
803. BABY CEREAL FOOD AND MILK POWDER
804. BACTERIA FOR CANE JUICE
805. BAKER'S YEAST
806. BAKERY INDUSTRY
807. BANANA PUREE
808. BEER & WINE
809. BEER PLANT (BREWERY)
810. BIDI
811. BIDI & CIGARETTE
812. BISCUIT PLANT

Choose & Start Your Own Industry
Out of 30,000 ready
Detailed Project Reports

813. BREAD (AUTOMATIC PLANT)
814. BLACK PEPPER (SPICES)
815. BREAD AND BISCUITS
816. BREEDING FARM
817. BROILER CHICKEN
819. BUTTON MUSHROOM CULTIVATION & PROCESSING
820. CANNING OF RASAGULLAS IN METAL CANS
821. CAFFEIN FROM TEA WASTE
822. CANNING OF FRUITS & VEGETABLES
823. CASEIN AND BY-PRODUCTS
824. CASHEW FRUIT JUICE FROM CASHEW FRUIT APPLE
825. CASHEWNUT KERNEL EXTRACTION FROM CASHEWNUT FRUIT
826. CASHEWNUT SHELL LIQUID & KERNEL PROCESSING
827. CASHEW FENI
828. CATECHEU (BY CHEMICAL PROCESS)
829. CATTLE FEED FROM TAPIOCA
830. CHEWING & BUBBLE GUM
831. CHICKEN/SHEEP MEAT PROCESSING
832. CHOCOLATE (MILK)
833. CIGARETTE AND BEEDIES
834. COCOA BUTTER FROM COCOA MASS
835. COCONUT PRODUCTS & BY PRODUCTS PROCESS COMPLEX
836. COLD/SOFT DRINKS
837. COLLECTION OF MILK AND MILK MAKING POWDER
838. COLLECTION OF MILK AND PACKING IN POLYTHENE POUCH (1/2 KG.1 KG. & 2 KG.)
839. CONDENSED MILK (SWEETNED)
840. CONFECTIONERY INDUSTRY (TOFFEE & CANDY, SEMI-AUTOMATIC PLANT)
841. COUNTRY LIQUOR FROM MOLASSES
842. CIGARETTE
843. DAIRY FARM AND DAIRY (MILK) PRODUCTS (PASTEURISED MILK, BUTTER, GHEE, PANEER)
844. DAIRY FARM TO PRODUCE MILK & PACKING IN POUCHES (50%) & CAN(50%)
845. DAIRY FOR MILK PROCESSING
846. DAIRY FARM (BUFALO)
847. DAL (PULSE) MILL UNIT
848. DEHYDRATION OF CARROT & GARLIC
849. DEHYDRATION & CANNING OF FRUITS & VEGETABLES
850. DEHYDRATION OF FIGS
851. DEHYDRATION OF FRUITS AND VEGETABLES
852. DEHYDRATED ONIONS AND ONION POWDER
853. DRY ICE BY BREAKING OF AIR
854. DRYING OF RED CHILLIES, HALDI, DHANIA, AND GREEN PEAS
855. EGG POWDER (40,000 EGGS PROCESSING PER DAY)
856. EXPORT OF PROCESSED FOODS AND MARINE PRODUCTS
857. FISH CANNING & POUCHING
859. FISH FARMING (PRAWN & OTHER MARINE PRODUCTS)
860. FISH MEAL
861. FLOUR MILL AND MUSTARD OIL
862. FOOD COLOUR & ORASTED GROUNDNUT GRAM PEAS, ETC IN POUCHES
863. FROG LEGS PROCESSING
864. FROZEN MEATS PROCESSING
865. FOOD FLAVOURS (WHISKY) VODKA, GRAPE, BUTTER SCOTCH)
866. FOOD PRODUCTS COMPLEX (DEHYDRATED ONIONS, GARLIC POWDER & FLAKES, CATTLE FEED, TOMATO POWDER, TOMATO PRODUCTS, CANNED FRUITS & VEGETABLES, TOMATO PURE, GROUN NUT OIL, REFIND OIL, DEHYDRATED GRAPES, BANANA POWDER & WAFFERS)
867. FRUIT JUICE, JAM, JELLIES & ALLIED PRODUCTS
868. FRUIT JUICE, PICKLES PROCESSING AND CANNING
869. FRUIT JUICE MAKING & PACKING IN PLASTIC CONTAINER/POUCHES
870. FRUIT PROCESSING (JAM & JELLIES)
871. FRUIT PULP & JUICE CONCENTRATES
872. FRUIT & VEGETABLE DRYING (FREEZE DRYING METHOD)
873. GOAT & SHEEP FARMING
874. GRAM DALL/PULSE MILL
875. GRAPE DEHYDRATION
876. HARD BOILED CANDY (TOFFEE & CANDY)
877. HERBAL CIGARETTES
878. HONEY PROCESSING & PACKAGING
879. ICE CREAM OF DIFFERENT FLAVOURS
880. ICE CREAM STABILIZER
881. ICE MAKING PLANT
882. INDIAN MADE FOREIGN LIQUOR (I.M.F.L)
883. INSTANT FOOD (IDLI MIX, DOSA MIX, GULAB JAMUN MIX)
884. INSTANT FOOD (INSTANT FOOD & FAST FOOD PARLOUR)
885. INSTANT NOODLES
886. INSTANT TEA
887. INSTANT TEA FROM BLACK TEA
888. INTEGERATED STARCH BAKING POWDER/YEAST INDUSTRY
889. IODIZED SALT
890. IODIZED SALT (ORDINARY MOISTURE-LESS/FREE FLOWING IN PLASTIC BAGS AND CONTAINERS)
891. JAM, JELLIES, FRUIT JUICE & ALLIED PRODUCTS
892. KATHA AND CUTCH
893. KHANDSARI SUGAR
894. KHANDSARI SUGAR & IMFL
895. LACTIC ACID FROM WHITE SUGAR BY FERMENTATION PROCESS
896. LACTOSE & BY PRODUCTS PROCESSING FROM MILK
897. LIQUID GLUCOSE AND ITS BYE PRODUCTS
898. MACRONI AND VERMICILLI
899. MALT EXTRACTION FROM BARLEY
900. MANGO PROCESSING (MANGO PULP, JUICE & SLICES)
901. MAYUR BRAND TYPE CHEWING TOBACCO
902. MINERAL WATER
903. MILK PRESERVATION & MARKETING TO WHOLE SELLERS (INPOUCH PACKING BY UHT TECHNOLOGY)
904. MILK PROCESSING AND PACKAGING OF MILK PRODUCTS
905. MILK PRODUCTS (CASEIN, LACTOSE, GHEE & WHEY POWDER)
906. MILK TOFFEE
907. MINI FLOUR MILL
908. MINI SUGAR PLANT
909. MISRI (PEARL SUGAR CANDIES)
910. MODERN RICE MILL
911. MURABBA
912. MUSTARD OIL EXTRACTION & REFINING
913. MUTTON TALLOW
914. NAMKEEN INDUSTRY (BHUJIA, CHANA CHUR ETC.)
915. NAMKEEN & SWEETS
916. NON-BASMATI RICE FROM PADDY
917. OLEORESIN, ESSENTIAL OIL, DYES & POWDER OF SPICES
918. OLEORESIN EXTRACTION FROM DIPTERO-CARPUT TURMINATUS AND PINUS KHASYANA
919. OLEORESIN EXTRACTION FROM CHILLI
920. PAN MASALA AND POUCH

Price Rs. 3675/- for each "Detailed Project Report" Payable in advance through Draft/Cash/M.O. in favour of *"ENGINEERS INDIA RESEARCH INSTITUTE"*. 4449, Nai Sarak (D), Main Road Delhi - 110 006 *OR Ask by V.P.P.* ● Ph : 3918117, 391 6431, 392 0361, 396 0797 ●Fax : 91-11- 391 6431 ●E-Mail : eirisidi@bol.net.in ● WebSite : www.startindustry.com

Apart from the above mentioned reports EIRI is also having other most lucrative projects (as many as 30,000). You just name it and we have that report

MAKING
921. PAN MASALA, TOBACCO, ZARDA & KIMAM
922. PANEER FROM MILK
923. PAPPAD PLANT
924. PAPAIN FROM PAPAYA (PAPAYA LATEX)
925. PECTIN FROM MANGO PEEL PECTIN FROM APPLE POMACE
926. PHYTO TEA (HERBAL TEA)
927. PICKLES AND SAUCES
928. PICKLES MURABBA ETC. (VEG. & NON. VEG. PICKLES)
929. PIGGERY MEAT PROCESS
930. PINE-APPLE JUICE PREPARATION & PACKAGING
931. POTATO CHIPS/WAFFERS
932. POTATO POWDER
933. POUCH FILLING & PACKAGING OF EDIBLE OIL & GHEE
934. POULTRY FEED
935. PROCESSED FOODS & SPICES (EOU)
936. PROCESSED READYMADE FOOD
937. PROCESSING OF FRUITS & VEGETABLES
938. RABBIT FARMING
939. RASGULLAS MAKING & CANNING IN METAL CANS
940. READY TO EAT PROCESSED COOKED FOOD
941. READY TO EAT SNACK FOOD (CRAX, ROLL & BALL TYPE)
942. RICE & CORN FLAKES
943. ROASTED/SALTED/ MASALA, CASHEW NUTS, ALMONDS & PEANUTS
944. ROLLER FLOUR MILL
945. SALT LICKS FOR CATTLE
946. SAUSAGES FOOD CASING
947. SOFT DRINKS
948. SOFT DRINKS ESSENCES
949. SOFT DRINKS (NON CARBONATED) MANGO, LICCHI, PINEAPPLE FLAVOURS FROOTI TYPE IN TETRAPACK)
950. SOFTY ICE CREAM CONES (FULLY AUTOMATIC)
951. SOFT/COLD DRINKS (COLA, ORANGE, LEMON ETC. FLAVOURS)
952. SOYABEAN PRODUCTS
953. SOYA MILK & PANEER
954. STARCH & ALLIED PROPDUCT FROM BROKEN RICE
955. STRAWBERRY CULTIVATION & PROCESSING
956. SUGARCANE JUICE PRESERVATION
957. SUGAR CUBES FROM CANE SUGAR
988. SUGAR PLANT
989. SWEET AROMA BETEL NUT
990. SYNTHETIC TALLOW
991. TAMARIND JUICE POWDER
992. TEA & COFFEE PROCESSING & PACKAGING
993. TOFFEES, GOLIES, CANDY (HARD BOILED)
994. TOMATO PRODUCTS
994. TRADING BUSINESS OF SPICES & PAN MASALA
995. TUITY FRUITY
996. VODKA FROM POTATOES
997. WINE, BRANDY, WHISKY & CHAMPAGNE
997. WINE FROM DATES
998. YEAST FROM MOLASSES
999. ZARDA, KIMAM NO. 60,90,120,160,240,300 & 400 (TOBACCO)
1000. ZARDA-ZAFRANI (BABACHHAP TYPE)

GUMS & ADHESIVE

1001. ACRYLIC ADHESIVE
1002. ADHESIVE (FEVICOL TYPE)
1003. ADHESIVE BASED ON POLYURETHANE
1004. ADHESIVE FOR BAND AID (JOHNSON & JOHNSON TYPE)
1005. ADHESIVE INDUSTRIES (LAMINATED, STICKER, DDL & OTHER TYPES)
1006. ADHESIVE FOR GASKET (LIQUID/PASTE)
1007. GUAR GUM
1008. GUM BOTTLE (PVC)
1009. GUM FOR PASTING LABELS
1010. OFFICE PASTE
1011. RUBBER ADHESIVE
1012. SURGICAL ADHESIVE PLASTER

LEATHER & LEATHER PRODUCTS

1013. HANDMADE LEATHER
1014. LEATHER AUXILLARIES & CHEMICALS
1015. LEATHER DYES
1016. LEATHER WASHERS
1017. LEATHER BOARD FROM LEATHER WASTE
1018. LEATHER FOR UPHOLSTRY (SOFA)
1019. LEATHER GARMENTS
1020. LEATHER GOODS
1021. LEATHER SHOES
1022. LEATHER SHOE & CHAPPAL
1023. LEATHER SUITCASES, BRIEFCASES & TRAVELLING BAGS
1024. LEATHER GOODS AND GARMENTS
1025. LEATHER GARMENTS, SHOE & CHAPPAL
1026. LEATHER TANNING
1027. LEATHER TANNING & GARMENTS (EOU)
1028. SHEEP SKIN PICKLING PLANT
1029. SHOE UPPER
1030. SPORT SHOES (PLASTIC)

MISCELLANEOUS PRODUCTS

1031. AGARBATTI (INSENCE STICK)
1032. AGARBATTI (Mosquito Repellent)
1033. AGARBATI BAMBOO STICK
1034. AGARBATTI SYNTHETIC PERFUMERY COMPOUND
1035. AIR FRESHNER (ODONIL TYPE)
1036. AIR TAXI
1037. AMUSEMENT PARK
1038. ANODIC ALUMINIUM LABEL
1039. AQUACULTURE PRAWN FARMING (100% EOU)
1040. AQUA CULTURE SHRIMP FARMING (100% EOU)
1041. ARTIFICIAL FLOWERS
1042. ARTIFICIAL JEWELLERY
1043. ASBESTOS YARN
1044. ASH TRAYS FOR MARUTI VEHICLE
1045. AIR BUBBLE PACKAGING
1046. ASPHALTIC ROOFING SHEET (METAL COMPONENTS)
1047. AUTOMATIC BOOK BINDING
1048. ALKYD RESIN
1049. APPLE JUICE CONCENTRATE
1050. BALL POINT PEN FEFILLS (JOTTER TYPE)
1051. BANK BRANCH BUILDING
1052. BANQUET HALL
1053. BIO-COAL BRIQUETTES FROM AGRICULTURAL CELLULOSE WASTE
1054. BOOT CREAM/POLISH
1055. BUFFING & POLISHING COMPOUND
1056. BRASS BADGES BY ETCHING
1057. BRIQUETTED FUEL FROM AGRO WASTE
1058. BRIQUETTING OF LIGNITE COAL

Price Rs. 3675/- for each "Detailed Project Report" Payable in advance through Draft/Cash/M.O. in favour of *"ENGINEERS INDIA RESEARCH INSTITUTE"*. 4449, Nai Sarak (D), Main Road Delhi - 110 006 *OR Ask by V.P.P.* ● Ph : 3918117, 391 6431, 392 0361, 396 0797 ●Fax : 91-11- 391 6431 ●E-Mail : eirisidi@bol.net.in ● WebSite : www.startindustry.com

1059. BUFFALO HORN TIP, HOOF
1060. BANQUET HALL
1061. BUTTON
1062. CALCINED PETROLEUM (C.P) COKE
1063. CANVAS SHOES
1064. CANVAS SHOES, JUNGLE BOOTS
1065. CARBON BRUSH, BRUSH HOLDER & SLIP RING
1066. CEMENT SHEETS WITH COIR FIBRE & OTHER SEGMENTS
1067. CERAMIC TILES (GLAZED) BY DOUBLE FIRING/HEATING
1068. CHILDREN RECREATION CENTRE
1069. COAL BRIQUETTES
1070. COLD STORAGE & ICE
1071. COLD STORAGE FOR FRUITS AND VEGETABLES
1072. COMPRESSOR (HERMETIC) FOR AIR CONDITIONER
1073. COSTUME JEWELLERY/ IMITATION JEWELLERY
1074. DECORATIVE LAMINATED SHEET (SUNMICA)
1075. DIAMOND CUTTING & EXPORTS
1076. DRINKING STRAW FROM PROPYLENE
1077. ENGINEERING COLLEGE
1078. ENTERTAINMENT CLUB
1079. FASHION TECHNOLOGY INSTITUTE
1080. FAST FOOD PARLOUR
1081. FAST FOOD (INSTANT FOOD & FAST FOOD PARLOUR)
1082. FIRE EXTINGUISHERS (SODA ACID TYPE)
1083. FISH NET
1084. FLORICULTURE (CUT FLOWER ROSE) WITH GREEN HOUSE
1085. FLOOR COVERING SHEET
1086. FILM STUDIO (VIDEO)
1087. FLUSH DOOR, CHIP BOARD, WOOD WOOL & OTHER INSULATING BOARDS
1088. GAS DETECTORS OF L.P.G
1089. GEMS MANUFACTURING
1090. GLASS BOTTLE BY SCRAP
1092. GOAT & SHEEP FARMING
1093. GOLD ELECTROPLATING
1094. GOLD JEWELLERY (E.O.U)
1095. GOLD PLATED SILVER JEWELLERY & CUTLERY
1096. GRANITE SLAB AND TILES
1097. GREEN HOUSE
1098. HARD CHROMIUM PLATING
1099. HEALTH CLUB AND BEAUTY PARLOUR CUM HAIR SALOON WITH SONA BATH
1100. HEALTH CLUB CUM BEAUTY PARLOUR TRAININGINSTITUTE
1101. HORN TIP,HOOVE BUTTON
1102. HOSPITAL
1103. HOSPITAL (100 BEDS)
1104. HOSPITAL (200 BEDS)
1105. ICE MAKING PLANT
1106. IMITATION AND COSTUME
1107. JEWELLERY (NECKLACE, EARRINGS EAR TOP ETC.)
1108. INITMATE SCENT CHEMICALS FROM ALL TYPES OF FLAVOUR
1109. INVESTMENT CASTING
1110. JUTE, COIR, GLASS ROPE/ SUTLI
1111. JUTE TWINE
1112. L.P.G BOTTLING PLANT
1113. L.P.G REGULATOR (DOMESTIC PURPOSE)
1114. LAMINATED PARTICLE BOARD & HARD BOARD
1115. LAMINATED SAFETY AND TOUGHENED GLASS
1116. LEASING & HIRE PURCHASE
1117. LICHEN (CHARILA)
1118. MANILA ROPES
1119. MEDICAL COLLEGE
1120. MATCH UNIT FROM WAXED PAPER
1121. MEDIUM DENSITY FIBRE BOARD
1122. MELAMINE CROCKERY
1123. MINERAL WATER
1124. MINI CEMENT PLANT
1125. MIRROR SILVER, GOLDEN, PINK, BLACK & SMOKES
1126. MODERN ADVERTISING AGENCY WITH DTP & FILM STUDIO
1127. MOTEL/SMALL HOTEL
1128. MULTI COLOUR PRINTING
1129. MULTI STOREY COMMERCIAL COMPLEX ALONGWITH RESIDENTIAL AND DELUX FLATS FOR FOREIGN TOURISTS & REVOLVING RESTAURENT AT THE TOP
1130. MULTIPLE LAMINATION INDUSTRY
1131. MUSHROOM GROWING AND PROCESSING (BY DEEP FREEZING METHOD)
1132. NEWS PAPER PRINTING
1133. NICKEL LINED INDUSTRIAL SCREEN
1134. OFFSET COLOUR PRINTING PRESS (SIX COLOUR)
1135. OFFSET PRINTING PRESS
1136. P.C.C ELECTRIC POLES
1137. PHOTOGRAPHIC DEVELOPER & FIXER
1138. PVC EXTRUSION PROFILE (DOOR & WINDOWS)
1139. POP-CORN
1140. PHOTO ETCHING OF S.S.
1141. PRE STRESSED CEMENT CONCRETE PIPES
1142. PILFER PROOF CAPS
1143. PILFER PROOF CAPS AND CROWN CAP
1144. POUCH MAKING & GRAVURE PRINTING (ROTO PRINTING)
1145. POULTRY & FISH FARMING (INTEGERATED UNIT)
1146. PRINTING OF TIN SHEETS
1147. READYMADE GARMENTS
1148. RESTAURANT
1149. ROSE PLANTATION AND ROSE OIL EXTRACTION
1150. ROTOGRAVURE PRINTING
1151. SAFETY BELTS
1152. SAFETY MATCHES
1153. SHOE LACES
1154. SILK COCOON CULTIVATION (GROWING OF SILK COCOON WARM)
1155. SILK SCREEN PRINTING FORMULATIONS FOR PLASTIC, PAPER & CLOTH
1156. SPIKENARD (JATAMANSI)
1157. STENCIL COATING SOLUTION
1158. SUGAR CANDY (MISRI)
1159. SUGAR CANE PLANTATION
1160. SUGAR CANE JUICE PRESERVATION
1161. SURAT ZARI
1162. SYNTHETIC SHOES & SOLES
1163. TEA PACKAGING INDUSTRY
1164. TENNIS BALLS
1165. THREE STAR HOTEL
1166. TRAVELLING AGENCY
1167. TRAYS, TROLLEYS FOR HOSPITAL WITH SCRATCHLESS COATING
1168. WAX EXTRACTS (TANNING POWDER)
1169. WIRE ROPE SLINGS
1170. WOOD WOOL SLAB
1171. WOODEN CANE FURNITURE WITH EXPORT POTENTIAL
1172. WOODEN FURNITURE
1173. WOODEN PANEL INCLUDING KILN SEASONING
1174. WOODEN FURNITURE
1175. WATCH CASE BUFFING
1176. WATCH DIAL
1177. WRIST WATCHES
1178. WATCHES (ELECTRONIC)
1179. ZEDOARY (KACHUR)

EDIBLE OILS, ESSENTIAL OILS LURICATIING OILS, GREASES, VEGETABLE OILS, WAXES, CAMPHOR, PERFUMES & PERFUMERY COMPOUNDS AND REFINED OILS ETC.

1180. AROMATIC PERFUMERY COMPOUND
1181. AEROSOL
1182. AGARBATTI PERFUMERY COMPOUND
1183. BEES WAX MANUFACTURE
1184. CAMPHOR
1185. CARDANOL FROM CASHEW NUT SHELL LIQUID
1186. CASTOR OIL
1187. CASTOR OIL DERIVATIVE OLEORESINS
1188. CHILLI OIL
1189. CITRONELLA OILS
1190. CLOVE OIL
1191. CONCENTRATE OF ROSE JASMINE & LILY ETC.
1192. COLOURED FLAME CANDLE

Price Rs. 3675/- for each "Detailed Project Report" Payable in advance through Draft/Cash/M.O. in favour of *"ENGINEERS INDIA RESEARCH INSTITUTE"*. 4449, Nai Sarak (D), Main Road Delhi - 110 006 *OR Ask by V.P.P.* ● Ph : 3918117, 391 6431, 392 0361, 396 0797 ●Fax : 91-11- 391 6431 ●E-Mail : eirisidi@bol.net.in ● WebSite : www.startindustry.com

1193. CANDLES (SEMI-AUTOMATIC)
1194. CORN OIL (MAIZE OIL)
1195. DEHYDRATED CASTOR OIL
1196. EUGENOL FROM CINNAMON LEAF OIL
1197. EXTRACTION OF ESSENTIAL OIL (CARDAMON, JEERA, AJOWAN, GINGER OILS ETC. & PACKAGING OF GROUND SPICES)
1198. EXTRACTION OF JASMINE ESSENCE
1199. EXTRACTION OF ESSENTIAL OILS BY SUPER CRITICAL FLUID METHOD FROM FLOWERS, HERBS & SPICES
1200. EUCALYPTUS OIL
1201. EXTRACTION OF OIL FROM OIL SEED EXPANDEREXTRUSION TECHNOLOGY)
1202. FAT LIQUOR SULPHATED OIL
1203. FLAVOURS FOR FOOD
1204. GARLIC OIL & POWDER
1205. GINGER OIL, SANDALWOOD OIL AND NAGARMOTHA OIL
1206. GINGER OIL
1207. GINGER OIL & GINGER DUST
1208. INTEGERATED WAX COMPLEX
1209. IONONE FROM LEMON GRASS OIL
1210. JASMINE & LILLY FLOWER OIL
1211. LEMON GRASS OIL
1212. LIQUID PARAFFIN
1213. LUBE OIL & GREASE
1214. LUBRICATING OIL
1215. MENTHOL CRYSTALS
1216. MENTHOL OIL & CRYSTAL
1217. MICRO CRYSTALLINE WAX
1218. MUSTARD OIL (EDIBLE OIL)
1219. OIL FROM ARTEMISIA HERBS
1220. PALM OIL CRUSHING UNIT
1221. PAN MASALA
1222. PARAFFIN WAX
1223. PARAFFIN WAX FROM SLACK WAX
1224. REFINED OIL-SUN FLOWER OIL, GROUNDNUT OIL, STAFF FLOWER OIL & COTTON SEED OIL
1225. REFINED VEGETABLE OIL
1226. RECLAMATION OF USED ENGINE OIL
1227. RICE BRAN OIL (R.B.O)
1228. ROSE OIL EXTRACTION
1229. SMOKE LESS CANDLE
1230. SPICE OIL & OLEORESINS
1231. SOLVENT EXTRACTION PLANT (OIL CAKE BASED)
1232. SYNTHETIC ALMOND OIL
1233. SYNTHETIC TALLOW
1234. SYNTHETIC GHEE
1235. VEGETABLE OIL EXTRACTION & REFINING
1236. WADDING OIL (100%) FOR WADDING OF COTTON HOSIERY CLOTH IN DYEING PROCESS
1237. WAX EMULSION FOR TEXTILE
1238. WAX FLOOR POLISH

PAINT, ENAMEL, SOLVENTS, THINNERS, INKS & VARNISH

1239. ACRYLIC EMULSION PAINTS
1240. ALUMINIUM PAINT
1241. AUTOMOBILE PAINTS
1242. BALL POINT PEN REFILL INK
1243. BITUMINIOUS ROAD EMULSION
1244. BITUMEN
1245. BITUMINIOUS FELTS FOR WATER & DAMP PROOFING
1246. BITUMINIOUS ROAD EMULSION RAPID MEDIUM & SLOW SETTING
1247. BUFFING & POLISHING
1248. CEMENT PAINT FOR WHITE & GREY CEMENT

1249. DISPERSANT
1250. DRY DISTEMPER
1251. DRY DISTEMPER & CEMENT PAINT
1252. DUPLICATING INK BLACK FOR GESTNER DUPLICATOR
1255. EMULSION PAINTS (WATER BASED)
1256. HAMMERTONE PAINT
1257. INSULATING VARNISH & WIRE ENAMEL
1258. IRON OXIDE PIGMENTS
1259. INSULATING VARNISH (POLY VINYL BUTYRAL BASED, FFC GRADE)
1260. LIME COLOUR (CEMENT COLOUR)
1261. SYNTHETIC RED OXIDE FOR FLOORINGS
1262. SOLVENT & THINNERS
1263. MARKING INKS (WATER PROOF)
1264. METAL NAPHTHANATE (AS DRIER FOR PAINTS)
1265. N.C.PUTTY
1266. OFFSET PRINTING INK
1267. OIL BOUND DISTEMPER PAINT
1268. PAINT BRUSHES
1269. PAINT REMOVERS
1270. PAINT INDUSTRY
1271. PAINT & VARNISH
1272. PICTURE VARNISH
1273. POWDER COATING PAINT
1274. PRINTING INKS (OFFSET, FLEXO & ROTO GRAVURE)
1275. PRIMER PAINT & ENAMEL PAINT
1276. PUTTY & WATER PROOFING PAINT
1277. PRINTING INKS (FLEXO-GRAPHIC INK)
1278. PUTTY (METAL CASEMENT)
1279. RED OXIDE PRIMER (ANTI CORROSIVE)
1280. REFRACTORY PAINT (GRAPHITE BASED)
1281. SCREEN PRINTING INKS
1282. SILK SCREEN PRINTING INK FORMULATION FOR PLASTIC, PAPER, CLOTH
1283. STAMP & PAD INK
1284. STOVING PAINT
1285. SPIRIT SOLUBLE MALEIC RESIN
1286. TEXTURE PAINT
1287. THINNERS AND ITS ALLIED PRODUCTS
1288. TONER INK
1289. VARNISH THINNER (SOLVENT)
1290. VACUUM METALLIZING LACQUERS
1291. WOOD PRIMER

PHARMACEUTICAL, DRUGS, AYURVEDIC/HERBAL COSMETICS & MEDICINES, HOMOEOPATHIC MEDICINES, DISPOSABLE SYRINGE, DENTAL COLLEGE & FINE CHEMICALS ETC.

1292. AROMATIC PILLS
1293. ASPIRIN
1294. AYURVEDIC PAIN BALM OINTMENTS
1295. AYURVEDIC CHURAN AND TABLETS
1296. AYURVEDIC TABLETS (HAJMOLA TYPE)
1297. AYURVEDIC/HERBAL PHARMACY
1298. AYURVEDIC SHERBATS
1299. AYURVEDIC PRODUCTS
1300. BULK DRUGS (E.O.U)
1301. BLOOD BAGS
1302. CALCIUM GLUCONATE
1303. CAPSULE, TABLET & INJECTION WITH MODERN INSTRUMENTS
1304. CASHEW FENI
1305. CHLOROQUINONE PHOSPHATE (BULK DRUGS)
1306. CLINICAL THERMOMETER
1307. DENTAL CLINIC

Price Rs. 3675/- for each "Detailed Project Report" Payable in advance through Draft/Cash/M.O. in favour of *"ENGINEERS INDIA RESEARCH INSTITUTE"*. 4449, Nai Sarak (D), Main Road Delhi - 110 006 *OR Ask by V.P.P.* ● Ph : 3918117, 391 6431, 392 0361, 396 0797 ●Fax : 91-11- 391 6431 ●E-Mail : eirisidi@bol.net.in ● WebSite : www.startindustry.com

1308. DENTAL COLLEGE
1309. DENTAL GRADE EUGENOL
1310. DEXTROSE MONOHYDRATE, LIQUID GLUCOSE
1311. DEHYDRATED ONION & ONION POWDER
1312. DEXTROSE POWDER (ANHYDROUS FROM STARCH)
1314. DEXTROSE SALINE SOLUTION
1315. DISTILLERY (I.M.F.L)
1316. DISPOSABLE NEEDLES FOR SYRINGES
1317. DISPRIN
1318. DISTILLED WATER
1319. EMPTY HARD GELATINE CAPSULES
1320. FILLING & PACKING OF CAPSULES
1321. GLUCOSE - D - POWDER
1322. GLYCERINE
1323. HERBAL COSMETICS
1324. HERBAL SHAMPOO
1325. HERBAL HAIR OILS (AYURVEDIC)
1326. HOMOE & BIO-MEDICINES WITH MOTHER TINCTURE
1327. HOMOEPATHIC MEDICINES
1328. HYPODERMIC NEEDLES
1329. I.V. FLUIDS
1330. IBUPROFEN
1331. INFUSION & TRANSFUSION SETS (I.V. SET)
1332. INJECTABLE FOR PHARMACEUTICALS
1333. INJECTION AMPOULES PACKAGING BOX
1334. INTEGERATED SURGICAL COTTON
1335. ICE MAKING PLANT
1336. ICE & COLD STORAGE
1337. LACTOSE & BY PRODUCTS PROCESSING FROM MILK
1338. LICHEN (JATAMANSI CHARILA)
1339. LIQUID GLUCOSE AND ITS BY-PRODUCTS
1340. L-LYSINE MONOHYDRO CHLORIDE
1341. LIQUID GLUCOSE FROM POTATOES
1342. MEDICAL COLLEGE
1343. NICOTINE FROM TOBACCO WASTE
1344. OINTMENT-AYURVEDIC (YELLOW & WHITE)
1345. PHARMACEUTICAL AND FOOD GRADE GELATINE
1346. PHARMACEUTICAL INDUSTRY (TABLETS, CAPSULES, LIQUID, GEL, OINTMENT POWDER INJECTABLE)
1347. PHARMACEUTICAL UNIT (EOU) WITH FORMULA TIONS, INJECTABLES, ETC. PYRIDINE & DERIVATIVES
1348. SALT (IODIZED SALT)
1349. SALINE & INJECTION WATER
1350. SALINE WATER & DEXTROSE SOLUTION (I.V. FLUID IN PLASTIC BOTTLES)
1351. SORBITOL
1352. STARCH (MAIZE)
1353. SURGICAL ADHESIVE PLASTER
1354. SURGICAL BANDAGES
1355. SURGICAL GLOVES
1357. SURGICAL COTTON
1358. SURGICAL COTTON AND BANDAGE
1359. SYNTHETIC CAMPHOR POWDER
1360. TABLETS & CAPSULES
1361. TISSUE CULTURE
1362. TINCTURE FROM RECTIFIED SPIRIT
1363. TRIMETHOPIME
1364. VETERENARY MEDICINES (ONLY FORMULATIONS)
1365. VITAMIN 'C', SORBITOL' ANHYDROUS DEXTROSE, STARCH

PULP, PAPER, STRAW/GREY BOARD, KRAFT PAPER, PACKAGING, PAPER CARRY BAGE, PAPER FROM AGRO WASTE & STATIONERY ETC.

1366. AMMONIA PAPER
1367. AUTOMATIC BOOK BINDING
1368. ADHESIVE (FEVICOL TYPE)
1369. ALL PIN & GEM CLIPS
1370. CARBON PAPER
1371. CARD BOARD
1372. CARBON LESS PAPER
1373. CELLPHANE PAPER
1374. COMPUTER FORMS & SECURITY PRINTING PRESS
1375. CORRUGATED BOARD & BOX (PRINTED & LAMINATED)
1376. CORRUGATED BOARD AND BOXES FROM FROM CARD BOARDS
13/7. CORRUGATED CARTONS FROM PLAIN PAPERS
1378. CORRUGATRED PACKING & MATERIAL (BULB & TUBES PACKING)
1379. DESK TOP PUBLISHING
1380. DEFOAMING AGENT FOR PAPER PLANT
1381. DRINKING STRAW PAPER
1382. D.T.P CUM OFFSET PRESS
1383. EGG TRAYS
1384. EXERCISE NOTE BOOK, REGISTER AND PAD
1385. FLEXOGRAPHIC INK
1386. GREETING CARD BY OFFSET PRESS
1387. HAND MADE PAPER FILTER PAPER
1388. HARD BOARD
1389. INJECTION AMPOULES PACKAGING BOXES
1390. INSULATIING PAPER
1391. KRAFT PAPER
1392. KRAFT PAPER FROM BAGASSE
1393. LAMINATED PACKAGING PAPER WITH PRINTING
1394. LAMINATION & COATING ON PAPER
1395 M.G PAPER FROM WASTE PAPER
1396. MILL PAPER FROM WASTE PAPER
1397. MILL BOARD FROM RICE & WHEAT STRAWS
1398. MILL BOARD FROM WASTE PAPER
1399. MINI PAPER PLANT FROM SISAL
1400. MINI PAPER PLANT
1401. MULTI WALL PAPER SACKS
1402. NEWS PAPER FOR CHILDREN
1403. NEWS PRINT PAPER FROM RICE STRAW BAGASSE
1404. NEWS PAPER CHILDRENS
1405. NEWS PRINT PAPER
1406. OFFSET AND TREADLE TYPE PRINTING PRESS
1407. MILL BOARD BASED ON RICE STRAW
1408. PAPER AND BOARD FROM STRAW
1409. PAPER & PAPER PRODUCTS
1410. PAPER ENVELOPES
1411. PAPER CARRY BAGS
1412. PAPER BOARD CARTON
1413. PAPER CONES FOR LOUD SPEAKERS
1414. PAPER FROM AKRA
1415. PAPER FROM BAGASSE WITH CORRUGATED BOARD & BOXES
1416. PAPER FROM BAMBOO
1417. PAPER GLASSES FOR BEVERAGES
1418. PAPER FROM RICE HUSK & WHEAT HUSK
1419. PAPER FROM TREE BARK, EUCALYPRUS WOOD
1420. PAPER PRODUCTS
1421. PAPER PLANT (WHITE WRITING & NEWS PAPER FOR PULP & WASTE PAPER)
1422. PAPER PLATES, PAPER GLASS
1423. PAPER CONES & TUBES
1425. PAPER PLANT WITH DTP & PRINTING & PUBLISHING UNIT
1426. PAPER BASED PHENOLIC SHEET
1427. PAPER CUP FOR ICE CREAM
1428. PAPER TUBES SPIRAL WINDING COMPOSIT CONTAINER
1429. PAPER LABLE FOR BEER BOTTLES
1430. PARTICLE BOARD & BLACK BOARD WITH SANDING & LAMINATION OF PARTICLE BOARD
1431. PARTICLE BOARD FROM RICE HUSK
1432. POUCH FILLING & MAKING FOR TOMATO SAUCE
1433. POUCH MAKING &

Price Rs. 3675/- for each "Detailed Project Report" Payable in advance through Draft/Cash/M.O. in favour of *"ENGINEERS INDIA RESEARCH INSTITUTE"*. 4449, Nai Sarak (D), Main Road Delhi - 110 006 *OR Ask by V.P.P.* ● Ph : 3918117, 391 6431, 392 0361, 396 0797 ●Fax : 91-11- 391 6431 ●E-Mail : eirisidi@bol.net.in ● WebSite : www.startindustry.com

GRAVURE PRINTING
1434. PROCESSING OF PAPER FOR FEEDING IN COMPUTER
1435. PULP FROM BAMBOO & WOOD
1436. PAPER FILES
1437. PLAYING CARDS
1438. ROSIN SIZING AGENT (FOR PAPER PLANT)
1439. SAND PAPER
1440. SANITRY NAPKINS
1441. SILICON COATED PAPER
1442. STENCIL PAPER
1443. STRAW BOARD AND GREY BOARD
1444. STRAW BOARD & MILL BOARD
1445. STRAW BOARD AND PAPER BOARD
1446. TISSUE PAPER FACIAL
1447. TISSUE MOIST TOILETERY CLEANSING TISSUE AND RELATED PRODUCTS
1448. TISSUE PAPER ROLLS
1449. TETRA PACK FOR MILK PACKAGING, GHEE & OTHER LIQUIDS
1450. TOILET PAPER ROLLS
1451. TOILET PAPER & NAPKINS
1452. WAX COATED PRINTED PAPER
1453. WET FACE FRESHNER TISSUE
1454. WHITE WRITING & PRINTING PAPER
1455. WRITING & PRINTING PAPER (PAPER MILLS)

PLASTIC, B.O.P.P, ACRYLIC, DISPOSABLE PLASTIC PRODUCTS, PET PRODUCTS, P.V.C, H.D.P.E, P.P, L.D.P.E., P.U, A.B.S, THERMOFOARMING, MASTER BATCHES, & POLYMER AND RUBBER PRODUCTS, TYRE, TUBE, ADHESIVE, SHEET, COIR & MANY OTHERS

1456. ABS GRANULES FROM ABS SCRAPS FROM OLD T.V. CABINETS, WHITE GOODS ETC.
1457. ACRYLIC BEADS
1458. ACRYLIC COPOLYMER EMULSION
1459. ACRYLIC LATEX
1460. ACRYLIC SHEET
1461. ACRYLIC SHEET & MOULDED PRODUCTS
1462. ACRYLIC TEETH
1463. AUTO TUBES
1464. AUTO FLAPS FOR TRUCKS & BUSES
1465. AUTO TYRES & TUBES
1466. BABY BOTTLES (PLASTIC) WITH WHITESILICON RUBBER NIPPLES
1467. B.O.P.P. FILM
1468. B.O.P.P. PRESSURE SENSITIVE SELF ADHESIVE TAPE
1469. BABY NIPPLE (SILICON)
1470. BABY NIPPLE (BIG SIZE)
1471. BALLOON PLASTIC ADVERTISING
1472. BLISTER FILM PVC
1473. BLISTER PACKAGING & POUCH PAKAGING
1474. BLOW MOULDING PLASTIC CONTAINER
1475. COATING ON METALIZED POLYESTER FILM/METALISED PAPER/ ALIMINIUM FOIL
1476. COATING ON PLASTIC (ELECTROLYSIS) & GLASS
1477. COIR FOAM (RUBBERISED)
1478. COLOUR COATING ON PLASTICS
1479. COLOUR MASTER BATCHES FOR VARIOUS PLASTICS
1480. CYCLE TYRES AND TUBES
1481. DISPOSABLE PLASTIC CUPS GLASSES, ETC.
1482. DISPOSABLE PLASTIC SYRINGES & NEEDLES
1483. DISPOSABLE PLASTIC SYRINGES
1484. DOUGH MOULDING COMPOUND (D.M.C)
1485. EPOXY RESIN
1486. EXPANDED POLYESTRENE MOULDING (THERMOCOLE)
1487. F.R.P AUTO,SCOOTER ROOFS & CEILINGS
1488. F.R.P PRODUCTS (HELMET, WASHBASIN SHEETS, ROOFING SHEETS)
1489. FIBRE REINFORCED PLASTIC (HIGH PRESSURE MOULDING WITH SMC BMC AND DMC)
1490. FIELD RUBBER CONVERTED TO THE 60% LATEX RUBBER
1491. FLEXIBLE P.U. FOAM
1492. FORMALDEHYDE CROCKERY & OTHER ITEMS
1493. FORMALDEHYDE RESIN (UREA, PHENOL, MELEMINE)
1494. GASKET SHEET
1495. GUM BOTTLE (PVC)
1496. GLASS BEADS
1497. HDPE COATED PAPER SACK
1498. H.D.P.E. BAGS
1499. H.D.P.E. CONTAINERS (BLOW MOULDING)
1500. H.D.P.E. CONTAINER, POLY JARS BY INJECTION MOULDING (FOOD GRADE)
1501. H.D.P.E. JERRY CANS
1502. HDPE MANUFACTURING FROM ETHYLALCOHOL
1503. H.D.P.E PIPE AND FITTINGS
1504. H.D.P.E. PIPES
1505. H.D.P.E PRINTED BAGS
1506. H.D.P.E TWINES AND ROPES
1507. H.D.P.E. & L.D.P.E PIPES AND FITTINGS
1508. H.D.P.E/PP BOX STRAPPING
1509. H.D.P.E/PP WOVEN SACKS USING PLAIN LOOMS
1510. HOLOGRAM STICKERS-3D
1511. H.M BAG PLANT WITH PRINTING UNIT
1512. HAWAI CHAPPALS (RUBBER)
1513. I.V PLASTIC BOTTLE
1514. ICE CREAM CUP (PLASTIC)
1515. INJECTION MOULDED AUTO COMPONENTS
1516. INJECTION & BLOW MOULDED PLASTIC PRODUCTS
1517. INJECTION MOULDED PLASTIC PRODUCTS
1518. INTEGERATED COMPLEX ESTER'S & ALLIED PRODUCTS (D.O.P,D.B.P, & ETHYL ACETATE, BUYTL ACETATE, WIRE ENAMELS, JELLY CABLE COMPOUND)
1519. L.D.P.E. (LOW DENSITY POLY ETHYLENE) GRANULES FROM VIRGIN (L.D.P.E. RESIN)
1520. INTEGERATED SURGICAL RUBBER GOODS INDUSTRY
1521. INJECTION MOULDED PLASTIC BALLS
1522. L.D.P.E FROM ETHYL ALCOHOL
1523. LDPE MOULDED PRODUCTS
1524. LAMINATION OF COEXTRUSION MULTILAYER FILM IN ROLL FORM
1525. LATEX RUBBER
1526. LATEX RUBBER CONDOM
1527. MASTER BATCHES (COLOURED, P.V.C, L.D.P.E, H.D.P.E, ETC.)
1528. MELAMINE FORMALHYDE RESIN
1529. MOULDED LUGGAGE
1530. MULTI-LAYER (3 LAYER BAGS)
1531. MULTI-LAYER (3 LAYER) FILM WITH LAMINATION & PRINTING
1532. OIL SEAL
1533. PET BOTTLE/CONTAINERS
1534. PET BOTTLES FROM PRE FORM
1535. PET BOTTLE & MINERAL WATER
1536. PET PRE-FORM FROM PET RESIN
1537. PET PRE-FORM CUM PET BOTTLES
1538. PET PRE-FORM PET BOTTLES CUM MINERAL WATERS
1539. POLY CARBONATE RESIN
1540. PTFE COMPONENTS
1541. PU/PVC SOLE FOR SPORT SHOE BY IMPORTED M/C.
1542. PVC BATTERY SEPARATOR
1543. P.V.C COMPOUNDS (FRESH)
1544. P.V.C COMPOUNDS (SCRAP)
1545. P.V.C ELECTRICAL INSULATING TAPE
1546. P.V.C. EXTRUSION PROFILES
1547. P.V.C FITTINGS
1548. P.V.C FLEXIBLE FUSIBLE POWDER HEAT FUSIBLE POWDER
1549. P.V.C GRANULES (FOR

Price Rs. 3675/- for each "Detailed Project Report" Payable in advance through Draft/Cash/M.O. in favour of *"ENGINEERS INDIA RESEARCH INSTITUTE"*. 4449, Nai Sarak (D), Main Road Delhi - 110 006 *OR Ask by V.P.P.* ● Ph : 3918117, 391 6431, 392 0361, 396 0797 ●Fax : 91-11- 391 6431 ●E-Mail : eirisidi@bol.net.in ● WebSite : www.startindustry.com

INSULATION & SHEETS GRADES)
1550. P.V.C GRANULES FROM PVC SCRAPS (WITH POLLUTION CONTROL)
1551. P.V.C HOSES
1552. P.V.C LEATHER CLOTH
1553. P.V.C FLEXIBLE PIPES
1554. P.V.C PIPES AND FITTINGS
1555. POLYTHENE BAGS (PRINTED)
1556. PVC PLASTICS FILM SHEET SOFT/RIGID
1557. PVC RESIN AND COMPOUND
1558. PVC RULAR
1559. PVC STABLIZERS (SINGLE PACK SYSTEM)
1560. PVC WIRE AND CABLES
1561. PAPER BASED PHENOLIC SHEET FOR ELECTRICAL
1562. PHENOL FORMALDEHYDE RESIN
1563. PHENOLIC RESIN
1564. PLASTIC BEADS FROM PLASTIC SCRAPS
1565. PLASTIC BUTTONS
1566. PLASTIC CANS
1567. PLASTIC COLLAPSIBLE TUBE
1568. PLASTIC CORRUGATED SHEET & BOXES
1569. PLASTIC FILM AND SHEETS WITH PRINTING FLEXO & ROTO/LDPE/HDPE/PP/HM/PVC
1570. PLASTIC FILTER MASTER BATCH & OTHER MASTER BATCHES FOR VARIOUS PLASTICS
1571. PLASTIC JERRY CANS
1572. PLASTIC GRANULES OR POWDER FROM PLASTIC SCRAP
1573. PLASTIC INJECTION MOULDED T.V. CABINETS
1574. PLASTIC ITEMS MANUFAC TURE FROM POWDER MELAMINE
1575. PLASTIC GOODS
1576. PLASTIC PIPES & TARPAULINES
1577. PLASTIC SHEET FROM SCRAP
1578. PLASTIC PLANT (BLOW MOULDING & INJECTION MOULDING)
1579. PLASTIC PRODUCTS (GOLD, SILVER, NICKEL)
1580. PLASTIC TOYS
1581. POLYESTER BEADING
1582. POLYESTER FILM
1583. POLYTHENE BAGS & AUTOMATIC PRINTING
1584. POLYTHENE PRINTED BAGS
1585. POLYURETHANE FOAM AND ITS PRODUCTS
1586. PROPYLENE FILM (PRINTED) & BAG MANUFACTURING
1587. PLASTIC MATS
1588. RAINBOW COLOUR ON PVC FILM & SHEET
1589. RED MUD PVC PIPES AND FITTINGS
1590. RE-RUBBERISED OF SOLID TYPE
1591. RESIN COATED SAND REXINE
1592. REXINE CLOTH & ALLIED PRODUCTS
1593. RUBBER ADHESIVE
1594. RUBBER AUTO PARTS
1595. RUBBER BELTING
1596. RUBBER MOULDING UNIT INCLUDING LINING RUBBER SHEETING
1597. RUBBER RECLAIMING
1598. RUBBER ROLLERS FOR TEXTILE MILLS & PAPER INDUSTRIES
1599. RUBBER & PLASTIC SHEETS, MATS & FLAPS
1600. RUBBER SHEET AND ALLIED HOSPITAL RUBBER GOODS
1601. RUBBERIZED PVC GASKET
1602. RUBBERISED COIR
1603. RUBBER COMPOUND FOR AUTOMOBILES
1604. SAFETY BELTS
1605. SILVER AND GOLD PLATING ON PVC AND NYLON-6
1606. SILICONE RUBBER NIPPLES/ TEATS
1607. SPECTACLE FRAMES (PLASTIC)
1608. SPUNGE RUBBER
1609. SURGICAL EXAMINATION GLOVES
1610. SYNTHETIC PEARL COATING ON POLYSTYRENE BEADS
1611. SYNTHETIC RUBBER ADHESIVE
1612. TEFLON MANUFACTURING
1613. TEFLON TAPE
1614. TEFLON TAPES & CABLES
1615. THERMOCOLE SHEET AND MOULDED PRODUCTS EXPANDED POLYESTERENE EXTRUSION PROFILES
1616. THERMOFORMED PACKAGING (BLISTER PACKAGING & POUCH PACKAGING)
1617. THERMOPLASTIC POLYURETHANE
1618. THERMOFORMED CUPS, PLATES & GLASS WITH HIPS SHEET
1619. THERMOCOLE
1620. THERMOCOLE BASED DISPOSABLE GLASS, CUPS & PLATES
1621. TOOTH BRUSHES
1622. TOY BALLOON, DECORA TIVE & INDUSTRIAL BALLOONS
1623. TREAD RUBBER
1624. TYRE RETREADING (HOT)
1625. TYRE RETREADING BY COLD PROCESS
1626. TYRE TUBES & FLAPS
1627. TYRE & TUBES
1628. UNSATURATED POLYESTER FOR REXINE
1629. V-BELT AND FAN BELT
1630. VINYL ASBESTOS AND PVC WALL PAPER
1631 VITON (FLUORO ELASTOMER)

SOAP, COSMETICS & PERFUMS

1632. ACID SLURRY, SYNTHETIC DETERGENT POWDER
1632. ACID SLURRY
1633. AGARBATTI SYNTHETIC, PERFUMERY COMPOUND
1634. AFTER SHAVE LOTION
1635. ANTISEPTIC CREAM
1636. BETA IONONE
1637. BLEACHING POWDER
1638. BLUE DETERGENT POWDER
1639. CLEANING POWDER (VIMTYPE)
1640. COLD CREAM
1641. COLOURED FLAME & PERFUMED CANDLES (RED, BLUE, GREEN FLAME)
1642. COSMETIC INDUSTRY (MODERN)
1643. COSMETIC INDUSTRY (SHAMPOO, SPRAY PERFUME, TALCUM POWDER
1644. DETERGENT POWDER (ARIEL TYPE)
1645. DETERGENT POWDER (NIRMA TYPE) FULLY AUTOMATIC PLANT
1646. DETERGENT WASHING POWDER
1647. FISH OIL SOAP
1648. GLYCERINE TRANSPARENT SOAP
1649. HAIR REMOVING CREAM
1650. HERBAL COSMETICS
1651. HERBAL SHAMPO & CREAM
1652. HERBAL/AYURVEDIC COSMETICS
1653. INCENSE POWDER, INCENSE STICKS & INCENSE CAKE
1654. OPTICAL WHITENERS
1655. ROSE OIL EXTRACTION
1656. SHAMPOOS (COCONUT OIL BASED COLD PROCESS)
1657. SHAVING CREAM
1658. SINDUR (KUMKUM)
1659. SOAP COATED PAPER
1660. SPRAY DRIED DETERGENT POWDER
1661. STAIN REMOVER
1662. TALCUM POWDER (FACE & TOILET POWDER)
1663. TOILET AND HERBAL SOAP
1664. TOOTH PASTE & POWDER
1665. WASHING DETERGENT POWDER AND WASHING SOAP
1666. WASHING POWDER LIQUID DETERGENTS, LOTION & SHAMPOO

Price Rs. 3675/- for each "Detailed Project Report" Payable in advance through Draft/Cash/ M.O. in favour of *"ENGINEERS INDIA RESEARCH INSTITUTE"*. 4449, Nai Sarak (D), Main Road Delhi - 110 006 *OR Ask by V.P.P.* ● Ph : 3918117, 391 6431, 392 0361, 396 0797 ●Fax : 91-11- 391 6431 ●E-Mail : eirisidi@bol.net.in ● WebSite : www.startindustry.com

TEXTILE INDUSTRIES, READYMADE GARMENTS, COTTON, DYEING, BLEACHING, CLOTH, HOSIERY, POWER LOOM, HAND LOOM, WOOLLEN, SILK, SOCKS, SURGICAL COTTON & MANY OTHERS

1667. ANGORA RABBIT WOOL
1668. BUCKRAM
1669. CANVAS SHOES, JUNGLE BOOT, BOOT RUBBER KNEES & BOOT COMBAT
1670. CARPET FROM COTTON WASTE
1671. CERAMIC THREAD GUIDE
1672. COTTON BUDS/SWABS
1673. COTTON FROM WASTE YARN
1674. COTTON ROLLS
1675. COTTON SPIDERS FOR LOUD SPEAKERS
1676. DENIM CLOTH
1677. DENIM CLOTH (INTEGERATED UNIT WITH BLEACHING, DYEING AND PRINTING)
1678. DISPERSENT FOR TEXTILE
1679. DYEING & BLEACHING
1680. DYEING OF HANK YARN
1681. EMULSIFIER FOR WOOL BATCHING OIL
1682. EMBROIDERY ON FABRICS
1683. GARMENT DYEING, WASHING & STITCHING (JEANS, JACKETS, SKIRTS & SHIRTS)
1684. GOVES KNITTING
1685. GUNNY BAGS
1687. HDPE WOVEN SACKS
1688. HDPE TARPAULINS USING PLAIN LOOM WITH LAMINATION
1689. HDPE/PP WOVEN SACKS USING CIRCULAR LOOMS
1690. HOSIERY CLOTH (COTTON) PROCESSING (BLEACHING, DYEING, FINISHING OF CLOTH)
1691. HOSIERY INDUSTRY
1692. HOSIERY MERCERISING
1693. HOSIERY PRODUCTS LIKE VEST, BRIEF, T-SHIRTS & SOCKS
1694. JACQUARD FABRICS
1695. JUTE COIR, GRASS ROPE/ SUTLI MAKING
1696. JUTE FELT
1697. JUTE TWINES
1698. KNITTED FABRICS
1699. LAMINATED JUTE BAGS
1700. LAMINATION OF HDPE WOVEN CLOTH (JUTE,COTTON, PAPER)
1701. NYLON YARN CRIMPING, DOUBLING AND BLEACHING
1702. PIGMENT BINDER FOR TEXTILE PRINTING
1704. POLYESTER RESIN FOR WIRE ENAMEL
1705. POLYESTER RESIN
1706. POLYESTER YARN FROM WASTE POLYESTER ZIP FASTENERS
1707. POWER LOOM
1708. READYMADE GARMENTS & HOSIERY
1709. READYMADE GARMENTS MERCHANDISE
1710. READYMADE GARMENTS & COVERS
1711. READYMADE GARMENTS & EMBROIDERY OF GOWNS, SHIRTS, BLOUSES, T-SHIRTS ETC. (ONLY LADIES)
1712. READYMADE SALWAR SUIT
1713. RECOVERY OF NYLON FROM NYLON WASTE
1714. ROTARY PRINTING AND DYEING ON COTTON, SYNTHETIC TEXTILE
1715. SANITARY NAPKINS
1716. SCREEN PRINTING ON COTTON CLOTH
1717. SEWING THREAD REELS & BALLS MAKING INDUSTRIES
1718. SCREEN PRINTING ON COTTON, POLYESTER & ACRYLIC
1719. SHAWLS (WOOLLEN)
1720. SHOE LACES
1721. SILK FABRICS ON HANDLOOM
1722. SOCKS KNITTING
1723. SPINNING, DOUBLING DYEING MERCERISING & BLEACHING OF COTTON YARN
1724. SPINNING & CARDING OF WOOL INTO YARNS
1725. STARCH BOOK BINDING CLOTH
1726. SURAT JARI
1727. SURGICAL COTTON & BANDAGE
1728. SYNTHETIC TEXTILE INDUSTRY(SUITING, SHIRTING, SAREES) TERRY CLOTH
1729. T-SHIRTS
1730. TOWELS, BED SHEET COVERS
1731. TERRY TOWEL
1732. TERRY FABRICS WEAVING UNIT
1733. TEXTILE AUXILLIARIES & CHEMICALS
1734. TEXTILE BLEACHING, DYEING & FINISHING & PRINTING OF COTTON FABRICS
1735. TEXTILE (HOSIERY)
1736. TEXTILE MILL
1737. TEXTILE DYEING & PRINTING
1738. TEXTILE PRINTING (JOB WORK)
1739. TEXTILE PIGMENT PRINTING BINDER
1740. TOWEL (TERRY)
1741. VELVET CLOTH BY FLOCKING PROCESS
1742. VISCOSE STAPLE FIBRE
1743. WADDING OIL (100%) FOR WADDING OF COTTON HOSIERY CLOTH IN THE DYEING PROCESS
1744. WEAVING OF DASUTI CLOTH WITH PRINTING, DYEING, EMBROIDERY & FINISHING
1745. WASHING OF JEANS & OTHER GARMENTS
1746. WORSTED WOOLLEN YARN CLOTH
1747. ZARI GLITTER SALMA SITARA OF PLASTIC FILM

INFOTECH/IT, HOSPITALITY, HOSPITAL, COLLEGE, SCHOOL, MEDICAL, ENTERTAINMENT CLUB, WARE HOUSING & REAL ESTATE, PROJECTS

1748. AMUSEMENT PARK
1749. AMUSEMENT PARK CUM WATER PARK
1750. BANQUET HALL
1751. CALL CENTER (DOMESTIC)
1752. CALL CENTER (INTERNATIONAL)
1753. CHILDREN RECREATION CENTRE
1754. COLD STORAGE
1755. COMMUNITY HALL
1756. COMPUTER EDUCATION INSTITUTE
1757. COMPUTER SOFTWARE
1758. COLLEGE
1759. CYBER CAFE
1760. DENTAL CLINIC
1761. DENTAL COLLEGE
1762. DIAGONOSTIC CENTRE
1763. E-COMMERCE/BUSINESS
1764. E-SCHOOL (Rs. 5000/-)
1765. ENGINEERING COLLEGE
1766. ENTERTAINMENT CLUB
1767. ENTERTAINMENT CLUB, HOLIDAY RESORT, 4 STAR HOTEL, AMUSEMENT PARK CUM WATER PARK, MUSHROOM & ITS PRODUCTS, FISH FARMING, LAKE FOR BOATING, DEER PARK
1768. FASHION TECHNOLOGY INSTITUTE
1769. FAST FOOD PARLOUR
1770. FIVE STAR HOTEL
1771. FOOD PARLOUR
1772. FRANCHISE TRAINING PROGRAMME FOR IIT & ENGINEERING ENTRANCE EXAMS.
1773. GOLF COURSE
1774. HEALTH CLUB, BEAUTY PARLOUR
1775. HEALTH CLUB AND FITNESS CENTER
1776. HEALTH RESORTS
1777. HOLIDAY RESORTS
1778. HOLIDAY RESORT CUM

Price Rs. 3675/- for each "Detailed Project Report" Payable in advance through Draft/Cash/ M.O. in favour of *"ENGINEERS INDIA RESEARCH INSTITUTE"*. 4449, Nai Sarak (D), Main Road Delhi - 110 006 *OR Ask by V.P.P.* ● Ph : 3918117, 391 6431, 392 0361, 396 0797 ●Fax : 91-11- 391 6431 ●E-Mail : eirisidi@bol.net.in ● WebSite : www.startindustry.com

ENTERTAINMENT CLUB WITH 4 STAR HOTEL
1779. HOSPITALS
1780. ICE CREAM PARLOUR
1781. INTERNET SERVICE PROVIDER (I.S.P.)
1782. MEDICAL COLLEGE
1783. MEDICAL COLLEGE, HOSPITAL & RESEARCH INSTITUTE
1784. MEDICAL TRANSCRIPTION CENTRE
1785. MENTAL RETARDATION HOSPITAL & CEREBRAL PALSY
1786. MOTEL/SMALL HOTEL
1787. MULTISTOREY COMMERCIAL COMPLEX
1788. MULTISTOREY RESIDENTIAL COMPLEX
1789. NURSERY SCHOOL
1790. NATURE CARE CENTRE
1791. NURSING HOME
1792. ONLINE SHOPPING MALL (RS. 5000/- REPORT)
1793. PORTAL
1794. REHABILITATION CENTRE FOR AGED & NEEDY PERSONS
1795. RESIDENTIAL CUM COMMERCIAL COMPLEX
1796. RESTAURANT
1797. RESTAURANT WITH PUB
1798. SCHOOL (PRIMARY)
1799. SCHOOL (HIGHER SECONDARY)
1800. THREE STAR HOTEL
1801. TOURIST CLUB
1802. TRAINING INSTITUTE FOR MEDICAL TRANSCRIPTION
1803. VIDEO FILM STUDIO
1804. WARE HOUSE
1805. WEBSITE DESIGN & E-MAIL REGISTERING

AGRO BASED INDUSTRIES

1806. COAL BRIQUETTES FROM AGROWASTE
1807. FURFURALFROM RICEHULL
1808. MUSHROOM CULTIVATION & PROCESSING (BUTTON)
1809. MUSHROOM GROWING & PROCESSING WITH AIR CONDITIONING
1810. MUSHROOM CULTIVATION & PROCESSING UNIT DEHYDRATION & PACKAGING OF OYSTER & PADDY STRAW MUSHROOMS
1811. ORGANIC MANURE
1812. PAPAYA CULTIVATION
1813. PAPAYA & TOMATO CULTIVATION
1814. PROCESSING & UTILISATION OF COCONUT
1815. PROCESSING OF SHEEP HAIR TO PRODUCE WOOL

BAKERY, CONFECTIONERY & FOOD PRODUCTS

1816. AGROLACTOR SOYA MILK
1817. APPLE FRUIT JUICE WITH CANNING BOTTLING
1818. AYURVEDIC SHARBAT
1819. BAKERY UNIT (PASTRIES, BREAD, BUNS, CAKE, TOFFEE ETC.)
1820. BAKING POWDER
1821. BANANA & ITS BY PRODUCTS
1822. BANANA POWDER
1823. BANANA WAFERS
1824. BANANA CULTIVATION
1825. BEER INDUSTRY
1826. DEHULLING OF JAUN FOR BEER
1827. BEER & WINE
1828. BEER, ALCOHOL, IMFL
1829. BESEN PLANT
1830. BISCUIT PLANT
1831. BREAD & BISCUIT PLANT
1832. BOTTLING PLANT COUNTRY LIQUOR FROM RECTIFIED SPIRIT
1833. BRANDY
1834. BREAD RUSKS
1835. CANNED FRUITS & VEGETABLES
1836. CANNING & PRESERVATION OF MEAT
1837. CANNING & PRESERVATION OF VEGETABLES
1838. CANNING OF MANGO PULP & MANGO SLICES
1839. CARBONATED BEVERAGS
1840. CASHEW FENI
1841. CASHEW NUT (DRIED & FRIED)
1842. CATTLE BREEDING
1843. CATTLE BREEDING & DAIRY FARM TO PRODUCE MILK
1844. CATTLE FEED FROM TAPIOCA
1845. CHEWING GINGER & AMLOKI
1846. CHEWING GUM
1847. CHILLI SAUCE
1848. CHILLI POWDER
1849. CHOCOLATE
1850. CIDER PLANT
1851. COCOA POWDER
1852. COCOA BUTTER & COCOA POWDER
1853. COCONUT SHELL POWDER
1854. COCONUT WATER
1855. COCONUT SWEET (WATERY)
1856. COCONUT MILK POWDER (DEHYDRATED)
1857. COCONUT PRODUCTS & BY PRODUCTS (INTEGRATED PLANT)
1858. COLD DRINK
1859. CURRY POWDER
1860. DAIRY FOR MILK PROCESSING (GHEE, BUTTER & PANEER)
1861. DAIRY PRODUCTS
1862. DAIRY PRODUCTS MILK PACKAGING IN POUCH (GHEE, BUTTER, ETC.
1863. DAIRY FARM TO PRDUCE MILK WITH PACKAGING (COW)
1864. DAIRY FARM TO PRDUCE MILK WITH PACKAGING (BUFALLOE)
1865. DAIRY FARM & MILK PRODUCTS
1866. DAL MOTH, CHANACHUR & BHUJIYA
1867. DEHYDRATION OF FRUITS & VEGETABLE
1868. DESICCATED COCONUT POWDER FROM COCONUTS
1869. DEHYDRATION & CANNINGOF FRUITS & VEGETABLES
1870. DRY FRUIT ROASTING & PACKAGING
1871. DRYING OF RED CHILLIES, HALDI, DHANIYA, PEAS & GROUND NUT
1872. EGG POWDER
1873. FISH CANNING IN TIN & POUCHES
1874. FISH DEHYRATION (DRYING OF FISH)
1875. FISH MEAL
1876. FISH PROCESSING (BEAST FREEZING PROCESSES)
1877. FLAVOURS FOR FOOD INDUSTRIES
1878. FLOUR MILL (ROLLER)
1879. FROZEN MEAT
1880. FOOD DEHYDRATION (FRUITS & VEGETABLES)
1881. FRIED & ROASTED GROUND NUT, GRAMS, PEAR ETC.
1882. FRUIT JUICE MAKING & PACKAGING IN PLASTIC CONTAINER
1883. FRUIT JUICE IN TETRA PACK (DRINKS)
1884. FRUIT JUICE, SQUASHES, SAUCE & KETCHUP, JAM, JELLY, VINEGAR ETC.
1885. GARLIC FLAKES
1886. GARLIC POWDER
1887. GHEE & BUTTER
1888. GINGER (PULVERISED)
1889. GINGER GLAZING & PRESERVATION
1890. GINGER STORAGE
1891. GINGER PROCESSING
1892. GINGER OIL & GINGER DUST
1893. GINGER POWDER (DRY) & OLEORESIN
1894. GRAPE DEHYDRATION
1895. GRAPE CULTIVATION
1896. GRAPE JUICE
1897. HONEY PROCESSING & PACKAGING
1898. ICE CREAM & ICE CANDY
1899. ICE CUBE
1900. INVERT SUGAR
1901. IDLI MIX, DOSA MIX SAMBHAR MIX, VADA MIX,GULAB JAMUN MIX
1902. INSTANT COFFEE & INSTANT TEA

Price Rs. 3675/- for each "Detailed Project Report" Payable in advance through Draft/Cash/ M.O. in favour of *"ENGINEERS INDIA RESEARCH INSTITUTE"*. 4449, Nai Sarak (D), Main Road Delhi - 110 006 *OR Ask by V.P.P.* ● Ph : 3918117, 391 6431, 392 0361, 396 0797 ●Fax : 91-11- 391 6431 ●E-Mail : eirisidi@bol.net.in ● WebSite : www.startindustry.com

1903. INSTANT NOODLES
1904. INSTANT SOUPS
1905. IODIZED SALT FROM CRUDE SALT
1906. JAM CHUTNEY PICKLES & SQUASHES
1907. KATHA MANUFACTURING
1908. LECITHIN (SOYA BASED)
1909. LEMON & ITS PRODUCTS
1910. MACARONI MANUFACTURING
1911. MACARONI, SPAGHETTI, VERMICELLI & NOODLES
1912. MAIZE & ITS BY PRODUCTS MALTING PLANT
1913. MANGO PAPPAD (AAM PAPPAD)
1914. MANGO POWDER RIPE
1915. MANGO POWDER
1916. MANGO PROCESSING & CANNING (MANGO PULP)
1917. MEAT PROCESSING (CHICKEN MUTTON)
1918. MEAT PROCESSING (BUFFALO)
1919. MENTHOL BOLD FROM MENTHOL FLAKES
1020. MILK POWDER
1921. MILK POWDER & GHEE
1922. MILK POWDER, GHEE & SPICES
1923. MILK PRESERVATION & MARKETING TO WHOLE SELLERS
1924. MILK PRESERVATION & MARKETING TO WHOLE SELLERS (IN POUCHES)
1925. MILK TOFFEE MANUFACTURES
1926. MINERAL WATER
1927. MINERAL WATER IN POUCHES
1928. MINI FLOUR MILL ATTA MAIDA, SUJI & WHEAT BRAN
1929. MITHAI/HALWAI (SWEET & NAMKEEN)
1930. MUTTON PROCESSING
1931. PAN MASALA (MEETHA, SADA, ZARDA) MAKING & PACKING
1932. PAN MASALA AND POUCH MAKING
1933. PANEER (CHEESE)
1934. PAPAD & BARIYAN
1935. PAPAD PLANT
1936. PEPSICOLA IN POLYTUBES
1937. PETHA PACKAGING
1938. PICKLES
1939. PIGGERY/MEAT/CHICKEN PROCESSING
1940. PINE APPLE JUICE CANNING
1941. POTATO & ONION POWDER
1942. POTATO & ONION FLAKES
1943. POTATO CHIPS
1944. POTATO GRANULES
1945. POUCH FILLING FOR SAUNF SUPARI ILAICHI ETC.
1946. PRESERVATION OF RAWS MANGO JUICE
1947. PROCESSED CHEESE & MARINE PDTS.
1948. PULP FROM TARMARIND
1949. READYMATE PROCESSED FOOD
1950. RICE & CORN FLAKES
1951. RICE BASMATI (TRADING)
1952. RICE POLISHING & PACKAGING IN POUCH
1953. ROASTED/SALTED/MASALA/ CASHEW NUTS ALMONDS & PEA NUT
1954. ROLLER FLOUR MILL

INFOTECH/IT PROJECTS

1955. MEDICAL TRANSCRIPTION
1956. E-COMMERCE
1957. CYBERCAFE
1958. INTERNET SERVICE PROVIDER (ISP)
1959. COMPUTER EDUCATION CENTRE
1960. PORTAL (WEBSITE DESIGN)
1961. CALL CENTRE

TERMS AND CONDITIONS

FOR INDIA

1. Price Rs. 3,675/- (Rs. Three Thousand Six Hundred Seventy Five Only) for Each *Market Survey Cum Detailed Techno Economic Feasibility Report.* Payable in advance through Draft/M.O./Cash in favour of 'ENGINEERS INDIA RESEARCH INSTITUTE', Delhi. Delivery by Regd.post within 2 Days. (Postage Free)

2. Reputed Firms/Companies may place their orders by V.P.P. for full amount in India Only.

FOR OVERSEAS

1. Price US$ 250/- (US Dollars Two Hundred Fifty Only) for Each *Market Survey Cum Detailed Techno Economic Feasibility Report.*

2. Payable fully in advance through Draft in favour of 'ENGINEERS INDIA RESEARCH INSTITUTE', Delhi (Payable in India) Delivery by Regd. Air Mail Post within 2 Days.

ENGINEERS INDIA RESEARCH INSTITUTE

4449, Nai Sarak (D), Main Road, Delhi - 110 006 (India)
Ph:. 91-11-3918117, 3916431, 3920361, 3960797
Fax: 91-11-3916431 E-Mail : eirisidi@bol.net.in
Website:www.startindustry.com
Also at : 4/27, Roop Nagar, Near Roop Nagar No. 1 School, Delhi - 110 007 (India) Ph:. 396 0797, 392 0361

New Detailed Project Reports available on FOOD & ALLIED INDUSTRIES @ Rs. 3675/-

LIST OF READILY AVAILABLE DETAILED PROJECT REPORTS

- ACTIVATED CARBON FROM COCONUT SHELL & RICE HUSK
- AGRICULTURE IMPLIMENTS
- AMALA PLANTATION & PROCESSING (E.O.U)
- AYURVEDIC MADICINES
- BAKERY (BREAD/BISCUIT)
- BEER PLANT (EOU)
- BANANA POWDER (EOU)
- BONE CRUSHING PLANT
- BEE KEEPING
- BIO-FERTILIZER
- BREWERY & DISTILLERY
- CASHEW NUT SHELL LIQUID & KERNEL
- CATTLE & POULTRY FEED
- COCONUT PRODUCT & BY PRODUCTS
- CURRY PASTE
- CONFECTIONERY
- CUSTARD POWDER
- COLD STORAGE & ICE
- DALL MILL
- DAIRY FARM & PRODUCTS
- DAIRY FARM (MILK)
- DEHYDRATION OF FRUITS & VEGETABLE BY FREEZE DRYING METHOD
- EGG POWDER (E.O.U)
- FISH FARMING
- FLORICULTURE (CUT FLOWER)
- FLOUR MILL
- FOOD PROCESSING UNIT
- FOOD DEHYDRATION
- FROZEN MEAT
- HERBS CULTIVATION
- HERBS DRYING
- GINGER PROCESSING
- GOAT & SHEEP FARMING
- GOAT FARMING
- GUAR GUM
- GRANULATED MIXED FERTILIZER
- HONEY PROCESSING
- HYBRID SEEDS
- ICE CREAM (FOR ALL TYPE)
- INSECTICIDES FROM NEEM SEEDS, NEEM OIL & LEAVE
- INSTANT FOOD
- INSTANT NOODLES
- INVERT SUGAR
- IODIZED SALT
- KATTHA & CUTCH
- MANGO JUICE BOTTLING
- MANGO PRODUCTS
- MANGO PULP
- MAIZE & ITS BY PRODUCTS
- MENTHOL FLAKES & BOLD
- MUSHROOM
- MINERAL WATER
- OLEORESINS FROM CHILLI
- PAPAYA
- PEANUT BUTTER
- PIGGERY FARM
- PORK FARMING
- POTATO CHIPS
- ONION FLAKES
- POPLAR TREE
- RICE MILL
- SOYA BEAN OIL
- SOFT DRINK
- SPICES
- STARCH FROM MAIZE
- STRAWBERRY CULTIVATION
- TEA & COFFEE
- TEAK PLANT

Each 'EIRI' ***Market Survey Cum Detailed Techno Economic Feasibility Report (Detailed Project Report)*** covers Introduction, Properties, Market Survey, Process of Manufacture, Cost Economics with Profitability Analysis, Suppliers of Plant & Machineries and Raw Materials, Cash Flow Statement, Repayment Schedule, Depreciation Chart, Projected Balance Sheet etc.

Price **Rs. 3675/-** (Rs. Three Thousand Six Hundred Seventy Five Only) for Each. Send Draft/M.O. in favour of **"ENGINEERS INDIA RESEARCH INSTITUTE", DELHI .**

ENGINEERS INDIA RESEARCH INSTITUTE

4449, Nai Sarak (D), Main Road, Delhi - 110 006 (India)

Ph:. 3918117, 3916431, 3920361, 3960797 Fax: 91-11-3916431

E-Mail : eirisidi@bol.net.in Website:www.startindustry.com

PRACTICAL PROJECT EXECUTION KNOW HOW REPORTS

The Project Report provides a proper way to meet the practical problems which pose difficulties, delays & hike in pre-evaluated project cost. The Cost of the Report is Rs. 10500/- EACH REPORT CONTAINS

☞ **INTRODUCTION :** Project Mix, Uses & Applications, Quality Control Measure & Their Introduction for Attaining Required Properties Economy & Productivity Competence

☞ **MARKET SURVEY :** Market Position, Installed Capacity Production, Anticipated Demand, Present Manufacturers, Statistics of Imports & Exports, Estimated demand, Demand & Supply Gap. LI/IL Issued Recently

☞ **PROCESS OF MANUFACTURE :** Inventory Controls & Tests, Comparative Study of Process for Manufacturing the Product, Process Detail in Stages from Raw Materials to Finished Products

☞ **RAW MATERIALS :** Raw Material Specifications & Tests, Market Codes & Raw Material Prices, Sources of Procurement of Raw Materials [Imported/Indigenous]

☞ **PLANT & MACHINERY :** Range of Machineries Required, Detailed Specifications of Machines & Equipmants, Prices as Actual with Concerned Quotations

☞ **LAND & BUILDING :** Total Land Area Requirement with Rates, Covered Area Break-up with Estimated Costs of Construction

☞ **PROJECT ECONOMICS :** Land & buildings, Plant, Machinery & Other Fixed Assets, Total Capital & Investment, Working Capital Assessment Raw Material & Consumable Stores, Staff Salaries & Wages, Utilities & Overheads, Total Cost of Project, Sources of Finance/ Refinance, Break Even Point Determination

☞ **ANNEXURES OF CHARTS :** Repayment Schedule for 5 Yrs., Result of Performance of the Project 5 Yrs., Cash Flow Statment for 5 Yrs., Projected Balance Sheet for 5 Yrs., Equity Balance Sheet, Land Man Ratio

LIST OF THE AVAILABLE PROJECT REPORTS @ Rs. 10,500/-

- ALCOHOL BEER STARCH LIQUID GLUCOSE DEXTROSE SORBITOL VITAMIN-C CATTLE FEED ETC.
- ACRYLIC SHEET
- AMMONIUM SULPHATE
- AL- HOT & COLD ROLLING MILL
- BEER PLANT
- CALCIUM CARBONATE
- CIGARETTE PLANT
- COLD STORAGE & ICE
- CYBER CAFE
- CALL CENTRE (INTERNATIONAL)
- CEMENT PLANT
- CORRUGATED BOARD & BOX (PTD. & LAMINATED)
- DI-CALCIUM PHOSPHATE (DCP)
- DISTRIBUTION TRANSFORMER
- DICLOFENAC GEL
- DENTAL COLLEGE
- DENTAL CLINIC
- DETERGENT CAKE, POWDER & TOILET SOAP
- EGG POWDER
- ENTERTAINMENT CLUB HOLIDAY RESORT 4* HOTEL AMUSEMENT PARK CUM WATERPARK,MUSHROOM & FISH FARM
- EMBROIDERY ON FABRIC
- EXTRACTION OF ESSENTIAL OIL BY SUPER CRITICAL FLUID
- FOAMED PVC COMPOUNDING & ITS PDTS. (PROFILE,BOARD,PIPE)
- FERRO ALLOYS
- FOOD PRODUCTS COMPLEX
- FRIED & ROASTED GROUNDNUT,GRAMS PEAS ETC. IN POUCHES
- FLOAT GLASS
- FIVE STAR HOTEL
- GOLD & SILVER JEWELLERY
- GREASES
- GOLD PLATING, SILVER PLATING CHEMICAL
- G.I. PIPES
- GUNNY BAGS
- GLASS SHEETS
- HYDRAZINE
- HOTEL (3 STAR/5 STAR)
- HOMOEOPATHIC MEDICINES
- HOSIERY
- IODIZED SALT
- INDIAN MADE FOREIGN LIQUOR (I.M.F.L)
- ICE PLANT
- INVERT SUGAR
- ICE CREAM
- JELLY FILLED CABLES
- JUTE BAGS
- JAM, JELLY, CHUTNEY, PICKLESS AND SQUASHES
- JUTE WASTE PRODUCTS
- KATTHA & CUTCH
- KNITTED CLOTH
- KALI MEHANDI
- LEMON GRASS OIL
- LATHER SHAVING CREAM
- PYHTO - TEA MANUFACTURING UNIT
- MEDICAL TRANSCRIPTION CENTRE
- MINERAL WATER & PET BOTTLES

- MASALA (SPICES)
- MINI CEMENT PLANT
- MINI FLOUR MILL (ROLLER)
- NURSING HOME
- NAMKEEN (BHUJIA ETC.)
- OFFSET PRINTING PRESS
- OLEORESINS FROM SPICES
- ORGANIC MANURE
- ONE TIME CARBON
- OXYGEN GAS
- PAPER BEVERAGE GLASSES
- POWER PLANT (THERMOL)
- PAPER CONE
- POTATO CHIPS
- PVC WIRE & CABLES
- PVC PIPES & FITTINGS
- POULTRY & BROILER FARMING
- P.V.C. FLEXIBLE PIPE
- PETROL PUMP
- PIGGERY FARM
- Q.S.S. PHOTO COLOUR LAB
- RUBBER RECLAIMING
- REFINED VEGETABLE OIL
- RESORCINOL
- RICE SORTING & GRADING PLANT
- SODIUM METASILICATE
- SYNTHETIC RED & YELLOW IRON OXDIE FROM IRON FILLING & PICKLE LIQUID
- SHAMPOO
- STAPLE PINS
- SCHOOL
- TIN CONTAINERS
- TOYS (ELECTRONIC)
- TEA PACKAGING
- TEXTILE PRINTING
- TOOL ROOM SHEET METAL PRODUCTS
- TOILET SOAP
- ULTRA MARINE BLUE (NEEL)
- UN-SATURATED POLYESTER RESIN
- U-BOLTS & CENTRE BOLTS
- VENETIAN BLIND
- VEGETABLE OIL
- WASHING & DYEING OF JEANS & OTHER GARMENTS
- WELDING ELECTRODESS
- WINE FROM DATES
- WHOLE WHEAT PORRIDGE
- YARA TARA
- XEROX PAPER
- ZARDA KIMAM & TOBACCO
- ZINC OXIDE
- ZEDOARY (KACHUR)

TERMS AND CONDITIONS

1. Price Rs. 10,500/- (Rs. Ten Thousand Five Hundredonly) for India or US $ 750/- for Overseas Client for each *Practical Project Execution Know How Report.* Payable in advance through Draft/M.O./Cash in favour of *'ENGINEERS INDIA RESEARCH INSTITUTE'*, Delhi, (India). Delivery by Registered Air Mail post within 2 days (Postage FREE).

2. Reputed Firms/Companies may place their orders by V.P.P. for full amount in India Only.

ENGINEERS INDIA RESEARCH INSTITUTE

4449, Nai Sarak (PPER), Main Road (Near Chandni Chowk), Delhi - 110 006 (India)

• Tel : 011- 391 8117, 391 6431, 392 0361, 396 0797

ALSO : 4/27, Roop Nagar, Nr. Roop Nagar No.1 School, Delhi - 110 007 • Ph : 91-11- 392 0361, 396 0797

• Fax : 91-11- 391 6431 • E-mail : eirisidi@bol.net.in

• website: www.startindustry.com

We are fully capable to prepare any ***Practical Project Execution Know-How Report @ Rs. 10,500/- each.*** Delivery of the report within 10 days. Above listed Reports are readily available with EIRI. Apart from the above, many others are also available. Just send a Draft/M.O. for Rs. 10,500/- in our favour ***(ENGINEERS INDIA RESEARCH INSTITUTE).***

Modern Packaging Technology for Processed Food, Bakery, Snack Foods, Spices & Allied Food Products

With Directory of Suppliers of Packaging Materials, Machinery & Equipments and other Important Relevant Addresses

The Book covers latest & Updated technology for food packaging including process food, fruits & vegetables, meat poultry & fish, edible oils, vanaspati & ghee, spices, biscuits, confectionery, snack foods, drinking water. Packaging laws & regulations, National standards of packaging code for food stuffs & perishables, food packaging, International Standards.

Fruits & Vegetables Processing Hand Book

The book covers Canning in Commercial Scale, Canning of Fruits, Canning of Vegetables, Fruit Juices, Squashes & Cordials, Fruit Beverages, Jams & Jellies, Tomato Products, Pickles, Sauces & Chutneys, Cashew Fruit Juice, Dehydration of Fruits & Vegetables, Frozen Foods, Fruits & Vegetables Juice with Other Products etc.

Hand Book of Perfume & Flavours

(With Directory of Plant & Equipment, Raw Material & Manufacturer/Exporters/ Suppliers of Perfumes)

The book covers new formulaes of various kinds of perfumes & flavours. The major chapters of the book are Perfume, Formulary of Perfume, Formulary of Flavour, Chemicals Specifications for Perfume & Flavour Components, Plant & Equipment Suppliers, Suppliers of Raw Materials, Manufacturer/Exporters/Suppliers of Perfumes. At the end of the book the last but not the least chapter project profiles has also included for the benefits of the new entrepreneurs.

Hand Book of Essential Oils Manufacturing & Aromatic Plants

The book covers trade of essential oils, rose oil distillation method, cultivation of matricaria chamomilla, extraction of essential oils, essential chemical constituents profile in tree spice, folk medicinal, essential oil bearing plants status, promising aromatic plants of industrial value, essential oil industry waste utilization, fractionation of essential oil in perfumery & turpentine industry, citronella oil, ginger oil, jasmine rose & lily oil, jasmine flower oil etc.

Hand Book of Spices & Packaging with Formulaes

(With Directories of Plant & Equipments & Importers/ Exporters/Mfrs. of Spices)

The Book covers new formulaes of various kinds of Spices. The major chapters of the book are Ajowan, Amchur, Aniseed, Asafoetida, Chilli, Caraway, Cardamom, Cassia, Celery Seed, Cinnamon, Clove, Coriander, Cumin Seed, Fennel, Fenugreek, Garlic, Ginger, Nutmeg, Pepper, Tamarind, Turmeric, Drying of Red Chilli, Dry Ginger, Onion Dehydration, Garlic Powder, Mustard Powder, Turmeric Powder, Formulaes of Different Kinds of Ground Spices, Packaging of Spices, Methods of Tests, Agmark, Details of Machinery, National Standards, Importers/Exporters of Spices, Plant & Equipment Suppliers & Manufacturers of Spices

Hand Book of Electroplating, Anodizing & Surface Finishing Technology

The book covers New & latest technology of Electro-plating, Anodizing & Metal Treatments. Various Project Profiles including Aluminium Anodizing, Gold Plating, Nickle Plating Brightner, Precious Metal Plating, Mirror, Hard Anodizing on Aluminium, Barrel Electroplating, Chrome Plating, Zinc Electroplating Brightner, Electrolating on Silver & Gold, Copper Plating on Metallic Parts etc.

ENGINEERS INDIA RESEARCH INSTITUTE

4449, Nai Sarak, Main Road, Delhi - 110 006 (INDIA)

Ph.: 391 8117, 391 6431, 396 0797, 392 0361 • Fax :91-11-391 6431

E Mail:eirisidi@bol.net.in • Website:www.startindustry.com

HAND BOOK OF DAIRY FORMULATIONS PROCESSES & MILK PROCESSING INDUSTRIES

The book is covering Introduction, Manufacturing, Technologies, Packaging, Statistical, Figures & Formulations of various Milk & Milk Based Products, Project Profiles on Dairy & Milk Products, Directory Section.

START YOUR OWN COLD STORAGE UNIT

The major chapters in the book are Special features of Cold Storage Project, Selection of the location for the Cold Storage production details and process of manufacture, Operating Conditions, Selection of the Refrigeration Plant Capacity & Machinery, Main Features of Ammonia Compressors

FOOD PROCESSING & AGRO BASED INDUSTRIES

The book is covering 31 detailed and exhaustive chapters including dairy, confectionery, fruit juice, chocolate, frozen desserts, honey, chewing gum, tomato products, jams and jellies, chutney, dehydration of fruit and vegetables, packing of food & alllied products, new development in technologies for food processing, aseptic packaging of food and beverages, packaging of dairy & milk products, breads, buns, pies, pasta products, cakes, biscuits and other allied bakery products. Among all the project profiles on different

HAND BOOK OF HERBS, MEDICINAL & AROMATIC PLANTS CULTIVATION

The book is covering allmost all the Herbs, Medicinal & Aromatic Plants cultivation details.

Manufacture of Snacks Food, Namkeen, Pappad & Potato Products

The book covers Manufacturing of Potato Chips, Pappad, Snacks Food, Namkeen, Ready to Eat Food Products, Project Profiles, Manufacturers of Machinery & Raw Materials.

AGRO BASED INDUSTRIES HANDBOOK (PLANTATION & FARMING)

The Book Covers almost all the lucrative Plantation Cultivation & Farming methods related with Piggery Farm, Aquaculture Shrimp Farming, Poultry & Broiler Farming, Dairy Farm & Dairy (Milk) Products (Pasteurised Milk, Butter Ghee & Paneer), Teak Tree Plantation, Suger Cane Plantation, Floriculture (Cut Flower-Rose) with Green House Technology, Silk Cocoon Cultivation (Growing of Silk Cocoon From Silk Worm), Mushroom Growing & Processing by Deep Freezing Method (Export Oriented), Papaya Cultivation and Papain Manufacture.

Hand Book of Essential Oils Manufacturing & Aromatic Plants

The book covers trade of essential oils, rose oil distillation method, cultivation of matricaria chamomilla, extraction of essential oils, essential chemical constituents profile in tree spice, folk medicinal, essential oil bearing plants status, promising aromatic plants of industrial value, essential oil industry waste utilization, fractionation of essential oil in perfumery & turpentine industry, citronella oil, ginger oil, jasmine rose & lily oil, jasmine flower oil etc.

World Importers Directory of Agro Based & Food Processing Industries

The Directory provides Importers addresses of food & Agro Based industries with their Phone and Fax number alongwith complete addresses. This will help to find global overseas customers to the traders/exporters/ manufacturers.

Books Available at :

ENGINEERS INDIA RESEARCH INSTITUTE

4449, Nai Sarak, Main Road, Delhi-6

Ph:. 3918117, 3916431, 3920361, 3960797 * Fax: 91-11- 3916431

***E-Mail : eirisidi@bol.net.in**

RUBBER CHEMICALS & PROCESSING INDUSTRIES

The Book covers Natural & Synthetic Rubber, Acrylic, ABR, Butyl, Nitrile, Silicone, Urethane, Rubber Powder, Reclamation, Pigments & Colour, Blowing Agents, Latex Dipped Goods, Latex Foam, Latex Based Adhesive, & Rubber Solution, Rubber Moulded Articles, Rubber Beltings, Rollers, Footwear, Tyre & Tubes, Gaskets, Seals, Washers, Auto Parts, Various Other Important Formulaes, Polymeras Related to Rubber, Compounding, Processing Methods, Testing, Trade Names & Chemical Compositions, Suppliers of Plant & Machinery, Suppliers of Raw Materials, Project Profiles, Details of Rubber Processing Equipments.

HAND BOOK OF SYNTHETIC & HERBAL COSMETICS

The Book covers Production Problems & Recommendations, Cosmetic, Face Powder, Variations of Face Powder, Toilet Powder, Creams, Vanishing Creams, Foundation Creams, Hand Lotions, After Shaving Lostions, Deodorants, Mascara-eyebrow Pencils-Eye Shadows, Lipstics, Shampoos, Depilatories, Shaving Creams, Cosmetics for the Nails, Tooth Powder, Oral Herbal Preparations, Govt. Rrgulations & Acts on Drugs & Cosmetics, Bath Preparations, Baby Preparations, Home Made Cosmetics, Herbal Preparations for Body, Skin Cleansing, Herbal Preparations for Feet & Hands, How to Layout a Cosmetic Factory, Project Profiles, Suppliers of Plant & Machinery, Suppliers of Raw Materials

START YOUR OWN COLD STORAGE UNIT

The book provides the informations as the name indicates. The major chapters in the book are Special features of Cold Storage Project, Brief about Refrigerated Cold Storage, B.I.S. Specifications, Selection of the location for the Cold Storage production details and process of manufacture, Operating Conditions, Principles of Fresh Food Storage, Refrigeration, Technical and Design Section, Selection of the Refrigeration Plant Capacity and Machinery, Details of Plant Equipments and Machineries, Project Profiles for different capacities of Cold Storage Unit, Plant Equipment and Machinery Suppliers for setting up Cold Storage Unit.

HAND BOOK OF PRINTING PROCESSES TECHNOLOGIES & INDUSTRIES

The printing Industry now-a-days in India are increasingly by day. New technologies, methods & processes are being developed gradually. The printing sector plays a vital role towards recording, disseminating, preserving and updating data,information, knowledge, news, views, opinions & expertise domestic and foreign sources. The book is in three parts. The first part of the book deals with the technologies of printing & printing processes, the second part of the book covers the various project profiles on printing which are most indispensable now-a-days for every entrepreneur and industrialist who are venturing for new unit. Part 3rd the last but most important covers various sources/ suppliers for plant & machinery, Raw materials & technologies.

Modern Packaging Technology for Processed Food, Bakery, Snack Food, Spices & Allied Food Products

HAND BOOK OF ESSENTIAL OILS MANUFACTURING & AROMATIC PLANTS

With Directory of Plant & Machinery Suppliers, International Importers & Exporters and Manufacturers & Exporters of Essential Oils & Aromatic Chemicals

SMALL MEDIUM & LARGE SCALE CHEMICAL INDUSTRY

The unique book on Chemical & Allied manufacturing industries containing the formulations and manufacturing processes of 27 lucrative chemicals & allied industries alongwith the addresses of plant, machinery and raw material suppliers with the valuable addresses of All India Trade & Industry Organisation.

INDUSTRIAL AND BUSINESS DIRECTORY WITH A CHECK LIST OF E-MAIL AND WEBSITE REFERENCES

AGRO BASED PLANTATION CULTIVATION & FARMING

Book covers Banana •, Bee Keeping, Coconut, Dairy , Eucalyptus, Floriculture, Ginger, Goat, Mushroom, Orchard, Papaya, Piggery, Poultry, Rabbit, Sheep, Tea , Teak, Tissue Culture.

Books Available At : ENGINEERS INDIA RESEARCH INSTITUTE, 4449 Nai Sarak, Main Road, Delhi - 6 Ph : 011 - 3918117, 3916431, 3920361, 3960797 * E-Mail : eirisidi@bol.net.in * Website : startindustry.com

New Detailed Project Reports available on
Electroplating Anodizing & Surface Finishing @ Rs. 3675/-

LIST OF READILY AVAILABLE DETAILED PROJECT REPORTS

- Anodized Aluminium Lable (Anodizing Print)
- Anodizing Name Plates
- Anodizing of Aluminium
- Anodizing of Aluminium
- Barrel Electroplating
- Brass Badges by Etching Process
- Barrel Plating Compound
- Coating on Metal Plastic (PVC)
- Chemical Etching of S.S
- Copper Plating on Metallic Parts
- Chrome Plating
- Corrugation of Plain Galvanized Sheet
- Di-Nickeling of Metals
- Electroplating on Utensils
- Electroplating Chemicals
- Electrolplating of Plastics
- Electroplating of Metal
- Electroplating Brightners
- Electroplating Scheme Plant for Nickel-Chrome-Copper Planting Articles
- Electropating of Various Metals
- Electroplating of Zinc on Wire
- Electrolytic Iron Powder
- Etching Process
- Etching of Stainless Steel & Other Materials
- Gold Coloured Metal Coating on Brass Button
- Gold Electroplating
- Gold Plated Silver Jewellery
- Gold Salt
- Gold Colour Powder
- Gold Potassium Cyanide
- Gold Plating on Glass
- HardChromium Plating
- Hard Anodizing on Al.
- Hot Dip Galvanizing
- Metal Pre Treatment Chemicals
- Metal Finishing
- Metal Separation Copper, Tin, Lead from Spent Wash
- Mirror (Silver, Golden Pink, Black etc.)
- Nickel Electroplating Salts
- Nickel Plating
- Nickel Plating on Glass Bangles
- Photo Etching of Stainless Steel
- Precious Metal Plating & Manufacturing of their Salt
- Rhodium Plating on Silver & Golden Jewellery
- Rainbow Colours on Metal
- Silvering of Glass
- Silver Brass & Gold Electroplating
- Titanium Jewellery Plating
- Transparent Anodizing Printing
- Vacuum Metallizing
- Tin Printing & Anodizing on Aluminium
- Wood Metal Polish
- Zinc Electroplating on Nut Bolt Washer etc.

Each 'EIRI' ***Market Survey Cum Detailed Techno Economic Feasibility Report (Detailed Project Report)*** covers Introduction, Properties, Market Survey, Present Manufacturers, Process Flow Sheet Diagram, Process of Manufacture, Formulations, Cost Economics with Profitability, Suppliers of Plant & Machineries and Raw Materials, Cash Flow Statement, Repayment Schedule, Depreciation Chart, Projected Balance Sheet etc.

*Price **Rs. 3675/-** (Rs. Three Thousand Six Hundred Seventy Five Only) for Each Report. Send Draft/M.O./Cash in favour of **"ENGINEERS INDIA RESEARCH INSTITUTE", DELHI. (Payable In India) (Delivery within Two Days)**

ENGINEERS INDIA RESEARCH INSTITUTE

4449, Nai Sarak (D), Main Road, Delhi - 110 006 (India)

Ph:. 3918117, 3916431, 3920361, 3960797 Fax: 91-11-3916431

E-Mail : eirisidi@bol.net.in * Website:www.startindustry.com

New Detailed Project Reports available on Soaps, Detergents & Allied Ind. @ Rs. 3500/- each

LIST OF READILY AVAILABLE PROJECT REPORTS

- AFTER SHAVE LOTION
- ALLETHRIN MOSQUITO REPELLENT OIL
- AGARBATTI SYNTHETIC PERFUMERY COMPOUND
- AMALA PLANTATION & PROCESSING (E.O.U)
- ARIAL TYPE DETERGENT POWDER
- AYURVEDIC MEDICINES
- ACID SLURRY (LABS)
- BLUE DETERGENT POWDER
- COLD CREAM
- COSMETIC INDUSTRY
- COLD WAVE FOR HAIR CURLING
- COLD CREAM
- COSMETICS
- CLEANING POWDER (VIM TYPE)
- DETERGENT PASTE
- DETERGENT CAKE
- DETERGENT POWDER
- DETERGENT POWDER (NIRMA TYPE)
- DOG SOAP
- DETERGENT POWDER (ARIEL TYPE)

- FACE POWDER
- HERBAL HAIR OIL
- HAIR SHAMPOO
- HAIR DYE POWDER
- HAIR FIXER (SPRAY)
- HAIR FIXER (GEL TYPE)
- HAIR STYLING GEL
- HERBAL COSMETICS
- HAIR OIL
- KALI MEHANDI (HAIR DYE)
- LAL DANT MANJAN (AYURVEDIC)
- LIPSTICS
- LIQUID DETERGENT
- LIQUID SOAP
- LAUNDRY DRY CLEANER
- MOSQUITO REPELLENT CANDLE
- MOSQUITO REPELLENT OIL
- MOSQUITO COILS & MATS
- MENTHOL FLAKES & BOLD
- NAIL ENAMEL
- NAIL POLISH & REMOVER
- NEUTRALIZER (FOR HAIR CURLING)
- NEROL LAUNDRY SOAP
- PERFUME
- PERFUME FOR SOAP

DETERGENT & AGARBATTI

- PETROLEUM JELLY
- POWDERED TALC FROM SOAP STONE
- RAZOR BLADES
- SOAP STONE POWDER
- SPRAY PERFUME
- SCENT & PERFUME
- SHAMPOO
- SHAVING CREAM
- SHAVING SOAP
- TOOTH PASTE & POWDER
- TALCUM POWDER
- TOOTH PASTE
- TOOTH PASTE (GEL TYPE)
- TOILET & HERBAL SOAP
- TOILET SOAP
- WASHING & LAUNDRY SOAP

Each 'EIRI' ***Market Survey Cum Detailed Techno Economic Feasibility Report (Detailed Project Report)*** covers Introduction, Properties, Market Survey, Process of Manufacture, Cost Economics with Profitability Analysis, Suppliers of Plant & Machineries and Raw Materials, Cash Flow Statement, Repayment Schedule, Depreciation Chart, Projected Balance Sheet etc.Price **Rs. 3500/-** (Rs. Three Thousand Five Hundred Only) for Each. Send Draft/M.O. in favour of **"ENGINEERS INDIA RESEARCH INSTITUTE", DELHI** or **Ask to Send by V.P.P.**

ENGINEERS INDIA RESEARCH INSTITUTE

4449, Nai Sarak (D), Main Road, Delhi - 110 006 (India)

Ph:. 3918117, 3916431, 3920361, 3960797 Fax: 91-11-3916431

E-Mail : eirisidi@bol.net.in Website:www.startindustry.com

New Publications from EIRI

1. HAND BOOK OF EXPORT ORIENTED INDUSTRIES
2. HAND BOOK OF PLASTIC PROJECTS (HI-TECH PLASTIC PROJECTS)
3. AGRO BASED & FOOD PROCESSING WITH EXPORT ORIENTED INDUSTRIES
4. HAND BOOK OF PACKAGING INDUSTRIES
5. ALL CHEMICALS AND ALLIED INDUSTRIES
6. HAND BOOK OF HOSIERY READYMADE GARMENTS & TEXTILE PROJECTS
7. AGRO BASED INDUSTRIES HAND BOOK (PLANTATION & FARMING)
8. REAL ESTATE PLAZAS, HOTEL, MOTEL, HOSPITAL & COMMERCIAL COMPLEXES
9. WORLD IMPORTERS DIRECTORY OF AGRO BASED & FOOD PROCESSING
10. WORLD IMPORTERS YELLOW PAGES (ALL TRADE BUYERS DIRECTORY)
11. HAND BOOK OF PRINTING PROCESSES TECHNOLOGIES & INDUSTRIES
12. SMALL MEDIUM & LARGE SCALE CHEMICAL INDUSTRES
13. DAIRY FORMAULATIONS, PROCESSES & MILK PACKAGING INDUSTRIES
14. PLASTIC PROCESSING AND PACKAGING INDUSTRIES
15. STATIONERY, PAPER CONVERTING & PACKAGING INDUSTRIES
16. INDUSTRIAL DIRECTORY (ALL INDIA TRADE DIRECTORY)
17. FOOD PROCESSING AND AGRO BASED INDUSTRIES
18. AGRO BASED PLANTATION CULTIVATION AND FARMING HAND-BOOK
19. RUBBER CHEMICALS AND PROCESSING INDUSTRIES
20. PAINT PIGMENT VARNISH AND LACQUER MANUFACTURING
21. MODERN INKS FORMULAES AND MANUFACTURING INDUSTRIES
22. HAND BOOK OF BAKERY INDUSTRIES
23. INDUSTRIAL DIRECTORY OF DELHI AND SURROUNDING AREAS ON CD-ROM
24. START YOUR OWN COLD STORAGE UNIT
25. GARMENTS EXPORT DIRECTORY OF DELHI AND AROUND
26. MOULDS DESIGN AND PROCESSING HAND BOOK
27. PROFITABLE SMALL SCALE MANUFACTURE OF SOAPS & DETERGENTS
28. PET PRE-FORM AND ITS PRODUCTS (BOTTLES ETC.) MFG.
29. INDIAN INDUSTRIAL AND BUSINESS DIRECTORY
30. ESSENTIAL OILS MANUFACTURING & AROMATIC PLANTS
31. MODERN PACKAGING TECHNOLOGY FOR PROCESSED FOOD, BAKERY, SPICE & ALLIED FOOD INDUSTRIES
32. AGRO BASED HAND BOOK ON CULTIVATION, PLANTATION & FARMING
33. HAND BOOK OF PERFUMES & FLAVOURS
34. HAND BOOK OF SPICES & PACKAGING WITH FORMULAES
35. HAND BOOK OF HERBAL & SYNTHETIC COSMETICS
36. HAND BOOK OF ADHESIVES WITH THEIR FORMULAES
37. HAND BOOK OF ELECTROPLATING ANODIZING & SURFACE TREATMENT TECHNOLOGY
38. HAND BOOK OF AYURVEDIC & HERBAL MEDICINES WITH FORMULAES
39. FRUITS & VEGETABLES PROCESSING HAND BOOK
40. HAND BOOK OF HERBS, MEDICINAL & AROMATIC PLANTS CULTIVATION
41. HAND BOOK OF CONFECTIONERY WITH & FORMULATIONS
42. MANUFACTURE OF SNACKS FOOD, NAMKEEN, PAPPAD & POTATO PRODUCTS
43. ESSENTIAL OIL PROCESSES AND FORMULATIONS HAND BOOK
44. SYNTHETIC RESINS TECHNOLOGY WITH FORMULATIONS
45. PAINT VARNISH SOLVENTS AND COATING TECHNOLOGY
46. COSMETICS PROCESSES AND FORMULATIONS HAND BOOK

Above all books available at :

ENGINEERS INDIA RESEARCH INSTITUTE

Regd. Off. :4449, Nai Sarak (B), Main Road, Delhi-110 006.(India)

Ph: 3916431, 3918117, 3920361, 3960797 * Fax: 91-11- 3916431

E-mail : eirisidi@bol.net.in, Website : www.startindustry.com